THE AFRICAN CHARTER ON HUMAN AND PEOPLES' RIGHTS
The System in Practice, 1986–2000

The African Charter is the regional mechanism for the promotion and protection of human rights on that continent and is in many ways unique. Yet there is very little scholarship available analysing the Charter as an operational system in practice. This volume provides an analytical overview by a range of expert collaborators – commissioners, NGOs and academics – many of whom have been actively involved in the implementation of the Charter since its establishment in 1981. Chapters cover the Charter's reporting system, the interpretation of different rights by the Commission, the prospects for the African Court on Human and Peoples' Rights and the role of NGOs. This authoritative, comprehensive and up-to-date book will interest lawyers acting for government and non-governmental organisations, academics and postgraduates.

MALCOLM EVANS is Professor of Public International Law at the University of Bristol and Director of the Bristol Centre for International Legal Studies. His chief areas of interest in the field of human rights concern the freedom of religion and torture prevention, and he has written extensively on these topics, with principal works including *Religious Liberty and International Law in Europe* (1997) and, as co-author, *Preventing Torture* (1998), *Protecting Prisoners* (1999) and *Combating Torture in Europe* (2001). He is a member of the Board of Management of the Association of the Prevention of Torture. With Rachel Murray he has co-edited a collection of *Documents of the African Commission on Human and Peoples' Rights* (2001) and also continues his long-standing research and writing interests in the international law of the sea.

RACHEL MURRAY is Lecturer in Law, Birkbeck College University of London and was previously Assistant Director at the Centre for Human Rights in the School of Law, Queen's University, Belfast. She has been researching the work of the African Commission on Human and Peoples' Rights for a number of years. She has written widely on the subject (*The African Commission on Human and Peoples' Rights and International Law*, 2000) and regularly contributes articles and information on this area to the *Human Rights Law Journal*, the *Netherlands Quarterly of Human Rights* and the *South African Journal of Human Rights*. She co-edited *Documents of the African Commission on Human and Peoples' Rights* (2001) with Malcolm Evans. She works closely with African and international NGOs operating in this area and regularly attends the Commission's sessions, liaising with its members.

THE AFRICAN CHARTER ON HUMAN AND PEOPLES' RIGHTS

The System in Practice, 1986–2000

EDITED BY

MALCOLM D. EVANS

AND RACHEL MURRAY

CAMBRIDGE
UNIVERSITY PRESS

CAMBRIDGE UNIVERSITY PRESS
Cambridge, New York, Melbourne, Madrid, Cape Town, Singapore, São Paulo

Cambridge University Press
The Edinburgh Building, Cambridge CB2 2RU, UK

Published in the United States of America by Cambridge University Press, New York

www.cambridge.org
Information on this title: www.cambridge.org/9780521802079

First published 2002
Third printing 2004

A catalogue record for this publication is available from the British Library

Library of Congress Cataloguing in Publication data

The African Charter on Human and Peoples' Rights: the system in practice, 1986–2000 /
edited by Malcolm D. Evans and Rachel Murray.
p.   cm.
Includes bibliographical references and index.
ISBN 0 521 80207 5
1. Human rights – Africa.   2. African Charter on Human and Peoples' Rights.
I. Evans, Malcolm.   II. Murray, Rachel, Dr.
JC599.A36 A36   2002
323′.096 – dc21   2001043851

ISBN-13 978-0-521-80207-9 hardback
ISBN-10 0-521-80207-5 hardback

Transferred to digital printing 2005

CONTENTS

v

Contents

CONTRIBUTORS

Professor Malcolm Evans is Professor of Public International Law at the University of Bristol and Director of the Bristol Centre for International Legal Studies. His chief areas of interest in the field of human rights concern the freedom of religion and torture prevention and he has written extensively on these topics, with principal works including *Religious Liberty and International Law in Europe* (CUP, 1997) and, as co-author, *Preventing Torture* (OUP, 1998), *Protecting Prisoners* (OUP, 1999) and *Combating Torture in Europe* (Council of Europe, 2001). He is a member of the Board of Management of the Association of the Prevention of Torture. With Rachel Murray he has co-edited a collection of *Documents of the African Commission on Human and Peoples' Rights* (Hart, 2001) and also continues his long-standing research and writing interests in the international law of the sea.

Dr Rachel Murray is Lecturer in Law at Birkbeck College, University of London and was previously the Assistant Director of the Centre for Human Rights and Lecturer in Law at the School of Law, Queen's University Belfast. She has written widely on the African human rights mechanism including a monograph (*The African Commission on Human and Peoples' Rights and International Law*, Hart Publishing, 2000), a collection of documents of the Commission with Professor Evans (*Documents of the African Commission on Human and Peoples' Rights*, Hart Publishing, 2001) and writes regularly for leading journals such as the *Human Rights Law Journal*, the *Netherlands Quarterly of Human Rights* and the *South African Journal of Human Rights*. She attends the sessions of the African Commission

vii

and works closely with NGOs and others involved in supporting its activities.

Professor Victor Dankwa is the outgoing Chairman of the African Commission on Human and Peoples' Rights and has been a member of the Commission since its inception in 1987. He is also Professor in Law at the University of Ghana.

Julia Harrington is the Co-Director of the Institute for Human Rights and Development, an NGO based in The Gambia which has closely supported the work of the Commission. She worked for several years as a legal officer at the Secretariat of the Commission before co-establishing this NGO. She holds degrees in social science and law from Harvard University.

Professor Christof Heyns is the Director of the Centre for Human Rights and Professor in Human Rights Law at the Law Faculty of the University of Pretoria, South Africa. He is editor of the *Human Rights Law in Africa* series and co-editor of the *African Human Rights Law Journal* and is on the editorial boards of the *African International and Comparative Law Journal* and the *East African Human Rights Law Journal*. He has published widely on human rights law in Africa, including (co-authored with Professor Frans Viljoen) *The Domestic Impact of the Main UN Human Rights Treaties*.

Tokunbo Ige is the Africa Team Co-ordinator with the UN High Commissioner for Human Rights in Geneva. She worked for many years as the Legal Officer for Africa for the International Commission of Jurists. She was the founder and first Executive Director of the Legal Research and Resource Development Centre, Lagos, Nigeria. She has authored and co-authored a number of articles on issues of women's rights, the African human rights system and legal services in rural areas in Africa.

Ahmed Motala is currently human rights officer at Save the Children UK. He has previously worked at the International Secretariat of Amnesty International as Legal Adviser for Africa. As a South African human rights lawyer and activist, he worked in that country during the apartheid years and contributed to the developments that led to the establishment of the first democratic government. He has also regularly contributed to the work of the African Commission on Human and Peoples' Rights over the past eleven years.

Dr Gino Naldi is Senior Lecturer at the University of East Anglia Law School. He was awarded an LLM in 1979 and a PhD in 1984 from the University of Birmingham. He has written widely, including publications on the Organization of African Unity (*The Organization of African Unity: An Analysis of its Role*, 2nd edn, 1999; and *Documents of the Organization of African Unity*, 1992) and on the African human rights system in journals such as the *North Carolina Journal of International Law and Commercial Regulation* and the *South African Journal of Human Rights*.

Chidi Anselm Odinkalu is Senior Legal Officer at Interights in London. Interights works closely to support the work of the African Commission. He has published a number of articles on the work of the Commission in leading legal journals.

Dr Nyamkeko Barney Pityana is a member of the African Commission on Human and Peoples' Rights and was the former Chairperson of the South African Human Rights Commission. After sixteen years in exile in both England and Geneva, Dr Pityana returned to South Africa in 1992. While in Geneva he served as director of the World Council of Churches' Programme to Combat Racism. Dr Pityana is an ordained Anglican priest and also an attorney. The University of Cape Town awarded him a PhD in religious studies in 1995. He is a trustee of a number of grass-roots development bodies such as the Eastern Cape-based Microprojects Trust and the Maths Centre for Professional Teachers in Johannesburg and is on the Board of the Geneva-based International Foundation for Human Rights Policy.

Professor Frans Viljoen is Professor of Law at the Faculty of Law in the University of Pretoria, South Africa and a member of its Centre for Human Rights. He completed his LLD on the topic 'The Realisation of Human Rights in Africa Through Inter-Governmental Institutions'. He teaches law and acts as academic co-ordinator of the LLM (Human Rights and Democratisation in Africa) presented by the Centre for Human Rights. He has published widely on topics related to the promotion and protection of human rights in Africa, and is co-editor of the *African Human Rights Law Journal*, published by the Centre for Human Rights.

PREFACE

The African human rights system has not generated the same degree of interest as other regional human rights systems. Although it is often compared with the European and Inter-American mechanisms – often unfavourably – comparatively little attention has been given to the details of its practical operation and it is rare indeed to find evaluations of the African system that are based on such material. This collection of essays aims to address this gap by presenting and examining the system from a practical perspective, drawing on the expertise of those who worked closely in or alongside it. The contributors have therefore largely been drawn from the small number of those actively involved in the practical work of the African Charter, including Commissioners, NGOs, those with connections with the Secretariat and those with interests of an academic nature. Each brings a different perspective and their experience ensures that their contributions move beyond presentation and speculation to provide informed comment and analysis of topics, which have been selected both for their individual interest and for their contribution towards a rounded understanding of the African system.

One reason why so few have written on these topics in the past was the paucity of information produced by the central organ, the African Commission on Human and Peoples' Rights, concerning its work. However, for a number of years now, the jurisprudence and material emanating from this body has been expanding and there now exists a considerable body of publicly available information, knowledge of which has hitherto largely remained restricted to those closely involved in its work. It is hoped that this collection of essays will play a useful role in bringing this to a wider audience, not only in Europe but also in Africa, in academic circles, and beyond. It is to be hoped that it will prove useful both to those who engage with the system, as individuals, NGOs and States themselves, and to those who study and teach human rights in universities and elsewhere. It is also to be hoped that those who carry the responsibility of making the system function will find food for thoughtful reflection. Through all these means, the overriding aspiration is to contribute in some modest way to the furtherance of the advancement of human rights within Africa.

ACKNOWLEDGMENTS

Thanks must, of course, go to all those who have contributed to this collection and for their willingness to comply with or acquiesce in the demands of the editorial process. Even this would be as nought but for the hard work of Pat Hammond at the University of Bristol Law Department in the preparation of the text, and in reassuring us that no computing calamity was ever truly irreparable. We are also extremely grateful to Diane Abraham for stepping in at the last moment and helping out with the final throes of preparation. Finola O'Sullivan at Cambridge University Press has been a constant source of encouragement and support and we are pleased to be able to acknowledge our considerable debt to her. Finally, we would like to thank the African Commission on Human and Peoples' Rights and its Secretariat for allowing attendance at its sessions and making available its material not only to us as editors, but to all contributors in their various roles and capacities. Our hope is that this collection will in its own way be of service in furthering the work of the human rights system within Africa.

TABLE OF CASES

Table of cases

Table of cases

ABBREVIATIONS

ACHPR	African Charter on Human and Peoples' Rights
AEC	African Economic Community
BYIL	*British Yearbook of International Law*
CAT	Convention Against Torture
CEDAW	Convention on the Elimination of All Forms of Discrimination Against Women
CERD	Convention on the Elimination of Racial Discrimination
CLB	*Commonwealth Legal Bulletin*
COMESA	Common Market for Eastern and Southern Africa
CSCE	Conference on Security and Co-operation in Europe
ECA	Economic Commission for Africa
ECHR	European Convention on Human Rights
ECOSOC	Economic and Social Council (of the United Nations)
ECOWAS	Economic Community of West African States
EHRR	*European Human Rights Reports*
HRC	Human Rights Committee (of the United Nations)
HRQ	*Human Rights Quarterly*
HRLJ	*Human Rights Law Journal*
IACHR	Inter-American Convention on Human Rights
ICCPR	International Covenant on Civil and Political Rights
ICESCR	International Covenant on Economic, Social and Cultural Rights
ICJ	International Commission of Jurists
ICLQ	*International and Comparative Law Quarterly*
ICTY	International Criminal Tribunal for the Former Yugoslavia
IHRR	*International Human Rights Reports*

ILM	*International Legal Materials*
ILO	International Labor Organization
IMF	International Monetary Fund
JAL	*Journal of African Law*
NGOs	non-governmental organisations
NQHR	*Netherlands Quarterly on Human Rights*
OAS	Organization of American States
OAU	Organization of African Unity
OSCE	Organization for Security and Co-operation in Europe
RADIC	*Revue Africaine de Droit International et Comparatif*
SAJHR	*South African Journal of Human Rights*
UDHR	Universal Declaration of Human Rights
UN	United Nations
UNDP	United Nations Development Programme
UNGA	United Nations General Assembly
UNTS	*United Nations Treaty Series*
WHO	World Health Organization
YB	Yearbook

1

FUTURE TRENDS IN HUMAN RIGHTS IN AFRICA: THE INCREASED ROLE OF THE OAU?

GINO J. NALDI[*]

Ex Africa semper aliquid novi.[1]

When the Organization of African Unity (OAU) was founded in 1963 the question of human rights did not feature prominently on its agenda. Unlike the Council of Europe the protection of human rights was not one of the OAU's principal aspirations.[2] Nevertheless, this is not to say that human rights were wholly neglected by the OAU Charter since it makes references, albeit slight, to human rights.[3] Accordingly, one of the purposes of the OAU is to promote international co-operation, having due regard to the Charter of the United Nations and the Universal Declaration of Human Rights.[4] However, almost twenty years were to elapse before the OAU felt able to adopt a human rights document proper.[5]

---

[*] The author dedicates this chapter to the memory of his father, Ferruccio Naldi.

[1] Pliny the Elder.

[2] On the objectives of the OAU, see G. J. Naldi, *The Organization of African Unity* (2nd edn, London: Mansell, 1999), pp. 2–18.

[3] ILM 2 (1963) 766; G. J. Naldi (ed.), *Documents of the Organization of African Unity* (London: Mansell, 1992), p. 3.

[4] Article 2(1)(e) of the OAU Charter. Furthermore, the Member States reaffirm their adherence to, *inter alia*, the Universal Declaration of Human Rights in the preamble to the OAU Charter.

[5] For the background leading to the adoption of the African Charter, see Naldi, *The Organization of African Unity*, pp. 109–13; E. A. Ankumah, *The African Commission on Human and Peoples' Rights* (The Hague: Kluwer, 1996), pp. 4–8; R. M. D'Sa, 'The African Charter on Human and Peoples' Rights: Problems and Prospects for Regional Action', *Australian Year Book of International Law* 10 (1981–3) 101 at 103–6; K. O. Kufuor, 'Safeguarding Human Rights: A Critique of the African Commission on Human and Peoples' Rights', *Africa Development* 18 (1993) 65 at 66–9.

The role of the OAU

The initial question that must be considered is why the OAU failed for many years to address adequately the issue of human rights. It must be clearly understood that the principal objectives of the OAU have been to defend the sovereignty and territorial integrity of its Member States and to rid Africa of colonialism and racialism.[6] Conceived and born during the Cold War and the liberation struggle, the OAU remained in that mindset for a generation.[7] Account must also be taken of the fact that the States of Africa, most newly independent, jealously guarded their freedom and deeply resented any measures which hinted at external interference with their internal affairs. Indeed, one of the basic principles of the OAU is that of non-interference in the internal affairs of States.[8] African States have traditionally insisted on rigorous compliance with this principle and have tended to regard international concern for human rights as a pretext for undermining their sovereignty.[9] However, the principle of domestic jurisdiction is a relative one, and as international law has evolved, particularly in the field of human rights, its scope and extent has been restricted accordingly.[10] It is now generally accepted that human rights assume priority over national sovereignty.[11] Thus African States have been compelled to accept international scrutiny of their human rights credentials.[12]

[6] Articles 2–3 of the OAU Charter. See further Naldi, *The Organization of African Unity*, pp. 2–18; C. O. C. Amate, *Inside the OAU: Pan-Africanism in Practice* (London: Macmillan, 1986), pp. 61–3; T. O. Elias, *Africa and the Development of International Law* (2nd edn by R. Akinjide, Dordrecht, Boston, London: Martinus Nijhoff, 1988), pp. 124–9.

[7] Amate, *Inside the OAU*, pp. 60–1.   [8] Article 3(2) of the OAU Charter.

[9] See, for example, the statement made by Swaziland to the UN Human Rights Commission in 1997, UN Doc. E/CN.4/1997/SR.4, paras. 46–7; and *Mika Miha v. Equatorial Guinea*, Communication 414/1990 (UN Human Rights Committee), UN Doc. CCPR/C/51/D/414/1990, where Equatorial Guinea argued, unsuccessfully, that the communication submitted to the UN Human Rights Committee constituted interference in its internal affairs even though Equatorial Guinea had recognised the jurisdiction of the UN Human Rights Committee.

[10] *Tunis–Morocco Nationality Decrees Case*, PCIJ, Series B, No. 4 (1923), p. 24; M. N. Shaw, *International Law* (4th edn, Cambridge University Press, 1997), p. 24. UN Secretary-General Boutros Boutros-Ghali has therefore remarked that 'the time of absolute and exclusive sovereignty' has passed, *An Agenda for Peace*, ILM 31 (1992) 953, para. 17.

[11] Vienna Declaration and Programme of Action, adopted by the UN World Conference on Human Rights 1993, ILM 32 (1993) 1661, Part I, paras. 1, 4 and 5; Shaw, *International Law*, p. 202.

[12] C. Clapham, *Africa and the International System: The Politics of State Survival* (Cambridge University Press, 1996), pp. 190–1. For examples of measures undertaken by the UN, see Naldi, *The Organization of African Unity*, p. 40 at note 22.

However, it must be conceded that the OAU institutionally has not generally conducted itself in a manner to suggest that the protection of human rights has been regarded as an overriding consideration. Rather, rightly or wrongly, the perception given to the wider world is one of slavish adherence to the principle of domestic jurisdiction regardless of the human rights abuses that may exist within Member States.[13] There has certainly been a reluctance to criticise leaders who fail to protect human rights.[14] The institutional defects of the OAU may be responsible for this pusillanimity. It should be observed that the OAU Assembly operates by consensus; its resolutions have no binding force.[15] Not only was the OAU designed to act only when assured of overwhelming support but a fear of divisiveness led to cravenness. Nonetheless, a question that must be addressed is whether the OAU is endowed, institutionally or otherwise, to investigate human rights problems.

Eschewing official and institutional modes of dispute settlement,[16] resort to informal procedures has been the preferred method of the OAU. International mediation, conciliation or recourse to the good offices of African statesmen have been regular features.[17] UN Secretary-General Kofi Annan has expressed the view that such efforts still have a valuable role to play.[18] They have the convenience of pragmatism, flexibility, persuasion and compromise. In the context of human rights it seems undeniable that such processes can have a useful role, particularly where the problem at issue is one on a large scale or where there are systematic violations of human

---

[13] Clapham, *Africa and the International System*, pp. 110–17; G. Robertson, *Crimes Against Humanity: The Struggle for Global Justice* (London: Penguin, 1999), p. 57.

[14] According to Amate, concern at human rights abuses was only expressed at the Assembly for the first time in 1979: Amate, *Inside the OAU*, p. 472.

[15] Naldi, *The Organization of African Unity*, p. 19.

[16] It is interesting to note that the Commission of Mediation, Conciliation and Arbitration, provided for by Article 19 of the Charter and the Protocol on the Commission of Mediation, Conciliation and Arbitration (see Naldi (ed.), *Documents of the Organization of African Unity*, p. 32) has never become operational. See Naldi, *The Organization of African Unity*, pp. 14 and 24–9.

[17] Amate, *Inside the OAU*, pp. 162–8; T. Maluwa, 'The Peaceful Settlement of Disputes Among African States, 1963–1983: Some Conceptual Issues and Practical Trends', ICLQ 38 (1989) 299 at 301; M. Shaw, 'Dispute Settlement in Africa', *Yearbook of World Affairs* 37 (1983) 149.

[18] 'United Nations, Report of the Secretary-General on: Causes of Conflict and the Promotion of Durable Peace and Sustainable Development in Africa', RADIC, 10 (1998) 549, para. 21.

3

rights. These methods remain underused, however, insofar as human rights are concerned.[19]

An important development at the institutional level has been the establishment of the Mechanism for Conflict Prevention, Management and Resolution. As has been observed, the OAU has usually relied on *ad hoc* arrangements of dispute settlement. However, among their drawbacks is that they are reactive and remedial rather than proactive and preventive. Considerable loss of life and property may have occurred before the OAU offered its services. It was therefore proposed that the OAU should commit itself towards the peaceful and speedy resolution of all conflicts in Africa.[20] Accordingly, the Mechanism was approved by the OAU Assembly in 1993.[21]

The Mechanism's primary objective is the anticipation and prevention of conflicts, including internal ones, with emphasis on anticipatory and deterrent measures.[22] Prompt and decisive action should prevent the emergence of conflicts, prevent conflicts from worsening, and preclude the need for complex and demanding peacekeeping operations.[23] However, the Mechanism operates subject to the fundamental principles of the OAU, especially respect for the sovereignty and territorial integrity of Member States and non-interference in the internal affairs of States. The consent and co-operation

[19] The OAU was involved in attempts at solutions to the ethnic conflicts in the Great Lakes region of Central Africa, P. J. Magnarella, *Justice in Africa: Rwanda's Genocide, Its Courts and the UN Criminal Tribunal* (Aldershot: Ashgate, 2000), pp. 30–1; A. Parsons, *From Cold War to Hot Peace: UN Interventions 1947–1995* (London: Penguin, 1995), p. 213. Most recently, Nelson Mandela has presided over efforts to moderate a peace agreement in Burundi.

[20] See 'Proposals for an OAU Mechanism for Conflict Prevention and Resolution', RADIC 4 (1992) 1072.

[21] Declaration of the Assembly of Heads of State and Government on the Establishment Within the OAU of a Mechanism for Conflict Prevention, Management and Resolution, AHG/Dec. 3 (XXIX) (the 'Cairo Declaration'), RADIC 6 (1994) 158.

[22] Para. 15 of the Cairo Declaration. The Mechanism seems to mirror in part UN Secretary-General Boutros Boutros-Ghali's vision for more effective preventive action in *An Agenda for Peace*, ILM 31 (1992) 953.

[23] Adequate funding and the political support of Member States will ultimately determine the success of the Mechanism, M. A. Hefny, 'Enhancing the Capabilities of the OAU Mechanism for Conflict Prevention, Management and Resolution: An Immediate Agenda for Action', *Proceedings of the African Society of International and Comparative Law* 7 (1995) 176 at 181–3. The OAU must co-ordinate its activities with other African organisations, co-operate, where appropriate, with neighbouring countries, and liaise with the UN with regard to peacekeeping and peace-making activities, and, when necessary, call upon the UN to provide financial, logistic and military support for the OAU's efforts, paras. 24–5 of the Cairo Declaration.

of the parties to a dispute is a prerequisite for OAU involvement.[24] It is encouraging to note that the Mechanism has mediated in a number of internal
conflicts.[25]

The Mechanism appears to herald a more resolute approach to dispute settlement by the OAU. At a conceptual level, the Mechanism may be regarded as
revolutionary in the sense that it demands a rethink of the rigid adherence of
African States to the principles of sovereignty and non-interference.[26] However, care should be taken not to overstate this assessment for, unlike the UN,
there does not appear to be any imminent prospects for peace-enforcement
which, as events in the Balkans and elsewhere suggest, can only be effective
where the warring parties genuinely seek peace and/or the UN forces have
the military resources and the political support necessary to act as a forceful
deterrent.[27] At a practical level, the Mechanism enhances the OAU's capacity
to solve disputes. Endowing it with a preventive role is especially welcome.
The Mechanism seems eminently capable of assuming an appropriate role,
more political than legal perhaps, over large-scale human rights concerns.

Notwithstanding these accomplishments, it does not seem that the OAU
is in a very strong position, as a political organisation, to protect the human
rights of the individual. Nevertheless, the fact should not be overlooked that
the OAU has taken concrete measures to improve the protection of human
rights through the adoption of various treaties and at the same time has
made a distinctive contribution to international human rights law.

The African Charter on Human and Peoples' Rights: fatally flawed?

The adoption of the African Charter on Human and Peoples' Rights (hereinafter the 'African Charter')[28] has largely proved to date to be a false dawn
for the promotion and protection of human rights in Africa. Obinna Okere

---

[24] Para. 14 of the Cairo Declaration.   [25] Naldi, *The Organization of African Unity*, p. 33.
[26] Hefny, 'Enhancing the Capabilities of the OAU Mechanism', p. 180.
[27] Parsons, *From Cold War to Hot Peace*, pp. 256–7.
[28] Adopted by the Eighteenth Assembly of Heads of State and Government of the Organization
of African Unity (OAU) at Nairobi in July 1981, entered into force on 21 October 1986,
ILM 21 (1982) 58; Naldi (ed.), *Documents of the Organization of African Unity*, p. 109.
All of the OAU's fifty-three Member States have now ratified the African Charter: see
R. Murray, 'Africa', NQHR 17 (1999) 350. For an analysis of the African Charter, see Naldi,
The Organization of African Unity, pp. 109–212; U. O. Umozurike, *The African Charter on
Human and Peoples' Rights* (The Hague: Kluwer, 1997).

describes the African Charter as 'modest in its objectives and flexible in its means'.[29] Certainly, there are a number of features about the African Charter which have given cause for concern. More so than other comparable instruments, the substantive provisions of the African Charter are equivocally phrased.[30] Moreover, extensive use is made of 'clawback' clauses[31] that seem to make the enforcement of a right dependent on municipal law or at the discretion of the national authorities. Article 10(1) is one such example.[32] It states that: 'Every individual shall have the right to free association *provided that* he abides by the law' (emphasis added). The attainment of this right therefore appears to be undermined because it is subject to the dictates of municipal law.[33] However, it is interesting to observe that in a recent

[29] B. Obinna Okere, 'The Protection of Human Rights in Africa and the African Charter on Human and Peoples' Rights: A Comparative Analysis with the European and American Systems', HRQ 6 (1984) 141 at 158. For other sceptical assessments, see R. Gittleman, 'The African Charter on Human and Peoples' Rights: A Legal Analysis', *Virginia Journal of International Law* 22 (1982) 667; P. Amoah, 'The African Charter on Human and Peoples' Rights – An Effective Weapon for Human Rights?', RADIC 4 (1992) 226; Robertson, *Crimes Against Humanity*, pp. 57–8.

[30] D'Sa, 'The African Charter', pp. 107–8; Gittleman, 'The African Charter', p. 685; C. A. Odinkalu, 'The Individual Complaints Procedures of the African Commission on Human and Peoples' Rights: A Preliminary Assessment', *Transnational Law and Contemporary Problems* 8 (1998) 359 at 398, who expresses little pessimism with this problem as he believes that the African Commission on Human and Peoples' Rights has been addressing this concern through its procedures and jurisprudence.

[31] See R. Higgins, 'Derogations Under Human Rights Treaties', BYIL 48 (1976–7) 281.

[32] See also Articles 8, 9(2), 12(1) and 13(1) of the African Charter. It does not seem appropriate to draw an analogy with the limitations contained in Articles 10 and 11 of the European Convention on Human Rights, for example, since these are strictly defined and are only permitted subject to stringent criteria: see D. J. Harris, M. O'Boyle and C. Warbrick, *Law of the European Convention on Human Rights* (London: Butterworths, 1995), pp. 285–301.

[33] Robertson, *Crimes Against Humanity*, pp. 57–8; Ankumah, *The African Commission*, pp. 176–7; D'Sa, 'The African Charter', pp. 109–11. Umozurike, who is less critical, divides the African Charter's civil and political rights into unrestricted and restricted rights: see Umozurike, *The African Charter*, Chapter 3. See also U. O. Umozurike, 'The Protection of Human Rights Under the Banjul (African) Charter on Human and Peoples' Rights', *African Journal of International Law* 1 (1988) 65 at 68. However, it is encouraging to note that the African Commission on Human and Peoples' Rights has interpreted this provision creatively, stating that there is a duty on the State to abstain from interfering with the free formation of associations, and that there must always be a general capacity for citizens to join, without State interference, in associations in order to attain various ends: Communication 101/93, *Civil Liberties Organisation in respect of Nigerian Bar Association v. Nigeria*, Eighth Activity Report 1994–1995, Annex VI (see R. Murray and M. Evans (eds.), *Documents of the African Commission on Human and Peoples' Rights* (Oxford: Hart Publishing, 2001), p. 394 (hereinafter *Documents of the African Commission*)).

opinion the African Commission on Human and Peoples' Rights (here-inafter the 'Commission') has rejected this interpretation and has asserted the supremacy of international human rights law.[34] The Commission's im-portant views on this issue, which although dealing with the specific question of freedom of expression state a principle of general application, deserve to be quoted at length.

> Governments should avoid restricting rights, and have special care with regard to those rights protected by constitutional or international human rights law. No situation justifies the wholesale violation of human rights. In fact, general restrictions on rights diminish public confidence in the rule of law and are often counter-productive . . .
>
> According to Article 9(2) of the Charter, dissemination of opinions may be restricted by law. This does not mean that national law can set aside the right to express and disseminate one's opinions; this would make the protection of the right to express one's opinions ineffective. To allow national law to have precedent over the international law of the Charter would defeat the purpose of the rights and freedoms enshrined in the Charter. International human rights standards must always prevail over contradictory national law. Any limitation on the rights of the Charter must be in conformity with the provisions of the Charter . . .
>
> In contrast to other international human rights instruments, the African Charter does not contain a derogation clause. Therefore limitations on the rights and freedoms enshrined in the Charter cannot be justified by emer-gencies or special circumstances . . .
>
> The only legitimate reasons for limitations to the rights and freedoms of the African Charter are found in Article 27(2), that is that the rights of the Charter 'shall be exercised with due regard to the rights of others, collective security, morality and common interest' . . .
>
> The reasons for possible limitations must be founded in a legitimate State interest and the evils of limitations of rights must be strictly proportionate with and absolutely necessary for the advantages which are to be obtained . . .
>
> Even more important, a limitation may never have as a consequence that the right itself becomes illusory.[35]

It needs to be recalled that a distinguishing characteristic of the African Charter is the fact that it imposes obligations upon the individual towards

---

[34] Communications 105/93, 128/94, 130/94 and 152/96, *Media Rights Agenda and Constitu-tional Rights Project* v. *Nigeria, Media Rights Agenda and Constitutional Rights Project,* Twelfth Activity Report 1998–1999, Annex V (*Documents of the African Commission,* p. 718).

[35] *Ibid.*

the State and the community.[36] As Ankumah points out, the duty provisions are generally 'problematic and could adversely affect enjoyment of the rights set forth in the Charter'.[37] Gittleman hence writes that the African Charter is 'incapable of supplying even a scintilla of external restraint upon a government's power to create laws contrary to the spirit of the rights granted'.[38] Umozurike's early assessment was that the African Charter may well be a paper tiger except for effective public opinion that may be whipped up against the offender.[39] The African Charter could aptly be described as a statist document. The suggestion has therefore been made that the African Charter be revised to make it more anthropocentric.[40]

However, lest it be thought that it is all doom and gloom with the African Charter its positive attributes should be acclaimed. A particularly constructive feature is the fact that the *locus standi* requirements before the Commission are relatively broad since individuals and organisations (such as NGOs) other than the victim can submit complaints.[41] Furthermore, second and third generation rights are listed as legally enforceable rights.[42] This step,

[36] Articles 27–29. See further Ankumah, *The African Commission*, pp. 170–2; Naldi, *The Organization of African Unity*, pp. 114 and 138–9; Umozurike, *The African Charter*, pp. 64–5; D'Sa, 'The African Charter', pp. 115–16; Makau wa Mutua, 'The Banjul Charter and the African Cultural Fingerprint: An Evaluation of the Language of Duties', *Virginia Journal of International Law* 35 (1995) 339.

[37] Ankumah, *The African Commission*, p. 171; Amoah, 'The African Charter', pp. 227–8.

[38] Gittleman, 'The African Charter', p. 159.

[39] Umozurike, 'The Protection of Human Rights', pp. 82–3.

[40] W. Benedek, 'The African Charter and Commission on Human and Peoples' Rights: How to Make it More Effective', NQHR 11 (1993) 25 at 31. Odinkalu, 'The Individual Complaints Procedures', p. 398, is sceptical whether such a development would necessarily result in greater protection of human rights.

[41] The Commission's Rule of Procedure 114(2), since deleted, made this clear, stating that: 'The Commission may accept such communications from any individual or organisation irrespective of where they shall be.' See Naldi (ed.), *Documents of the Organization of African Unity*, p. 151. See Umozurike, 'The Protection of Human Rights', p. 78; Benedek, 'The African Charter', pp. 27–8. In any event, this procedure is now clearly established in the Commission's practice.

[42] Naldi, *The Organization of African Unity*, pp. 127–38; Umozurike, *The African Charter*, pp. 45–9 and 51–61; D'Sa, 'The African Charter', pp. 113–15 and 116–22. Umozurike has expressed doubts as to the wisdom of this approach which he believes confuses legally enforceable rights with desirable political rights. Since the integrity of the former could therefore be undermined, he would have preferred that the second and third generation rights have been declared merely hortatory. See Umozurike, 'The Protection of Human Rights', p. 81; and Umozurike, 'The African Charter on Human and Peoples' Rights', in M. Theodoropoulas (ed.), *Human Rights in Europe and Africa* (Athens: Hellenic University Press, 1992), pp. 114–15. Nevertheless, the Commission has had occasion to pronounce

radical for its time, attracted considerable criticism, fuelling the debate about the nature of human rights, which traditionally has focused exclusively on an individualistic approach.[43] However, the ideological distinction between the different categories of rights now seems less important in light of the Vienna Declaration on Human Rights which stresses that all human rights are universal, indivisible and interdependent.[44]

It is common knowledge that the African Charter has created a safeguard mechanism. The Commission, mandated under the African Charter with promoting and ensuring the protection of human and peoples' rights,[45]

on these rights. Thus in Communications 25/89, 47/90, 56/91 and 100/93 (joined), *Free Legal Assistance Group, Lawyers' Committee for Human Rights, Union Interafricaine des Droits de l'Homme, Les Témoins de Jehovah* v. *Zaire*, Ninth Activity Report 1995–1996, Annex VIII (*Documents of the African Commission*, p. 444), a violation of the right to health enshrined in Article 16 of the African Charter was established when the State failed to provide safe drinking water, electricity and medicines. The Commission additionally found that the closure of universities and secondary schools for a number of years constituted a violation of the right to education in Article 17 of the African Charter. In Communication 39/90, *Annette Pagnoulle (on behalf of Abdoulaye Mazou)* v. *Cameroon*, Eighth Activity Report 1994–1995, Annex VI; Tenth Activity Report 1996–1997, Annex X (*Documents of the African Commission*, pp. 384 and 555), the Commission held that the right to work guaranteed by Article 15 of the African Charter had been violated when the applicant, a magistrate, who had been imprisoned without trial, failed to be reinstated when others who had been condemned in similar conditions had been reinstated. In Communications 105/93, 128/94, 130/94 and 152/96, *Media Rights Agenda and Constitutional Rights Project, Media Rights Agenda and Constitutional Rights Project* v. *Nigeria*, Twelfth Activity Report 1998–1999, Annex V (*Documents of the African Commission*, p. 718), the Commission found a violation of Article 16 when a detainee in deteriorating health was denied medical assistance. The Commission had to consider the nature and scope of the right to self-determination under Article 20(1) of the African Charter in Communication 75/92, *Katangese Peoples' Congress* v. *Zaire*, Eighth Activity Report 1994–1995, Annex VI (*Documents of the African Commission*, p. 389).

[43] See, e.g., R. Higgins, *Problems and Process: International Law and How We Use it* (Oxford: Clarendon Press, 1994), pp. 99–103; P. Sieghart, *The Lawful Rights of Mankind* (Oxford: Oxford University Press, 1986), p. 161.

[44] Vienna Declaration and Programme of Action, Part I, para. 5; UN Commission on Human Rights, Resolution 1999/25, para. 3(d), UN Doc. E/CN.4/1999/167, p. 105. The Limburg Principles also describe economic, social and cultural rights as an integral part of international human rights law. See *The Review* (International Commission of Jurists), No. 37 (1986) 43–55. Significantly, the UN Committee on Economic, Social and Cultural Rights has stated that States Parties to the International Covenant on Economic, Social and Cultural Rights 1966 have assumed clear obligations in respect of the full realisation of the rights in question which require them to move expeditiously and effectively towards that goal. See General Comment 3, UN Doc. HRI/GEN/1/Rev.2, pp. 55–9.

[45] Articles 30 and 45 of the African Charter. Ankumah, *The African Commission*, p. 8, prefers to describe the Commission as a 'supervisory institution'.

has relatively weak powers of investigation and enforcement.[46] Lack of an effective remedy has been identified as a particular deficiency.[47] Its decisions do not formally have the binding force of a ruling of a court of law but have a persuasive authority akin to the Opinions of the UN Human Rights Committee.[48] However, an expectation of compliance does appear to have been engendered.[49] It is also important to note that the Commission

[46] Kufuor, 'Safeguarding Human Rights', p. 74; Z. Motala, 'Human Rights in Africa: A Cultural, Ideological, and Legal Examination', *Hastings International and Comparative Law Review* 12 (1989) 373 at 405. Articles 47–54 of the African Charter make provision for inter-State communications; one has been submitted to date. 'Other' communications, i.e. from individuals and NGOs, are governed by Articles 55–59 of the African Charter, although, as Odinkalu, 'The Individual Complaints Procedures', p. 371, has observed, the infelicitous wording of Article 55 of the African Charter has led some to question whether the Commission has the capacity to receive individual communications. However, this procedure is now well established in the Commission's practice. According to the Commission, the main aim of this procedure is 'to initiate a positive dialogue, resulting in an amicable resolution, which remedies the prejudice complained of. A prerequisite for amicably remedying violations of the Charter is the good faith of the parties concerned, including their willingness to participate in a dialogue.' See Communications 25/89, 47/90, 56/91 and 100/93 (joined), *Free Legal Assistance Group, Lawyers' Committee for Human Rights, Union Interafricaine des Droits de l'Homme, Les Témoins de Jehovah* v. *Zaire*, Ninth Activity Report 1995–1996, Annex VIII (*Documents of the African Commission*, p. 444). See further Odinkalu, 'The Individual Complaints Procedures', pp. 374–8. A State reporting procedure is also required under Article 62. See further Naldi, *The Organization of African Unity*, pp. 139–47; and Ankumah, *The African Commission*, pp. 20–8, 51–77 and 79–110.

[47] Benedek, 'The African Charter', pp. 31–2; and Kufuor, 'Safeguarding Human Rights', pp. 71–4. However, as has been noted, the Commission has stated that one of its principal objectives is to remedy the prejudice complained of: Communications 25/89, 47/90, 56/91 and 100/93 (joined), *Free Legal Assistance Group, Lawyers' Committee for Human Rights, Union Interafricaine des Droits de l'Homme, Les Témoins de Jehovah* v. *Zaire*, Ninth Activity Report 1995–1996, Annex VIII (*Documents of the African Commission*, p. 444). Hence Odinkalu, 'The Individual Complaints Procedures', p. 374, comments that the Commission 'thus recognises that the bottom line of the communications procedure is the redress of the violations complained of'.

[48] See Article 59 of the African Charter and Rule 120 of the Commission's Rules of Procedure, as amended, HRLJ 18 (1997) 154; Ankumah, *The African Commission*, pp. 24 and 74–5; D'Sa, 'The African Charter', p. 126. Murray writes that the Commission has relied on these provisions enabling it to declare that there have been violations of the African Charter: R. Murray, 'Decisions by the African Commission on Individual Communications Under the African Charter on Human and Peoples' Rights', ICLQ 46 (1997) 412 at 428.

[49] This approach would appear to be required under Article 1 of the African Charter: see Communications 129/94, *Civil Liberties Organisation* v. *Nigeria*, Ninth Activity Report 1995–1996, Annex VIII (*Documents of the African Commission*, p. 452). See further C. Anyangwe, 'Obligations of States Parties to the African Charter on Human and Peoples'

is effectively subordinate to the OAU and concerns were raised that its supervisory mandate could thereby be neutered. Although the Commission's independence does not appear to have been compromised,[50] it has nevertheless been criticised as being generally unable to act as a forceful guardian of rights.[51] However, an analysis of the Commission's decisions in recent times does suggest that the Commission is generally becoming more robust in performing its mandate.[52] Thus Odinkalu expresses the view that on

Rights', RADIC 10 (1998) 625. It may be that the Commission has come to regard its decisions on communications as binding: see Communications 137/94, 139/94, 154/96 and 161/97, *International Pen, Constitutional Rights Project, Interights on behalf of Ken Saro-Wiwa Jr and Civil Liberties Organisation* v. *Nigeria*, Twelfth Activity Report 1998–1999, Annex V (*Documents of the African Commission*, p. 729); Murray, 'Decisions by the African Commission', p. 431; and further Murray, 'Africa', p. 93 at p. 94, and p. 516 at p. 519.

[50] Kufuor, 'Safeguarding Human Rights', p. 70; I. Badawi El-Sheikh, 'The African Commission on Human and Peoples' Rights: Prospects and Problems', NQHR 7 (1989) 272 at 274–5.

[51] The failings appear to be both institutional and personal: Ankumah, *The African Commission*, pp. 179–98; Robertson, *Crimes Against Humanity*, pp. 58–9. Makau wa Mutua, 'The Banjul Charter', p. 11, thus describes the Commission as 'a facade, a yoke that African leaders have put around our necks'. Oloka-Onyango, although not as critical, is also unimpressed: J. Oloka-Onyango, 'Beyond the Rhetoric: Reinvigorating the Struggle for Economic and Social Rights in Africa', *California Western International Law Journal* 26 (1995) 1 at 52–6. See also Amoah, 'The African Charter', pp. 232–7; C. E. Welch, Jr, 'The African Commission on Human and Peoples' Rights: A Five-Year Report and Assessment', HRQ 14 (1992) 43. For a more favourable assessment, see Umozurike, *The African Charter*, pp. 67–85; R. Murray, *The African Commission on Human and Peoples' Rights and International Law* (Oxford: Hart Publishing, 2000). Ankumah, while acknowledging its failings, is nevertheless of the view that the Commission has the potential to become an effective body: see Ankumah, *The African Commission*, p. 9. More recently, Odinkalu writes that 'any conclusions . . . about the work of the Commission . . . must remain tentative and probably lie somewhere between the extremes of opinion', but that 'any temptation to dismiss it as a worthless institution today must be regarded as premature, ill-informed, or both': see Odinkalu, 'The Individual Complaints Procedures', pp. 401 and 402.

[52] See, for example, Communications 27/89, 46/91, 49/91 and 99/93, *Organisation Mondiale Contre la Torture and the Association Internationale des Juristes Democrates, Commission Internationale des Juristes, Union Interafricaine des Droits de l'Homme* v. *Rwanda*, Tenth Activity Report 1996–1997, Annex X (*Documents of the African Commission*, p. 551); Communications 105/93, 128/94, 130/94 and 152/96, *Media Rights Agenda and Constitutional Rights Project* v. *Nigeria*, Twelfth Activity Report 1998–1999, Annex V (*Documents of the African Commission*); Communications 137/94, 139/94, 154/96 and 161/97, *International Pen, Constitutional Rights Project, Interights on behalf of Ken Saro-Wiwa Jr and Civil Liberties Organisation* v. *Nigeria* Twelfth Activity Report 1998–1999, Annex V (*Documents of the African Commission*, p. 718). See further Murray, 'Decisions by the African Commission', pp. 428–32.

'its interpretation of the Charter, the Commission has been mostly positive and sometimes even innovative'.[53] He adds that the Commission has been successfully addressing the deficiencies in the African Charter through its practice, evolving procedures and jurisprudence.[54]

An important practical consideration that is universally believed to be hampering the Commission's ability to perform its role is the lack of financial resources.[55] The Commission must be adequately resourced to enable it to fulfil its mandate.

Whatever its failings, the Commission was assigned the role of safeguarding human rights under the African Charter. The suggestion of strengthening the protection of human rights by establishing a court like other regional human rights regimes was initially rejected.[56] This decision was justified on the ground that the African conception of dispute settlement is based on negotiation and conciliation rather than an adversarial or confrontational system.[57] However, the real reason may have been less prosaic. It appears there was widespread reluctance among OAU Member States to subordinate themselves to a supranational judicial organ.[58]

---

[53] Odinkalu, 'The Individual Complaints Procedures', p. 402.

[54] Ibid., p. 398.

[55] The Office of the UN High Commissioner for Human Rights has identified the limited resources allocated by the OAU to the Commission as one of the major obstacles to its effective functioning: UN Doc. E/CN.4/1999/93, para. 6. See also Ankumah, The African Commission, pp. 32–3; Murray, 'Decisions by the African Commission', p. 414; Odinkalu, 'The Individual Complaints Procedures', pp. 398–400; C. M. Peter, 'The Proposed African Court of Justice – Jurisprudential, Procedural, Enforcement Problems and Beyond', East African Journal of Peace and Human Rights 1 (1993) 117 at 132–3; Robertson, Crimes Against Humanity, p. 58; and Shaw, International Law, p. 294.

[56] Amoah, 'The African Charter', p. 237.

[57] Ibid., pp. 237–8. On the African philosophy of rights which emphasises the nexus between individual and community, see A. A. Naim and F. M. Deng (eds.), Human Rights in Africa (Washington DC: Brookings Institution, 1990); T. Maluwa, International Law in Post-Colonial Africa (The Hague: Kluwer, 1999), pp. 130–7; Umozurike, The African Charter, pp. 12–19; J. A. M. Cobbah, 'African Values and the Human Rights Debate: An African Perspective', HRQ 9 (1987) 309. It should be observed that the preamble to the African Charter stresses that the concept of human and peoples' rights should be inspired by African values and historical tradition.

[58] Ankumah, The African Commission, p. 9. Umozurike, 'The Protection of Human Rights', p. 78, has also been critical of this omission, writing that it 'was an attempt to avoid exposing a government or the head of State closely identified with the government for its wrong doings'.

The African Court on Human and Peoples' Rights

The creation of an African Court on Human and Peoples' Rights[59] (here-inafter the 'Court') with the specific task of reinforcing the role of the Commission[60] enhances in theory the prospects of promoting the protection of human rights in Africa. The possibility of jurisdictional disputes between the two organs does exist, and will be discussed in Chapter 10.

In addition, it must be pointed out that the Court will not be the only judicial organ with sole responsibility for the protection of human rights in Africa. Thus the Court of Justice set up by the OAU's Treaty Establishing the African Economic Community (AEC Treaty)[61] is directed to protect human rights.[62] Similarly, a Court of Justice has been established under the Revised Treaty of the Economic Community of West African States (ECOWAS),[63] as has a Court of Justice of the Common Market for Eastern and Southern Africa.[64] Although the subject-matter of these treaties is economic affairs, the experience of the European Community proves that economic law has a justiciable human rights dimension[65] and it therefore seems only a matter

---

[59] Protocol to the African Charter on Human and Peoples' Rights on the Establishment of an African Court on Human and Peoples' Rights, adopted by the OAU Assembly of Heads of State and Government at its 34th Ordinary Session in Ouagadougou in 1998, RADIC 9 (1997) 953. The Protocol requires fifteen ratifications to enter into force: see Article 34(3). At the time of writing, five States have ratified. For an analysis of the Protocol, see G. J. Naldi and K. D. Magliveras, 'Reinforcing the African System of Human Rights: The Protocol on the Establishment of a Regional Court of Human and Peoples' Rights', NQHR 16 (1998) 431. For further discussion of the Court, see Chapter 10 below.

[60] Article 2 of the Protocol.

[61] Naldi (ed.), *Documents of the Organization of African Unity*, p. 203; ILM 30 (1991) 1241. On the AEC, see Naldi, *The Organization of African Unity*, pp. 240–58; G. J. Naldi and K. D. Magliveras, 'The African Economic Community: Emancipation for African States or Yet Another Glorious Failure?', *North Carolina Journal of International Law and Commercial Regulation* 24 (1999) 601.

[62] According to Article 3(g) of the AEC Treaty, one of the principles of the AEC is the 'recognition, promotion and protection of human and peoples' rights in accordance with the provisions of the African Charter on Human and Peoples' Rights'. The Court of Justice has jurisdiction to adjudicate upon this provision under Article 18 of the AEC Treaty.

[63] Article 4(g) of the Revised ECOWAS Treaty, RADIC 8 (1996) 187.

[64] Article 6(e) of the COMESA Treaty, ILM 33 (1994) 1111. On the jurisdiction of the Court of Justice, see in particular Articles 19, 23–26 and 32.

[65] *Internationale Handelsgesellschaft* v. *Einfuhr und Vorratstelle fur Getreide und Futtermittel* [1970] ECR 1125. In *Opinion 2/94 on Accession by the Community to the European Convention on Human Rights* [1996] ECR I-1759, paras. 33–4, the European Court of Justice

---

of time before these courts pronounce on human rights issues. This raises the issue of conflicting interpretations and conclusions arising concerning the application and definition of Charter rights.

The African Charter on the Rights and Welfare of the Child

The African Charter only makes the briefest of express references to the rights of children.[66] In the years following the adoption of the African Charter, however, the question of children's rights came to the fore in the international arena leading to the adoption of the UN Convention on the Rights of the Child in 1989.[67] Although the UN Convention attracted the support of many African States,[68] it was felt that the African child was exposed to a particular set of dangerous circumstances[69] which called for additional measures of protection but in an African perspective.[70] The result was the 1990 African Charter on the Rights and Welfare of the Child.[71]

The Charter may be said to complement the UN Convention on the Rights of the Child. It seeks to guarantee a number of civil, political, economic, social and cultural rights comparable to those protected by the UN Convention, although it would seem that such protection is not generally as effective as under the UN Convention.[72] However, the Charter yields in those situations where it may be considered not to equal national or international standards.[73] Furthermore, in keeping with the African concept

stated that 'it is well settled that fundamental rights form an integral part of the general principles of law whose observance the Court ensures. Respect for human rights is therefore a condition for the lawfulness of Community acts.'

[66] Article 18(3) of the African Charter.   [67] ILM 28 (1989) 1448.

[68] Somalia is one of only two States not to have ratified the UN Convention.

[69] K. C. J. M. Arts, 'The International Protection of Children's Rights in Africa: The 1990 OAU Charter on the Rights and Welfare of the Child', RADIC 5 (1993) 139 at 141–3.

[70] B. Thompson, 'Africa's Charter on Children's Rights: A Normative Break with Cultural Traditionalism', ICLQ 41 (1992) 434.

[71] Naldi (ed.), *Documents of the Organization of African Unity*, p. 183. The Charter requires fifteen ratifications to enter into force (Article 47(3)); it became operational on 29 October 1999.

[72] Arts, 'The International Protection of Children's Rights in Africa', pp. 147–9, identifies the freedom of expression, the freedom of thought, conscience and religion, the right to privacy, the right of access to information, the right to benefit from social security, and explicit rights for minorities as especially problematic since they are subordinate to the rights of parents, legal guardians or the State.

[73] Article 1(2); Arts, 'The International Protection of Children's Rights in Africa', pp. 154–5.

of rights, the Charter imposes responsibilities on the child towards his or her family, the community and the State.[74] Yet there are progressive features in the Charter. It should be observed initially that a child is defined as a person below the age of eighteen years.[75] The best interests of the child is *the* primary consideration.[76] The participation and recruitment of children in armed conflicts is prohibited.[77] Harmful social and cultural practices are to be eliminated.[78] It seems that female genital mutilation is included in this proscription.[79] Child marriages are expressly prohibited[80] but curiously the age bar is set somewhat high at eighteen years.[81] In relation to refugee children Article 23(4) of the Charter adheres to the broad definition of refugee status in the OAU Convention on Refugees 1969.[82] The prohibition on child labour is somewhat equivocal, however.[83] Requiring States Parties only to take legislative and administrative measures to combat this problem has been criticised as inadequate.[84] On the other hand, the

---

[74] Article 31. See Arts, 'The International Protection of Children's Rights in Africa', pp. 153–4.

[75] Article 2. Cf. Article 1 of the UN Convention on the Rights of the Child, which is less conclusive. See Arts, 'The International Protection of Children's Rights in Africa', p. 145.

[76] Article 4. By way of contrast, the best interests of the child is simply *a* primary consideration according to Article 3(1) of the UN Convention on the Rights of the Child.

[77] Article 22. The UN Convention on the Rights of the Child has come in for particular criticism because Article 38 permits recruitment as from age fifteen years. See now the Optional Protocol (2000) and notes 135, 138 and 139 below.

[78] Article 21(1). See further the UN Fourth World Conference on Women (Beijing Platform for Action), ILM 35 (1996) 401, paras. 113, 115, 118, 124, 224, 276 and 277; the Vienna Declaration and Plan of Action, Part I, para. 18(2), Part II, paras. 38 and 4. See also Article 1(3) of the Charter, which states that any custom, tradition, cultural or religious practice inconsistent with the Charter shall to the extent of the inconsistency be discouraged. In *Dow* v. *Attorney-General* [1992] 2 LRC (Const) 623, the Botswana Court of Appeal, addressing the issue of sex discrimination, held that custom and tradition must always yield to the Constitution and express legislation.

[79] Arts, 'The International Protection of Children's Rights in Africa', p. 151. This practice has been condemned by the Beijing Platform for Action, para. 283(d). It has been reported that female circumcision exists in at least twenty-five countries in Africa: UN Doc. E/CN.4/Sub.2/1991/6, p. 3. A WHO Regional Plan of Action to Accelerate the Elimination of Female Genital Mutilation was launched in many African countries in March 1997: UN Doc. E/CN.4/Sub.2/1997/SR.14, para. 15. See further below.

[80] Article 21(2); Beijing Platform for Action, paras. 93 and 274(e).

[81] Arts, 'The International Protection of Children's Rights in Africa', p. 149. See further below.

[82] Article 1(2), in Naldi (ed.), *Documents of the Organization of African Unity*, p. 101. For discussion, see Naldi, *The Organization of African Unity*, pp. 79–80.

[83] Article 15. Cf. Article 32 of the UN Convention.

[84] Arts, 'The International Protection of Children's Rights in Africa', pp. 149–50. By comparison, Article 32(2) of the UN Convention additionally requires social and educational measures.

measures required of States Parties is more extensive than those of the UN Convention.[85]

The Charter makes provision for an implementation mechanism, the African Committee of Experts on the Rights and Welfare of the Child,[86] which, while it must meet at least once a year, can be convened whenever necessary.[87] The mandate of the Committee, which has been praised as 'positive', broader and better defined than that of the UN Committee on the Rights of the Child,[88] is to promote and protect the rights and welfare of the child, especially to collect and document information, to assess problems relating to children, to organise meetings, to encourage national and local institutions concerned with child welfare, to advise governments, to formulate and draft rules aimed at protecting children, to co-operate with African, regional and international institutions and organisations concerned with the rights and welfare of children, to monitor the implementation and ensure protection of the rights enshrined in the Charter, and to perform any other tasks entrusted to it by the OAU.[89] As part of the monitoring activities, there is a reporting procedure that requires States to submit a report to the Committee every three years.[90]

A potentially significant achievement, which is not mirrored in the UN Convention, confers upon the Committee jurisdiction to entertain communications from persons, groups or NGOs relating to the Charter.[91] This provision would seem to allow the Committee to consider complaints in the manner of the African Commission or the UN Human Rights Committee. In addition, the Committee has been granted broad powers of investigation.[92] It may therefore resort to any appropriate method of investigating any matter falling within the ambit of the Charter, including measures a State Party has taken to implement the Charter, and request from the States Parties any information relevant to the implementation of the Charter. However, in formal terms of enforcement the Committee's principal weapon under the Charter is publicity, the OAU having ultimate responsibility.[93] Nevertheless, the Committee thus has at its disposal considerable powers to hold States to

---

[85] Arts, 'The International Protection of Children's Rights in Africa', p. 150.
[86] Article 32.   [87] Article 37(3).
[88] Arts, 'The International Protection of Children's Rights in Africa', pp. 155–7, who considers the African Commission to be a better comparison.
[89] Article 42.
[90] Article 43(1)(b). Under the UN Convention, the time period is five years: Article 44(1)(b).
[91] Article 44(1).   [92] Article 45(1).   [93] Article 45(2)–(4).

account for their failings in relation to the rights and welfare of children. If exercised properly, the Committee could become a formidable guardian of children's rights.

The Charter must be viewed as a positive development on the whole. It does not detract from the UN Convention; rather it complements it. The mandate of the Committee compares favourably with that of the UN Committee. Since the Charter has just entered into force, it is still too early to say what its impact will be. It may be that the Charter is simply too radical and progressive for many African States to attract widespread support since it challenges established traditions and customary and religious laws.[94]

The Grand Bay Declaration

In addition to the failings of the African institutional mechanisms for the protection of human rights, much of Africa has been racked in recent years by a series of events, civil wars, international conflicts, dictatorial rule, the collapse of civil society, economic crises and natural disasters,[95] which have contributed to the deterioration of the human rights situation. The OAU therefore decided that the root causes of human rights violations had to be reappraised with a view to improving strategies for the promotion and protection of human rights. The result was the OAU's First Ministerial Conference on Human and Peoples' Rights, held in Mauritius on 12–16 April 1999, which adopted the Grand Bay (Mauritius) Declaration and Plan of Action.[96]

The Declaration is significant in a number of ways. It seeks to integrate human rights policies throughout the activities of the OAU. It calls for the

---

[94] In particular, family law: Arts, 'The International Protection of Children's Rights in Africa', p. 158; Thompson, 'Africa's Charter on Children's Rights', pp. 438–42.

[95] United Nations, Report of the Secretary-General on Causes of Conflict and the Promotion of Durable Peace and Sustainable Development in Africa, Part II. See also Resolution on the Human Rights Situation in Africa, Eighth Annual Activity Report (*Documents of the African Commission*, p. 402).

[96] CONF/HRA/DECL (I), reprinted in RADIC 11 (1999) 352. The Office of the UN High Commissioner for Human Rights was instrumental in providing assistance to the Commission in the preparation of the Conference: UN Doc. E/CN.4/1999/93, pp. 2–4. It should be observed that, although the Declaration is not a legally binding document, it could be viewed, *inter alia*, as an authoritative interpretation and elaboration of the meaning of human rights in the OAU Charter, the African Charter and the African Charter on the Rights and Welfare of the Child.

strengthening of the Commission. It encourages OAU Member States to ratify and implement all major OAU and UN human rights conventions. It reaffirms the evolution of our contemporary understanding of human rights as expressed in documents such as the Vienna Declaration and Programme of Action, although it cannot be said that the Declaration is revolutionary in expanding the frontiers of human rights. Therefore only those provisions that emphasise this assessment will be discussed.

The Declaration must be viewed in the wider context of the legitimate aspirations of the peoples of Africa to secure full enjoyment of human rights.[97] Hence the Declaration rightly considers the promotion and protection of human rights a priority for Africa,[98] acknowledging that observance of human rights is indispensable for maintaining national and international peace and security and encouraging sustainable development.[99] It therefore seeks to consolidate and build upon the gains already made in Africa in the field of human rights.[100]

The Conference 'affirms the principle that human rights are universal, indivisible, interdependent and inter-related' and calls for parity to be given to economic, social and cultural rights as well as civil and political rights.[101] In addition, the right to development, the right to a generally satisfactory, healthy environment and the 'right to national and international peace and security' are held to be 'universal and inalienable rights which form an integral part of fundamental human rights'.[102] It will be recalled that one of the distinctive features of the African Charter has been its inclusive nature, guaranteeing, *inter alia*, economic, social and cultural rights, or second generation rights, and peoples' rights, or third generation or group rights.

---

[97] Preambular para. 8. See also para. 5(c).   [98] *Ibid.*, para. 1.

[99] *Ibid.*, paras. 3, 7, 9 and 10. Preambular para. 4 recognises that violations of human rights constitute a burden for the international community. See also the Vienna Declaration and Programme of Action, Part I, para. 6.

[100] Preambular paras. 12 and 15. The Declaration accepts that a multi-faceted approach is needed to tackle the causes of human rights violations in Africa: para. 8.

[101] Para. 1; preambular para. 12; and further African Charter, preambular para. 8. See also the Vienna Declaration and Programme of Action, Part I, paras. 5 and 8.

[102] Para. 2; see also preambular para. 9. See further Vienna Declaration and Programme of Action, Part I, paras. 10(1) and 11(1) and Part II, para. 74. With specific reference to the right to development, the Declaration on the Right to Development 1986, UN General Assembly Resolution 41/128, which describes this right as 'inalienable', reiterates the interdependence and indivisibility of all human rights.

Taking the opportunity to reinforce its support for second and third generation rights, the Conference condemns poverty,[103] disease,[104] ignorance and illiteracy,[105] certain structural adjustment programmes giving rise to social dislocation and the debt problem[106] as inimical to the enjoyment of human rights.[107] It calls upon the international community to alleviate the debt burden in order to allow the maximisation of human rights.[108] It reaffirms its concern for the environment by identifying environmental degradation as a violation of human rights.[109]

---

[103] It is estimated that 40 per cent of the population of sub-Saharan Africa lives in poverty: UN Doc. E/C.12/1997/SR.27, para. 27. The Vienna Declaration and Programme of Action establishes a link between poverty and the inhibition of human rights: Part I, para. 14. See also para. 25 thereof. The rights especially affected include the right to food, the right to health and the right to education.

[104] See Article 16 of the African Charter. According to the Economic Commission for Africa (ECA), access to healthcare is generally poor in Africa: *African Economic Report – 1998*, paras. 78 and 80.

[105] According to the ECA, the literacy rate in Africa seems to be 61 per cent: *African Economic Report – 1998*, para. 75. Article 17 of the African Charter guarantees the right to education.

[106] UN Commission on Human Rights, Resolution 1999/22, UN Doc. E/CN.4/1999/167, p. 96.

[107] Para. 8(c), (e) and (f).

[108] Para. 26. A concerted, albeit limited, response by the international community has been the Heavily Indebted Poor Countries Initiative developed jointly in 1996 by the IMF and the World Bank: *African Economic Report – 1998*, Part I. A.6.

[109] Para. 8(n). The link between the two is well established in international law: *Lopez Ostra v. Spain* EHRR 20 (1995) 277; *Gabcikovo-Nagymaros Project Case*, ILM 37 (1998) 162 at 206 *per* Judge Weeramantry; Vienna Declaration and Programme of Action, Part I, para. 11(1); Stockholm Declaration on the Human Environment 1972, ILM 11 (1972) 1416; UN Commission on Human Rights, Adverse Effects of the Illicit Movement and Dumping of Toxic and Dangerous Products and Wastes on the Enjoyment of Human Rights, Progress Report of the Special Rapporteur, UN Docs E/CN.4/Sub.2/1991/8, E/CN.4/Sub.2/1992/7, pp. 22–31, E/CN.4/Sub.2/1993/7, E/CN.4/Sub.2/1994/9 and E/CN.4/Sub.2/1996/17, pp. 33–5. See further J. Downs, 'A Healthy and Ecologically Balanced Environment: An Argument for a Third Generation Right', *Duke Journal of Comparative and International Law* 3 (1993) 351; W. P. Gormley, 'The Legal Obligation of the International Community to Guarantee a Pure and Decent Environment: The Expansion of Human Rights Norms', *Georgetown International Environmental Law Review* 3 (1990) 85; D. Shelton, 'Human Rights, Environmental Rights, and the Right to the Environment', *Stanford Journal of International Law* 28 (1991) 103. It must be recalled that the OAU paved the way in international law by establishing a satisfactory environment as a human right in Article 24 of the African Charter. This provision of the African Charter has been criticised for its vagueness: see R. R. Churchill, 'Environmental Rights in Existing Human Rights Treaties', in A. E. Boyle and M. R. Anderson (eds.), *Human Rights Approaches to Environmental Protection* (Oxford: Clarendon Press, 1996), p. 89 at pp. 104–7. Africa suffers from a number of environmental problems: see UN General Assembly Resolution A/RES/S-19/2.

The Conference 'affirms the interdependence of the principles of good governance, the rule of law, democracy and development'.[110] Despite recent advances in constitutionalism across parts of Africa, liberal democratic values have not set deep roots.[111] Many ruling regimes lack popular support or democratic mandate.[112] Rather, bad governance and abuses of human

[110] Para. 3; preambular para. 8. The OAU had paved the way by endorsing these principles in two resolutions adopted at its 35th Ordinary Summit in Algiers in July 1999: see Murray, 'Africa', p. 518. Cf. Articles 13(1) and 20(1) of the African Charter, and see Umozurike, *The African Charter*, pp. 36–8. See also Vienna Declaration and Programme of Action, Part I, para. 9. The Vienna Declaration and Programme of Action establishes a link between democracy, respect for human rights and development: Part I, paras. 8 and 10(3). In its Resolution 1999/57, entitled 'Promotion of the Right to Democracy', UN Doc. E/CN.4/1999/167, p. 194, the UN Commission on Human Rights declared that democracy fosters the full realisation of human rights. See further Communication 129/94, *Civil Liberties Organisation* v. *Nigeria*, Ninth Activity Report 1995–1996, Annex VIII (*Documents of the African Commission*, p. 452), where the Commission sought to uphold the rule of law.

[111] M. Sinjela, 'Constitutionalism in Africa: Emerging Trends', *The Review* (International Commission of Jurists) No. 60 (1998) 23. The Commonwealth has been instrumental in setting an agenda of democracy and human rights: see the Harare Commonwealth Declaration 1991, *Commonwealth Law Bulletin* 18 (1992) 347–9; A. Duxbury, 'Rejuvenating the Commonwealth: The Human Rights Remedy', ICLQ 46 (1997) 344. Thus Nigeria's membership of the Commonwealth was suspended in 1995 as a result of human rights abuses: see K. D. Magliveras, *Exclusion from Participation in International Organisations* (The Hague: Kluwer, 1999), pp. 188–92. The Commission also condemned the abuse of human rights in Nigeria, Resolution on Nigeria, Eighth Annual Activity Report (*Documents of the African Commission*, p. 400). The case of Sierra Leone is also instructive. The international community imposed sanctions on Sierra Leone following the *coup d'état* in 1997 which overthrew the democratically elected government. Under Resolution 1132 (1997) the UN Security Council imposed sanctions on Sierra Leone and authorised ECOWAS to enforce them. Moreover, the OAU authorised ECOMOG to remove the military junta by force: see *Keesing's* 43 (1997) 41674. In addition, Sierra Leone was suspended from the Commonwealth: Magliveras, *Exclusion from Participation*, pp. 192–4.

[112] It is interesting to observe that the Commission has opined that the forcible assumption of power is in breach of Articles 13(1) and 20(1) of the African Charter and that the best form of government is one elected by and accountable to the people and has thus called upon military governments to hand over power to democratically elected representatives. Resolution on the Military, Eighth Annual Activity Report (*Documents of the African Commission*, p. 399). Moreover, it has condemned the planning or execution of *coups d'état* and any attempt to seize power by undemocratic means and has called upon African Governments to ensure that elections are transparent and fair. Eighth Annual Activity Report, Resolution on the Human Rights Situation in Africa (*Documents of the African Commission*, p. 559). See also Communication 44/90, *Peoples' Democratic Organisation for Independence and Socialism* v. *The Gambia*, Tenth Activity Report 1996–1997, Annex X (*Documents of the African Commission*, p. 402); Communication 102/93, *Constitutional*

rights have been common events. Indeed, the Conference acknowledges the link between these situations and violations of human rights.[113]

The Conference acknowledges that these objectives cannot be easily achieved without an independent and impartial judiciary.[114] The role of the judiciary in Africa has not been easy, particularly as its independence has often been under threat from the executive or military.[115] The Commission has therefore called for the independence of the judiciary to be respected.[116]

The Conference proceeds to identify the shared core values on which human rights are based and calls for account to be taken of positive traditional and cultural values.[117] Clearly, the basic aspirations of the human condition are thereby articulated and it must be observed that the instability that prevails in much of Africa cannot create the conditions necessary to satisfy these basic desires. The former include, first, respect for the sanctity of life. It is unlikely that this phrase is to be read literally since the African

---

Rights Projects and Civil Liberties Organisation v. *Nigeria,* Twelfth Activity Report 1998–1999, Annex V (*Documents of the African Commission,* p. 712).

[113] Para. 8(g)–(i), (p) and (r).

[114] Para. 4. The lack of an independent judiciary is considered as contributing to the violation of human rights in Africa: para. 8(k). See further the Vienna Declaration and Programme of Action, Part I, para. 27; UN Basic Principles on the Independence of the Judiciary, *The United Nations and Human Rights 1945–1995* (New York: United Nations, 1995), p. 313.

[115] Pressure on the judiciary from the executive is common in much of Africa most recently in Zimbabwe notwithstanding Article 26 of the African Charter: Ankumah, *The African Commission,* pp. 125–6. See further the opinion of the UN Human Rights Committee in Communication 468/91, *Olo Bahamonde* v. *Equatorial Guinea,* UN Doc. A/49/40, Annex IX, BB; and the report of Special Rapporteur Mr Param Cumaraswamy on the independence of judges and lawyers, UN Doc. E/CN.4/2000/61. For further discussion, see B. Ajibola and D. Van Zyl (eds.), *The Judiciary in Africa* (Cape Town: Juta, 1998), pp. 105–81.

[116] Resolution on The Gambia, Eighth Annual Activity Report (*Documents of the African Commission,* p. 405); Resolution on Nigeria, Eighth Annual Activity Report (*Documents of the African Commission,* p. 404); Communication 129/94, *Civil Liberties Organisation* v. *Nigeria,* Ninth Activity Report 1995–1996, Annex VIII (*Documents of the African Commission,* p. 452); Communication 60/91, *Constitutional Rights Project (in respect of Wahab Akamu, G. Adega and others)* v. *Nigeria,* Eighth Activity Report 1994–1995, Annex VI (*Documents of the African Commission,* p. 385); Communication 87/93, *Constitutional Rights Project (in respect of Zamani Lakwot and others* v. *Nigeria),* Eighth Activity Report 1994–1995, Annex VI (*Documents of the African Commission,* p. 391); Communications 137/94, 154/96 and 161/97, *International Pen, Constitutional Rights Project, Interights on behalf of Ken Saro-Wiwa Jr and Civil Liberties Organisation* v. *Nigeria,* Twelfth Activity Report 1998–1999, Annex V (*Documents of the African Commission,* p. 729).

[117] Para. 5. Cf. Article 17(3) of the African Charter.

Charter itself does not provide an absolute guarantee.[118] Rather it is the prohibition on the arbitrary deprivation of life that is reinforced. Thus the Commission has condemned arbitrary[119] and extrajudicial killings.[120] Naturally, as the Declaration itself recognises, respect for life has inextricable links with other human rights, the most obvious being second and third generation rights such as health, food, development and a healthy environment. These all have resource implications which African countries have difficulty meeting for a variety of reasons. Respect for human dignity is also emphasised.[121]

[118] Article 4 of the African Charter; and see Naldi, *The Organization of African Unity*, pp. 117–18. Thus the majority of African States retain the death penalty. Angola, Cape Verde, Guinea-Bissau, Mauritius, Mozambique, Namibia, Sao Tomé and Principe, Seychelles and South Africa have abolished the death penalty. Mozambique, Namibia and Seychelles have ratified the Second Optional Protocol to the ICCPR. A number of other States are abolitionist *de facto*: see further R. Hood, *The Death Penalty* (2nd edn, Oxford: Oxford University Press, 1996), pp. 241–6; UN Doc. E/CN.4/1999/52. It should also be observed that Article 5(3) of the African Charter on the Rights and Welfare of the Child prohibits the sentence of death being pronounced on a child. As to abortion, the practice varies across Africa: see Naldi, *The Organization of African Unity*, p. 170 at note 59.

[119] Communications 64/92, 68/92 and 78/92, *Krischna Achutan (on behalf of Aleke Banda)*; *Amnesty International*; *Amnesty International (on behalf of Orton and Vera Chirwa) v. Malawi*, Seventh Activity Report 1993–1994, Annex IX; Eighth Activity Report 1994–1995; Annex VI (*Documents of the African Commission*, pp. 347 and 387); Communications 137/94, 139/94, 154/96 and 161/97, *International Pen, Constitutional Rights Project, Interights on behalf of Ken Saro-Wiwa Jr and Civil Liberties Organisation v. Nigeria*, Twelfth Activity Report 1998–1999, Annex V (*Documents of the African Commission*, p. 729). Communication 194/85, *Miango v. Zaire* (UN Human Rights Committee), UN Doc. A/43/40, p. 218.

[120] Communications 25/89, 47/90, 56/91 and 100/93 (joined), *Free Legal Assistance Group, Lawyers' Committee for Human Rights, Union Interafricaine des Droits de l'Homme, Les Témoins de Jehovah v. Zaire*, Ninth Activity Report 1995–1996, Annex VIII (*Documents of the African Commission*, p. 444); Communications 27/89, 46/91, 49/91 and 99/93, *Organisation Mondiale Contre la Torture and Association Internationale des Juristes Democrates, Commission Internationale des Juristes (CIJ), Union Interafricaine des Droits de l'Homme v. Rwanda*, Tenth Activity Report 1996–1997, Annex X (*Documents of the African Commission*, p. 551). See also Communication 542/93, *Tshishimbi v. Zaire*, Communication 542/93 (UN Human Rights Committee).

[121] Cf. Article 5 of the African Charter. The Commission has found violations of this provision to have been established on a number of occasions: see Communications 64/92, 68/92 and 78/92, *Krischna Achutan, Amnesty International, Amnesty International v. Malawi*, Seventh Activity Report 1993–1994, Annex IX; Eighth Activity Report 1994–1995, Annex VI (*Documents of the African Commission*, pp. 347; 387); Communication 25/89, *Free Legal Assistance Group and Others v. Zaire*, HRLJ 18 (1997) 32; Communication 74/92, *Commission Nationale des Droits de l'Homme et des Libertes v. Chad*, Ninth Activity Report

Secondly, seeking to promote the values associated with cultural and other diversity, and a tolerance of differences, is a distinguishing feature of liberal pluralist democracies.[122] In this context, the Conference accepts that the

1995–1996, Annex VIII (*Documents of the African Commission*, p. 449); Communications 27/89, 46/91, 49/91 and 99/93, *Organisation Mondiale Contre la Torture and Association Internationale des Juristes Democrates, Commission Internationale des Juristes (CIJ), Union Interafricaine des Droits de l'Homme* v. *Rwanda*, Tenth Activity Report 1996–1997, Annex X (*Documents of the African Commission*, p. 551); Communication 97/93, *Modise* v. *Botswana*, Seventh Activity Report 1993–1994, Annex IX; Tenth Activity Report 1996–1997, Annex X (*Documents of the African Commission*, pp. 349 and 567); Communications 137/94, 139/94, 154/96 and 161/97, *International Pen, Constitutional Rights Project, Interights on behalf of Ken Saro-Wiwa Jr and Civil Liberties Organisation* v. *Nigeria*, Twelfth Activity Report 1998–1999, Annex V (*Documents of the African Commission*, p. 729); Communication 212/98, *Amnesty International* v. *Zambia*, Twelfth Activity Report 1998–1999, Annex V (*Documents of the African Commission*, p. 745). See also Communications 241/87 and 242/87, *Birhashwirwa and Mulumba* v. *Zaire* (UN Human Rights Committee), UN Doc. A/45/40, Annex IX, I; Communication 428/90, *Bozize* v. *Central African Republic* (UN Human Rights Committee), UN Doc. HR/94/24; Communication 440/90, *El-Megreisi* v. *Libya* (UN Human Rights Committee), UN Doc. HR/94/24; Communication 326/88, *Kalenga* v. *Zambia*; Communication 366/89, *Kanana* v. *Zaire* (UN Human Rights Committee), UN Doc. A/49/40, Annex IX, J; Communication 49/79, *Marais* v. *Madagascar* (UN Human Rights Committee); Communication 414/90, *Mika Miha* v. *Equatorial Guinea* (UN Human Rights Committee), UN Doc. CCPR/C/51/D/414/1990; Communication 458/91, *Mukong* v. *Cameroon* (UN Human Rights Committee), UN Doc. CCPR/C/51/D/458/1991. Ankumah, *The African Commission*, p. 116, is therefore moved to write that torture is practised with 'impunity' in Africa.

[122] In *South African National Defence Union* v. *Minister of Defence and Another* 1999 (6) BCLR 615 (CC) at 623, O'Regan J emphasised the importance of tolerance of different views by society, saying that: 'Tolerance, of course, does not require approbation of a particular view. In essence, it requires the acceptance of the public airing of disagreements and the refusal to silence unpopular views.' See also *National Coalition for Gay and Lesbian Equality* v. *Minister of Justice and Others* 1998 (12) BCLR 1517 (CC) at 1574–7 *per* Sachs J; Communication 468/91, *Olo Bahamonde* v. *Equatorial Guinea* (UN Human Rights Committee), UN Doc. A/49/40, Annex IX, BB. See also the Vienna Declaration and Programme of Action, Part II, B.1. In its Resolution 1998/21, entitled 'Tolerance and Pluralism as Indivisible Elements in the Promotion and Protection of Human Rights', UN Doc. E/CN.4/1998/177, p. 84, the UN Commission on Human Rights recognised that tolerance and pluralism strengthen democracy, facilitate the full enjoyment of all human rights and thereby constitute a sound foundation for civil society, social harmony and peace. It should be observed that in much of Africa little tolerance of alternative lifestyles is shown, e.g. Zimbabwe, where President Mugabe has made homophobic statements on a number of occasions: see Communication 136/94, *William Courson* v. *Zimbabwe*, Eighth Activity Report 1994–1995, Annex VI (*Documents of the African Commission*, p. 397), and Ankumah, *The African Commission*, p. 174. Cf. section 9(3) of the Constitution of South Africa and *National Coalition for Gay and Lesbian Equality* v. *Minister of Justice and Others* 1998 (12) BCLR 1517 (CC).

exploitation of ethnicity, racism and religious intolerance contributes to the violation of human rights.[123]

The Conference therefore takes the opportunity to express its deep concern about acts of genocide, crimes against humanity and war crimes that have been perpetrated in parts of Africa, and calls for both their elimination and adequate handling.[124] The African Charter does not expressly address such massive violations of human rights which, in the light of the recent history of communal violence and 'ethnic cleansing' in parts of Africa, exemplified by the genocidal atrocities in the Great Lakes region, seems regrettable.[125] However, under Article 58(1) of the African Charter, the Commission is allowed to draw to the OAU's attention cases revealing 'the existence of a series of serious or massive violations of human and peoples' rights'.[126] Thus the Commission has been able to rely on this provision to

---

[123] Para. 8(b) and (s). See also Articles 8 and 28 of the African Charter. According to Umozurike, *The African Charter*, pp. 53–4, Article 19 of the African Charter protects minorities. See also Communications 27/89, 46/91, 49/91 and 99/93, *Organisation Mondiale Contre la Torture and Association Internationale des Juristes Democrates, Commission Internationale des Juristes (CIJ), Union Interafricaine des Droits de l'Homme* v. *Rwanda*, Tenth Activity Report 1996–1997, Annex X (*Documents of the African Commission*, p. 551); Communication 56/91, *Les Témoins de Jehovah* v. *Zaire*, Ninth Activity Report 1995–1996, Annex VIII (*Documents of the African Commission*, p. 444). See also *Prosecutor* v. *Akayesu*, ILM 37 (1998) 1399.

[124] Para. 11. See also preambular paras. 6 and 8(s). See also the Vienna Declaration and Programme of Action, Part I, para. 28. See further the Statement on Africa adopted by the UN Committee on the Elimination of Racial Discrimination, UN Doc. A/54/18, pp. 11–12. It is interesting to note that Hissene Habre, former President of Chad was indicted in Senegal under the UN Convention Against Torture 1984 for human rights abuses: *International Enforcement Law Reporter* 16 (2000) 634.

[125] It should be observed that the International Criminal Tribunal for Rwanda has found as proven accusations of genocide and crimes against humanity: *Prosecutor* v. *Akayesu*, ILM 37 (1998) 1399; *Prosecutor* v. *Kambanda*, ILM 37 (1998) 1411; and, most recently, *Prosecutor* v. *Rutaganda*, ILM 39 (2000) 557; *Prosecutor* v. *Musema*, *International Enforcement Law Reporter* 16 (2000) 652. Rwanda itself is trying suspects before a special genocide court, but in an effort to expedite justice the introduction of a traditional form of trial known as *gacaca* is contemplated: Report on the Situation of Human Rights in Rwanda Submitted by the Special Representative, Mr Michel Moussalli, UN Doc. E/CN.4/2000/41, pp. 27–32. According to the UN Commission on Human Rights, violations of human rights and international humanitarian law continue in the Democratic Republic of the Congo, Resolution 1999/56, UN Doc. E/CN.4/1999/167, p. 189.

[126] Communications 25/89, 47/90, 56/91 and 100/93 (joined), *Free Legal Assistance Group, Lawyers' Committee for Human Rights, Union Interafricaine des Droits de l'Homme, Les Témoins de Jehovah* v. *Zaire*, Ninth Activity Report 1995–1996, Annex VIII (*Documents*

find that events in Rwanda amounted to, *inter alia*, gross violations of human rights.[127]

Recognising that the family unit as the basis of society needs to be strengthened,[128] better protection of women's and children's rights is also sought,[129] and the abolition of discrimination against women[130] and children[131] and cultural practices which dehumanise or demean women and children is called for.[132] Furthermore, the Conference calls upon States to adopt measures to eradicate violence against women[133] and children.[134]

---

of the African Commission, p. 444); Communication 74/92, *Commission Nationale des Droits de l'Homme et des Libertés* v. *Chad*, Ninth Activity Report 1995–1996, Annex VIII (*Documents of the African Commission*, p. 449). On this question, see R. Murray, 'Serious or Massive Violations Under the African Charter on Human and Peoples' Rights: A Comparison with the Inter-American and European Mechanisms', NQHR 17 (1999) 109.

[127] Communications 27/89, 46/91, 49/91 and 99/93, *Organisation Mondiale Contre la Torture and Association Internationale des Juristes Démocrates, Commission Internationale des Juristes (CIJ), Union Interafricaine des Droits de l'Homme* v. *Rwanda*, Tenth Activity Report 1996–1997, Annex X (*Documents of the African Commission*, p. 551).

[128] Communication 212/98, *Amnesty International* v. *Zambia*, Twelfth Activity Report 1998–1999, Annex V (*Documents of the African Commission*, p. 745).

[129] Para. 6. Cf. Article 18(3) of the African Charter. According to the Vienna Declaration and Programme of Action, Part I, para. 18, and the Beijing Platform for Action, para. 213, the human rights of women and of the girl-child are an inalienable, integral and indivisible part of human rights. It has been seen above that the OAU had already adopted a comprehensive set of children's rights in the form of the African Charter on the Rights and Welfare of the Child, which came into force a few months after the adoption of the Declaration. With regard to women's rights, the Commission forwarded to the OAU a draft protocol in September 2000, see pp. 31–4 below.

[130] Cf. Article 18(3) of the African Charter; UN Convention on the Elimination of All Forms of Discrimination Against Women 1979; Vienna Declaration and Programme of Action, Part I, para. 18; Beijing Platform for Action, para. 214.

[131] See Articles 3, 21(1)(b) and 26 of the African Charter on the Rights and Welfare of the Child, in Naldi, *Documents of the Organization of African Unity*, p. 183; Article 2(1) of the UN Convention on the Rights of the Child; Beijing Platform for Action, para. 93.

[132] Para. 8(j) accepts that harmful traditional practices violate human rights, whereas para. 10 sees their removal as contributing to the promotion of human rights.

[133] See the Vienna Declaration and Programme of Action, Part II, para. 38; Beijing Platform for Action, paras. 99 and 113.

[134] See Article 16 of the African Charter on the Rights and Welfare of the Child; Articles 19 and 37(a) of the UN Convention on the Rights of the Child; Beijing Platform for Action, paras. 99 and 283(b) and (d). It should be observed that many African States retain judicial corporal punishment for juveniles although it has been declared unconstitutional by the Constitutional Court of South Africa in *S* v. *Williams and Others* 1995 (7) BCLR 861 (CC), the Supreme Court of Namibia in *Ex Parte Attorney-General, Namibia: Re Corporal*

In particular, the Conference wants to see an end to the use of child soldiers and urges better protection of peoples in conflict situations.[135]

In addition, the Conference, recognising that contemporary forms of slavery contribute to the violation of human rights in Africa,[136] recommends that steps be taken to eradicate child labour,[137] sexual exploitation of children[138] and trafficking in children,[139] and for the protection of children in conflict with the law[140] and refugee children.[141]

Punishment by Organs of State 1991 (3) SA 76 (NmS) and the Supreme Court of Zimbabwe in *S* v. *Juvenile* 1990 (4) SA 151 (ZS) (although reversed by the Constitution of Zimbabwe Amendment (No. 11) Act 1990).

[135] See Article 22 of the African Charter on the Rights and Welfare of the Child; Article 38 of the UN Convention on the Rights of the Child; and note the Optional Protocol to the UN Convention on the Rights of the Child on involvement of children in armed conflict, UN Doc. A/54/49 (2000). See further UN Security Council Resolution 1261 (1999). It is estimated that there are some 120,000 child soldiers in Africa: UN Doc. E/CN.4/2000/3, para. 38. See also Vienna Declaration and Plan of Action, Part I, para. 29, Part II, para. 50; and Beijing Platform for Action, paras. 131–40.

[136] Para. 8(a). The Vienna Declaration and Programme of Action has condemned these examples of contemporary forms of slavery: Part I, para. 21.

[137] See Article 15 of the African Charter on the Rights and Welfare of the Child; Article 32 of the UN Convention on the Rights of the Child; Beijing Platform for Action, para. 282; ILO Convention No. 182 Concerning the Prohibition and Elimination of the Worst Forms of Child Labour, ILM 38 (1999) 1207. There appears to have been a sharp increase in the exploitation of child labour across Africa in recent years as a result of unfavourable economic conditions, including the use of children in crime and drugs-related activities, UN Docs E/CN.4/Sub.2/1993/30, para. 39; and E/CN.4/Sub.2/1993/30, paras. 97–8.

[138] See Article 27 of the African Charter on the Rights and Welfare of the Child; Article 34 of the UN Convention on the Rights of the Child; Vienna Declaration and Plan of Action, Part II, para. 48; Beijing Platform for Action, para. 283(d); and note the Optional Protocol to the UN Convention on the Rights of the Child on the sale of children, child prostitution and child pornography, UN Doc. A/54/49 (2000).

[139] See Article 29 of the African Charter on the Rights and Welfare of the Child; Beijing Platform for Action, para. 99; and note the Optional Protocol to the UN Convention on the Rights of the Child on the sale of children, child prostitution and child pornography, UN Doc. E/CN.4/1998/103. The abduction, sale and trafficking in children seems widespread in Sudan, UN Doc. A/54/49 (2000), para. 47; and the Protocol to Prevent, Suppress and Punish Trafficking in Persons, Especially Women and Children, Supplementing the UN Convention against Transnational Organised Crime, ILM 40 (2001) 377.

[140] See Article 17 of the African Charter on the Rights and Welfare of the Child; Articles 37 and 40 of the UN Convention on the Rights of the Child. It appears that many African countries lack special jurisdictions for juveniles: UN Doc. E/CN.4/Sub.2/1991/50, para. 32. See further Naldi, *The Organization of African Unity*, p. 183 at note 134.

[141] See Article 23 of the African Charter on the Rights and Welfare of the Child; Article 22 of the UN Convention of the Rights of the Child. See further Naldi, *The Organization of African Unity*, p. 90.

The Conference further urges full respect for the rights of people with disability[142] and people living with HIV and AIDS.[143] The impact of this disease on the fabric of African society must not be underestimated,[144] straining already limited resources.[145]

The Conference, acknowledging the link between human rights violations and population displacement,[146] calls for the problem of refugees and displaced persons to be addressed.[147] Notwithstanding the progressive nature

[142] See Article 18(4) of the African Charter; Article 13 of the African Charter on the Rights and Welfare of the Child; Article 23 of the UN Convention on the Rights of the Child. See also the Vienna Declaration and Plan of Action, Part II, paras. 63–5. The UN Committee on Economic, Social and Cultural Rights has stated that it must now be widely accepted that the rights of people with disabilities must be protected and promoted through legislation and policies, General Comment 5, UN Doc. HRI/GEN/1/Rev.2, pp. 66–70. Note Zimbabwe's Disabled Persons Act, UN Doc. CCPR/C/74/Add.3, para. 6(c).

[143] See also the Vienna Declaration and Plan of Action, Part I, para. 21; Beijing Platform for Action, paras. 98 and 281(d)–(e).

[144] *African Economic Report – 1998*, Economic Commission for Africa, para. 79, which states that 14 million people are affected by HIV/AIDS in sub-Saharan Africa. According to the World Bank, there are 23 million people with HIV/AIDS in Africa: *The Guardian* (London), 14 April 2000, p. 27. See also UN Doc. E/CN.4/2000/51, p. 12. As Zambia has acknowledged, social and economic development is threatened as HIV/AIDS hits the productive age group, UN Doc. E/CN.4/2000/SR.8, para. 87; UN Doc. E/CN.4/2000/51. James Wolfensohn, President of the World Bank, is quoted as stating that checking the speed of AIDS has probably become the 'most important development challenge facing us in Africa today': *ibid.* UN Secretary-General Kofi Annan has sought to draw attention to the adverse impact of HIV/AIDS in Africa, UN Doc. E/CN.4/1999/76.

[145] United Nations, Report of the Secretary-General on Causes of Conflict and the Promotion of Durable Peace and Sustainable Development in Africa, RADIC 10 (1998) 549, para. 87. According to the ECA, access to healthcare in Africa is generally poor: *African Economic Report – 1998*, paras. 78 and 80. The right to health is protected by Article 18 of the African Charter and Article 14 of the African Charter of the Rights and Welfare of the Child. In Communications 25/89, 47/90, 56/91 and 100/93 (joined), *Free Legal Assistance Group, Lawyers' Committee for Human Rights, Union Interafricaine des Droits de l'Homme, Les Témoins de Jehovah v. Zaire*, Ninth Activity Report 1995–1996, Annex VIII (*Documents of the African Commission*, p. 444), the Commission found that a shortage of medicine constituted a violation of Article 16.

[146] See preambular para. 8(d); Vienna Declaration and Plan of Action, Part I, para. 23(2). See further Naldi, *The Organization of African Unity*, p. 99, at note 1.

[147] Para. 9. It should be observed that the UN Commission on Human Rights has adopted the Guiding Principles on Internal Displacement setting out the rights and guarantees under international law relevant to the protection of internally displaced persons: UN Doc. E/CN.4/1998/53/Add.2. In Communications 27/89, 46/91, 49/91 and 99/93, *Organisation Mondiale Contre la Torture and Association Internationale des Juristes Democrates, Commission Internationale des Juristes (CIJ), Union Interafricaine des Droits de l'Homme*

of the OAU Convention on Refugees,[148] many African States have found that human dislocations have stretched their ability to cope.[149]

The Conference condemns terrorism as a violation of human rights, in particular the right to life.[150] It also urges African States to adopt an African convention to combat this problem.[151]

The Conference seeks to safeguard the values that promote civil society.[152] Recognising the role of the media as a public watchdog, the Conference urges States to guarantee a free and independent press.[153] Lack of freedom of association is also identified as a source of violations of human rights.[154]

In this regard, the lack of independent human rights institutions is considered as contributing to the violation of human rights.[155] The Conference

v. *Rwanda*, Tenth Activity Report 1996–1997, Annex X (*Documents of the African Commission*, p. 551), the Commission stated that Article 12 of the African Charter included 'a general protection of all those who are subject to persecution, that they may seek refuge in another State'.

[148] See Naldi, *The Organization of African Unity*, pp. 79–88.

[149] See *ibid.*, pp. 84 and 85–6.

[150] Para. 12; see also para. 8(q). It should be observed that Article 3(5) of the OAU Charter condemns political assassinations and subversive activities. This proscription was reinforced by the adoption in 1965 of the Declaration on the Problem of Subversion (text in Naldi (ed.), *Documents of the Organization of African Unity*, p. 57), according to which Member States undertake not to tolerate any acts of subversion against the OAU or its Member States. See further Naldi, *The Organization of African Unity*, p. 11.

[151] The OAU adopted the Convention on the Prevention and Combating of Terrorism at its Thirty-Fifth Ordinary Session held in Algiers in July 1999, RADIC 11 (1999) 777.

[152] Para. 17. See also para. 10, where the Conference recognises that 'the development and energisation' of civil society contributes to the creation of an environment conducive to human rights.

[153] Para. 21; preambular para. 8(m). Cf. Article 9 of the African Charter. The Commission has upheld the freedom of the press in Communication 102/93, *Constitutional Rights Project v. Nigeria*, Twelfth Activity Report 1998–1999, Annex V (*Documents of the African Commission*, p. 712); Communications 105/93, 128/94, 130/94 and 152/96, *Media Rights Agenda and Constitutional Rights Project v. Nigeria*, Twelfth Activity Report 1998–1999, Annex V (*Documents of the African Commission*, p. 712). See also Communications 422–424/90, *Aduayom et al. v. Togo* (Human Rights Committee).

[154] Para. 8(m). Cf. Article 10 of the African Charter; and see Communication 101/93, *Civil Liberties Organisation in respect of the Nigerian Bar Association v. Nigeria*, Eighth Activity Report 1994–1995, Annex VI (*Documents of the African Commission*, p. 394); Communications 105/93, 128/94, 130/94 and 152/96, *Media Rights Agenda and Constitutional Rights Project v. Nigeria*, Twelfth Activity Report 1998–1999, Annex V (*Documents of the African Commission*, p. 718); Communication 212/98, *Amnesty International v. Zambia*, Twelfth Activity Report 1998–1999, Annex V (*Documents of the African Commission*, p. 745).

[155] Para. 8(l).

therefore urges the establishment of adequately financed national independent human rights institutions.[156] However, many African States have already set up statutory commissions with jurisdiction over human rights issues.[157] It therefore calls for co-operation between such bodies and the Commission so as to enhance respect for human rights in Africa.[158] In this context, the Conference stresses the importance of promoting an African civil society, particularly NGOs, as a prerequisite for the healthy development of a State governed by the rule of law.[159] It therefore calls upon all international organisations to co-operate with the OAU in order to maximise the co-ordinated approach to the implementation of human rights in Africa.[160] Furthermore, the Conference appeals to the Commission, the OAU Secretary-General and the media to raise awareness of human rights among the people of Africa.[161]

The Conference reaffirms the importance of the promotion, protection and observance of human rights obligations.[162] The Conference proposes a multi-faceted approach in order to fulfil this commitment. It reiterates the fact that primary responsibility for the promotion and protection of

---

[156] Para. 15. See further Vienna Declaration and Programme of Action, Part I, para. 36; Principles Relating to the Status of National Institutions, UN General Assembly Resolution 48/134 (Paris Principles); Declaration on the Right and Responsibility of Individuals, Groups and Organs of Society to Promote and Protect Universally Recognised Human Rights and Fundamental Freedoms (Declaration on Human Rights Defenders), adopted by the UN General Assembly in Resolution 53/144 of 9 December 1998; the Durban Declaration, adopted by the Second Conference of African National Institutions, UN Doc. E/CN.4/1999/95, pp. 4–5. And see Article 26 of the African Charter.

[157] For example, Lesotho, UN Doc. HRI/CORE/1/Add.98, para. 77; Mauritius, UN Doc. CERD/C/362/Add.2, paras. 4–7; Senegal, UN Doc. CCPR/C/102/Add.2, paras. 28–31; South Africa, UN Doc. HRI/CORE/1/Add.92, para. 16; Uganda, UN Doc. HRI/CORE/1/Add.69, paras. 29 and 30; Zambia, UN Doc. E/CN.4/2000/SR.8, para. 79.

[158] Para. 25.

[159] Paras. 17–19; preambular para. 13. See also the Johannesburg Declaration, a declaration of principles adopted by NGOs in 1998 which recognises the role, rights and protection due to human rights defenders, AI Index: AFR 01/10/98; and further the Declaration on Human Rights Defenders. In May 1999, however, Egypt adopted a restrictive law on NGOs: UN Doc. E/CN4/2000/NGO/132, para. 7. Welch believes that a dearth of African NGOs could seriously undermine the efficacy of the Commission's protective and promotional mandate: Welch, 'The African Commission', pp. 55–6.

[160] Para. 18. The Office of the UN High Commissioner for Human Rights, for instance, has provided technical, financial and other assistance to the Commission and the OAU: UN Doc. E/CN.4/1999/93, pp. 2–4.

[161] Paras. 20–21.   [162] Para. 13. Cf. Article 25 of the African Charter.

human rights lies with the State.[163] It thus urges all OAU Member States to ratify the principal OAU and UN human rights conventions. However, the Conference accepts that what is important is that these instruments be implemented in domestic law and made effective.[164] Thus Article 1 of the African Charter imposes a binding legal obligation on the States Parties to recognise the rights, duties and freedoms set out therein which must be given effect through the adoption of legislative or other measures.[165] Furthermore, the Conference recommends that States formulate and adopt national action plans for the promotion and protection of human rights.[166] In addition, the Conference calls on all States Parties to meet their reporting obligations under the African Charter.[167]

With regard to the OAU, the Conference stresses the need for human rights to be at the forefront of all OAU activities.[168] Noting the crucial role played by the Commission in the observance of human rights, the Conference feels that the structure and functioning of the Commission must be re-evaluated with a view to removing all obstacles to the effective discharge of its mandate.[169] How this is to be achieved is not specified, but it might be addressed at some future stage, although the Conference makes an

---

[163] Para. 15.   [164] Para. 14.

[165] Thus in *Nemi and Others* v. *The State* [1994] 1 LRC 376, the Supreme Court of Nigeria found that the African Charter had been made part of domestic law by the legislation ratifying it. And see Anyangwe, 'Obligations of States Parties to the African Charter', pp. 627–35. See also General Comment 3 adopted by the Human Rights Committee, UN Doc. HRI/GEN/1/Rev.2, pp. 4 and 55–9; Communication 414/90, *Mika Miha* v. *Equatorial Guinea*, UN Doc. CCPR/C/51/D/414/1990. In Communication 74/92, *Commission Nationale des Droits de l'Homme et des Libertés* v. *Chad*, Ninth Activity Report 1995–1996, Annex VIII (*Documents of the African Commission*, p. 449), the Commission stated that 'if a State neglects to ensure the rights in the African Charter, this can constitute a violation'. It is interesting to note that attempts by the Nigerian military regime to limit or revoke the domestic effect of the African Charter were condemned by the Commission, Communication 129/94, *Civil Liberties Organisation* v. *Nigeria*, Ninth Activity Report 1995–1996, Annex VIII (*Documents of the African Commission*, p. 452). See also Communications 137/94, 139/94, 154/96 and 161/97, *International Pen, Constitutional Rights Project, Interights on behalf of Ken Saro-Wiwa Jr and Civil Liberties Organisation* v. *Nigeria*, Twelfth Activity Report 1998–99, Annex V, (*Documents of the African Commission*, p. 729), paras 113–16.

[166] Para. 28.

[167] Para. 16. On the State reporting system, see Article 62 of the African Charter. Ankumah, *The African Commission*, p. 25, writes that most States have not taken this obligation seriously, but it may be that the Commission is finally losing patience with defaulters: Murray, 'Africa', p. 94.

[168] Para. 22.   [169] See note 6 above.

urgent plea for increased resources for the Commission.[170] Furthermore, in seeming recognition of the pusillanimous approach of the OAU Assembly to the Commission's activity reports, the Conference hopes that the Assembly considers delegating this task to the Council of Ministers.[171]

The Declaration does not propose any new or revolutionary principles or category of rights. It may be considered disappointing in that it does not expand our understanding of human rights. It is nonetheless important because it constitutes a reaffirmation of the commitment to promote and protect human rights by the OAU and its Member States. It also updates the OAU's exposition of human rights as set out in the African Charter, bringing it more into line with the current thinking and interpretation of human rights. The references to contemporary forms of slavery, women's and children's rights, poverty, HIV and AIDS, democracy and the rule of law, for example, are all to be welcomed. In this respect the Declaration seems to have been inspired by, and to reflect, such soft law international documents as the Vienna Declaration and Programme of Action. The Declaration, while accepting the universality of human rights, is also notable in seeking to give human rights an African dimension so as to make the issue more relevant to the peoples of Africa. However, lest the Conference be accused of grandstanding, some modest practical proposals are made to secure more effective protection of fundamental rights and freedoms. Proper resourcing of the Commission is crucial, but there is still scope for improving its mandate, particularly with regard to enforcement, although such a step may be less urgent once the African Court on Human and Peoples' Rights comes into being.

The draft protocol on women's rights

In September 2000, the Commission adopted and submitted to the OAU for consideration a draft protocol to the African Charter on women's rights.[172] Notwithstanding the fact that the African Charter enshrines the principle of non-discrimination on the grounds of, *inter alia*, sex[173] and that it

---

[170] Para. 23. The Office of the UN High Commissioner for Human Rights has identified the limited resources allocated by the OAU to the Commission as one of the major obstacles to its effective functioning: UN Doc. E/CN.4/1999/93, para. 6.

[171] Para. 24.

[172] I am grateful to Dr Rachel Murray for providing me with a copy of this document.

[173] Article 2. Cf. section 16 of the Constitution of Mauritius, Article 10(2) of the Constitution of Namibia, and section 9(3) of the Constitution of South Africa.

specifically calls for the elimination of all discrimination against women and the protection of women's rights,[174] it was felt that insufficient progress had been made in these regards. Women in many African countries, often described as 'junior males', routinely suffer discrimination in areas such as succession, marriage and divorce.[175] In many instances, such unfavourable treatment is compounded by recourse in traditional societies to customary or religious laws that confer upon women a status inferior to men.[176] The draft protocol seeks to address these, and other, problems.

The draft protocol asserts first, second and third generation rights. The salient features of the draft protocol include provision for 'positive action',[177] a prohibition on the implementation of the death penalty on pregnant women,[178] a prohibition on the commercial exploitation of women,[179] which should cover prostitution and trafficking in women, a prohibition on traditional and cultural practices harmful to women and girls, including female genital mutilation,[180] protection for women and girls against rape and sexual violence[181] (which, if perpetrated in times of war or conflict,

---

[174] Article 18(3).

[175] As Ankumah points out, in many African countries the husband is considered the custodian of the wife's person and property: Ankumah, *The African Commission*, pp. 153–4. See the recent controversial judgment of the Supreme Court of Zimbabwe in *Magaya* v. *Magaya* [1999] 3 LRC 35, noted in JAL 43 (1999) 248. But cf. *Dow* v. *Attorney-General* [1992] LRC (Const) 623; and *Ephrahim* v. *Pastory* [1990] LRC (Const) 757. See also *Aumeeruddy-Cziffra* v. *Mauritius* HRLJ 4 (1983) 139. The UN Human Rights Committee has stated that such sex-based discrimination is prohibited under the ICCPR, General Comment 19, UN Doc. HRI/GEN/1/Rev.2, para. 6. And See further the Vienna Declaration and Plan of Action, Part II, para. 39; and the report of Special Rapporteur Ms Radhika Coomaraswamy on violence against women, UN Doc. E/CN.4/2000/68/Add.5, pp. 4–6.

[176] See, for example, *Magaya* v. *Magaya* (Supreme Court of Zimbabwe) [1999] 3 LRC 35. UN committees have expressed concern about the existence of dual legal systems in a number of African States, for example, Tanzania, UN Doc. E/CN.4/Sub.2/1997/SR.14, para. 5; Zambia, UN Doc. CCPR/C/79/Add.62, para. 9; and Zimbabwe, UN Doc. CERD/C/304/Add.3.

[177] Draft Article 2. It is not clear whether positive discrimination, or affirmative action, would be permissible under the African Charter, but see Umozurike, *The African Charter*, p. 30.

[178] Draft Article 4(a). Cf. Article 6(5) of the ICCPR. See also Article 30(e) of the African Charter on the Rights and Welfare of the Child.

[179] Draft Article 4(b). See also draft Article 4(c) which prohibits the sexual exploitation of children. Cf. Article 6 of the Convention on the Elimination of Discrimination Against Women, ILM 19 (1980) 33.

[180] Draft Article 6(b). See further above.

[181] Draft Article 4(c). See also the Beijing Platform for Action, para. 113; *Aydin* v. *Turkey*, ECHR, Reports 1997-VI, para. 83. And note section 24(2)(a) of the Constitution of Malawi.

should be considered a war crime[182] as understood by the Rome Statute of the International Criminal Court[183]), the principle of marriage based on consent,[184] a minimum age of 18 for a valid marriage,[185] a prohibition on polygamy,[186] the right to be regarded as equal partners in marriage,[187] the right of a married woman to retain and use her maiden name,[188] the right to acquire and administer property,[189] the right to divorce,[190] equal rights with respect to the children and property of the marriage upon divorce or separation,[191] a widow's rights to her children, to live in the matrimonial

---

[182] Draft Article 4(d).

[183] ILM 37 (1998) 999, Article 7(1)(g) (crimes against humanity). See further *Prosecutor* v. *Furundzija* ILM 38 (1999) 317, paras. 165–86 (ICTY); Vienna Declaration and Programme of Action, Part II, para. 38.

[184] Draft Article 7(a). Cf. Article 23(3) of the ICCPR; Article 16(1)(b) of the Convention on the Elimination of Discrimination Against Women. See also section 22(4) of the Constitution of Malawi, and Article 14(2) of the Namibian Constitution. Nonetheless, such a requirement is problematic for some societies, e.g. The Gambia, UN Doc. E/C.12/1994/9, para. 14.

[185] Draft Article 7(b). The practice of early marriage is prevalent in parts of Africa, UN Doc. E/CN.4/Sub.2/1991/6, p. 7, and has been condemned by the Beijing Platform for Action. Furthermore, the age at which marriage may be entered into in many traditional societies is discriminatory (e.g. in Togo, UN Doc. CCPR/C/63/Add.2, para. 85(a), and Zimbabwe, UN Doc. CRC/C/SR.294, para. 3) or dependent on common or customary law (e.g. Ghana, UN Doc. CRC/C/15/Add. 73, para. 7) or religion (e.g. Egypt, UN Doc. E/1990/5/Add.38, para. 143(c)).

[186] Draft Article 7(c). Polygamy, associated both with customary practices and Islam, may give rise to problems with regard to parallel legal systems, customary, religious and secular, in many African countries, e.g. The Gambia, UN Doc. E/C.12/1994/9, para. 14, Nigeria, UN Doc. CCPR/C/79/Add.65, para. 25, Senegal, UN Doc. E/C.12/1993/SR.37, para. 65, Zambia, UN Doc. CCPR/C/63/Add.3, para. 93, and Zimbabwe, UN Doc. CRC/C/SR.294, para. 3. Tunisia's Code of Personal Status prohibits polygamy, UN Doc. CCPR/C/84/Add.1, para. 54. In *Bhewa* v. *Government of Mauritius* (1990) MR 79, the Supreme Court of Mauritius upheld the exclusive status of monogamous marriages.

[187] Draft Article 7. Under Tunisia's Code of Personal Status, the wife enjoys full legal personality on an equal footing with the husband, UN Doc. CCPR/C/84/Add.1, para. 55.

[188] Draft Article 7(f).

[189] Draft Article 7(i). Cf. Articles 15(2) and 16(h) of the Convention on the Elimination of Discrimination Against Women. Under Article 24 of Tunisia's Code of Personal Status, the husband is prohibited from administering the wife's personal property, UN Doc. CCPR/C/84/Add.1. However, in most African countries the husband is the guardian of the wife's property: Ankumah, *The African Commission*, pp. 153 and 154.

[190] Draft Article 8. In Togo, women have the right to initiate divorce, UN Doc. CCPR/C/63/Add.2, para. 85(d).

[191] Draft Article 8(c) and (d). Cf. Article 23(4) of the ICCPR; Article 16(1)(c) of the Convention on the Elimination of Discrimination Against Women; and Article 19(2) of the African Charter on the Rights and Welfare of the Child.

home and to inherit property,[192] the right to participate equally in the political process,[193] rights to education and training,[194] employment rights, including equal remuneration,[195] and reproductive rights, although termination of pregnancy is not explicitly mentioned.[196]

Significantly, no provision is made for an enforcement or supervisory mechanism,[197] although the rights guaranteed will be capable of being interpreted and applied by the African Court on Human and Peoples' Rights, the African Economic Community Court and the regional courts of justice.

In terms of substantive rights, the draft protocol on women's rights is far-reaching and seems to reflect the Beijing Platform for Action. It must be considered revolutionary because it challenges many entrenched traditional, cultural, societal and religious views and values. It is unlikely that the draft will survive review by the OAU unscathed. Whether the draft protocol is adopted with or without significant amendments, early ratification seems questionable.

Conclusion

It can be seen from the above exposition that Africa, through the OAU, has erected a comprehensive framework for the promotion and protection of human rights which has the potential to become an effective regional system.[198]

---

[192] Draft Articles 20 and 21. Customary law often adversely affects the women's rights to succession: see, for example, *Magaya* v. *Magaya* (Supreme Court of Zimbabwe), [1999] 3 LRC 35 noted, Ankumah, *The African Commission*, pp. 153 and 154.

[193] Draft Article 10. Cf. Article 7 of the Convention on the Elimination of Discrimination Against Women.

[194] Draft Article 12. Cf. Article 10 of the Convention on the Elimination of Discrimination Against Women. Problems exist in many African countries in relation to equal opportunities in education: see Naldi, *The Organization of African Unity*, p. 195 at note 223.

[195] Draft Article 13. Cf. Article 11 of the Convention on the Elimination of Discrimination Against Women.

[196] Draft Article 14. Cf. Articles 11(2) and 12 of the Convention on the Elimination of Discrimination Against Women.

[197] Cf. the Committee on the Elimination of Discrimination Against Women established under the Convention on the Elimination of Discrimination Against Women which considers national reports. An Optional Protocol, ILM 38 (1999) 763, enables the Committee to consider individual petitions and to investigate systematic violations.

[198] It should not be overlooked that there are other African regional organisations with a tangential human rights mandate. In addition, a number of African States have recognised the jurisdiction of the UN Human Rights Committee to consider individual petitions.

In terms of substantive rights, the standards set by the OAU generally conform to international standards. Where content falls short of international standards, it is encouraging to observe that the Commission is interpreting the provisions of the African Charter in ways that meet such principles. Where the rights of certain groups have been inadequately addressed, such as women and children, additional instruments are being drafted to seal the gaps. Weaknesses in the enforcement arena are also being addressed, principally through the establishment of the African Court. Certainly, it does not seem to be an exaggeration to assert that the OAU, though a latecomer to this field, has made an important contribution to the development of human rights law, at least at a theoretical level. Regrettably, much still remains to be done. The realisation of international human rights standards is inhibited by a variety of factors, including lack of political will, inter- and intra-State conflicts, and resource constraints. The commitment of many African States to upholding fundamental rights and freedoms is still suspect. The ratification of the existing treaties, especially the protocol on the African Court, would be a significant step towards attaining greater regard for human rights in practice. Ultimately, the best guarantor of fundamental rights is the development of a culture that respects the rule of law and human rights norms.

In March 2001, the OAU declared the establishment of a new pan-African body, the African Union,[199] which in due course will replace the OAU. Unlike the OAU Charter, the Union's objectives and fundamental principles include commitments to democratic principles and institutions, popular participation, the rule of law, good governance and the promotion and protection of human rights.[200] A 'democracy clause' condemns and rejects unconstitutional changes of government,[201] which the Union can reinforce through the imposition of punitive measures, and by prohibiting those regimes that come to power through unconstitutional means from participating in the Union's activities.[202]

A new Court of Justice will have jurisdiction in Article 26 to interpret the implementation and application of the Act, and its competence must surely extend over human rights controversies. The relationship between the Court and the African Court of Human and Peoples' Rights will thus have to be addressed.

---

[199] The Constitutive Act entered into force on 26 May 2001, 12 RADIC (2000) 629.
[200] *Ibid.*, Articles 3(g), (h) and 4(g).   [201] *Ibid.*, Article 4(p).   [202] *Ibid.*, Article 30.

2

THE REPORTING MECHANISM OF THE AFRICAN CHARTER ON HUMAN AND PEOPLES' RIGHTS

MALCOLM EVANS, TOKUNBO IGE AND RACHEL MURRAY

It was as long ago as 1961 that the idea of an African human rights court was put forward as a possible mechanism for addressing the issue of human rights abuses in Africa,[1] but at that time it was considered to be too controversial a proposition to gain endorsement from the Member States of the Organization for African Unity (OAU). This is a reflection of attitudes which have long underpinned the African system and which have led many African leaders over a considerable period of time to believe that sensitive issues of human rights violations could only be dealt with within a non-confrontational atmosphere. This approach is reflected in the procedures under the African Charter on Human and Peoples' Rights. The African Commission is the organ with the primary responsibility for promotion and protection of human rights under the African Charter[2] and it was confidently expected that such an atmosphere would prevail at its sessions once it was established. The two main mechanisms used by the Commission to monitor State compliance with their Charter obligations and to address human rights issues within Africa are the communication, or complaints system,[3] and the State reporting procedure established in Article 62 of the Charter.

Ultimately, the degree to which confrontation can be eliminated from the operation of a reporting procedure is determined by the quality of the participation of both sides. It is not sufficient for a State to produce timely

---

[1] See International Commission of Jurists, African Conference on the Rule of Law, Lagos, 3–7 January 1961.

[2] Articles 30 and 45 of the ACHPR.

[3] Articles 47–54 provide for an inter-State complaints system, Articles 55–59 for an individual communications procedure: see Chapter 3 below.

and accurate reports and to present them in a balanced and open fashion if the form of scrutiny to which they are subjected is perfunctory, ill-informed or hostile. However, it is certainly the case that a non-confrontational process cannot even get off the ground if the State does not meet its basic obligations under the Charter. The particular substantive obligations are considered elsewhere in this volume, but for current purposes it is necessary to recall the more general obligations which are assumed by States Parties. Article 1 places States Parties under a mandatory obligation to give effect to the rights, freedoms and duties which are set out in the Charter,[4] and in Article 62 it is provided that:

> Each State Party shall undertake to submit every two years, from the date the present Charter comes into force, a report on the legislative measures taken with a view to giving effect to the rights and freedoms recognised and guaranteed by the present Charter.

There is little doubt that the Charter's effectiveness depends primarily on the willingness of States Parties to carry out their solemn treaty obligations and it is upon their contribution to the reporting process that this chapter will focus.

The objectives of the reporting procedure under the African Charter

As international concern for the promotion and protection of human rights around the world has increased, different strategies have been developed to ensure compliance with international norms. The most basic of all of these procedures is that of State reporting. This is found in all the principal UN human rights treaties and, indeed, is the only procedure that is compulsory in all instruments. It has long been regarded as the lowest common denominator and has been derided for being inadequate to force States to comply with their treaty obligations. As is well known, such criticisms miss the point. Reporting procedures are intended to oversee compliance and are not a form of enforcement mechanism as such. To be sure, the potency of a reporting system as a catalyst for change and as a point of pressure upon States should not be underrated but the essence of the process lies in the State

---

[4] Article 1 reads: 'The Member States of the Organization of African Unity parties to the present Charter shall recognise the rights, duties and freedoms enshrined in this Charter and shall undertake to adopt legislative or other measures to give effect to them.'

presenting its record of compliance to the monitoring body and receiving the benefit of external scrutiny. A spirit of collaboration could be considered to pervade the entire concept: a joint exploration of compliance which fully reflects the underlying premise of the African model. On this interpretation it is hardly surprising that such an approach would be accorded priority within the Charter.

Of course, in the light of the practice under the UN system, this portrayal of the ideal reads as a cruel parody of reality. Recent in-depth examinations of the functioning of the UN reporting system have pointed to the 'corrosive' effects of the backlog of reports which are still awaiting submission to the supervisory bodies and to the time it takes for those bodies to consider reports.[5] The various treaty bodies within the UN system have themselves taken a variety of measures to address a number of problems with the operation of the reporting system.[6] Indeed, the current position is seen by some as being so seriously inadequate that the entire system should be overhauled. This notwithstanding, the reporting system has evolved over the years into an important component of the human rights framework and has acquired a certain potency that can play an important part in bringing out compliance with human rights standards and treaty obligations. Some international experts believe that the process of reporting, for all the bureaucratic baggage that it carries, 'should be treated as an opportunity rather than a chore or a formality. It is an opportunity to reaffirm a government's commitment to respect the human rights of its own citizens and to reassert that commitment in the domestic political forum.'[7] While acknowledging that conscientious compliance with reporting requirements can be time-consuming and expensive, an effective reporting procedure which enables periodic examination and evaluation of the human rights situation within a country against the backdrop of a specific set of legally framed obligations can hardly fail to

---

[5] See, for example, the report of Philip Alston, as independent expert, 'Effective Functioning of Bodies Established Pursuant to United Nations Human Rights Instruments', E/CN.4/1997/74; and J. Crawford, 'The UN Human Rights Treaty System: A System in Crisis?', in P. Alston and J. Crawford (eds.), *The Future of UN Human Rights Treaty Monitoring* (Cambridge: Cambridge University Press 2000), p. 1 at pp. 4–6.

[6] It should be noted that it is not the purpose of this chapter to explore these developments nor to offer a comparative account of the reporting procedures. Indeed, given the calls for change within the UN system, the merits of such an exercise at the current time are open to doubt since it hardly provides a stable comparator.

[7] P. Alston, 'Purposes of Reporting', *United Nations Manual on Human Rights Reporting* (New York: 1991), p. 13.

augment and enhance the degree of protection accorded to those within the scope of the African Charter.

The practice concerning the reporting obligation under the African Charter

Under the UN system, it is expressly provided that it is the monitoring bodies established under the treaties which receive and consider the reports submitted by States Parties and it is therefore natural to assume that this is inevitably the case as regards reports submitted in accordance with Article 62 of the African Charter. However, Article 62 merely requires that a State submit reports: it is entirely silent on the issue of who is to receive and review them and on the related question of who is to determine whether the resulting picture is satisfactory. Some commentators have suggested that this silence was deliberate, so as not to jeopardise the prospects for ratification.[8] Such conclusions could well be justified when one takes into consideration the political context and climate that prevailed during the period leading to the adoption of the Charter. As with the individual communication procedure, the very existence of which is concealed within the text of the Charter, it was the Commission that gave itself the mandate to consider the reports submitted under Article 62. At its Third Ordinary Session in 1988 the Commission took the view that 'the African Commission is the only appropriate organ of the OAU capable not only of studying the said periodic reports but also of making pertinent observations to States Parties' and recommended that the OAU mandate it with the power to examine them.[9] Not only did the Assembly of Heads of State and Government of the OAU do so, but it also entrusted the Commission with the responsibility for preparing guidelines on the form and content of the periodic reports,[10] and it is in pursuance of this mandate that the Commission has been endeavouring to develop an effective system for the operation of the reporting procedure.

---

[8] C. Heyns, *Human Rights Law in Africa*, vol. II, *1997* (The Hague: Kluwer, 1999), p. 56.

[9] Recommendation on Periodic Reports, First Annual Activity Report of the African Commission on Human and Peoples' Rights, 1987–1988, ACHPR/RPT/1st, Annex IX, in R. Murray and M. Evans (eds.), *Documents of the African Commission on Human and Peoples' Rights* (Oxford: Hart Publishing, 2001), p. 168 (hereinafter *Documents of the African Commission*).

[10] At its 24th Ordinary Session. See Second Annual Activity Report of the African Commission on Human and Peoples Rights, para. 31 (*Documents of the African Commission*, p. 176).

The Commission's view on the purpose of reporting is reflected in the introductory notes to the Guidelines for National Periodic Reports which it adopted in 1988.[11] According to the Commission, the elaboration and acceptance of human rights instruments by States 'important as they are, are by themselves a mere beginning in the essential exercise of promotion, protection and restoration of human and peoples' rights; implementation of those instruments, by word and deed, is of parallel significance and is equally needed'.[12] It was the desire of the Commission that the reports 'show not only achievements made on the statute books' but that they also 'reveal the extent of implementation in terms of how far the rights and freedoms of the Charter are being fulfilled and how far the duties are successfully carried out'.[13] Thus, 'the aim of the exercise is to show the degree of actual satisfaction of the rights, duties, and freedoms of the Charter; the reporting obligation therefore extends to the practices of the courts and administrative organs of the State Party, and other relevant facts'.[14]

On the face of it, the obligations imposed on States by virtue of Article 62 are disarmingly straightforward. Each State Party is required to submit a report every two years from the date on which the Charter entered into force[15] which is to 'report on the legislative measures taken with a view to giving effect to the rights and freedoms recognised and guaranteed' by the Charter'.[16] They will then be invited to send a representative to the next

[11] Guidelines for National Periodic Reports, Second Annual Activity Report of the African Commission on Human and Peoples' Rights 1988–1989, ACHPR/RPT/2nd, Annex XII (*Documents of the African Commission*, p. 49).

[12] *Ibid.*, para. 1.   [13] *Ibid.*   [14] *Ibid.*, para. 9.

[15] Although it does not make it clear, it is evident that this period runs from the date at which the Charter entered into force *for each State Party.*

[16] This rather odd and restrictive wording could be taken to imply that there is no obligation to report on legislative measures that concerned the areas of the rights, etc. in question that was not enacted with the express purpose of giving effect to Charter rights (which might, for example, include legislation which predated the entry into force of the Charter or, more significantly, subsequent legislation that, while affecting the enjoyment of such rights, etc., was not intended to give effect to them but, perhaps, erode them). There is certainly a marked contrast with the wording of the equivalent obligation in Article 40 of the ICCPR which calls for reports 'on measures they have adopted which give effect to the rights recognised therein and on the progress made in the enjoyment of those rights'. However, it is unlikely to be understood in so restrictive a sense. Indeed, the most obvious difference concerns the restriction on the African Charter to legislation, as opposed to other forms of administrative or judicial acts, but, as will be seen below, the Commission has made it clear in its Guidelines that the reporting obligation is to be understood to include

session of the Commission where the report will be examined in public. There is no doubt that the existing system is far from effective in attaining even these minimal prescribed and desired goals. After almost fifteen years of its being in operation, only a small number of States have discharged their Charter obligations by submitting periodic State reports and sending representatives to respond to the Commission's questions on their reports.

As at April 2001, twenty-three States had not submitted any report at all, eighteen States had submitted only an initial report and eleven States a subsequent report, but still owed more. The Commission records that twelve States have submitted all their reports[17] but this is somewhat misleading since it includes those States whose overdue reports have been 'rolled up' into the most recently submitted and consolidated report. Although it is true to say that these States are now deemed to be 'up to date' with their reporting obligations, this does not mean that they have been acting in compliance with their reporting obligations across the period that the Charter has been in force for them. To put these figures another way, at April 2001 the fifty-three States Parties to the Charter should have submitted a total of 301 reports between them but only forty-one had actually been submitted. Three States were at least four years behind in the submission of reports, nine were at least six years behind, one was at least eight years behind and sixteen were at least ten years behind.

The Commission's response to this situation has been limited, amounting to little more than adopting resolutions calling on States to submit their reports, writing letters to countries who have failed to do so[18] and requiring the individual Commissioners to raise the issue of compliance with reporting obligations in the course of their promotional visits to countries. One development which has certainly improved awareness of the extent to which States have been failing to comply with Article 62 has been the decision of the Commission to compile a list setting out the status of each State

the latter, indicating thus a preference for a broad, inclusive and purposive approach to the nature of the reporting obligation.

[17] See *Documents of the African Commission.*

[18] Letter by Mr Isaac Nguema, Second Annual Activity Report of the African Commission on Human and Peoples' Rights 1988–1989, ACHPR/RPT/2nd, Annex XIII (*Documents of the African Commission*, p. 187); Draft Resolution on Overdue Reports for Adoption, Fifth Annual Activity Report of the African Commission on Human and Peoples' Rights 1991–1992, ACHPR/RPT/5th, Annex IX (*Documents of the African Commission*, p. 226).

regarding its rate of compliance.[19] A more practical step, taken in order to facilitate the clearing of the backlog of overdue reports, was the decision of the Commission in 1995 that several reports could be combined into one. This gesture has met with some limited success and some fifteen States have since submitted consolidated reports which combine those overdue, reducing by sixty-five the number of reports outstanding.[20]

As indicated above, the timely submission of reports is only the first element of the reporting process. The next concerns the presentation and discussion of that report and the Commission has been faced with the difficulty of States who have submitted a report not sending a representative to the sessions when the report was due to be examined. After much discussion about how to respond to this, the Commission decided at one stage that it would examine the reports at subsequent sessions even if a representative of the State was not present. It might be that the Commission sees this as a way of putting pressure on States which have submitted reports to send a representative to a subsequent session but it does not appear to have had much effect, principally because the Commission has failed to act on its threat. The most persistent offender to date has been Seychelles which submitted its first report in 1995 but has so far failed to send a representative to a session of the Commission, but the Commission seems content to continually defer the examination of its report while negotiations continue to attempt to ensure their presence.[21]

The failure of many States to comply with their obligations and the subsequent – arguably, lack of – reaction by the Commission can perhaps be explained by the emphasis which the Commission places upon the element of 'dialogue' within the reporting process. The Commission's Reporting

---

[19] Although intended as a source of potential embarrassment, there is also the danger that, in revealing just how widespread non-compliance is, it may serve only to reassure States in their delinquency.

[20] Algeria (combining 1989–95), Angola (combining 1992–8), Burkina Faso (combining 1988–99), Burundi (combining 1991–9), Chad (combining 1988–99), Ghana (combining 1995–9), Guinea (combining 1988–98), Libya (combining 1993–7), Mali (combining 1988–98), Mozambique (combining 1991–5), Namibia (combining 1994–8), Rwanda (combining 1990–2000), Sudan (combining 1988–96), Swaziland (combining 1997–9): see *Documents of the African Commission.*

[21] Another example concerns Chad, which submitted its report in 1997 but failed to send a representative until the 25th Session in 1999. Recently, the examination of the reports submitted by Ghana in March 2000 and Namibia in May 2000 have had to be postponed because representatives have not attended the sessions at which their reports were due to be considered (27th Session, April 2000 and 28th Session, October 2000 respectively).

Guidelines identify the goal of the reporting procedure as being to 'create a channel for constructive dialogue between the States and [the Commission] on human and peoples' rights'[22] and conceives its relationship with States as being between equals.[23] It would appear that the desire to ensure that a 'constructive dialogue' takes place is considered to be more important than simply holding an examination of the report. Laudable as this preference for substance over form may be, it does nevertheless remain the case that the Commission has failed to adopt and put into practice a coherent policy on how to deal with this situation should it arise again.

Alternatively, the approach of the Commission to this particular problem could be seen in the broader context of its approach to the reporting process as a whole. As will be seen below, the Commission has hitherto taken a restrained approach when considering the substance of State reports. Given the lack of enthusiasm for the Charter in numerous States, the Commission has tended to view the reporting mechanism as a means of involving States in its work and as a way of encouraging their attendance at the sessions rather than as an effective monitoring tool. As such, the Commission appears to be trying to foster the interest of States in its work and building a relationship with them before taking a more critical approach to a State's compliance with human rights. But it is questionable whether the correct balance has been struck. The human rights situation in Africa is in large part a reflection of the lack of political will on the part of several States Parties to carry out their Charter obligations. Unless steps are taken to improve the situation, the goals and aspirations of the African Charter will remain a pipe dream. Placed against this background, the reporting mechanism provides a fleeting opportunity to raise the shutters, casting light and allowing the gaze of fellow African States to fall upon the situation. A refusal to respond to this most minimal of opportunities could be seen as reflecting a lack of desire to build confidence between the Commission and the State in order that a richer and more fruitful relationship will subsequently flourish, and a desire instead to avoid the charge of intrusion and intervention into the affairs of the States concerned not for

---

[22] Guidelines, note 11 above, para. 2.

[23] This is reflected in the Guidelines which, for example, provide in para. 2 that: 'The States being invited to report on the measures they have adopted and the progress made in achieving the objectives of the Charter, as well as indicating any factors and difficulties affecting the degree of fulfilment. The Commission, on the other hand, furnishing suggestions, advice and other assistance on satisfying the requirements of the Charter.'

legal reasons – human rights now not being solely a matter of domestic concern – but for broader political considerations. The independence of Commissioners from government influence has been a constant source of concern[24] and where procedures rely on amicable methods for their success there is inevitably an increased risk that political considerations will outweigh human rights concerns. To the extent that this is the case, it is unlikely that the legitimate and indeed welcome emphasis upon constructive dialogue can provide a convincing rationale for the failure of the Commission to respond effectively to the problems of non-submission and non-appearance.

The content of State reports

The Commission has adopted the approach found in the UN treaty bodies of calling for the submission of an initial report to be followed by periodic reports which provide updates on progress and on obstacles encountered. It its Guidelines for National Periodic Reports, the Commission recommends that 'the initial report' will constitute the background. In the first report the governments should describe the basic conditions prevailing in their countries as well as the basic programmes and institutions relevant to the rights and duties covered in the Charter.[25] As such, it is expected to be general in nature, containing an overview of the human rights situation and including details of the laws and other forms of domestic action that have been taken pertaining to human rights. This initial report is 'to be the foundation on which the subsequent reports will be based'.[26] As required by Article 62 of the Charter, the initial report is to be followed every two years by a periodic report which is to set out the progress being made in a much more detailed and precise fashion. This is spelt out in the Reporting Guidelines which provide that:

> In the following periodic reports the governments would indicate the measures taken, the progress made in achieving the observance of the rights and duties in the Charter, and spell out the difficulties limiting success which they encountered in their efforts. A report on the new measures such as new

---

[24] The degree to which those Commissioners who are simultaneously State officials, such as ambassadors, or who are serving government ministers can act in a fully independent capacity is clearly a matter of legitimate debate, not to say doubt.

[25] Guidelines, note 11 above, para. 4.   [26] *Ibid.*

legislation, new administrative decisions or judicial judgments passed to uphold these rights since the submission of the initial report would also be added.
This means that the subsequent reports will follow the topics as discussed in
the initial reports.[27]

The actual content of the reports are expected to follow the pattern laid out
in the Guidelines. The primary reason for this was to ensure that reports were
uniform in content which would, among other things, assist the Commission
in obtaining a global view of the human rights situation in Africa in addition
to the position in each reporting country.[28]

This would appear to be straightforward enough. Unfortunately, there
are currently two sets of Guidelines and the relationship between them is far
from clear. The original Guidelines produced and adopted by the Commission in 1988 are complex, repetitive and lengthy. In 1998, the Commission
adopted an amendment to the Guidelines which is brief to the point of being
vacuous.[29] Inevitably, practice lies somewhere between these two extremes.
Since both sets of Guidelines may now be sent to States, they are left with the
conundrum of knowing which to follow and can hardly be blamed for not
conforming to the full rigours of the original set. To make matters worse, it
is also entirely unclear from the text of the amendments whether the revised
set are intended to apply only to initial reports or to periodic reports as
well. In this state of confusion, the only sensible approach is to present an
overview of both the Guidelines and the amendments, although this should
be sufficient to make it clear that the amendments provide far too skimpy a
framework for the satisfactory development of periodic as opposed to initial
reports.

There is, however, one common feature of both the Guidelines and the
amendments which needs to be highlighted at the outset. Although the
Charter does not formally classify the rights it contains into rigid categories
such as 'civil and political rights' and 'economic, social and cultural rights',
the Guidelines and amendments call for various forms of rights to be addressed separately within the body of reports.[30]

---

[27] *Ibid.*   [28] *Ibid.*, Section I, para. 2.

[29] Amendment of the General Guidelines for the Preparation of Periodic Reports by States
Parties, DOC/OS/27 (XXIII). These are reproduced in full in the text below, at p. 48.

[30] The rights which are to be regarded as civil and political for the purposes of the reporting
procedure, are set in the Guidelines, note 11 above, Section I, para. 3. These correspond to
Articles 2–13 of the Charter.

REPORTS UNDER THE REPORTING GUIDELINES

According to the Guidelines, initial reports are to address civil and political rights in two distinct parts. The first part should contain a general section giving a brief description of the general legal framework within which civil and political rights are protected in the reporting State. In the course of doing so, a number of distinct issues are to be addressed: whether civil and political rights are protected by a 'Bill of Rights' in the Constitution and the extent to which derogation is possible; whether the Charter can be invoked in the national courts and has become part of the domestic law; which judicial, administrative or other authorities have jurisdiction affecting human rights; which remedies are available for victims of human rights violations; and any other measures taken to implement the Charter.[31] In its second part, addressing civil and political rights, the initial report should give a 'description of the basis of the applicable Articles of the Charter' relating to: the legislative and other measures in force with regard to the provisions of the Charter; any restrictions or limitations imposed on the enjoyment of rights; any factors or difficulties affecting the implementation of the Charter; and any other information concerning progress.[32] Periodic reports are expected to follow almost the same pattern as the initial reports but are to give more detailed information on the implementation of each of the rights, duties and freedoms contained in the Charter.[33]

The Guidelines for reporting on economic, social and cultural rights are similar to those of the civil and political rights, but are more specific and require the provision of technical information on a range of issues. Three general categories of such rights are identified and then detailed guidance – in many cases very detailed guidance – is provided on the matters to be addressed in initial and then periodic reports. The three basic areas are: (a) the right to work as provided for in Article 15: (b) matters pertaining to family and health as provided for in Articles 16 and 18; and (c) matters pertaining to education as provided for in Article 17(1).[34] By way of illustration, and

---

[31] Guidelines, note 11 above, Section I, para. 4(a)(i)–(vi).

[32] *Ibid.*, Section I, para. 4(b)(i)–(iv).   [33] *Ibid.*, Section I, paras. 7–8.

[34] No one would describe the Guidelines as well drafted. In sheer presentational terms, the first of these three social and economic concerns are addressed in Section II of the Guidelines, whereas the second and third are addressed in Sections II.A and II.B. The rights provided for in Article 17(2) are covered in the section dealing with 'peoples' rights'. Article 17(3) does not appear to be directly addressed by the Guidelines. Moreover, the guidance concerning the right to education in Section II.B is only given in relation to initial reports and, unlike

taking the first of these three categories by way of example, States are expected to describe in general the basic conditions prevailing in their countries as well as programmes and institutions relevant to the rights concerned and with emphasis upon information concerning programmes directed at economic advancement,[35] and then to consider a series of questions concerning: remuneration, safe and healthy working conditions, equal opportunity for promotion, and rest, leisure, limitation of working hours, and holiday with pay.[36] A similar approach and level of specificity is required of the other areas of social and economic concern. The following two sections of the Reporting Guidelines work through the substantive rights found in Articles 18–25, concerning Peoples' Rights[37] and Articles 26–29, concerning specific duties of both States and individuals under the Charter.[38] Compared with the previous sections, these are in the main couched in much more general terms and lack the same degree of specificity. There then follow three sections requesting information on what might be termed themes not directly addressed within the Charter but implicit within the human rights framework: the elimination of all forms of racial discrimination,[39] apartheid[40] and discrimination against women.[41] In all of these instances, the Guidelines appear to have been more than merely inspired by those relating to the relevant UN instruments.

THE AMENDMENT TO THE GUIDELINES

The divisions in the Guidelines are so formal that they could be taken as suggesting that separate reports might be required on each of these areas. In fact, the Commission has not taken this view and no State has presented its reports in this way. This categorisation does, however, add to the confusion of what is required, since each section calls for separate styles of reporting to be applied to the various sets of rights. Whatever other merits the Guidelines may have in terms of providing concrete guidance and potentially shedding light upon the favoured approach to their interpretation by the Commission,

---

the other subdivisions, there is no mention of the manner in which it is to be considered in periodic reports.

[35] *Ibid.*, Section II, para. 2.   [36] *Ibid.*, Section II, paras. 6–9.

[37] *Ibid.*, Section III, paras. 1–19. The bulk of this section, paras. 14–19, is in fact comprised of very detailed guidelines relating to Article 17(2) concerning cultural life.

[38] *Ibid.*, Section IV, paras. 1–8.   [39] *Ibid.*, Section V, paras. 1–20.

[40] *Ibid.*, Section VI, paras. 1–2.   [41] *Ibid.*, Section VII, paras. 1–9.

the overwhelming feeling is that their length and detail is inappropriate for the practical exercise of State reporting.

Thus, at the request of Member States and at the insistence of NGOs, discussion took place on amendments to the Guidelines, and this resulted in the adoption of the amendments in 1997.[42] These amended Guidelines were inspired by the recommendations of two seminars organised in Harare and Tunis.[43] They are just over a page long and provide as follows:

1. An initial report (the first report) should contain a brief history of the State, its form of government, the legal system and the relationship between the arms of government.
2. The initial report should also include basic documents such as the constitution, the criminal code and procedure and landmark decisions on human rights.
3. The major human rights instruments to which the State is a party and the steps taken to internalise them should be set out.
4. How well is the party implementing the following rights protected by Charter:
   (a) civil and political rights;
   (b) economic, social and cultural rights; and
   (c) group rights?
5. What is the State doing to improve the condition of the following groups mentioned in the Charter:
   (a) women;
   (b) children; and
   (c) disabled?
6. What steps are being taken to protect the family and encourage its cohesion?
7. What is being done to ensure that individual duties are observed?
8. What are the problems encountered in implementing the Charter having regard to the political, economic or social circumstances of the State?
9. How is the State carrying out its obligations under Article 25 of the Charter on human rights education?

---

[42] Amendment of the General Guidelines see note 29 above.
[43] Seminar on State Reporting for the English Speaking Countries, Harare, Zimbabwe 23–27 August 1993; Seminar on State Reporting for Francophone, Arabophone and Lusophone Countries, Tunis, Tunisia, 24–27 May 1994.

10. How is the State, as an interested party, using the Charter in its international relations, particularly in ensuring respect for it?
11. Any other relevant information relating to the implementation and promotion of the Charter.

EVALUATION

There is no doubt that these shorter guidelines would be easier for States to use in preparing their reports but, despite this, the pattern of reporting has been far from uniform. Reports have always varied hugely in their quality, style and length, and this has continued under the new Guidelines. It is thus not clear that States have in fact obtained or followed the simplified Guidelines. Indeed, some States say that they have not obtained a copy of them. However, it may be that the Commission is itself less concerned about the uniformity of reports than with their actually being submitted with sufficient detail and critique. Nevertheless, the amended Guidelines are now so vaguely constructed that they might fail to give sufficient guidance on the material which the Commission requires – or should be requiring – if the dialogue is to have substance. Thus it is very much in the hands of the States themselves to make of this situation what they will. This was the case before the adoption of the amended Guidelines and their adoption has merely served to underline this practice and, arguably, legitimate it. In practice, however, it appears that the position is very much as it always was, with some States, such as Seychelles (1995) and Chad and Guinea (1998), producing reports which are very limited in scope, while others, such as Burkina Faso, Zimbabwe (1997) and South Africa (1999), have produced very detailed reports. The latter is clearly the Commission's preference and the reports of Zimbabwe and South Africa were held up by the Commission as models of their kind.

The Zimbabwe report in question was a combination of its second and third reports[44] and was separated into sections reflecting the rights within the Charter, detailing within each section constitutional provisions and legislation adopted that was relevant to those rights. There were some indications that the government saw shortcomings in its approach and statistics and tables were included, such as on the number of AIDS cases and access to safe drinking water, for example. It was over sixty pages long. South Africa's

---

[44] Zimbabwe's Second and Third Report in Terms of Article 62 of the African Charter on Human and Peoples' Rights.

initial report was nearly 150 pages in length.[45] It included detail on the structure of government, the legal system and international instruments, before going on to consider each of the provisions of the Charter separately. It included separate sections on South Africa's approach to Article 25 and its relations with other States in respect of the Charter. The sections on the rights included constitutional provisions, legislation and programmes. There was a recognition throughout of shortcomings in certain respects. The report of Burkina Faso followed a similar structure and length.[46] By way of comparison, that of Chad was only thirteen pages long and briefly dealt with certain, but not all, rights, omitting discussion of peoples' rights and duties altogether.[47] Where some States have been praised for the quality of their reports, this has actually prompted other States being examined at the same session of the Commission, to make comparisons with their own, often less satisfactory, reports.[48] Thus, States can prompt each other to improve their practice regarding the reporting obligation.

At the end of the day, however, it is difficult to see that the adoption of the amended Guidelines has made a great deal of difference. Although much has been made of the complexity of the original Guidelines and this certainly prompted the Commission to review them, the more recently submitted reports tend to be more rather than less detailed. The most important factor is not the Guidelines but the will of the State to fully engage with the reporting process. What, for example, is to be made of the incident in which one State asked a Commissioner who was its national to present its report to the Commission?[49] It is arguable that the Commission focused too much on amending the Guidelines rather than the actual practicalities and efficiency of the procedure which the report feeds into. So, for example, it has not paid equal attention to ensuring that it contacts the relevant government

---

[45] Initial Country Report 1998, Government of South Africa.

[46] Rapport Initial du Burkina Faso sur la Promotion et la Protection des Droits de l'Homme, October 1998.

[47] Mesures d'Ordre Legislatif ou Autres Prises en Vue de Donner effet aux Droits et Libertés Reconnus et Garantis dans la Charte Africaine des Droits de l'Homme et des Peuples, Rapport adressé à la Commission Africaine des Droits de l'Homme et des Peuples, October 1998.

[48] For example, Burkina Faso's report was examined after that of South Africa which was considerably more detailed in its content and its presentation. The representatives expressed embarrassment at having to follow this report.

[49] See R. Murray, 'The 1997 Sessions of the African Commission on Human and Peoples' Rights', HRLJ 19 (1998) 169–87 at 184 and note 101.

personnel and examines whether the procedure of examining the report could be improved. Above all else, the Commission seems to have simply assumed that States have access to and pay attention to the reporting Guidelines and that amending the Guidelines would have the effect of encouraging States to submit reports. There is no evidence to support this, and the Commission has no clear strategy for ensuring that the Guidelines are properly disseminated and influence the composition of the reports. Clearly, its strategy has failed. In truth, it seems that the position is very much as follows: whereas previously States were largely unaware of a complicated, lengthy set of guidelines on reporting, they are now largely unaware of a simplified version. The Commission must rethink its approach to the whole of the State reporting process.

Methods to encourage the submission of reports by States have been debated, including ideas such as the Commission taking the initiative to produce reports on the human rights situation in particular countries, visits by Commissioners on a periodic basis or the Commission sending regular reminders to States.[50] In this respect, the recent decision to require Commissioners to ask States about the fulfilment of their reporting obligations during their promotional missions is an important initiative and does appear to have prompted some reports from States and the subsequent attendance of their representatives at the session. Although the Commission might also consider taking the initiative and adopting its own reports on particular countries, this would not solve the problem of bringing about a constructive dialogue. Indeed, it might have quite the opposite effect. Moreover, the material upon which such a report could be based is likely to be limited and this would inevitably devalue the nature of the exercise, rendering it politically sensitive and potentially damaging. For example, where States have not responded to requests for a report, they are likely to be equally reluctant to accept a fact-finding visit from the Commission. It has also been suggested that the Commission might base its considerations upon reports obtained from the UN. Once again, there are difficulties with this approach. Not only does it not facilitate dialogue, but the scope of the African Charter is not matched by the UN treaties, either individually or collectively, and, even where the same rights are addressed, such an approach simply presumes that their content is the same. In the final analysis, there is no effective substitute for the timely submission of an appropriately constructed report produced

[50] *Ibid.*, pp. 184–5.

in the spirit of constructive engagement with the Charter, its obligations and its mechanisms. For its part, the Commission must be alert to its own shortcomings in its dealings with States Parties. On the available evidence, it seems that both the States Parties and the Commission have a long way to go.

The process of examining State reports

State reports are considered in public during the two ordinary sessions which the Commission holds annually. This gives rise to a number of issues.

LANGUAGE AND TRANSLATION

Upon receipt of a State's report, copies should be made and sent to members of the African Commission who are to apprise themselves of its content. This has not always proven possible. At the sessions themselves, simultaneous translation is normally provided between English and French, and sometimes also Arabic. However, reports are usually only made available in the original language in which they were submitted. This has the practical consequence of preventing some Commissioners from being able to read particular reports at all. After a futile struggle to seek additional resources to enable the Secretariat to translate the reports, the Commission decided to appoint rapporteurs from among themselves who would have the task of studying the report thoroughly, making a summary of its contents and setting out the main questions on which clarification or additional information is required from the State Party. However, while this may have had considerable benefits in terms of organisation, it still does not enable all Commissioners to have the benefit of familiarising themselves with the report itself. It should be self-evident that all members of the Commission should be able to have access to the contents of the reports and be able to involve themselves fully in the examination process. At one stage the Commission considered asking States to provide translations of their reports but this does not seem to have met with a positive response and the Commission has not raised this request since. For the time being, the problem remains insuperable.

THE LEVEL OF STATE REPRESENTATION

Once the State has submitted its report to the Commission it is invited to send a representative to the next session, wherever it may be. There has been a recent trend towards examining the report of the country in which the session is being held since this has facilitated the attendance of representatives.[51] Difficulties have arisen concerning the level and competence of the delegate sent. If the persons sent are not sufficiently senior, there may be problems in answering the questions posed by the Commission fully and with authority. In recent years, it has been usual for States to send a delegation comprised of two or three senior officials from the State capital, usually from the Ministry of Foreign Affairs and / or Justice.[52] While often well placed to speak on policy issues, they may not always have at their disposal the detailed information that is required to respond adequately to the questions posed to them.

EXAMINATION

The procedure followed by the Commission for the actual presentation is again a reflection of its desire that reporting be a channel through which it creates and maintains a 'constructive dialogue' with States. Indeed, the Chair usually stresses this at the start of the examination.[53] The representative of the State briefly introduces the report and this oral presentation usually takes the form of a summary of the report, enhanced by some supplementary information where necessary. The representative usually talks for under half an hour. The rapporteur Commissioner will then pose a number of questions, following which the other Commissioners take turns to ask questions or make comments on the report. The amount of time spent on this phase of the proceedings largely reflects the length and content of the report and the Commissioners' willingness to probe the report in detail in the light of information from other sources such as NGOs. Rarely, however, does this phase go beyond an hour. Over the years, there does appear to have been an increased willingness by the Commissioners to seek information from additional sources and use such information when posing their

---

[51] For example, the report of Benin was examined at the 28th Session in October 2000 in Cotonou. See p. 42 above as regards States who do not send representatives.

[52] For example, the South African delegation presenting its report during the 25th Session of the Commission in April 1999 was headed by the Deputy Minister of Justice. Clapham notes similar difficulties in relation to the UN systems: see A. Clapham, 'UN Human Rights Reporting Procedures: An NGO Perspective', in P. Alston and J. Crawford (eds.), *The Future of UN Human Rights Treaty Monitoring*, pp. 175–200 at p. 189.

[53] See Murray, 'The 1997 Sessions'.

questions. As a result, there has been some evidence that some Commissioners' questions are increasingly probing, detailed and critical.[54] The State representative is then given a short time in which to formulate the responses to the questions. This can be as little as the break period of 15–30 minutes or may be as long as overnight, depending on the time of day at which the report is being examined. The representative will then answer the questions posed.

In addition, an important advance was made at the 29th Session[55] where, for the first time, the Commission followed up the examination of the reports with concluding comments, sometimes oral and in all cases written, on the reports. While these comments were brief and in general not directed towards specific questions which may not have been answered, at least this was a move towards a more critical use of the reporting procedure.

Although the basics of this procedure are familiar from the UN context, there are a number of concerns with the manner in which this procedure is conducted. There is clearly insufficient time to prepare the responses. This is exacerbated by the fact that, although questions are supposed to be sent to the State prior to the session, in the past this often did not occur or the questions posed were not the same as those of which the State had been notified, although there does seem to have been some improvement in this regard more recently. In addition, the formalism of a procedure in which all the questions are first read out before the answers are provided diminishes the effectiveness of the reporting procedure as a constructive dialogue. In effect, it is an oral exchange of written documentation and it is difficult to discern much evidence of genuine 'dialogue'. Declamation would be a more apposite description. The bulk of the time is made up of the State representatives presenting the written report (which may, of course, be the first time that some have been able to be properly appraised of its contents by virtue of the simultaneous translation) and the Commissioners asking questions which ought already to have been made known to the delegation. Comparatively little time is taken up by the delegation considering and giving their responses, or the Commissioners responding to them. Indeed, the latter is a comparatively rare phenomena: it is unusual for the Commissioners to return to the fray and take up the issues raised by the responses provided

---

[54] See in relation to UN procedures, Clapham, 'UN Human Rights Reporting', p. 188.
[55] 23 April to 7 May 2001, Tripoli, Libya.

and, although there have occasionally been requests for further details where the answers first provided were inadequate, even this is not consistently or often done.

TIMING

The whole process of examining a report, then, usually takes in the order of three hours. This is clearly insufficient time to deal with the situation of human rights, engage in a clear dialogue and probe further the concerns of the human rights community. Although the length of the sessions has recently been increased to fifteen days, the Commission does not appear to have made full use of this additional time. At the moment, the Commission usually only receives and examines two or three reports per session. It would therefore seem worthwhile considering whether more time could be devoted to the examination of those reports. The Commission should seriously consider revising its overall time allocations during its sessions to facilitate this. The agenda items are often the same from session to session and the necessity for some items is questionable. For example, there is usually considerable discussion on the promotional reports of Commissioners. The Commission has produced most of these reports recently in written format during the session. Although oral statements may reflect and ensure the accountability of Commissioners for their promotional activities, it would be worth considering whether providing written reports, coupled with a brief session for any questions to be raised, might be more appropriate and in keeping with the essential purposes of the Commission's activities.[56] Even within the existing timeframes devoted to the consideration of reports, there is plenty of scope for more effective use of the time devoted to the exercise. The efficiency of the procedure could be enhanced by ensuring that questions are indeed sent to the State in advance of the session and that only additional questions need be raised orally by the Commissioners after the initial presentation of the State report. Time should be used productively and not ritualistically. At the very least, this would send a signal to those States attending the session that the Commission takes its role as a human rights institution

[56] Similarly, the procedure whereby applications for observer status by NGOs and now national human rights commissions are examined is also time-consuming. Commissioners could consider only noting in detail those whose applications were not accepted and the reasons why this is the case.

seriously, even if it makes it a more uncomfortable experience for the States themselves.

CONCLUSIONS AND FOLLOW-UP

Perhaps one of the most important elements of any reporting procedure is the feedback that the State receives on its report and the comments and suggestions that are made by the treaty body. There have been limited attempts to provide some documentary record of the exchanges,[57] but there are no official summary records of the discussions and the annual activity reports tend merely to record the fact that the exchange took place rather than distil the essence of it. Until recently, therefore, the Commission's procedures have been wholly deficient in this respect. However, the decision at the Commission's 29th Session, to adopt concluding observations on the four State reports which were examined,[58] is a welcome advance. The comments, some of which were also delivered orally in the presence of the State, were brief and related to positive as well as negative aspects of the report and included a number of recommendations which the Commission then called on the State to respond to. This approach does appear to be an attempt to be more critical and to delve further into matters which were of particular concern or which were not answered by the State. It is a pity that there was no consistency: for example, not all questions which the State failed to answer were piched up on. Despite these flaws, this recent change does appear to be an attempt to move away from the perception that the examination is the end of the process and that the obligations of the State have been fulfilled for another two years. Indeed, the adoption of concluding observations has been accompanied by questions asked by the Commission on the State's initial report which had not been adequately answered the first time.[59]

It is hoped that the Commission will repeat this procedure with further reports, and will use this change in direction to provide more detailed comments and a comprehensive appraisal of a State's report. The information garnered in the reporting process should not be lost to view.

---

[57] For example, distribution of copies of the questions submitted to the States and answers provided at the sessions. This has been haphazard, however, and still fails to present the views of the Commission on the topics raised.

[58] Algeria, Ghana, Namibia and Congo.

[59] Commissioner Chigovera in relation to Namibia's first periodic report: see R. Murray, 'Report of 29th Session of the African Commission', on file with the author.

The role of other actors

NGOS AND ALTERNATE/SHADOW REPORTS

In accordance with the spirit of Article 45(1)(a) of the Charter, the Commission has over the years developed a working relationship with international and African NGOs. More than 230 NGOs have been granted observer status which has the effect of creating a formal relationship between them.[60]

Given their knowledge of the actual human rights situation in the various States Parties to the Charter or concerning various groups, NGOs can be a reliable source of information which the Commission could utilise, particularly to verify aspects of States' reports. In order to facilitate its work, the Commission encourages national NGOs to prepare alternate or shadow reports or commentaries to their country reports and to make these available to the Commission.[61]

The problem, already mentioned above, is that the Commission is reluctant to allow bodies such as NGOs to see the State reports in advance of the session. Indeed, rarely are copies of reports readily available before or during the sessions themselves, although some NGOs will seek and be given a copy of the report from the State. This clearly places great difficulties in the way of NGOs seeking meaningfully to contribute to the process since they may be left to guess at what needs to be challenged. There are clear examples of the Commissioners using NGO information when posing questions and there seems to be no reason why the reports themselves could not be disseminated to participants and other interested parties before the sessions. They should obviously be readily available during the sessions themselves, although this may be too late for the NGOs to be able to make an effective contribution to the process. Although consideration of States' reports takes place in open session, only members of the Commission and the State concerned are involved in the dialogue, and, although NGOs have asked that they be permitted to pose questions, they have been refused by the Commission, the latter stressing the need to maintain a constructive dialogue. There may, of course, be other opportunities to raise matters informally during the period of the session, and lively exchanges can and do occur,

---

[60] See Chapter 8 for further information on the role of NGOs in the work of the Commission.
[61] See in relation to UN systems, Clapham, 'UN Human Rights Reporting', pp. 190–2; and generally G. Lansdown, 'The Reporting Process Under the Convention on the Rights of the Child', in P. Alston and J. Crawford (eds.), *The Future of UN Human Rights Treaty Monitoring*, pp. 118–22.

albeit indirectly rather than directly through the conduct of the reporting procedure.

THE ROLE OF THE OAU

The African Charter was adopted by OAU Member States 'firmly convinced of their duty to promote and protect human and peoples' rights and freedoms taking into account the importance traditionally attached to these rights and freedoms in Africa'.[62] As its parent body therefore, the OAU has an obligation to ensure the implementation of the provisions of the Charter. Unfortunately, minimal efforts have hitherto been made to ensure meaningful implementation of these obligations by the OAU, although the First Ministerial Conference on Human Rights organised by the OAU in April 1999 also laid emphasis on the need for Member States to comply with their Charter obligations.[63] This unpalatable situation is constantly brought to the attention of all stake holders, and especially the States Parties and the OAU itself, not least by the Commission which has begun the practice of providing information on the status of reporting under the Charter as part of its report to the Council of Ministers and Assembly whenever they meet. This is now engendering a positive response which counters the notion that there is a total lack of political will on the part of States to engage with the system. That being said, while an encouraging number of States have expressed a genuine desire to collaborate with the African Commission and implement their Charter obligations by trying to overcome the obstacles facing them, a goodly number still appear unwilling to do so.

Conclusion

In-depth evaluations of the effectiveness of the reporting procedure and, indeed, the objectives of the exercise are yet to be carried out by the Commission, States Parties or the OAU. The Commission does not appear to have seriously considered how to tackle the problems of non-submission of reports or non-attendance at sessions other than by the adoption of an alternative set of Guidelines, the relevance and impact of which as a strategy

---

[62] African Charter, preamble.
[63] Grand Bay (Mauritius) Declaration and Plan of Action, OAU First Ministerial Conference on Human Rights in Africa, 12–16 April 1999, Grand Bay, Mauritius, CONF/HRA/ DECL (I).

is open to doubt. It is clear that the actual modalities of the dialogue – the examination process itself – are also in need of serious reassessment since it does not promote a constructive dialogue with States Parties or contain sufficient checks and balances to ensure consistency in approach between delegates and Commissioners. At the moment, its success is almost entirely dependent upon the ability and willingness of the Commissioners to seek additional information and to probe the manner, honesty and depth in which the State representatives are willing to answer the questions. This is a difficult task and the Commission could do much to help itself by drawing on resources that domestic and international civil society is willing to place at its disposal. There is, however, still a reluctance to do so. The recent move to adopt concluding comments and to follow up on initial reports in later examinations is to be welcomed and, if continued, should help States appreciate that merely conducting the examination process is not the aim of the exercise and that the Charter obligation is not satisfied by the two-yearly submission of reports. The idea that this is the start rather than the end of the process is almost entirely absent. It must be realized that it is a means to an end, not an end in itself.

The reporting mechanism has the potential to enable the Commission to monitor over an extended time period the human rights situation in States Parties to the Charter, a possibility not afforded by the individual communication procedure. Currently, however, its principal function appears to be as a device to encourage States' attendance at the sessions. A number of easily achieved and inexpensive amendments, however, might enhance the usefulness of the procedure.

As regards encouraging the timely submission of adequately prepared reports, the Commission should continue with its practice of requiring Commissioners to raise the question of reporting obligations during their promotional visits to States. It would also be useful if the Secretariat were to ensure that up-to-date details of the State representative responsible for the report were obtained and to make known whether it is anticipated that they will attend the session. This would facilitate the establishment of an ongoing relationship rather than the haphazard contacts that are currently the norm. The Commission might also consider preparing a State reporting pack for dissemination to States, containing the Guidelines (both the original and amended versions), the name of a contact person at the Commission's Secretariat, the obligations of the State, and a list of those States which have submitted their reports. States could later be told who is the rapporteur

Commissioner for the report, provided with the list of questions to be posed, be informed of any additional information required and given some details of the procedure for examination of the report at the session.

In terms of dissemination, the Secretariat could ensure that the reports are distributed to Commissioners and NGOs prior to the session at which they will be examined and that reports are translated by States themselves or by the Commission at least into English and French. Certainly, most other documents of the Commission seem now to be translated into these two languages and there is no clear reason why this should not be done for the State reports. It is essential that when a report is received from a State it is disseminated to relevant NGOs in the country and with observer status together with a brief letter requesting their comments.

The Commission must also reconsider the examination procedure itself and should show a greater willingness to provide a detailed critique of the report and not assume that 'constructive dialogue' is a synonym for 'polite exchange'. There is no point in a dialogue that does not attempt to address the real issues. In the past, so great a premium has been placed upon securing the cooperation and avoiding confrontation that there has been a danger of the process spilling over into collaboration, with weaknesses in reports and unanswered questions passed over and no concluding comments or criticisms made.[64] The recent changes, if strengthened, signal some hope for the reporting procedure becoming a 'constructive dialogue'. It might also be worthwhile considering seriously the frequency with which States should submit reports. Clearly, a two-yearly cycle has not on the whole been complied with and is perhaps an unrealistic expectation. What is not unrealistic is the belief that the reporting mechanism under the Charter can and should play an important role within the system of human rights protection within Africa. That it is yet to do so is a problem that for the time being lies with the Commission to solve.

---

[64] Indeed, Commissioners have found the process particularly acute at sessions where it is the host State's report that is being examined and they have expressed 'embarrassment' at having to do this: see R. Murray, 'Report of the 2000 Sessions of the African Commission on Human and Peoples' Rights', HRLJ, forthcoming.

3

ADMISSIBILITY UNDER THE AFRICAN CHARTER

FRANS VILJOEN

Introduction

Numerous international treaties for the protection of human rights have been adopted at the global and regional levels since the end of the Second World War. Individuals may bring complaints against their governments under a limited number of these instruments. At the global level, the United Nations (UN) adopted optional mechanisms in the Convention on the Elimination of Racial Discrimination (CERD),[1] the First Optional Protocol to the International Covenant on Civil and Political Rights (ICCPR), the Convention Against Torture (CAT)[2] and more recently the Convention on the Elimination of All Forms of Discrimination Against Women.[3] At the regional level, individual complaints are allowed under the European Convention on Human Rights and Fundamental Freedoms (ECHR),[4] the Inter-American Convention on Human Rights (IACHR)[5] and the African Charter on Human and Peoples' Rights (African Charter).[6]

In an era of increased judicial resolution of disputes, monitoring bodies have been established to deal with complaints (usually called 'communications') under each of these treaties. These monitoring bodies range from judicial to quasi-judicial, but all have to decide whether communications are

---

[1] CERD, Article 14.   [2] CAT, Article 22.

[3] The General Assembly adopted the Optional Protocol to CEDAW in October 1999 (A/RES/54/4). The Optional Protocol entered into force on 22 December 2000, after ten States had become party thereto. As at end November 2001, thirteen African States had become party to this Optional Protocol.

[4] ECHR, Article 34.   [5] IACHR, Article 44.

[6] Article 55 of the African Charter provides for compulsory acceptance of communications 'other than those of States Parties'.

admissible. The European Commission and Court of Human Rights became the first human rights institutions to grapple with issues of admissibility.[7] The CERD Committee, the Human Rights Committee under the ICCPR,[8] the Inter-American Commission and Court on Human Rights,[9] the CAT Committee and the African Commission[10] to some extent all followed in or deviated from the foundation laid by the European human rights institutions.

The principle that communications before these bodies have to comply with certain admissibility requirements before they may be 'admitted' serves as a screening or 'filtering' mechanism between national and international institutions. The continued importance of sovereignty to States is reflected in the fact that all complaints mechanisms under UN human rights treaties are optional. The admissibility requirement places a further divide between sovereign States and international supervision. Disputes between nationals and their States should, in the first instance, be resolved through non-judicial and judicial mechanisms at the national level. A dispute needs to be of a specific nature or character for it to proceed to the international level. At the international level these prerequisites are included in each of the human rights instruments and there is an apprehension that, without such a filter, international institutions may become overburdened with cases.

[7] See e.g. T. Zwart, *The Admissibility of Human Rights Petitions* (The Hague: Kluwer, 1994) who compares the European Commission on Human Rights and the UN Human Rights Committee in respect of admissibility.

[8] See e.g. D. McGoldrick, *The Human Rights Committee. Its Role in the Development of the International Covenant on Civil and Political Rights* (Oxford: 1991), pp. 160–98.

[9] See e.g. S. Davidson, *The Inter-American Court of Human Rights* (Dartmouth, 1992), pp. 61–79; and C. Cerna, 'The Inter-American Commission on Human Rights: Its Organisation and Examination of Petitions and Communications', in D. Harris and S. Livingstone (eds.), *The Inter-American System of Human Rights* (Oxford: 1998), pp. 79–96.

[10] See e.g. E. A. Ankumah, *The African Commission on Human and Peoples' Rights* (The Hague: Martinus Nijhoff, 1996), pp. 61–70; O. Gye-Wado, 'The Rule of Admissibility Under the African Charter on Human and Peoples' Rights', *African Journal of International and Comparative Law* 3 (1991) 742–55; C. A. Odinkalu, 'The Individual Complaints Procedures of the African Commission on Human and Peoples' Rights: A Preliminary Assessment', *Transnational Law and Contemporary Problems* 8 (1998) 359–405, especially 378–86; F. Ouguergouz, *La Charte Africaine des Droits de l'Homme et des Peuples* (Presses Universitaires de France, 1993), pp. 314–18 (where he deals with the 'competence' of the Commission), and 324–88 (where he deals with 'recevabilité'); F. Viljoen, 'Review of the African Commission on Human and Peoples' Rights: 21 October 1986 to 1 January 1997', in C. Heyns (ed.), *Human Rights Law in Africa 1996* (The Hague: Kluwer, 1997), pp. 47–116.

The African Charter provides for both individual[11] and inter-State communications. As the African Commission has thus far only finalised individual communications, the admissibility of these communications is the focus of attention here, with inter-State communications being discussed only briefly.[12]

Admissibility findings play an important role in the work of international human rights treaty bodies. Under the Optional Protocol to the ICCPR, 248 (or 29.3 per cent) of the 844 finalised communications were declared inadmissible up to January 1999.[13] From its inception in 1987, up to its 25th Session in May 1999, the African Commission finalised eighty-five communications. Of these, fifty-four (or 64 per cent) have been declared inadmissible.[14]

Rigorous analysis of the Commission's findings on admissibility is often difficult, due mainly to the lack of substantiation in the reasoning of the African Commission, especially in its initial years of operation.[15] Subsequent findings on communications have become more elaborate and extensive and, more recently, a summary of the chronological background to the procedure at the level of the Commission has been added. This has contributed to a clearer picture of the issues related to admissibility.[16] Sometimes the reason for a finding remains unclear, however, because the factual basis for the finding is not disclosed. Often facts are merely listed, the applicable law is stated in a general way, and the conclusion announced. This may be explained partly with reference to the influence of civil law judicial

---

[11] The Charter refers to 'other communications'.   [12] See below.

[13] M. Nowak, 'The International Covenant on Civil and Political Rights', in R. Hanski and M. Suksi (eds.), *An Introduction to the International Protection of Human Rights: A Textbook* (Abo Akademi University, Institute for Human Rights, 1997), p. 95.

[14] If the cases in which admissibility findings were made due to States not being party to the Charter are left out of the equation, the percentage of inadmissible cases drops to 50 per cent (or thirty-one out of sixty-two cases). These cases were initially treated as 'inadmissible', but have later, correctly, been treated as 'irreceivable'.

[15] For example: the 'judgment' in Communication 45/90, *Civil Liberties Organisation* v. *Nigeria*, Seventh Activity Report 1993–1994, Annex IX; R. Murray and M. Evans (eds.), *Documents of the African Commission on Human and Peoples' Rights* (Oxford: Hart Publishing, 2001), p. 345 (hereinafter *Documents of the African Commission*), reads as follows: 'The Commission declares that local remedies have not been exhausted as required by Article 56 of the Charter and Rule 114 of the Rules of Procedure and declares the communication inadmissible.'

[16] See e.g. Communication 102/93, *Constitutional Rights Project* v. *Nigeria*, Twelfth Activity Report 1998–1999, Annex V (*Documents of the African Commission*, p. 712).

style,[17] which is more concise and less reasoned than the common law style.

Procedure for consideration of admissibility

The issue of admissibility is considered separately from, and before, the substantive consideration of a communication.[18] The Commission, or a working group of its members, decides on the admissibility of communications. As the number of communications was initially not very high, the Commission did not make use of working groups until 1999, when a communications working group was designated to deal with the preparation of communications in the period between the 27th and 28th Sessions. In practice, every communication is assigned to a particular commissioner, who acts as rapporteur. When communications are received they are dealt with by the Secretariat. The Secretary prepares a list of all communications, with a brief summary of their contents. The Rules of Procedure provide that the 'Commission, through the Secretary, may request the author of a communication to furnish clarifications' of his or her communication.[19] Unfortunately, this provision has sometimes been interpreted to mean that the Secretary placed the communications as they had been received before the Commission, and awaited its instructions, even in cases where there clearly was information lacking. In other words, the Secretary did not ensure that all the information pertaining to admissibility had been gathered before referring the communication to the Commission.

The Commission must decide 'as early as possible' on the admissibility of communications.[20] Unfortunately, delay rather than promptness has characterised findings on admissibility. Long periods of delay often occur in the process of obtaining information, and it is not always clear whether these delays should be ascribed to the Commission or the Secretariat. Communication 44/90, *Peoples' Democratic Organisation for Independence and*

---

[17] For emulation of the civil law (French) style, see e.g. Communication 43/90, *Union des Scolaires Nigeriens, Union Generale des Etudiants Nigeriens au Benin* v. *Niger*, Seventh Activity Report 1993–1994, Annex IX (*Documents of the African Commission*, p. 345), using the formula 'meeting at . . .', 'by petition dated . . .', 'considering that . . .', 'declares . . .'.

[18] See e.g. Communication 212/98, *Amnesty International* v. *Zambia*, Twelfth Activity Report 1998–1999, Annex V; para. 28 (*Documents of the African Commission*, p. 745).

[19] Rules of Procedure, Rule 104.   [20] Rules of Procedure, Rule 113.

Socialism v. *The Gambia* was received in 1990 and a finding on admissibility was made in 1995: 'from 1990 to 1995, the Commission proceeded to verify the exhaustion of local remedies.'[21] It is unclear whether the Commission formally considered admissibility, or whether it was functioning through its Secretariat. Be that as it may, the five-year delay is unacceptable.

More recently, some communications have proceeded to a finding on admissibility much more speedily. Communication 212/98, *Amnesty International* v. *Zambia* was, for example, declared admissible within about a month of being received by the Commission.[22] The inclusion of the names of the Commissioners who act as rapporteurs in respect of a particular communication as part of the Commission's finding may be a factor enhancing greater commitment to the speedy resolution of communications.

If the communication is defective or incomplete, the Commission will request the author to clarify the uncertainties or to provide missing details. When such a request is made, the Commission must fix an 'appropriate' time limit.[23]

The Commission must request additional information from the State complained against before it can decide the issue of admissibility. A time limit for compliance with the request must also be set 'to avoid the issue dragging on too long'.[24] The Rules of Procedure require that the Commission decide on the issue of admissibility where the State does not respond within three months 'from the date of notification of the communication'.[25] Finding Communication 159/96, *Union Interafricaine des Droits de l'Homme and others* v. *Angola* admissible in April 1997, the Commission explained that its decision was based on 'information furnished by the complainants'. It deplored 'the fact that the defendant State did not respond to the notification sent to it in December 1996'.[26]

---

[21] Communication 44/90, *Peoples' Democratic Organisation for Independence and Socialism* v. *The Gambia*, Tenth Activity Report 1996–1997, Annex X, para. 13 (*Documents of the African Commission*, p. 559).

[22] Communication 212/98, *Amnesty International* v. *Zambia*, Twelfth Activity Report 1998–1999, Annex V (*Documents of the African Commission*, p. 745).

[23] Rules of Procedure, Rule 104(2).   [24] Rules of Procedure, Rule 117(1).

[25] Rules of Procedure, Rule 117(4).

[26] Communication 159/96, *Union Interafricaine des Droits de l'Homme, Féderation International des Ligues des Droits de l'Homme, Rencontre Africaine des Droits de l'Homme, Organisation Nationale des Droits de l'Homme au Sénégal and Association Malienne des Droits de l'Homme* v. *Angola*, Eleventh Activity Report 1997–1998, Annex II (*Documents of the African Commission*, p. 615).

To avoid delays in the processing of communications, several issues should be borne in mind. Communications should be as detailed as possible from the outset. A communication must also be in one of the working languages of the OAU, Arabic, English or French. As a practical consideration, because few of the secretarial staff or the commissioners speak Arabic, it is best to submit Arabic communications with an English or French translation. Translation practices at the level of the Secretariat have been lacking in the past. For this reason, even English or French communications should be submitted preferably in both languages. Although this is desirable in order for all Commissioners to be able to read the communication, it must be stressed that this is by no means a formal or absolute requirement. The language of communications should be clear and simple and the facts stated concisely.

A decision of inadmissibility may be reconsidered at a later date if the Commission is requested to reconsider its previous decision.[27] Sometimes the Commission invites the author to do so, as in *Alberto T. Capitao* v. *Tanzania*,[28] where the Commission observed that the 'case can be resubmitted when the local remedies have been properly exhausted or if the complainant proves that local remedies are unavailable, ineffective or unreasonably prolonged'.[29]

The Commission should make its findings on admissibility known 'as soon as possible' to the author of the complaint and the State Party concerned.[30]

Grounds for admissibility

Admissibility requirements to which communications under the Charter have to conform are set out in Article 56 of the Charter, although these are supplemented by the Commission's Rules of Procedure and its jurisprudence.

IDENTITY OF THE AUTHOR

Article 56(1) stipulates that communications must 'indicate their authors even if the latter requests anonymity'. The phrase 'indicate their authors'

---

[27] Rules of Procedure, Rule 118(2).
[28] Communications 53/90 and 53/91, *Alberto T. Capitao* v. *Tanzania*, Seventh Activity Report 1993–1994, Annex IX; Eighth Activity Report 1994–1995, Annex VI (*Documents of the African Commission*, pp. 346 and 384).
[29] *Ibid.*, para. 3.   [30] Rules of Procedure, Rule 118(1).

should be understood broadly to include full particulars to enable the Commission's Secretary to remain in contact with the author, to keep him or her informed about the status of the communication, and to request further information if it is required.[31] Therefore an 'indication' of the author means not only his or her full name, but at least also an address where the author can be contacted.[32] This should preferably be a street address, postal address, telephone number, fax number and e-mail address, should these be available.[33] The Commission has found a communication inadmissible due to the absence of the author's address.[34] Communication 108/93, *Monja Joana* v. *Madagascar*, illustrates the difficulties involved in obtaining such details where there are insufficient means of communication.[35] In this case, the Commission lost contact with the complainant, and unsuccessfully tried various means in an attempt to contact the complainant through other individuals. Later, it transpired that the complainant had died. Even attempts to contact his legal successor bore no results.

No communication may be submitted anonymously.[36] The author may request anonymity but still needs to state his or her name and other particulars as part of the communication. It will sometimes be difficult to maintain the anonymity of the complainant, as the State needs to be alerted to the specific situation that gave rise to the complaint against it. This aspect has not been raised explicitly in any finding of the Commission, and so far the Commission has received no communications from individuals who requested anonymity. Where NGOs brought communications, they usually stipulated on whose behalf these communications were

---

[31] Communication 70/92, *Ibrahim Dioumessi, Sekou Kande, Ousmane Kaba* v. *Guinea*, Seventh Activity Report 1993–1994, Annex IX; Ninth Activity Report 1995–1996, Annex VIII (*Documents of the African Commission*, pp. 347, 448), which emphasised that the identity of the authors must be known in order for them to 'be sent notifications'.

[32] In Communication 57/91, *Tanko Bariga* v. *Nigeria*, Seventh Activity Report 1993–1994, Annex IX (*Documents of the African Commission*, p. 346), the Commission made it clear that an address is required because 'for practical reasons it is necessary that the Commission is able to contact the author'.

[33] The Inter-American Convention goes further by requiring that individual petitions must contain 'the name, nationality, profession, domicile, and signature of the person or persons or the legal representative of the entity lodging the petition', IACHR, Article 46(1)(d).

[34] Communication 57/91, *Tanko Bariga* v. *Nigeria*, Seventh Activity Report 1993–1994, Annex IX (*Documents of the African Commission*, p. 346).

[35] Communication 108/93, *Monja Joana* v. *Madagascar*, Tenth Activity Report 1996–1997, Annex X (*Documents of the African Commission*, p. 573).

[36] There exists a similar requirement for communications under the Optional Protocol to the ICCPR, Article 3 and CAT, Article 22(2).

brought.[37] This did not happen in some instances, probably because the communication alleged situations of massive or widespread violations of human rights.[38]

THE COMMUNICATION MUST BE COMPATIBLE WITH THE OAU CHARTER AND THE AFRICAN CHARTER

At first glance, it appears that communications are required by Article 56(2) to be compatible with either the OAU Charter[39] or the African Charter, and not with both.[40] It does not, however, make sense to require that allegations of violations of the Charter should be compatible with the OAU Charter, and not with the African Charter. The OAU Charter is the founding document of the OAU, a political organisation, and sets out the aims and objectives of the OAU and the mandate and functioning of the OAU institutions. The main points of departure of this Charter that are in conflict with the ethos of the African Charter are State sovereignty and non-interference in the domestic affairs of Member States. The only mention of human rights is made as part of its purpose, namely, 'to promote international co-operation, having due regard to the Charter of the United Nations and the Universal Declaration of Human Rights'.[41] The African Charter, on the other hand, sets out the rights of individuals and peoples in States Parties and places the duty on States Parties to recognise and give effect to these rights. The word 'or' in Article 56(2) should therefore be read conjunctively, joining the two instruments, making it a requirement that communications have to be compatible with both the OAU Charter and the African Charter.

---

[37] See e.g. Communication 87/93, *Constitutional Rights Project (in respect of Zamani Lakwot and 6 Others)* v. *Nigeria,* Eighth Activity Report 1994–1995, Annex VI (*Documents of the African Commission,* p. 391).

[38] See e.g. Communication 74/92, *Commission Nationale des Droits de l'Homme et des Libertés* v. *Chad,* Ninth Activity Report 1995–1996, Annex VIII (*Documents of the African Commission,* p. 449), in which reference is to '15 . . . people detained', '200 wounded' and 'several tortured'. The communication refers by name to two individuals, Bisso Mamadou and Joseph Betudi, who had allegedly been assassinated: paras. 5 and 6.

[39] Charter of the Organization of African Unity, 25 May 1963, 47 UNTS 45, reprinted ILM 8 (1969) 1288.

[40] Article 56(3) reads as follows: 'are compatible with the Charter of the OAU or with the present Charter.'

[41] OAU Charter, Article 2(1). In fact, this formulation also suggests that the OAU Charter and the African Charter should be read cumulatively in Article 56 of the African Charter, as it is in respect of the UN Charter and its main human rights instrument at the time, the Universal Declaration of Human Rights.

Compatibility with the OAU Charter received attention in Communication 75/92, *Katangese Peoples' Congress* v. *Zaire*.[42] Without explicitly referring to the OAU Charter, the Commission took into account the 'sovereignty and territorial integrity of Zaire'. Given that these concepts are never mentioned in the African Charter but form the basis of the OAU Charter, this decision could lend support to the contention that communications have to be compatible with both the OAU Charter and the African Charter.

Even if one accepts this conclusion, the essence of Article 56 is that the Commission considers communications only if they are 'compatible with' the African Charter. Compatibility with the African Charter has four main aspects. First, the communication must allege that a right set out in the Charter has been violated (the 'substantive' requirement). Secondly, the communication must be directed at a State Party and must be submitted by someone who is competent to do so (the 'personal' requirement). Thirdly, the communication must be based on events that have occurred within the period of the Charter's application (the 'temporal' requirement). Lastly, the communication must be based on events that took place within the territorial sphere in which the Charter applies (the 'territorial' requirement). These will be examined in turn.

To be admissible, a communication must be based on an alleged violation of the Charter.[43] Similar prerequisites exist under all international human rights systems.[44] Allegations set out in a communication should provide *prima facie* evidence that a provision of the African Charter has been violated. In *Frederick Korvah* v. *Liberia*,[45] the author based the communication on a lack of discipline in the Liberian Security Police, corruption, immorality of the Liberian people generally and a national security risk caused by American financial experts. The Commission, finding that the matters 'described in

---

[42] Communication 75/92, *Katangese Peoples' Congress* v. *Zaire*, Eighth Activity Report 1994–1995, Annex VI (*Documents of the African Commission*, p. 388).

[43] An example under the Optional Protocol to the ICCPR is that an alleged breach of the collective right to strike cannot be brought under the ICCPR: see Communication 118/82, *J. B. and others* v. *Canada*, Doc. A/41/40, p. 151.

[44] See e.g. Optional Protocol to the ICCPR, Article 1 where the Human Rights Committee can entertain communications alleging violations of 'any of the rights set forth in the Covenant'; CAT, Article 22(2) and IACHR, Article 47(b) where a petition which does not state 'facts that tend to establish a violation of the rights guaranteed' by the Convention are inadmissible.

[45] Communication 1/88, *Frederick Korvah* v. *Liberia*, Seventh Activity Report 1993–1994, Annex IX (*Documents of the African Commission*, p. 337).

the communication do not amount to violations of human rights under the provisions of the Charter',[46] declared the communication inadmissible.

Although there is no need for the complainant to mention the specific provisions of the Charter that are allegedly violated, there must be a sufficient indication of the factual basis on which the alleged violation is based.[47] The Commission will otherwise not know which incident to investigate, about which specific incident to require information from the State, or on which particular violation to base its finding. Communications 104/94 and 109–126/94, *Centre for Independence of Judges and Lawyers* v. *Algeria* were declared inadmissible for a lack of specificity about places, dates and times on which incidents had allegedly occurred.[48]

At least one communication, found to be inadmissible for not revealing a violation of a right under the Charter, gave rise to some analysis of a substantive Charter provision. In Communication 75/92, *Katangese Peoples' Congress* v. *Zaire*, the Commission found that the communication had 'no merit under the African Charter'.[49] The Katangese Peoples' Congress, a liberation movement working towards achieving independence of the Katanga region from the then Zaire, brought a communication under Article 20(1) of the African Charter, requesting that the Commission recognise that it was entitled to independence, and therefore allow it to secede from Zaire. The Commission found that the claim did not amount to a violation of Article 20(1). The reasoning of the Commission was that, under the OAU Charter, the Commission must uphold the sovereignty and territorial integrity of all OAU Member States, including Zaire. Self-determination, referred to in Article 20, may be exercised in a variety of ways including independence, self-government, local government, federalism and unitarism. As a general rule, nationals of a State have to make use of one of these alternatives, without undermining the sovereignty and territorial integrity

---

[46] *Ibid.*

[47] Communication 162/97, *Mouvement des Réfugiés Mauritaniens au Sénégal* v. *Senegal*, Eleventh Activity Report 1997–1998, Annex II (*Documents of the African Commission*, p. 613), which was found inadmissible on the ground that the facts do not reveal a *prima facie* violation of the Charter. The Commission mentioned, in addition, that the specific provisions of the Charter allegedly violated had not been stipulated.

[48] Communications 104/93 and 109–126/94, *Centre for Independence of Judges and Lawyers* v. *Algeria and others*, Eighth Activity Report 1994–1995, Annex VI (*Documents of the African Commission*, pp. 349 and 396).

[49] Communication 75/92, *Katangese Peoples' Congress* v. *Zaire*, Eighth Activity Report 1994–1995, Annex VI (*Documents of the African Commission*, p. 388).

of the State. The Commission hints at two possible justifications that would entitle nationals to self-determination in the form of independence or secession. These are instances where there is 'concrete evidence of violations of human rights to the point that the territorial integrity of the State should be called to question', and where there is evidence that the group concerned is denied the right to participate in government, as guaranteed in the Charter. As neither of these prerequisites was present in the facts giving rise to the communication, the allegations could not be regarded as constituting a violation of Article 20.

Socio-economic rights under the Charter are in principle placed on a par with other rights as far as their justiciability is concerned. No threshold objection by respondent States that these rights are non-justiciable should therefore be countenanced at the admissibility stage. Two socio-economic rights under the Charter place obligations on States: the right to education and the right to health. The right to health is limited by the phrase 'best attainable state of physical and mental health'.[50] In the right to 'work under equitable and satisfactory conditions',[51] 'work' should be understood to be a verb, rather than a noun.[52] Such an understanding means that this right does not place obligations to fulfil on the State, causing the right to be civil or political in nature, rather than socio-economic.

The question arises whether a respondent State may argue that a communication is inadmissible on the basis that the alleged violation is allowed by the clawback clause.[53] This issue will only arise in respect of those rights containing a clawback clause. For example, is a communication alleging a violation of the right to association admissible if the right is curtailed by domestic law?[54] The practice of the Commission indicates that such issues do not raise questions of admissibility. The Commission has considered communications on their merits in instances where clawback clauses have come into play. This is in line with the Commission's interpretation of the word 'law', which does not equate 'law' with 'domestic law'. Rather, 'law' is understood as incorporating, presumably through Articles 60 and 61 of

---

[50] African Charter, Article 16(1).   [51] African Charter, Article 15.

[52] The French version of the Charter uses the verb *travailler* (to work) as the equivalent of 'work'.

[53] Such as the terms 'laid down by law', Article 6; 'subject to law and order', Article 8; and 'provided he abides by the law', Article 12(1).

[54] Article 10(1) of the Charter: 'Every individual shall have the right to free association provided he abides by the law.'

the Charter, international standards and therefore cannot lead to curtailment of rights. A clear articulation of this view is found in Communication 212/98, *Amnesty International* v. *Zambia*, where the Commission stated that '"clawback" clauses must not be interpreted against the principles of the Charter' and 'recourse to these should not be used as a means of giving credence to violations of the express provisions of the Charter'.[55] The same may be said of findings pertaining to admissibility – recourse to clawback clauses should not be allowed as a means of denying the African Commission jurisdiction.

The fact that the allegation must reveal a violation of the human rights treaty also implies that the treaty body does not review factual findings made by national tribunals. The UN's Human Rights Committee has held that it is 'beyond its competence to review findings of fact made by national tribunals or to determine whether national tribunals properly evaluated new evidence submitted on appeal'.[56] The European institutions have also made it clear that they do not establish a court of fourth instance.[57]

The second requirement is that a communication must be directed at a State that is a party to the Charter. Numerous petitioners in the early years of the Commission overlooked this rather obvious requirement resulting in it initially taking a substantial amount of the Commission's attention. It is preferable to deal with such matters administratively, at the level of the Secretariat.

In the first few years, this requirement was the cause of most findings of inadmissibility: twenty-three of the fifty-four cases found to be inadmissible until May 1999. There are four categories of countries against whom these communications were directed: non-African States,[58] OAU Member States

---

[55] Communication 212/98, *Amnesty International* v. *Zambia*, Twelfth Activity Report 1998–1999, Annex V (*Documents of the African Commission*, p. 745).

[56] Communication 174/84, *J.K.* v. *Canada*, Doc. A/40/40, p. 251.

[57] See e.g. K. Reid, *A Practitioner's Guide to the European Convention on Human Rights* (London: 1998), p. 31: 'The Convention organs are not . . . a court of appeal from domestic courts and cannot intervene on the basis that a domestic court has come to the "wrong" decision or made a mistake. Their role is to ensure compliance with the provisions of the Convention by the Contracting Parties.'

[58] Non-African States complained against are Bahrain (Communication 7/88, *Committee for the Defence of Political Prisoners* v. *Bahrain*, Seventh Activity Report 1993–1994, Annex IX (*Documents of the African Commission*, p. 339)); Indonesia (Communication 38/90, *Wesley Parish* v. *Indonesia*, Seventh Activity Report 1993–1994, Annex IX (*Documents of the African Commission*, p. 344)); the USA (Communication 2/88, *Iheanyichukwu A. Ihebereme* v. *USA*, Seventh Activity Report 1993–1994, Annex IX (*Documents of*

that had not yet become States Parties to the Charter;[59] the only African non-OAU member, Morocco[60] and the OAU itself.[61] When the Rules of Procedure were amended in 1995, this was one of the issues to be addressed. Rule 102(2) now provides as follows: 'No communication concerning a State

the African Commission, p. 337); Communication 5/88, *Prince J. N. Makoge* v. *USA*, Seventh Activity Report 1993–1994, Annex IX (*Documents of the African Commission*, p. 338)); and Yugoslavia (Communication 3/88, *Centre for the Independence of Judges and Lawyers* v. *Yugoslavia*, Seventh Activity Report 1993–1994, Annex IX (*Documents of the African Commission*, p. 337)). One communication was directed at two such States simultaneously, Haiti and the USA (Communication 37/90, *Georges Eugene* v. *USA, Haiti*, Seventh Activity Report 1993–1994, Annex IX (*Documents of the African Commission*, p. 344)).

[59] African States complained against before they had become party to the Charter are: Angola (Communication 24/89, *Union Nationale de Liberation de Cabinda* v. *Angola*, Seventh Activity Report 1993–1994, Annex IX (*Documents of the African Commission*, p. 342)); Burundi (Communication 26/89, *Austrian Committee Against Torture* v. *Burundi*, Seventh Activity Report 1993–1994, Annex IX (*Documents of the African Commission*, p. 342)); Ethiopia (Communication 9/88, *International Lawyers Committee for Family Reunification* v. *Ethiopia*, Seventh Activity Report 1993–1994, Annex IX (*Documents of the African Commission*, p. 339); Communication 10/88, *Getachew Abebe* v. *Ethiopia*, Seventh Activity Report 1993–1994, Annex IX (*Documents of the African Commission*, p. 339); Communication 14/88, *Dr Abd Eldayem AE Sanussi* v. *Ethiopia*, Seventh Activity Report 1993–1994, Annex IX (*Documents of the African Commission*, p. 340); Communication 21/88, *Centre Haitien des Libertés Publiques* v. *Ethiopia*, Seventh Activity Report 1993–1994, Annex IX (*Documents of the African Commission*, p. 342); Communication 28/89, *Association Internationales des Juristes Democrates* v. *Ethiopia*, Seventh Activity Report 1993–1994, Annex IX (*Documents of the African Commission*, p. 343); Communication 29/89, *Commission Française Justice et Paix* v. *Ethiopia*, Seventh Activity Report 1993–1994, Annex IX (*Documents of the African Commission*, p. 343)); and Ghana (Communication 4/88, *Co-ordinating Secretary of the Free Citizens Convention* v. *Ghana*, Seventh Activity Report 1993–1994, Annex IX (*Documents of the African Commission*, p. 338); Communication 6/88, *Dr Kodji Kofi* v. *Ghana*, Seventh Activity Report 1993–1994, Annex IX (*Documents of the African Commission*, p. 338)); Lesotho (Communication 33/89, *Simon B. Ntaka* v. *Lesotho*, Seventh Activity Report 1993–1994, Annex IX (*Documents of the African Commission*, p. 343)). One communication was directed at four States simultaneously, none of them a party to the Charter at the time (Communication 19/88, *International Pen* v. *Cameroon, Ethiopia, Kenya, Malawi*, Seventh Activity Report 1993–1994, Annex IX (*Documents of the African Commission*, p. 341)).

[60] Two communications were directed at Morocco, who at that stage was not a member of the OAU (Communication 20/88, *Austrian Committee Against Torture* v. *Morocco*, Seventh Activity Report 1993–1994, Annex IX (*Documents of the African Commission*, p. 341); Communication 41/90, *Andre Houver* v. *Morocco*, Seventh Activity Report 1993–1994, Annex IX (*Documents of the African Commission*, p. 344)).

[61] A further communication was directed at the OAU (Communication 12/88, *Mohamed El-Nekheily* v. *OAU*, Seventh Activity Report 1993–1994, Annex IX (*Documents of the African Commission*, p. 339)).

which is not a party to the Charter shall be received by the Commission or placed on a list under Rule 103 of the present Rules.'

Communications should not be directed against individuals. This may seem trite, but the language of the Charter invites an interpretation that, by including duties of individuals owed to other individuals, individuals may also be bound, and be found to 'violate' the Charter. The starting point is that the Charter is open only for ratification by States, and not individuals. The concept of duties should be used as a guideline by States to fulfil their general obligation under Article 1 of the Charter. States may be in breach of the Charter if they do not give effect to the duties of individuals under the Charter. But then it remains that it is the State that will be in breach, and not an individual. An inter-State communication may, for example, be brought against a State in respect of its failure to adopt legislative or other measures to give effect to individual duties. Individual duties may give rise to a communication in such a roundabout way, but not directly against individuals.

On the other hand, States may be held responsible for violations by non-State actors, such as guerrilla groups, multinationals, private enterprises and para-statals under the doctrine of State responsibility. A State may be in violation of the Charter if it is complicit in the violations of the Charter with a non-State actor, if it has sufficient control over the 'private actor',[62] or if it fails to investigate violations by non-State actors. Under such circumstances, violations by non-State actors of rights guaranteed under the Charter are imputed to the State. A communication may consequently be brought against a State under such circumstances. In Communication 74/92, *Commission Nationale des Droits de l'Homme et des Libertés v. Chad*,[63] the Government of Chad conceded that massive violations were taking place in Chad, but ascribed it to a situation of civil war, over which it and its agents had no control. Invoking Article 1 of the Charter, the Commission found that if a State neglects to ensure the rights in the Charter, it violates the Charter 'even if the State or its agents are not the immediate cause of the violation'. The Commission reiterated that the government 'had a responsibility to secure

---

[62] Communication 61/79, *Hertzberg and others* v. *Finland*, Doc. A/37/40, p. 161, in which the Human Rights Committee pointed out that Finland was responsible for the actions of a broadcasting company in which it had a dominant stake (90 per cent) and which was placed under specific government control.

[63] Communication 74/92, *Commission Nationale des Droits de l'Homme et des Libertés* v. *Chad*, Ninth Activity Report 1995–1996, Annex VIII (*Documents of the African Commission*, p. 449).

the safety and the liberty of its citizens, and to conduct investigations into murders'.

It is possible for a communication to be submitted against a new government for violations of the previous government given the doctrine of State responsibility. In respect of the situation in Malawi, the Commission observed as follows: 'Principles of international law stipulate ... that a new government inherits the previous government's international obligations, including the responsibility for the previous government's mismanagement.'[64] 'Inherited responsibility' derives from the fact that States, rather than governments, ratify the African Charter and, therefore, a communication may be submitted against the new government. The outcome of the case may be a finding of violation, or a finding that the matter has been amicably settled.[65]

In respect of the question by whom may a communication be lodged, the African Commission has made it clear that the author of a communication under the African Charter need not be a victim or a member of the victim's family. The rationale for this broad approach to standing is the practical difficulties that individuals face in Africa. These obstacles include the existence of serious or massive violations that may preclude individual victims from pursuing remedies on their own behalf, and the fact that victims are often obstructed or have difficulty in submitting communications themselves. Consequently, the Commission has declared admissible numerous communications submitted by African NGOs from a specific country, such as the Civil Liberties Organisation and the Constitutional Rights Project (both in Nigeria) or NGOs with a regional focus, such as the *Union Interafricaine des Droits de l'Homme*.

The lack of a 'victim' requirement has two additional consequences. First, communications may be filed by individuals from countries that are not States Parties to the Charter. This happened, for example, in Communication

---

[64] Communications 64/92, 68/92 and 78/92, *Krischna Achuthan, Amnesty International, Amnesty International* v. *Malawi*, Seventh Activity Report 1993–1994, Annex IX; Eighth Activity Report 1994–1995, Annex VI (*Documents of the African Commission*, pp. 347 and 387).

[65] As in Communications 16/88, 17/88 and 18/88, *Comité Culturel pour la Democratie au Benin, Badjogoume Hilaire, El Hadj Boubacar Diawara* v. *Benin*, Seventh Activity Report 1993–1994, Annex IX, Eighth Activity Report 1994–1995, Annex VI (*Documents of the African Commission*, pp. 340 and 381). The Commission observed that 'the present government of Benin has satisfactorily resolved the issue of violations of human rights under the previous administration'.

31/89, *Maria Baes* v. *Zaire*,[66] where Maria Baes, a Danish national, submitted a communication on behalf of a Zairean colleague at the University of Zaire, Dr Kondola. The Commission declared the communication admissible. Secondly, communications may be filed by international organisations. Examples of international NGOs that have successfully submitted cases to the Commission are Amnesty International, the International Commission of Jurists, International Pen and the *Organisation Mondiale Contre la Torture*.

The absence of a 'victim requirement' also means that authors may complain to the Commission about the compatibility of national laws or practices without being themselves directly affected by that particular law or practice. Under the ICCPR, the Human Rights Committee observed that: 'It is not the task of the Human Rights Committee, acting under the Optional Protocol, to review *in abstracto* national legislation or practices as to their compliance with obligations imposed by the Covenant.'[67] Some other international human rights instruments enable a third party to submit the communication on behalf of the victim.[68] By not requiring the author to be a 'victim', the Inter-American system shows the closest resemblance to the position under the African Charter. Indeed, the Inter-American Convention on Human Rights provides that 'any person or group of persons, or any non-governmental entity legally recognised in one or more Member States' of the OAS, may lodge complaints.[69]

Regarding the 'temporal' requirement, a general principle of international law is that treaties 'do not bind a party in relation to any act or fact which took place in any situation which ceased to exist before the date of the entry into force of the treaty in respect to that party'.[70] Exceptions to this are where the treaty itself provides otherwise, by expressly allowing for retroactive effect,

---

[66] Communication 31/89, *Maria Baes* v. *Zaire*, Eighth Activity Report 1994–1995, Annex VI (*Documents of the African Commission*, p. 383).

[67] Communication 187/85, *J.H.* v. *Canada*, Doc. A/40/40, p. 230, declared the communication inadmissible as there was 'no specific indication in the communication that the author himself has been adversely affected by the policy which he complains about'. See also Communication 35/78, *Aumeeruddy-Cziffra and others* v. *Mauritius*, Doc. A/36/40, p. 134, in which the Human Rights Committee held that a complainant must actually be affected to bring a complaint under the Optional Protocol to the ICCPR.

[68] CAT, Article 22(1) provides that its Committee will consider communications in light of information 'made available to it by *or on behalf of* the individual' (and the State Party concerned) (emphasis added).

[69] Article 44.   [70] Article 28 of the Vienna Convention on the Law of Treaties.

or where there are 'continuous violations'.[71] A 'continuous violation' is an action that started before the entry into force of the treaty, but where it or its effects continue after the entry into force of the treaty and, at that stage, therefore, may constitute an infringement of the treaty.

Because the African Charter does not deal explicitly with this aspect, the Commission has applied the general principles to the Charter. As far as the interpretation of the African Commission is concerned, one may distinguish between two possibilities. First, regarding States who were original parties to the Charter and for whom the date of entry into force coincided with the entry into force of the Charter (21 October 1986), the Commission has competence only to consider violations that are alleged to have occurred from the date of entry into force of the Charter. Issues relating to retroactivity have not arisen in the period after 1986, and are now unlikely to arise as the Charter has entered into force. Secondly, in relation to States that became parties after the entry into force of the Charter, the Commission has the competence to consider communications that have originated after the date of entry into force for a particular State. The date of entry into force is three months after the deposit by that State of its instrument of adherence.[72]

These principles were accepted in Communication 142/94, *Muthuthirin Njoka v. Kenya*.[73] This communication was originally submitted in 1991, and was declared inadmissible because Kenya was not a State Party to the Charter at the time the communication was submitted. Kenya acceded to the Charter on 23 January 1992. Thereafter the complainant resubmitted his communication but it was once again found to be inadmissible. This time the Commission observed that the 'cause of the complaint arose at a time when Kenya was not a party to the Charter'. The Commission also implicitly accepted the possibility of the 'continuous violation' exception when it remarked that there was 'no evidence of a continuing damage in breach of the Charter'. Similarly, in Communication 39/90, *Annette Pagnoulle v. Cameroon*,[74] the Commission reiterated that it 'cannot pronounce on the

---

[71] See the Human Rights Committee's views in Communication 117/81, *M. A. v. Italy*, Doc. A/39/40, p. 190, and the European Court in *De Becker v. Belgium*, Series A, No. 4, Judgment of 27 March 1962, I EHRR 43.

[72] Article 65 of the Charter.

[73] Communication 142/94, *Muthuthirin Njoka v. Kenya*, Eighth Activity Report 1994–1995, Annex VI (*Documents of the African Commission*, p. 398).

[74] Communication 39/90, *Annette Pagnoulle (on behalf of Abdoulaye Mazou) v. Cameroon*, Eighth Activity Report 1994–1995, Annex VI; Tenth Activity Report 1996–1997, Annex X (*Documents of the African Commission*, pp. 384 and 555).

quality of court proceedings that took place before the African Charter entered into force in Cameroon', but added: 'If, however, irregularities in the original sentence have consequences that constitute a continuing violation of any of the Articles of the African Charter, the Commission must pronounce on these.'[75]

Lastly, the 'territorial' requirement[76] provides that States Parties to the African Charter are in principle only responsible for violations that occur within their territory. There are exceptions, though, such as a refusal of a visa by a diplomatic post in a foreign country.[77] Although that action (the refusal) took place outside the State, the State is still responsible, and may be found in violation of its obligations.

The territorial requirement derives from the fact that States are responsible only for actions or events under their control. A State will, consequently, be responsible for an extra-territorial incident or event in cases where the State has *de facto* control over that incident or event. The European Court on Human Rights has held, for example, that a government can exercise its control 'directly', 'through its armed forces', or 'through a subordinate local administration', in that case finding Turkey in violation of the ECHR in respect of actions by its security forces in Northern Cyprus.[78]

COMMUNICATIONS MUST NOT BE WRITTEN IN DISPARAGING LANGUAGE

The African Charter disqualifies communications that are written in 'disparaging or insulting language',[79] directed at the State complained against and its institutions, or the OAU. This requirement is not found in other international human rights instruments.[80]

The Commission has on one occasion based a finding of inadmissibility, at least partly, on this ground. An NGO, the *Ligue Camerounaise des Droits de l'Homme*, submitted a communication in which it alleged that the

---

[75] *Ibid.*, para. 15.   [76] Also referred to as jurisdiction *ratione loci*.

[77] Case 5961/72, *Amekane* v. *UK*, 16 YB 356 (1973).

[78] *Loizidou (Preliminary Objections)* v. *Turkey*, Series A, No. 310, 23 March 1995, 23 EHRR 513.

[79] Article 56(3) of the Charter.

[80] The closest resemblance is the requirement that a complainant must not abuse the right to submit a communication, found in both the Optional Protocol to the ICCPR (Article 3) and the CAT (Article 22(2)).

Cameroon Government was committing serious and massive human rights violations.[81] The communication contained statements such as 'Paul Biya must respond to crimes against humanity', '30 years of the criminal neo-colonial regime incarnated by the duo Ahidjo/Biya', 'regime of torturers' and 'government barbarism'.[82] The government argued that the communication should be declared inadmissible because the allegations therein 'are posed in disparaging and insulting language'. The Commission agreed and declared the communication inadmissible. This decision is unfortunate and regrettable. At most, the Commission should have struck out the offending phrases, or should have referred the matter back to the author, including a reference to Article 56(3). Although the author may now resubmit the communication, this will require great determination. The original communication was submitted in March 1992, and the admissibility decision was taken only in April 1997. It is unlikely that the author will resume a process that has proven unsuccessful after more than five years. The allegations in this communication relate to the situation of human rights in Cameroon. These remarks should not be viewed as 'insulting' to the State, but as part of a passionate plea to focus attention on the situation in Cameroon. The Commission should have adopted the narrowest possible meaning of the words 'disparaging', 'insulting' and 'State concerned'. It is something quite different to use insulting language towards a 'State', as the Charter requires, from insulting a head of State, yet this distinction is not referred to in the Commission's finding. One cannot but agree with Odinkalu that Article 56(3) provides 'an artifice for distraction, obfuscation, and subterfuge'.[83]

It seems as if the decision really did not turn on the issue of disparaging language. The Commission observed that the information available to it 'did not give evidence of *prima facie* violations of the African Charter', that it lacked 'specificity' and declared the communication inadmissible. The language of the communication was only mentioned as an afterthought. But by stating clearly that this is a factor that the Commission considered, the Commission sent out a clear signal that it may 'censure' communications to cater for the sensibilities of heads of States. In this regard, it is instructive to note the reference, for the first time in a finding of the Commission, to the fact that the Commission takes decisions on admissibility by majority vote. One

---

[81] Communication 65/92, *Ligue Camerounaise des Droits de l'Homme* v. *Cameroon*, Tenth Activity Report 1996–1997, Annex X (*Documents of the African Commission*, p. 562).

[82] Paul Biya is the current President of Cameroon, while Ahmadou Ahidjo was his predecessor.

[83] Odinkalu, 'The Individual Complaints Procedure', p. 382.

can only guess why this fact was mentioned in this communication, when so many communications have already been decided about admissibility. No general clarification on this issue seemed required in that particular case, unless in fact some of the Commissioners disagreed.[84]

COMMUNICATIONS MUST NOT BE BASED SOLELY ON NEWS

The African Charter stipulates that communications are only to be considered if they 'are not based exclusively on news disseminated through the mass media'.[85] There is no similar requirement under the UN treaties or other regional human rights systems. This requirement was inserted in the African Charter especially because the Charter does not have the same individualistic focus. The fact that a complainant does not have to be personally affected (be a 'victim'), and that there is express provision for the submission of cases alleging serious or massive human rights violations, provide the possibility that communications may be based on reports by the mass media. But the media may be biased and media misrepresentation is not uncommon. As the possibilities of the electronic age increase global awareness of and information about human rights violations, the submission of communications as a result of media-based outrages alone may become more prevalent. The Charter, although not necessarily drafted against this backdrop, deals sufficiently with the demands of globalised communication. It does not rule out media reports as further substantiation or support, but they may not be the only basis for the allegations.

In Communications 147/95 and 149/96, *Sir Dawda K. Jawara v. The Gambia*,[86] the Commission emphasised the importance of the media in revealing human rights violations, referring to the role of the media in Burundi, Congo, Rwanda and Zaire. However, the Commission also pointed out that the Charter makes use of the word 'exclusively'. Because the communication under consideration was in part, but not exclusively, based on news disseminated through the mass media, the Commission found it to be admissible. The Commission's approach is summarised by the following statement: 'While it would be dangerous to rely exclusively on news disseminated from the mass media, it would be equally damaging if the Commission were to

---

[84] The reason for the reference to 'majority vote' is, however, not a matter of public record.
[85] Article 56(4) of the African Charter.
[86] Thirteenth Activity Report 1999–2000, Annex V.

reject a communication because some aspects of it are based on news disseminated through the mass media.'[87] Adopting this approach, the Commission
correctly focuses on the reliability of the information, rather than its source.

COMMUNICATIONS MUST BE SENT AFTER LOCAL REMEDIES HAVE BEEN EXHAUSTED

Article 56(5) requires that communications should be sent to the Commission only 'after exhausting local remedies, if any, unless it is obvious that
this procedure is unduly prolonged'. The rationale for the existence of this
rule derives from the consensual nature of international law. It is only fair
that a State must be afforded full opportunity to give effect to its international law obligations, something it has consented to do.[88] The African
Commission observed that this requirement is based 'on the principle that
a government should have notice of a human rights violation in order to
have the opportunity to remedy such violation before [being] called before
an international body'.[89] According to the International Court of Justice,
the rule is founded upon the principle 'that the responsible State must first
have an opportunity to redress by its own means within the framework of its
own domestic system the wrong alleged to be done to the individual'.[90] The
requirement of exhaustion of local remedies conforms with the principle
that international law is subsidiary to national law. It does not replace, but
rather supplements, national institutions. The requirement of exhaustion of
local remedies is part of the admissibility requirements of all international
human rights systems.[91]

---

[87] Para. 24.
[88] See, generally, C. F. Amerasinghe, *Local Remedies in International Law* (Grotius, 1990).
According to Amerasinghe, the principle of exhaustion of local remedies originated in the
context of the diplomatic protection of aliens, where the host State was allowed to settle
the matter internally before international mechanisms were invoked.
[89] Communications 25/89, 47/90, 56/91 and 100/93, *Free Legal Assistance Group, Lawyers'
Committee for Human Rights, Union Interafricaine des Droits de l'Homme, Les Témoins de
Jehovah v. Zaire*, Ninth Activity Report 1995–1996, Annex VIII (*Documents of the African
Commission*, p. 444). For another expression of the rationale, see Communication 71/92,
Rencontre Africaine pour la Defense de Droits de l'Homme v. Zambia, Tenth Activity Report
1996–1997, Annex X, para. 9 (*Documents of the African Commission*, p. 563).
[90] *Interhandel Case (Switzerland v. USA)*, ICJ Reports (1959) 6 at 27.
[91] The Optional Protocol to the ICCPR, Article 5(2) refers to 'available' domestic
remedies that need to be exhausted, unless their exhaustion is 'unreasonably prolonged'. CAT, Article 22(5)(b) also makes reference to 'available' local remedies, restates

Regarding the phrase 'after exhausting' in Article 56(5), if a complaint is 'pending' before the local courts, domestic remedies have not been exhausted.[92] In other circumstances, whether internal remedies have in fact been exhausted is mainly a factual question about which the Commission may request further information. This raises the question of onus. The complainant must at least lay a foundation for a finding that local remedies have been exhausted. Where the complainant in Communication 198/97, *SOS-Esclaves* v. *Mauritania* did not respond as to whether local remedies had been exhausted, the case was declared inadmissible.[93]

Under the Optional Protocol to the ICCPR a three-phased process seems to have developed.[94] Initially, the onus, although not a heavy one, is on the complainant. The complaint must merely set out a basis for a potential finding of admissibility, that is, that the victim or complainant has exhausted or tried to exhaust local remedies. Thereafter, if the State denies the allegations, and declares that there is a further effective remedy that is available, the State must prove this. Lastly, should the State meet this onus, the author of the communication has the duty to prove that this remedy is either unavailable under the particular circumstances, that it is ineffective, or that other exceptional circumstances exist.

That the African Commission seems to follow a similar approach may be seen from Communication 71/92, *Rencontre Africaine pour la Defense des Droits de l'Homme* v. *Zambia*.[95] The complainant seemingly met the initial burden. It then fell to the State to prove the existence of an unused remedy: 'When the Zambian Government argues that the communication must be declared inadmissible because the local remedies have not been exhausted, the government then has the burden of demonstrating the existence of such

the 'unreasonably prolonged' exemption, and adds the exemption that local remedies need not be exhausted if they are 'unlikely to bring effective relief to the person who is a victim'.

92 Communication 18/88, *Diawara* v. *Benin*; see Communications 16/88, 17/88 and 18/88, *Comité Culturel pour la Democratie au Benin, Badjogoume Hilaire, El Hadj Boubacar Diawara* v. *Benin*, Seventh Activity Report 1993–1994, Annex IX, Eighth Activity Report 1994–1995, Annex VI (*Documents of the African Commission*, pp. 340 and 381).

93 Communication 198/97, *SOS-Esclaves* v. *Mauritania*, Twelfth Activity Report 1998–1999, Annex V. (*Documents of the African Commission*, p. 742).

94 See e.g. McGoldrick, *The Human Rights Committee*, pp. 145–50.

95 Communication 71/92, *Rencontre Africaine pour la Defense de Droits de l'Homme* v. *Zambia*, Tenth Activity Report 1996–1997, Annex X (*Documents of the African Commission*, p. 563).

remedies.'[96] This the State did by indicating that legislation, the Immigration and Deportations Act, provided for an appeal against expulsion orders. Referring to the testimony of the complainant, implying that the onus has shifted back onto the complainant, the Commission found that the remedy was not available as a practical matter.[97]

Findings of inadmissibility on the basis of non-exhaustion of local remedies are often made because the communication does not reveal a sufficient factual basis to indicate otherwise. In Communication 127/94, *Sana Dumbaya v. The Gambia*,[98] the complainant failed, on two occasions, to respond to requests for further clarification about the exhaustion of local remedies. Faced with this uncertainty, and having given the author an opportunity to clarify the matter, the Commission assumes that if local remedies had been exhausted, the complainant would have made it known. In Communication 198/97, *SOS–Esclaves v. Mauritania*,[99] for example, the complainant indicated that the supposed victims have initiated internal procedures, without saying 'anything about the status of those procedures'. Since the Commission was unable to determine whether the procedures had been concluded, it declared the communication inadmissible. The complainants must be taken not to have met the initial onus. As a practical matter, in order to enable the Commission to arrive at a decision in respect of admissibility within the shortest possible period, copies of any relevant national decisions should be attached to communications.[100]

A 'local remedy' for the purposes of Article 56 has been described as 'any domestic legal action that may lead to the resolution of the complaints at the

---

[96] *Ibid.*, para. 12.

[97] See also Communication 53/90 and 53/91, *Alberto T. Capitao v. Tanzania*, Seventh Activity Report 1993–1994, Annex IX; Eighth Activity Report 1994–1995, Annex VI (*Documents of the African Commission*, pp. 346 and 384), where the Commission noted that an inadmissible communication may be resubmitted if 'the complainant proves that the local remedies are unavailable, ineffective or unreasonably prolonged'.

[98] Communication 127/94, *Sana Dumbaya v. The Gambia*, Eighth Activity Report 1994–1995, Annex VI (*Documents of the African Commission*, p. 397).

[99] Communication 198/97, *SOS-Esclaves v. Mauritania*, Twelfth Activity Report 1998–1999, Annex V (*Documents of the African Commission*, p. 742).

[100] For an example where this had been done, see Communication 212/98, *Amnesty International v. Zambia*, Twelfth Activity Report 1998–1999, Annex V (*Documents of the African Commission*, p. 745). Judgments from the High Court of Malawi in Lilongwe, the High Court in Zambia in Chipata and the Supreme Court of Zambia in Lusaka were attached. This clear documentary basis accounts in part for the apparent ease with which a finding of admissibility was taken.

local or national level'. The remedy must be of a judicial nature ('action before the law courts'),[101] and includes all avenues of appeal or review.[102] It is not sufficient that a complainant alleges that the matter has been investigated by a quasi-judicial institution at the domestic level, such as the national human rights institution. In Communication 221/98, *Alfred B. Cudjoe* v. *Ghana*,[103] the complainant submitted a complaint to the Ghanaian national human rights institution, the Commission on Human Rights and Administrative Justice, which found that the complainant's dismissal without benefits was invalid and that he was entitled to compensation. The complainant then submitted the same matter as a communication to the African Commission. The African Commission declared the communication inadmissible, as remedies of a judicial nature had not been exhausted.

The complainant in Communication 92/93, *International Pen* v. *Sudan*[104] was detained incommunicado in 1992. By the time he submitted a communication to the Commission he had not exhausted any remedies. He argued that remedies would not be effective because the government had denied the existence of any incommunicado detention. The Commission observed that 'the fact that the Government has in general terms denied the existence of incommunicado detentions in Sudan does not amount to saying that the case has been tried in Sudanese courts'.[105]

Communication 39/90, *Annette Pagnoulle* v. *Cameroon*[106] mentions several stages pursued by the complainant including petitioning the President of Cameroon; approaching the Ministry of Justice with an out of court settlement offer; submitting the case to the Administrative Chamber of the Supreme Court; and subsequently approaching the Supreme Court. The Commission held that local remedies had been exhausted, because none of the steps taken yielded any results.

---

[101] Communication 221/98, *Alfred B. Cudjoe* v. *Ghana*, Twelfth Activity Report 1998–1999, Annex V, para. 14 (*Documents of the African Commission*, p. 753).

[102] See e.g. Communication 40/90, *Bob Ngozi Njoku* v. *Egypt*, Eleventh Activity Report 1997–1998, Annex II, para. 57 (*Documents of the African Commission*, p. 604).

[103] Communication 221/98, *Alfred B. Cudjoe* v. *Ghana*, Twelfth Activity Report 1998–1999, Annex V (*Documents of the African Commission*, p. 753).

[104] Communication 92/93, *International Pen* (*in respect of Kemal al-Jazouli*) v. *Sudan*, Eighth Activity Report 1994–1995, Annex VI (*Documents of the African Commission*, p. 394).

[105] *Ibid.*

[106] Communication 39/90, *Annette Pagnoulle* (*on behalf of Abdoulaye Mazou*) v. *Cameroon*, Eighth Activity Report 1994–1995, Annex VI; Tenth Activity Report 1996–1997, Annex X (*Documents of the African Commission*, pp. 384 and 555).

The question may also arise whether a colonial judicial remnant is part of 'local remedies'. In Communication 44/90, *Peoples' Democratic Organisation for Independence and Socialism* v. *The Gambia*,[107] the government contested its admissibility on the basis that the communication 'could be taken through the courts to the level of the [UK] Privy Council'. The Commission found the communication admissible on the basis that 'the exhaustion of local remedies had been unduly prolonged'. It is not clear to what extent the provision of the relevant legislation,[108] making appeal to the Privy Council impossible, played any role. The role of recourse to the Privy Council is unclear in other communications against The Gambia, which were found to be inadmissible on the basis of non-exhaustion of local remedies.[109] Ankumah is of the opinion that appeal to the Privy Council should not be regarded as a 'local remedy', because making use thereof will cause undue hardships, such as travelling to England, and will be inconsistent with the idea that the African Charter represents a forum to cater for the special needs of Africans.[110] On the other hand, the fact remains that Gambian Governments have thus far elected to retain this extraordinary remedy as part of its 'local remedies'.

It would appear from the wording 'if any', in Article 56(5), that only remedies that are in fact available, adequate and efficient need to be exhausted. It is worth questioning whether the subjective perception (or belief) of the complainant is sufficient to meet this requirement, or whether an objective test should be applied. In Communication 192/85, *S. H. B.* v. *Canada*,[111] a complainant before the UN Human Rights Committee argued that the remedy open to him, namely, further appeal to the Court of Appeal, was not 'effective', exhaustion would be 'futile' and it therefore did not need to be exhausted. The Human Rights Committee found that 'the author's doubts about the effectiveness of these remedies are not warranted and do

---

[107] Communication 44/90, *Peoples' Democratic Organisation for Independence and Socialism* v. *The Gambia*, Tenth Activity Report 1996–1997, Annex X (*Documents of the African Commission*, p. 559).

[108] Section 22(5) of the (Gambian) Elections Act provides that, on issues pertaining to elections, judgments of The Gambian Supreme Court are final and conclusive.

[109] See e.g. Communication 86/93, *M. S. Ceesay* v. *The Gambia*, Eighth Activity Report 1994–1995, Annex VI (*Documents of the African Commission*, p. 390), in which the Commission noted the following under the heading 'Decision': 'The Government notified the Commission that the complainant had not had recourse to the local remedies . . . [T]he Commission declared the communication inadmissible.'

[110] Ankumah, *The African Commission*, p. 69.   [111] Doc. A/42/40, p. 174.

not absolve him from exhausting them', therefore, seeming to opt for an objective standard to determine whether local remedies 'exist'.

The same may be said about the practice of the African Commission. In Communication 135/94, *Kenya Human Rights Commission* v. *Kenya*,[112] the complainant challenged the refusal of the Registrar of Trade Unions to register the Universities Academic Staff Union (UASU) as a trade union. Court proceedings were initiated to overturn this decision. Although these proceedings were still pending at the time when the African Commission determined the issue of admissibility, the Kenyan President, Moi, had publicly stated that the government would never register the UASU despite the fact that the matter was already in court. This factor, which supposedly influenced the complainant to bring the communication, was not regarded as sufficient to indicate that remedies were unavailable. It is not clear from the Commission's finding whether this factor was explicitly considered as such, but the decision indicates that the Commission applied an objective test, (implicitly) finding that the perception of the complainant was not sufficient to exempt the complainant from exhausting local remedies.

Under the Inter-American system, the requirement of exhaustion of local remedies is not applicable in certain circumstances, namely:[113] when the domestic legislation of the State concerned does not afford due process of law for the protection of the right or rights that have allegedly been violated; the party alleging violation of his rights has been denied access to the remedies under domestic law or has been prevented from exhausting them; or there has been unwarranted delay in rendering a final judgment. Similarly, under the African Charter, one can also identify a number of grounds for exemption from exhausting local remedies: cases of massive or serious violations; where clauses oust the jurisdiction of national courts; where the remedy is of a non-judicial nature, such as a request for clemency; where local remedies are not available, due to the death of the complainant; when it is illogical to require exhaustion of local remedies; and, possibly, when a complainant is indigent. Each of these will be examined in turn.

As a practical matter, local remedies are *prima facie* not available or effective in instances of serious or massive violations. The complainants in Communications 25/89, 47/90, 56/91 and 100/93, *Free Legal Assistance Group and*

---

[112] Communication 135/94, *Kenya Human Rights Organisation* v. *Kenya*, Ninth Activity Report 1995–1996, Annex VIII (*Documents of the African Commission*, p. 455).
[113] IACHR, Article 46(2).

others v. *Zaire*[114] alleged widespread arrests, detention, extrajudicial executions, torture, unfair trials, restrictions of press freedom, deprivation of
property and denial of access to education.[115] After bringing the situation
to the attention of the OAU Assembly under Article 58 of the Charter, the
Commission unsuccessfully attempted to undertake a visit to Zaire. Finding
the communication(s) admissible, the Commission remarked as follows:

> The Commission has never held the requirement of local remedies to apply
> literally in cases where it is impractical or undesirable for the complainant to
> seize the domestic courts in the case of each violation. This is the situation
> here, given the vast and varied scope of the violations alleged and the general
> situation prevailing in Zaire.[116]

It would appear, therefore, that domestic remedies need not be exhausted
if the violations to which they relate occur within the context of serious or
massive violations of rights.[117] The Commission has in fact taken judicial

---

[114] Communications 25/89, 47/90, 56/91 and 100/93, *Free Legal Assistance Group, Lawyers'*
Committee for Human Rights, Union Interafricaine des Droits de l'Homme, Les Témoins de
Jehovah v. *Zaire*, Ninth Activity Report 1995–1996, Annex VIII (*Documents of the African*
Commission, p. 444).

[115] See also Communications 27/89, 46/91, 49/91 and 99/93, *Organisation Mondiale Contre la*
Torture and Association Internationale des Juristes Democrates, Commission Internationale
des Juristes (CIJ), Union Interafricaine des Droits de l'Homme v. *Rwanda*, Tenth Activity
Report 1996–1997, Annex X (*Documents of the African Commission*, p. 346), where the
Commission noted again 'the vast and varied scope' of violations and the 'large number
of individuals involved'. Alleging widespread massacres and arbitrary arrests of members
of the Tutsi group between 1989 and 1992, this communication predates the 1994 genocide. The decision was, however, only finalised in October 1996. One of the reasons for
this disturbing delay is the number of unsuccessful attempts by the Commission, from
1990 to 1995, to send a mission to Rwanda to investigate, among others, these cases. See
further Communication 71/92, *Rencontre Africaine pour la Defense de Droits de l'Homme*
v. *Zambia*, Tenth Activity Report 1996–1997, Annex X (*Documents of the African Com-*
mission, p. 563), also found to be admissible, based on the massive nature of the arrests,
the fact that the victims were kept in detention prior to their expulsions, and the speed
with which the expulsions were carried out which gave the complainants no opportunity
to establish the illegality of these actions in the courts.

[116] Communications 25/89, 47/90, 56/91 and 100/93 (joined), *Free Legal Assistance Group,*
Lawyers' Committee for Human Rights, Union Interafricaine des Droits de l'Homme, Les
Témoins de Jehovah v. *Zaire*, Ninth Activity Report 1995–1996, Annex VIII (*Documents of*
the African Commission, p. 444).

[117] See also Communication 159/96, *Union Interafricaine des Droits de l'Homme, Féderation*
International des Ligues des Droits de l'Homme, Rencontre Africaine des Droits de l'Homme,
Organisation Nationale des Droits de l'Homme au Sénégal and Association Malienne des
Droits de l'Homme v. *Angola*, Eleventh Activity Report 1997–1998, Annex II (*Documents*
of the African Commission, p. 615).

notice of the fact that domestic remedies are ineffective in such circumstances as the result of two factors: more than one right is violated at the same time and such situations involve numerous victims. These factors led the Commission to accept that the State would have had ample notice of the violations but did nothing to redress them. It therefore becomes unnecessary for victims to exhaust local remedies, which are clearly not sufficient in the circumstances.

The second situation in which complainants may be exempted from exhausting local remedies is where there has been an attempt to oust the jurisdiction of the courts. The military government in Nigeria adopted a number of ouster clauses in decrees which placed a blanket exclusion on the judicial review of certain decisions or actions taken in terms of military decrees and on the judicial review of 'special' (military) tribunals, or insulated the decrees themselves from any form of review. The Constitution (Suspension and Modification) Decree 107 of 17 November 1993, for example, specified that no question 'as to the validity of this Decree . . . shall be entertained by a court of law in Nigeria'. The Commission has found that 'ouster' clauses render local remedies 'non-existent, ineffective or illegal',[118] or 'illusory' and create a legal situation in which 'the judiciary can provide no check on the executive branch of government'.[119] The Commission consequently held that local remedies were ineffective and need not be exhausted when such ouster clauses applied.[120]

---

[118] See also the advisory opinion of the Inter-American Court in *Habeas Corpus in Emergency Situations*, OC-8/87, 30 January 1987, reprinted ILM 27 (1988) 517, where the Court held that derogation from *amparo* and *habeas corpus* orders is prohibited under the Inter-American Convention (Article 27(2)).

[119] Communications 137/94, 139/94, 154/96 and 161/97, *International Pen, Constitutional Rights Project, Interights on behalf of Ken Saro-Wiwa Jr and Civil Liberties Organisation* v. *Nigeria*, Twelfth Activity Report 1998–1999, Annex V, para. 76 (*Documents of the African Commission*, p. 729).

[120] See also Communication 87/93, *Constitutional Rights Project (in respect of Zamani Lakwot and 6 Others)* v. *Nigeria*, Eighth Activity Report 1994–1995, Annex VI (*Documents of the African Commission*, p. 391); Communication 129/94, *Civil Liberties Organisation* v. *Nigeria*, Ninth Activity Report 1995–1996, Annex VIII (*Documents of the African Commission*, p. 452), where the Commission agreed with the complainant's argument that 'it is reasonable to presume that domestic remedies will not only be prolonged but are certain to yield no results'. Also Communications 105/93, 128/94, 130/94 and 152/96, *Media Rights Agenda and Constitutional Rights Project* v. *Nigeria*, Twelfth Activity Report 1998–1999, Annex V (*Documents of the African Commission*, p. 718).

The third ground for exemption from exhausting local remedies is illustrated by Communication 60/91, *Constitutional Rights Project* v. *Nigeria*,[121] where the Commission declared a communication admissible because remedies of a non-judicial nature were not required to have been exhausted. In that instance, the relevant 'remedy' was a request for non-confirmation (clemency) of the death sentence by the (military) governor. Describing this power as a 'discretionary extraordinary remedy of a non-judicial nature', of which the aim is to 'obtain a favour and not to vindicate a right', the Commission found that it would be inappropriate to insist that the complainants seek remedies 'from sources which do not operate impartially and have no obligation to decide according to legal principles'.

The Commission added a ground for exemption of the requirement of local remedies in the case relating to the treatment and execution of Ken Saro-Wiwa.[122] Noting that the subjects of the communication (including Ken Saro-Wiwa) were deceased, the Commission declared the communication admissible as 'no domestic remedy can now give the complainants the satisfaction they seek'.[123]

Another ground which exempts a complainant from exhausting local remedies is when it would be illogical to require exhaustion. It is sensible that a complainant alleging a violation by way of imprisonment, who escaped the imprisonment and fled to another country, need not exhaust local remedies in the country from which he fled.[124]

Lastly, it is debatable whether a local remedy is 'available' to an individual who does not have the financial means to make use of it and, therefore, whether indigence should absolve a complainant from exhausting local remedies. This question was posed by the Inter-American Commission to its Court,[125] which concluded that 'if legal services are required . . . and a person

---

[121] Communication 60/91, *Constitutional Rights Project (in respect of Wahab Akamu, G. Adega and others)* v. *Nigeria*, Eighth Activity Report 1994–1995, Annex VI (*Documents of the African Commission*, p. 385).

[122] Communications 137/94, 139/94 and 154/96 and 161/97, *International Pen, Constitutional Rights Project, Interights on behalf of Ken Saro-Wiwa Jr and Civil Liberties Organisation* v. *Nigeria*, Twelfth Activity Report 1998–1999, Annex V (*Documents of the African Commission*, p. 729).

[123] *Ibid.*, para. 77.

[124] Communication 103/93, *Alhassan Abubakar* v. *Ghana*, Tenth Activity Report 1996–1997, Annex X (*Documents of the African Commission*, p. 571).

[125] *Exceptions to the Exhaustion of Local Remedies*, Inter-American Court, OC-11/90, Judgment of 10 August 1990, reprinted at *Human Rights Law Journal* 12 (1991) 20.

is unable to obtain such services because of his indigence, then that person would be exempted from the requirement to exhaust local remedies'.[126] The Court based its opinion on the reality that to require such a person to exhaust local remedies may infringe his or her right to equal protection before the law. Equal protection before the law includes the right not to be discriminated against on the basis of economic status.[127] A similar solution may be arrived at under the African Charter. The lack of legal aid is a reality in many African countries.[128] Even where such a system exists, it is highly unlikely that it would extend to support an individual lodging a complaint to the African Commission. The African Charter provides that every individual 'shall be entitled to the enjoyment of the rights and freedoms recognised and guaranteed in the present Charter without distinction of any kind such as social origin, fortune, or other status'.[129] The possibility that a legal aid system will be created under the Charter, as part of the Commission framework, seems remote. In order for access not to be denied to individuals on the basis of their indigence alone, admissibility requirements should be relaxed.

Complainants are not exempted from exhausting local remedies if they did not make use of existing local remedies due to their own 'default or negligence'.[130]

The wording of Article 56(5) of the Charter makes it clear that complainants do not have to exhaust domestic remedies if the procedure is 'unduly prolonged'. In Communication 135/94, *Kenya Human Rights Commission* v. *Kenya*[131] court proceedings were initiated on 23 December 1993, the communication was submitted on 8 March 1994 and declared inadmissible by the Commission in October 1995. The question arises as to how the period of 'undue delay' is to be determined. Is it the period between initiating proceedings locally (23 December 1993) and submission of the communication (8 March 1994), which amounts to less than three months? Or is it the period between the start of proceedings locally (23 December 1993) and

---

[126] *Ibid.*, para. 33.   [127] *Ibid.*, para. 22.

[128] See A. S. Butler, 'Legal Aid Before Human Rights Treaty Monitoring Bodies', *International and Comparative Law Quarterly* 49 (2000) 360–89.

[129] African Charter, Article 2.

[130] Communication 90/93, *Paul S. Haye* v. *The Gambia*, Eighth Activity Report 1994–1995, Annex VI (*Documents of the African Commission*, p. 393).

[131] Communication 135/94, *Kenya Human Rights Organisation* v. *Kenya*, Ninth Activity Report 1995–1996, Annex VIII (*Documents of the African Commission*, p. 455).

the finding of the Commission (October 1995), which amounts to about one year and ten months? A strict reading of the Charter seems to favour the first method, since Article 56(5) refers to communications 'sent' (submitted) after exhausting local remedies. However, another interpretation is also possible. It surely is relevant to consider whether local remedies have not yet been exhausted at the time the Commission considers the communication (especially if the complainant has kept on trying to exhaust local remedies, after submission of the communication). The phrase 'unless it is obvious that this procedure is unduly prolonged' is not qualified by an indication of the time when the communication was sent. In this case, the Commission based its finding on the fact that the communication was 'still pending', clearly adopting an approach in which the period up to consideration by the Commission is taken into account. In any event, the periods involved (about three months, or one year and ten months) were not considered to constitute 'undue delay'. Under the Inter-American system, 'undue delay' is also an exception to the rule that local remedies have to be exhausted. The Inter-American Commission has found a delay of three years and six months,[132] and of twenty months[133] after the institution of proceedings to be 'undue delay'.

COMMUNICATIONS MUST BE SUBMITTED WITHIN A REASONABLE TIME AFTER LOCAL REMEDIES HAVE BEEN EXHAUSTED

Article 56(6) requires that communications must be submitted 'within a reasonable period from the time local remedies are exhausted or from the date the Commission is seized of the matter'. As with the UN human rights treaties, no time limit for submission of communications has been imposed.[134] This is contrary to the requirements under the European and Inter-American systems, which require that a complainant submit a communication within six months after the date the 'final decision was taken'[135] or after he or she had 'been notified of the final judgment'.[136]

---

[132] Report 14/89, Case 9641 (Ecuador), 12 April 1989, Annual Report of the Inter-American Commission on Human Rights 1988–1989, OEA/Ser.L/V/II/76, Doc. 10, 104–15.

[133] Report 1a/88, Case 9755 (Chile), 12 September 1988, Annual Report of the Inter-American Commission on Human Rights, 1987–1988, OEA/Ser.L/V/II/74, Doc. 10 rev.1, 132–9.

[134] There is no such rule under the Optional Protocol to the ICCPR or under CAT.

[135] ECHR, Article 35.   [136] IACHR, Article 46(1)(b).

Given the lesser accessibility and visibility of the African Charter and Commission, it is certainly realistic not to make the six months rule a rigid requirement in Africa. Indeed, the situation in Africa is similar to that under the Inter-American system when a complainant is unable to obtain redress locally, and is not required to exhaust local remedies. In such instances, the Inter-American Commission has applied a 'reasonable time' test between the date of violation and the date of eventual submission. The African Commission has so far not interpreted the relative flexible standard of 'reasonable period' to the detriment of any author. No cases explicitly invoking this ground have so far been decided.

COMMUNICATIONS MUST NOT HAVE BEEN SETTLED ALREADY IN TERMS OF INTERNATIONAL LAW

According to Article 56(7) of the Charter a communication is inadmissible if it has already been 'settled' under the African Charter. In other words, the rule *ne bis in idem* applies. This is clearly sound, because a State should not be found in violation twice for one violating action or conduct and a complaint that has been finalised on the merits should not be reopened. This principle is similar to those of *autrefois acquit* and *autrefois convict*, which entail that an accused in a criminal trial may not be tried again for an offence for which he or she has already been either acquitted or convicted. Questions may, however, arise as to whether complaints submitted at the international level are 'similar'.

Article 56(7) further provides that a communication is inadmissible if it has already been 'settled' in terms of the principles of the UN Charter. International human rights bodies functioning internationally operate either at the regional or global level. The problem of concurrent jurisdiction arises especially in respect of allegations of violations that are covered by both a regional, in this case, the African Charter, and global instrument, such as the UN Charter or the ICCPR, with a supervisory body at each level. It is necessary that the interrelationships of these institutions be clearly defined.

While the African Charter allows for the simultaneous submission of communications to both the African Commission and a UN treaty body such as the UN Human Rights Committee, the complainant has to abide by the first decision or finding. This approach eliminates the unsettling possibility of divergent 'conclusions' to the matter before different bodies, and prevents forum shopping until, ultimately, relief is obtained somewhere.

Before submitting Communication 40/90, *Bob Ngozi Njoku* v. *Egypt*[137] to the African Commission, the complainant submitted the same matter to the UN Sub-Commission on Human Rights. The latter decided not to entertain the matter or to make any pronouncement on it and the African Commission found that the (in)action by the UN Sub-Commission 'does not boil down to a decision on the merits of the case and does not in any way indicate that the matter' has been 'settled', as required by Article 56(7). The communication was consequently declared admissible.

Under some treaties it is not the 'settlement' of the matter by another international body, but the fact that it is 'being examined' by such a body that renders the matter inadmissible. According to this approach, a complainant is bound to await the outcome of the matter in the first forum to which the matter was submitted.[138] Some States, especially those party to the ECHR, have made declarations when accepting the Optional Protocol to the ICCPR, for example, in terms of which the 'settlement' principle ('already having been considered') is incorporated. These States declare that they do not accept the Optional Protocol procedure if a communication has already been examined under the European human rights system. Only one African State, Uganda, has made a similar declaration when ratifying the Optional Protocol to the ICCPR.[139]

Despite the fact that the African Charter prescribes that communications that have already been 'settled' by the States involved in accordance with the UN or OAU Charter should not be considered,[140] the original Rules of Procedure, which in general restated the admissibility requirements in the Charter, deviated from this requirement. They stated that the Commission must ensure that 'the same issue is not already *being considered* by another

---

[137] Communication 40/90, *Bob Ngozi Njoku* v. *Egypt*, Eleventh Activity Report 1997–1998, Annex II (*Documents of the African Commission*, p. 604).

[138] Optional Protocol to the ICCPR, Article 5(2)(a) and see also the CAT.

[139] The full text of the declaration reads as follows: 'The Republic of Uganda does not accept the competence of the Human Rights Committee to consider a communication under the provisions of Article 5(2) from an individual if the matter in question has already been considered under another procedure of international investigation or settlement.' See www.un.org/ENGLISH/bible/englishinternetbible/partI/chapterIV/treaty6.asp (accessed on 21 January 2001).

[140] African Charter, Article 56(7).

international investigating or settlement body'.[141] In Communication 69/92, *Amnesty International* v. *Tunisia*,[142] the Commission expressed the view that the purpose of the relevant rule, Rule 114(3)(f), was to 'avoid usurpation of the jurisdiction of another body'. The Commission found the communication to be inadmissible because it had already been examined in terms of the procedure established under ECOSOC Resolution 1503. In addition, under these same Rules of Procedure, the Commission declared Communication 15/88, *Mpaka-Nsusu Andre Alphonse* v. *Zaire*[143] inadmissible, as the communication had already 'been referred for consideration to the Human Rights Committee'.[144] There was no indication and neither did the Commission require, that the matter should have been 'settled' by either the Human Rights Commission or the UN Human Rights Committee. The African Commission's revised Rules of Procedure reflect the provisions of the Charter: Rule 116 now specifies that admissibility issues are in all respects to be determined 'pursuant to Article 56 of the Charter'.

Article 56(7) also prohibits the African Commission from admitting communications that have been 'settled' in accordance with the OAU Charter. An example may be a human rights matter being resolved through the Mechanism for Conflict Prevention, Management and Resolution, an OAU Charter organ established by a resolution of the Assembly of Heads of State and Government.[145] Although the competence of the Central Organ of the Mechanism extends to the resolution of conflicts 'within States',[146] it is likely that it would be used more in respect of conflicts between States.

---

[141] Rule 114(3)(f) (emphasis added).

[142] Communication 69/92, *Amnesty International* v. *Tunisia*, Seventh Activity Report 1993–1994, Annex IX (*Documents of the African Commission*, p. 347).

[143] Communication 15/88, *Mpaka-Nsusu Andre Alphonse* v. *Zaire*, Seventh Activity Report 1993–1994, Annex IX (*Documents of the African Commission*, p. 340).

[144] See also the Human Rights Committee's views in Communication 157/83, *Mpaka-Nsusu* v. *Zaire*, Doc. A/41/40, p. 106, in which a number of violations of the Covenant were found. The Human Rights Committee recommended that the government provide the victim with 'effective remedies, including compensation, for the violations that he has suffered, and to take steps to ensure that similar violations do not occur in the future'.

[145] See S. Gutto, 'The New Mechanism of the Organization of African Unity for Conflict Prevention, Management and Resolution, and the Controversial Concept of Humanitarian Intervention in International Law', *South African Law Journal* 113 (1996) 314 at 315.

[146] Article 22 of the Resolution establishing the Mechanism.

Admissibility under the Protocol establishing the Court

On the ratification of the Protocol establishing the African Court on Human and Peoples' Rights[147] by fifteen States, this organ will be created. What follows are some tentative remarks about issues pertaining to admissibility that the Court may have to address.

The Court is mandated to (re)consider the question of admissibility under Article 6(2) of the Protocol which provides as follows: 'The Court shall rule on the admissibility of cases taking into account the provisions of Article 56 of the Charter.' One should bear in mind that cases may reach the Court by way of two different avenues; first, in respect of a State that has accepted the Protocol, but has not made a declaration accepting the right of individuals to approach the Court directly;[148] or secondly, in respect of States that have accepted the direct petition before the Court, and where such a petition is in fact brought. Of the five States that have so far ratified the Protocol, only one has made the optional declaration. It therefore seems relatively unlikely that that procedure will play a significant role in the future. The focus should therefore be on the procedure of a communication first being submitted to the Commission, and thereafter by the Commission to the Court. This procedure has important implications for the way in which the Court may be expected to deal with admissibility.

As always, the first hurdle for the applicant is the admissibility phase at the level of the Commission under Article 56 of the African Charter. The Court is not mandated to 'consider' the issue of admissibility, but to 'rule' on the issue, 'taking into account the provisions of Article 56'. In other words, the Court should not apply or implement Article 56, but must merely *take it into account*. The wording seems to suggest that the Court may negate the strict requirements of Article 56 if, for example, more pressing considerations arise. The Court should remain conscious of the traditional admissibility requirements, but need not rigorously apply and enforce them. This leaves the Court with a wider margin of discretion to consider other relevant factors, and consequently to deviate from the Commission's finding.

---

[147] OAU/LEG/EXP/AFCHPR/PROT(III). See I. Österdahl, 'The Jurisdiction Ratione Materiae of the African Court of Human and Peoples' Rights', *Review of the African Commission on Human and Peoples' Rights* 7 (1998) 132–50; N. Kirsch, 'The Establishment of an African Court on Human and Peoples' Rights', *Zeitschrift für auslandisches offentliches Recht und Volkerrecht* 58 (1998) 713, with the Protocol reprinted at *ibid.*, p. 727.

[148] In terms of Article 34(6) of the Protocol.

A distinction must be drawn between the Court's contentious[149] and advisory jurisdiction.[150] As far as its contentious jurisdiction is concerned, it must be kept in mind that most, if not all, cases will emanate from the Commission. To be admissible before the Commission, the case will have to allege a violation of the African Charter. The Protocol states that the 'jurisdiction' of the Court is not only based on the African Charter, but extends to other human rights instruments ratified by the States concerned.[151] This seems to be a curious provision, with uncertain consequences. Does the provision intend that the African Court has jurisdiction to decide cases on the basis of, for example, the International Covenant on Civil and Political Rights? That is, does the Court usurp the jurisdiction of treaty supervisory bodies? If reference is made to 'instruments ratified by States concerned', is that a reference to the fact that a treaty is ratified, or does it refer also to the acceptance of individual complaints mechanisms provided for under CERD, the Optional Protocol to the ICCPR, and CAT? If a literal reading is followed, the answer seems to be that reference is made only to the treaties, and not to the acceptance of the optional complaints mechanisms.

In answering these questions, one must note the purpose of the Court, namely, that it was established to 'complement'[152] and 'reinforce' the mandate of the Commission.[153] The Court was, therefore, intended to support an existing system where communications are based on the African Charter and not on other human rights instruments.

As for its advisory jurisdiction, the Court's material jurisdiction is based, first, on 'any legal matter relating to the African Charter',[154] but also, in this case, the jurisdiction is extended to 'any relevant human rights instrument'.[155] The extension of the Court's material competence is less problematic in respect of advisory opinions.[156]

In respect of the advisory jurisdiction, Article 4 of the Protocol extends the list of those entitled to approach the Court to any OAU Member State, the OAU, any OAU organ, as well as any 'African organisation recognised by the OAU'. The last of these categories is not very clear, but should at least include all NGOs that have observer status with the African Commission.

---

[149] Protocol, Article 5.   [150] Protocol, Article 4.
[151] Protocol, Article 3(1).   [152] Protocol, Article 2.
[153] Preamble to the Protocol.   [154] Protocol, Article 4(1).   [155] *Ibid.*
[156] See the advisory opinion of the Inter-American Court of Human Rights, '"Other Treaties" Subject to the Advisory Jurisdiction of the Court (Article 64 of the Inter-American Convention on Human Rights)', IACHR, OC-1/82, 24 September 1982, Series A, Judgments and Opinions 1.

The African Commission should submit to the Court all cases in which it has made a finding that a State had violated the Charter, to enable the Court to make the Commission's recommendatory finding binding. The Protocol further permits the State against which a complaint had been lodged also to submit a case.[157] This will be an opportunity to appeal the finding of the Commission if the Commission found against the State, either in an individual or in an inter-State communication. Similarly, a State Party whose citizen is a victim of human rights violations may also submit a communication.[158] This provision may be valuable in respect of inter-State communications, but its significance in respect of individual communications remains limited, as States cannot be expected to 'appeal' against Commission findings that favour them.

Issues relating to the timeframe of the Court's jurisdiction arise from the fact that States may opt into both the Court's jurisdiction and the acceptance of direct access to the Court. The Court may have to decide whether its jurisdiction extends to matters that have arisen before a State had ratified the Protocol, or before the entry into force of the Protocol. With regard to the former, is it possible for the State to deny the jurisdiction of the Court on the ground that it had not at the time explicitly accepted the Court's jurisdiction over this matter? If a matter arises during the period after a State had ratified the Protocol but before Protocol had entered into force, may that State deny the Court jurisdiction over communications arising in the period between when it adopted the Protocol and the later entry into force of the Protocol, even if it had already accepted the competence of the Court?

Inter-State communications

If, for good reason, a State Party considers that another State Party 'has violated the provisions of the Charter', it may lodge an inter-State complaint against that State.[159] The African Charter and the Commission's Rules of Procedure emphasise the importance of trying to resolve such matters through negotiations or other peaceful procedures (friendly settlement).[160] Exhaustion of friendly settlement procedures is not a prerequisite for submitting an inter-State communication to the African Commission.[161] As in the case of individual communications, there is a requirement that domestic

---

[157] Protocol, Article 5(1)(c).   [158] Protocol, Article 5(1)(d).
[159] African Charter, Article 47.   [160] African Charter, Article 48.
[161] African Charter, Articles 49 and 52; Rules of Procedure, Rule 98.

remedies must have been exhausted, unless it is obvious to the Commission 'that the procedure of achieving these remedies would be unduly prolonged'.[162] It is not quite clear whether this should be understood to mean that the complainant *State* needs to have exhausted the remedies available to it in the State against which it complains, or whether the *affected individuals* need to have exhausted these remedies. In the ordinary course of events, the duty to exhaust remedies falls on the shoulders of the individual in the State, rather than on other States. Sometimes remedies may be of a nature which makes them unsuited to exhaustion by individuals, as in cases of massive and widespread violations. In such instances, the requirement that the complainant State should exhaust at least some form of remedy is implied in the wording of the Rules of Procedure, which require the State to provide information about 'measures taken to exhaust local procedures for appeal'.[163] The exhaustion of local remedies has not played an important role in respect of inter-State communications brought under the ECHR, most of which relate to instances of massive or widespread violations.[164]

A second, implicit, admissibility requirement is that the matter should not have been settled by another procedure for international investigation or settlement.[165] A question arises as to whether the competence of the Commission is excluded where the case is 'considered' before another relevant international mechanism. This seems to be an important factor in the sole inter-State communication to be submitted so far.[166] By the 30th Session, in October 2001, this communication had not yet been finalised.

Conclusion

Drawing on provisions in UN and regional human rights treaties, the African Charter deals quite elaborately with admissibility in Article 56. Compared to other international human rights instruments, its most positive features are

---

[162] African Charter, Article 50. [163] Rules of Procedure, Rule 93(2)(b).

[164] See e.g. the decisions of the European Court of Human Rights in *Ireland* v. *UK* (1979–80) 2 EHRR 25, and the European Commission on Human Rights in *Denmark, France, The Netherlands, Norway, Sweden* v. *Turkey* (1967) 11 *Yearbook* 764.

[165] Rules of Procedure, Rule 93(2)(c).

[166] Communication 227/99, *Democratic Republic of Congo* v. *Burundi, Rwanda and Uganda*. The same matter has also been submitted to the International Court of Justice: *Case Concerning Armed Activities on the Territory of the Congo* (*Democratic Republic of Congo* v. *Uganda*) Request for the Indication of Provisional Measures 116, 1 July 2000 at http://icj-cij.org/icjwww/idocket/ico/icoframe.htm.

the fact that authors of communications are not required to be victims and that there is no fixed period within which communications have to be submitted. It is a pity, however, that there is a requirement that communications should not be written in disparaging language.

Admissibility has played an important role in the findings of the African Commission. More than half of the communications finalised so far by the Commission failed at this hurdle. Initially, the Commission dealt falteringly with admissibility. Numerous communications were declared inadmissible due to the fact that the States complained against had not been States Parties. Long delays between the submission of communications and admissibility findings occurred. The reasoning of the Commission was scant and ambiguous. There was some confusion about how to deal with communications submitted to more than one international forum.

However, the Commission has improved over the years. Communications against non-State Parties have later been dealt with administratively. Delays have decreased. The reasoning of the Commission has become much more elaborate and informative. The position in respect of communications submitted to different fora was clarified.

The Commission did not adopt an overly formalistic stance on the issue of admissibility. With a few exceptions, the Commission has interpreted the requirements of Article 56 of the Charter progressively, favouring complainants. The Commission, for example, interpreted the phrase 'local remedies, if any' to refer to remedies that are available, adequate and effective. Complainants in numerous instances, including those in situations of massive human rights violations and those facing domestic law containing clauses ousting the jurisdiction of national courts, were exempted from availing themselves of domestic remedies.

Complainants are likely to face issues about admissibility from the respondent State or the Commission. In particular, the non-exhaustion of domestic remedies is likely to be raised, as it is the requirement most frequently cited in admissibility findings. Because of this, communications should deal carefully and comprehensively with all issues relating to admissibility, and not concentrate only on the merits of the case. The better a communication is prepared before submission, the more likely the Commission is to come to a prompt decision favouring the complainant.

4

EVIDENCE AND FACT-FINDING BY THE AFRICAN COMMISSION

RACHEL MURRAY

Introduction

The outcomes of communication procedures, namely, the findings of violations of particular provisions of the instrument, are well analysed and documented. Yet an analysis of how international human rights bodies examine evidence presented before them has received little attention, usually being considered in passing during examination of the complaints procedures.[1] In a number of recent communications, the African Commission has had to analyse issues of evidence in coming to its decision. This chapter will examine these cases and the general approach of the Commission to issues of evidence and fact-finding in the communication procedure.

While the discussion will draw upon the experience of other international and regional bodies, there are a number of caveats that must be borne in mind when making comparisons. State-only courts such as the International Court of Justice may apply different considerations and although the African

---

[1] However, see D. Sandifer, *Evidence Before International Tribunals* (Charlottesville, VA: 1975); C. N. Brower, 'Evidence Before International Tribunals: The Need for Some Standard Rules', *International Law* 28 (1994) 47; J. J. Paust, 'The Complex Nature, Sources and Evidence of Customary Human Rights', *Journal of International and Comparative Law* 25 (1995–6) 235; K. Highet, 'Evidence and the Proof of Facts', in L. F. Damrosch (ed.), *The International Court of Justice at a Crossroad* (New York: 1987), pp. 355–75; H. Thirlway, 'Evidence Before International Courts and Tribunals', in R. Bernhardt (ed.), *Encyclopaedia of Public International Law* (Elsevier Science, 1995), vol. II, p. 302; M. Reisman and J. K. Levit, 'Fact-Finding Initiatives for the Inter-American Court of Human Rights', in R. Navia (ed.), *La Corte y el Sistema Interamericanos de Derechos Humanos* (Costa Rica: 1994), pp. 443–57; T. Buergenthal, 'Judicial Fact-Finding: Inter-American Human Rights Court', in R. Lillich (ed.), *Fact-Finding Before International Tribunals* (New York: 1991), pp. 261–74.

Charter has provision for inter-State communications[2] it has yet to produce a decision on such a case. The focus of this chapter is on communications which have been submitted by individuals or, often, NGOs. Similarly, the approaches of the international criminal tribunals for Rwanda and Yugoslavia must be treated with caution given that not only are they conducting criminal procedures but these are with the aim of determining the guilt of an individual.

The individual communication procedure is provided for in Articles 55–59 of the Charter. Cases can be submitted by individuals even if they are not victims themselves of a violation, and many cases have been submitted by NGOs acting on behalf of others. On receipt of a letter from an individual or NGO at the Secretariat of the Commission, the legal officers will register it with a number.[3] The Secretariat will then send a copy of the communication to the State against which it is brought with time limits for the State's response. A Commissioner will be appointed as rapporteur for the case. At its session the Commission will examine the admissibility of the case on the basis of the information received.[4] The parties will be informed of the decision on admissibility. If the communication is inadmissible, the case will be closed; if it is declared admissible, the parties will be asked for further information on the merits,[5] any responses will be transmitted to the other party,[6] and the parties will subsequently be invited to attend the session of the Commission at which the case will be heard. After an oral hearing[7] at the session, the Commission will deliberate in private on the matter. It will then produce a written decision which will be forwarded to the parties and subsequently made public in its yearly report after adoption by the Assembly of Heads of State and Government of the OAU. The manner in which the Commission assesses the information before it in coming to these decisions has never been examined in detail. This is the intention of this chapter.

Types of evidence and their collection

Article 46 of the Charter permits the Commission to 'resort to any appropriate method of investigation' and to call upon the Secretary-General of the

---

[2] Articles 47–54.

[3] The first digit is the number of the case received, the second is the year. The first digit does not restart at 1 at the start of each new year. Thus 3/88 was the third case *ever* received by the Commission and it was received in 1988.

[4] For discussion of the admissibility conditions, see Chapter 3.

[5] See the time limits below.   [6] Rule 119(3).   [7] See below.

OAU 'or any other person capable of enlightening it'. This is a wide provision which provides the Commission with potentially a great deal of flexibility and discretion in all aspects of its work,[8] enabling it to obtain information from a variety of sources as it deems appropriate.[9] Indeed, it has displayed a willingness to accept any form of evidence such as 'documentary proofs of the violation . . . for example, letters, legal documents, photos, autopsies, tape recordings, etc. to show proof of the violation'[10] as well as oral hearings. Its Special Rapporteurs appear to have been equally open, stating that he may:

> for the execution of his mandate, have recourse to all methods of investigation, specifically by requesting the assistance of States and national, international and African NGOs. He can be assisted in his mission by any person whom he judges competent to perform his task well.[11]

WRITTEN MATERIAL

In coming to its decisions, however, the Commission has, as have other international bodies,[12] relied primarily on written documents. Besides written correspondence from the parties, this has included copies of the relevant

---

[8] Rules 71–76 enable the Commission to consult or invite the participation of States, specialised institutions, intergovernmental organisations, NGOs and others.

[9] Inter-American organs have also accepted a wide variety of forms, including immigration cards, passport applications, dental records, opinions of pathologists on autopsies, explanations from the Bar Association and opinions of handwriting experts: see Inter-American Court, *Fairén Garbi and Solís Corrales*, Series C, No. 6, Judgment of 15 March 1989, paras. 38–40. Regulations of the Inter-American Commission on Human Rights, Article 46(1); and *Velàsquez Rodriguez*, Series C, No. 4, Judgment of 29 July 1988, para. 29. The ICJ will consider submissions, applications, oral and other documents: see *Nuclear Tests Cases*, ICJ Reports (1974) 253, 457 at 466–7. See also paras. 436 *et seq.*

[10] African Commission on Human and Peoples' Rights, Information Sheet No. 2: Guidelines on the Submission of Communications, p. 17.

[11] Report on Extrajudicial, Summary or Arbitrary Executions, Tenth Annual Activity Report of the African Commission on Human and Peoples' Rights, 1996–7, ACHPR/RPT/10th, Annex VI; R. Murray and M. Evans (eds.), *Documents of the African Commission on Human and Peoples' Rights* (Oxford: Hart Publishing, 2001), p. 508 (hereinafter *Documents of the African Commission*).

[12] In relation to the Inter-American Convention, see C. Cerna, 'The Inter-American Commission on Human Rights: Its Organisation and Examination of Petitions and Communications', in D. Harris and S. Livingstone (eds.), *The Inter-American System of Human Rights* (Oxford: 1998), pp. 65–114 at p. 97; Inter-American Court, *Godínez Cruz*, Series C, No. 5, Judgment of 20 January 1989, at para. 40; Inter-American Court, *Fairén Garbi and Solís Corrales*, Series C, No. 6, Judgment of 15 March 1989, para. 47. See also *Ireland* v. *UK* (1978) Series A, vol. 25, 2 EHRR 25, para. 161.

laws,[13] court judgments,[14] post-mortem reports,[15] photocopied newspaper articles describing the judgments,[16] transcripts of judgments,[17] affidavits,[18] expert opinion,[19] opinion from NGOs,[20] and 'scholarly' articles.[21]

The Commission has also accepted information from the media. Article 56(4) requires that communications are 'not based exclusively on news disseminated through the mass media', and the Commission has said, albeit in relation to proving a *prima facie* case for admissibility, that 'the author must be able to investigate and ascertain the truth of the facts before requesting the Commission's intervention'.[22] In Communications 147/95 and 149/96, *Sir Dawda K. Jawara* v. *The Gambia*,[23] although the government alleged the allegations were based on the media, the Commission declared the important issue was not whether the information was obtained from the media 'but whether the information is correct. Did the complainant try to verify the truth about these allegations? Did he have the means or was it possible for him to do so, given the circumstances of the case?' The Commission

---

[13] Communication 40/90, *Bob Ngozi Njoku* v. *Egypt*, Eleventh Activity Report 1997–1998, Annex II (*Documents of the African Commission*, p. 604).

[14] *Ibid.*

[15] Communications 147/95 and 149/96, *Sir Dawda K. Jawara* v. *The Gambia*, Thirteenth Activity Report 1999–2000, Annex V.

[16] Communication 40/90, *Bob Ngozi Njoku* v. *Egypt*, Eleventh Activity Report 1997–1998, Annex II (*Documents of the African Commission*, p. 604). See the treatment of press clippings by the Inter-American Court in *Velàsquez Rodriguez*, Series C, No. 4, Judgment of 29 July 1988, para. 146; *Nicaragua Case* (Merits), ICJ Reports (1986) 14, paras. 62–4.

[17] Communication 212/98, *Amnesty International* v. *Zambia*, Twelfth Activity Report 1998–1999, Annex V, para. 28 (*Documents of the African Commission*, p. 745).

[18] *Ibid.*, para. 28.

[19] Communication 71/92, *Rencontre Africaine pour la Defense de Droits de l'Homme* v. *Zambia*, Tenth Activity Report 1996–1997, Annex X, para. 16 (*Documents of the African Commission*, p. 563), where a letter from an expert on refugee law at Oxford University was submitted and cited. The ICJ does not often look at expert opinion, although it can do so: *Corfu Channel Case (UK* v. *Albania)*, Merits, ICJ Reports (1949) 4 at 9.

[20] Communications 105/93, 128/94, 130/94 and 152/96, *Media Rights Agenda and Constitutional Rights Project* v. *Nigeria*, Twelfth Activity Report 1998–1999, Annex V, at para. 39 (*Documents of the African Commission*, p. 718), letter from Olisa Agbakoba on 'Preliminary Objections and Observations to the Mission of the Commission'.

[21] Communications 105/93, 128/94, 130/94 and 152/96, *Media Rights Agenda and Constitutional Rights Project* v. *Nigeria*, Twelfth Activity Report 1998–1999, Annex V, para. 41 (*Documents of the African Commission*, p. 718).

[22] African Commission on Human and Peoples' Rights, Information Sheet No. 3, Communication Procedure, p. 9.

[23] Communications 147/95 and 149/96, *Sir Dawda K. Jawara* v. *The Gambia*, Thirteenth Activity Report 1999–2000, Annex V.

found, on the facts of the case, the communication should be admissible. The International Court of Justice has taken a flexible approach to this, being willing to take into account 'matters of public knowledge which have received extensive coverage' in the media,[24] but not if the information comes from one source alone.[25]

Documents and other information may be provided by the parties in their original submissions to the Commission or may have been prompted by the Commission later in its request for additional information. To what extent the Commission or any human rights body has a duty to seek out information that does not come to it is not clear, although it has been suggested by Kokott[26] that in human rights proceedings international courts themselves have a 'duty' to find the truth.[27] In this respect, although not taking the initiative to do so but mostly being prompted by NGOs, the Commission has shown itself willing to obtain information from the holding of oral hearings and, to a certain extent, undertaking on-site visits.

ORAL HEARINGS[28]

Although there is an explicit right of hearing in relation to inter-State cases in the Charter and the Commission's Rules of Procedure,[29] no equivalent exists for non-State Parties. However, since hearing an individual at the 16th Session,[30] the Commission has developed a practice of offering both parties the opportunity to attend a hearing when the merits are considered.[31] The Commission has heard from parties in a number of cases.[32] Although both

---

[24] *US Diplomatic and Consular Staff in Tehran Case* (*US* v. *Iran*), ICJ Reports (1980) 3 at 9.

[25] *Nicaragua Case* (Merits), ICJ Reports (1986) 14 at 41.

[26] J. Kokott, *The Burden of Proof in Comparative and International Human Rights Law. Civil and Common Law Approaches with Specific Reference to American and German Legal Systems* (The Hague: Kluwer Law International, 1998), p. 209, although this is in relation to hearings.

[27] This is particularly the case for *jus cogens* rights as they require the most protection: *ibid.*

[28] Thanks must go to Chidi Anselm Odinkalu for his insights and experience of the oral hearings.

[29] Rule 100: the Commission is to determine the procedure.

[30] Embga Louis Mekongo himself and on his behalf, Communication 59/91, *Embga Mekongo Louis* v. *Cameroon*, Eighth Activity Report 1994–1995, Annex VI (*Documents of the African Commission*, p. 385).

[31] Information Sheet No. 3, p. 12.

[32] For example, Communication 144/95, *William Courson (acting on behalf of Severo Moto)* v. *Equatorial Guinea*, Eleventh Activity Report 1997–1998, Annex II (*Documents of the African Commission*, p. 609); Communication 65/92, *Ligue Camerounaise des Droits de*

are invited to attend a hearing, sometimes only one party will appear,[33] which may be due in part to the lack of financial assistance to attend the sessions. NGOs have represented some individuals before the Commission in such oral hearings, even if the organisation is not necessarily the one which submitted the case[34] and the Commission itself has referred cases to NGOs to provide this representation.[35] Sometimes high level delegates from governments have appeared before the Commission.[36] Their contributions have varied from mere repetition of the information supplied in written documents,[37] to making a particular written submission or an oral statement without any written documents.[38]

---

l'Homme v. *Cameroon,* Tenth Activity Report 1996–1997, Annex X (*Documents of the African Commission,* p. 562); Communications 105/93, 128/94, 130/94 and 152/96, *Media Rights Agenda and Constitutional Rights Project* v. *Nigeria,* Twelfth Activity Report 1998–1999, Annex V (*Documents of the African Commission,* p. 718); Communication 71/92, *Rencontre Africaine pour la Defense de Droits de l'Homme* v. *Zambia,* Tenth Activity Report 1996–1997, Annex X (*Documents of the African Commission,* p. 563); Communications 137/94, 139/94, 154/96 and 161/97, *International Pen, Constitutional Rights Project, Interights on behalf of Ken Saro-Wiwa Jr and Civil Liberties Organisation* v. *Nigeria,* Twelfth Activity Report 1998–1999, Annex V (*Documents of the African Commission,* p. 729).

[33] For example, Communication 17/88, *Hilaire Badjogoume* v. *Benin,* Seventh Activity Report 1993–1994, Annex IX; Eighth Activity Report 1994–1995, Annex VI (*Documents of the African Commission,* pp. 340 and 381), where only the representative of the government of Benin appeared.

[34] For example, Communication 97/93, *John K. Modise* v. *Botswana,* Seventh Activity Report 1993–1994, Annex IX; Tenth Activity Report 1996–1997, Annex X (*Documents of the African Commission,* pp. 349 and 567).

[35] For example, Communications 83/92, 88/93 and 91/93, *Jean Y. Degli (on behalf of N Bikagni), Union Interafricaine des Droits de l'Homme, Commission Internationale des Juristes* v. *Togo,* Seventh Activity Report 1993–1994, Annex IX (*Documents of the African Commission,* pp. 348 and 390), where the Commission referred the complainant to the Botswana Centre for Human Rights which had observer status.

[36] For example, in Communication 212/98, *Amnesty International* v. *Zambia,* Twelfth Activity Report 1998–1999, Annex V (*Documents of the African Commission,* p. 745), the government was represented by the Senior Advocate in the Ministry of Legal Affairs and accompanied by the Deputy Permanent Secretary of the Home Affairs Department and an individual from the Foreign Affairs Department with responsibility for African and OAU relations.

[37] For example, Communication 74/92, *Commission Nationale des Droits de l'Homme et des Libertés* v. *Chad,* Ninth Activity Report 1995–1996, Annex VIII (*Documents of the African Commission,* p. 449), who 'reiterated the information in the original communication, both verbally and by way of a memoire'.

[38] For example, see Communications 105/93, 128/94, 130/94 and 152/96, *Media Rights Agenda and Constitutional Rights Project* v. *Nigeria,* Twelfth Activity Report 1998–1999, Annex V (*Documents of the African Commission,* p. 718).

The procedure at the session is that the hearings will take place in private.[39] Whether there are possibilities of holding hearings without the presence of the other parties, for example for security reasons, is not clear. The Inter-American Court has provided for this possibility.[40] The Commission will invite the parties to enter the room and the Chair will then introduce the rapporteur Commissioner for the case. This Commissioner will introduce the case to the Commission. Each party, if present, will then be given the opportunity to make a statement. The complainant is usually given around 15–20 minutes, the State a little longer but not more than an hour. The complainant is then provided with the opportunity to respond to the government's submission. The Commissioners will then ask questions[41] which can be probing and last for several hours. They can request clarification of the facts or domestic law and any remedies expected from the Commission. The parties are not permitted to ask each other questions. If the party has submitted a written document as well as their oral statement, this is often used as the foundation for interrogating the party present. The parties are then asked to leave the room during which time the Commission will deliberate on its findings in private. The manner in which the process is conducted is aimed to place 'complainants and the States which are alleged to have violated human and/or peoples' rights on an equal footing throughout the proceedings'.[42] It is there to enable the State 'to refute allegations'[43] and to give 'the Commission and the State Party an opportunity to discuss how areas of difficulties could be tackled. The Commission assured the State that it was ready at all times to offer its good offices to assist in matters of human and peoples' right.'[44]

---

[39] Rule 106.

[40] See Inter-American Court, *Fairén Garbi and Solís Corrales*, Series C, No. 6, Judgment of 15 March 1989, paras. 32–6.

[41] The ICJ follows the procedure of common law countries with examination and cross-examination: see *Corfu Channel Case (UK v. Albania)*, Merits, ICJ Reports (1949) 4; *Land, Island and Maritime Frontier Boundary Dispute Case*, ICJ Reports (1990) 92; ICJ Reports (1992) 351.

[42] Information Sheet No. 3, p. 12.

[43] Information Sheet No. 3, p. 14. The Inter-American Commission appears to hold hearings 'in order to verify the facts': Article 43 of the Inter-American Commission Regulations.

[44] Report of the Mission to Mauritania of the African Commission on Human and Peoples' Rights, Nouakchott, 19–27 June 1996, Tenth Annual Activity Report of the African Commission on Human and Peoples' Rights 1996–7, ACHPR/RPT/10th, Annex IX, p. 5 (*Documents of the African Commission*, p. 538), where the government sent a representative to the session.

On some occasions the Commission, often on matters of domestic law,[45] has heard witnesses,[46] although they have been called by the parties, rather than the Commission itself.[47] Whether there has been any incident where the Commission itself has requested the attendance of a witness is not clear.[48] There have been situations where complainants and those representing victims were not informed of the precise day and time that the case would be examined. This caused difficulties in ensuring witnesses who had travelled from far were able to arrive on time or to stay for longer periods if necessary.

How much original information is provided by oral hearings is not clear due to their confidential nature and the lack of clear indication in the reports on the decisions as to whether such material was an element within the reasoning. Probing questions by Commissioners enable them to challenge information received, but the extent of such depends on the individual Commissioner and his or her willingness to push the State to respond.

MISSIONS[49]

The Commission has undertaken on-site missions to Togo,[50] Sudan, Senegal, Nigeria and Mauritania. Visits to other States have also been suggested but

---

[45] Communication 97/93, *John K. Modise* v. *Botswana*, Seventh Activity Report 1993–1994, Annex IX; Tenth Activity Report 1996–1997, Annex X (*Documents of the African Commission*, pp. 349 and 567), where a witness was called.

[46] For example, in Communication 212/98, *Amnesty International* v. *Zambia*, Twelfth Activity Report 1998–1999, Annex V (*Documents of the African Commission*, p. 745), a relative of one of the victims, Mr William Steven Banda, was heard.

[47] The International Court of Justice has the ability to call witnesses if necessary (Article 62(2) of its Rules of Court) as can the parties (Rules 57 and 63). Witnesses are required to give evidence on oath (Article 64). It can also appoint experts to prepare a report for it (see *Delimitation of the Maritime Boundary in the Gulf of Maine Area*, ICJ Reports (1984) 246) to assist it in examining the technical aspects. In this case. However, the appointment of an expert was provided for in the special agreement.

[48] Witnesses have failed to appear before the Inter-American Court of Human Rights (see, for example, Inter-American Court, *Fairén Garbi and Solís Corrales*, Series C, No. 6, Judgment of 15 March 1989, para. 29).

[49] For discussion of missions in general, see R. Murray, 'On-Site Visits by the African Commission on Human and Peoples' Rights: A Case Study and Comparison with the Inter-American Commission on Human Rights', *African Journal of International and Comparative Law* 11 (1999) 460–73.

[50] See Communications 83/92, 88/93 and 91/93, *Jean Y. Degli (on behalf of N. Bikagni), Union Interafricaine des Droits de l'Homme, Commission Internationale des Juristes* v. *Togo*, Seventh Activity Report 1993–1994, Annex IX (*Documents of the African Commission*, pp. 348 and 390), in relation to alleged grave and massive violations.

not undertaken.[51] The basis on which the Commission decides to make such a visit is not clear but it does appear to do so only in more serious cases.[52]

From the information available,[53] members of the Commission's mission delegation visit various places other than just the capitals and speak with both complainants and the authorities. As there is no clear set of guidelines by which the Commission conducts these visits and its independence and impartiality have been questioned,[54] the use of missions in the collection of reliable information is questionable. This is compounded by the paucity of information about the way in which the missions have been conducted, with reports providing only minimal information on which places were visited and who was met, if a report is provided at all. Recent decisions adopted in relation to Sudan and Mauritania illustrate the Commission's difficulty with the relationship between missions and communications. Although it was clear that the mission to Mauritania was prompted by communications against that country,[55] the Commission held in its decisions that it was a mission:

> of good offices . . . to discuss the overall human rights situation in the coun-
> try . . . The mission was undertaken at the initiative of the Commission in its
> capacity as promoter of human and peoples' rights. It was not an inquiry
> mission; and while it permitted the Commission to get a better grasp of the
> prevailing situation in Mauritania, the mission did not gather any additional
> specific information on the alleged violations, except on the issue of slavery.
> The present decision is therefore based on the written and oral declarations
> made before the Commission over the past six years.[56]

[51] For example, to what was then Zaire, Communications 25/89, 47/90, 56/91 and 100/93 (joined), *Free Legal Assistance Group, Lawyers' Committee for Human Rights, Union Inter-africaine des Droits de l'Homme, Les Témoins de Jehovah v. Zaire*, Ninth Activity Report 1995–1996, Annex VIII, para. 5 (*Documents of the African Commission*, p. 444), the objective of which was 'discovering the extent and cause of human rights violations and endeavouring to help the government to ensure full respect for the African Charter' (*ibid.*, para. 6).

[52] See Murray, 'On-Site Visits'.

[53] See Report on Mission to Mauritania; and Report on Mission of Good Offices to Senegal of the African Commission on Human and Peoples' Rights (1–7 June 1996), Tenth Activity Report 1996–1997, Annex VIII (*Documents of the African Commission*, p. 538).

[54] See Murray, 'On-Site Visits'; see also Interights, Constitutional Rights Project, Rencontre Africaine des Droits de l'Homme (RADDHO), *Missions for Protective Activities* (London: Interights, 1997).

[55] See Report of the Mission to Mauritania, 'after receiving communications that revealed disturbing violations of human rights . . . the African Commission . . . decided to send a fact-finding and investigation mission'.

[56] Communications 54/91, 61/91, 98/93, 164/97 and 210/98, *Malawi African Association; Amnesty International; Ms Sarr Diop, Union Interafricaine des Droits de l'Homme and*

Similarly, in its decision on communications against Sudan the Commission held that the mission sent to the country:

> must be considered as part of its human rights promotion activities and does not constitute a part of the procedure of the communications, even if it did enable it to obtain information on the human rights situation in that country. Consequently, this decision is essentially based on the allegations presented in the communications and analysed by the African Commission.[57]

It is a pity that the Commission does not seem willing to use these visits to their full potential to obtain information on the cases before them. Such visits could achieve some of the successes of the Inter-American Commission[58] and provide the Commission with alternative and insightful information in its decisions and the ability to meet and liaise with key figures in the communications.

Rules of evidence

One would not wish to advocate strict rules of evidence or to transplant domestic rules 'automatically' to the international level,[59] but a clearer indication as to how material is dealt with is essential to an understanding of the outcome of the case and the ability of the communication procedure to provide a suitable remedy for the victim.

International bodies have acknowledged that, in contrast to domestic laws, there is flexibility in the admission of evidence[60] to which they have

---

RADDHO; Collectif des Veuves et Ayants-droits; Association Mauritanienne des Droits de l'Homme v. *Mauritania*, Thirteenth Activity Report 1999–2000, Addendum, para. 87.

[57] Communications 48/90, 50/91, 52/91 and 89/93, *Amnesty International; Comité Loosli Bachelard; Lawyers' Committee for Human Rights; Association of Members of the Episcopal Conference of East Africa* v. *Sudan*, Thirteenth Activity Report 1999–2000, Addendum, para. 46.

[58] C. Medina, 'The Role of Country Reports in the Inter-American System of Human Rights', in D. Harris and S. Livingstone (eds.), *The Inter-American System of Human Rights* (Oxford: 1998), pp. 115–32; and Cerna, 'The Inter-American Commission'.

[59] See *Velàsquez Rodriguez*, Series C, No. 4, Judgment of 29 July 1988, paras. 132–3; Inter-American Court, *Fairén Garbi and Solís Corrales*, Series C, No. 6, Judgment of 15 March 1989, para. 134.

[60] *Nicaragua Case* (Merits), ICJ Reports (1986) 14 at paras. 57–74; *Ireland* v. *UK* (1978) Series A, vol. 25, 2 EHRR 25, para. 209; see also Highet, 'Evidence and Proof of Facts', p. 357; Sandifer, *Evidence Before International Tribunals*; T. Franck, *Fairness in International Law and Institutions* (Oxford: 1995), pp. 335 *et seq.*; C. Parry, *The Sources and Evidence of International Law* (Manchester University Press, 1965); D. McGoldrick, *The Human Rights*

often taken an *ad hoc* approach.[61] It has been said that international tribunals 'generally admit virtually any evidence presented and impose few restrictions on its form . . . the weight varies from judge . . . to judge and is heavily influenced by the judge's own legal background'.[62] Furthermore:

> investigatory commissions evince no uniformity of practice with respect to evidentiary principles. Rather, their more informal nature allows them to operate with even less strict rules concerning the admissibility and weight of evidence than those of international tribunals. Standards of proof have varied across commissions, and in some cases their mandates and reports have been completely silent on the issue.[63]

It is clear, therefore, that there is no one set of international rules of evidence and that the manner in which evidence is dealt with will vary depending on the particular organ. Criticisms of the African Commission's apparent failure on some occasions to consider evidentiary matters in any detail must be considered in this context, and, in this sense, the African Commission is not unlike its European, Inter-American or UN counterparts.

BURDEN OF PROOF[64]

Issues of burden of proof are important in relation to not only the merits of the case but also at the admissibility stage, most notably concerning exhaustion of domestic remedies. In this respect, the general approach of the African Commission is that, while the individual complainant has the duty to provide a *prima facie* case of exhaustion, if the State wishes to contest this or raise the matter it then has the burden of proving that remedies were adequate or effective.[65] These admissibility matters are examined in detail

---

Committee. Its Role in the Development of the International Covenant on Civil and Political Rights (Oxford: 1991), p. 143.

[61] S. R. Ratner and J. S. Abrams, *Accounting for Human Rights Atrocities in International Law – Beyond the Nuremberg Legacy* (Oxford: 1997), p. 216.

[62] *Ibid.*, p. 217. Highet, 'Evidence and Proof of Facts', p. 357: parties before the ICJ 'have freedom to introduce, more or less, whatever evidence they may consider appropriate to prove their cases'.

[63] Ratner and Abrams, *Accounting for Human Rights Atrocities*, p. 218.

[64] In general, see Kokott, *Burden of Proof.*

[65] See Communication 40/90, *Bob Ngozi Njoku* v. *Egypt*, Eleventh Activity Report 1997–1998, Annex II (*Documents of the African Commission*, p. 604); Communication 71/92, *Rencontre Africaine pour la Defense de Droits de l'Homme* v. *Zambia*, Tenth Activity Report 1996–1997, Annex X (*Documents of the African Commission*, p. 563). The Inter-American Court

by Professor Frans Viljoen in Chapter 3. It is necessary here to deal with the burden of proof relating to the substantive aspects of the case on the merits.[66]

The African Commission, as with other international bodies,[67] requires that the complainant submit a '*prima facie* case' in order to be admissible:

> For the purpose of seizure and admissibility the author of the communication can confine himself or herself to presenting a *prima facie* case and satisfying the conditions laid down in Article 56 of the Charter.[68]

The approach of other international bodies seems to be that the burden will then shift to the government to determine that the allegations are not true.[69] The UN Human Rights Committee, for example, has held:

> the burden of proof . . . cannot rest alone on the author of the communication, especially considering that the author and the State Party do not always have equal access to the evidence and that frequently the State Party alone has access to the relevant information. It is implicit in Article 4(2) of the Optional Protocol that the State Party has the duty to investigate in good faith all

has warned against presuming against the State: *Godínez Cruz*, Series C, No. 5, Judgment of 20 January 1989 at para. 62. See also Inter-American Court, *Fairén Garbi and Solís Corrales*, Series C, No. 6, Judgment of 15 March 1989, para. 83; *Akdivar and Others* v. *Turkey*, Reports 1996-IV, 23 EHRR 143, para. 68; *Austria* v. *Italy*, Application No. 788/60, 11 January 1961, *Yearbook*, vol. 4, pp. 166–8; *Donnelly and Others* v. *United Kingdom* (first decision), Application No. 5577–5583/72, 5 April 1973, *Yearbook*, vol. 16, p. 264. See also *Mukong* v. *Cameroon*, Communication 458/91, Decision of 21 July 1994, *Revue Universalle des Droits de l'Homme* 6 (1994) No. 9(2) 457–63, CCPR/C/51/D/458/1991, 10 August 1994, CCPR/C/51/D/458/1991, Fifty-First Session, before the United Nations Human Rights Committee under the ICCPR.

[66] The Inter-American Court has suggested proceeding on a case-by-case basis: Inter-American Court, *Fairén Garbi and Solís Corrales*, Series C, No. 6, Judgment of 15 March 1989, para. 97; and the European Court of Human Rights, although not followed in subsequent decisions, on one occasion suggested that there is no burden of proof as such: *Ireland* v. *UK* (1978) Series A, vol. 25, 2 EHRR 25, para. 60.

[67] For example, the UN's Human Rights Committee has said that there is a burden on the author to submit 'sufficient evidence in substantiation of the allegations as will constitute a *prima facie* case': Doc. A/39/40, para. 588; see McGoldrick, *The Human Rights Committee*, pp. 145–6. See also *Nicaragua Case* (Provisional Measures), ICJ Reports (1984) 169 at 437.

[68] Information Sheet No. 3, pp. 13–14. See also Communication 65/92, *Ligue Camerounaise des Droits de l'Homme* v. *Cameroon*, Tenth Activity Report 1996–1997, Annex X, para. 13 (*Documents of the African Commission*, p. 562), and Communication 107/93, *Academic Staff of Nigerian Universities* v. *Nigeria*, Seventh Activity Report 1993–1994, Annex IX (*Documents of the African Commission*, p. 350). For what amounts to a *prima facie* case, see below.

[69] *Velàsquez Rodriguez*, Series C, No. 4, Judgment of 29 July 1988, para. 79.

allegations of violation of the Covenant . . . especially when such allegations are corroborated by evidence submitted by the author of the communication, and to furnish to the Commission the information then available to it.[70]

In respect of the African Commission it would appear that the response of the government to the allegations dictates the subsequent burden. It would appear that the party making the allegations has the burden of proving them.[71] So the African Commission has stated that 'the onus is on the State to prove that it is justified to resort to the limitation clause'.[72]

If 'there has been no substantive response from the government . . . only a blanket denial of responsibility', this will not be sufficient to discharge the burden:[73]

> since the government . . . does not wish to participate in a dialogue, that the Commission must, regrettably, continue its consideration of the case on the basis of facts and opinions submitted by the complainants alone. Thus, in the absence of a substantive response by the government, in keeping with its practice, the Commission will take its decisions based on the events alleged by the complainants.[74]

What amounts to a 'substantive response' was not clarified in this case, although the Commission has stated on other occasions that the State should

---

[70] *Bleir* v. *Uruguay*, Doc. A/37/40, p. 130, paras. 13.1–13.3.

[71] Inter-American Court, *Fairén Garbi and Solís Corrales*, Series C, No. 6, Judgment of 15 March 1989, para. 126; see also Inter-American Court, *Velàsquez Rodriguez*, Series C, No. 4, Judgment of 29 July 1988, para. 123.

[72] Communication 212/98, *Amnesty International* v. *Zambia*, Twelfth Activity Report 1998–1999, Annex V, para. 42 (*Documents of the African Commission*, p. 745). This is the same before the UN's Human Rights Committee: see *Silva* v. *Uruguay*, Doc. A/36/40, p. 130; *Hertzberg* v. *Finland*, Doc. A/37/40, p. 161.

[73] This is in line with the approach of other international bodies: see for example UN Human Rights Committee, *Santullo (Valcada)* v. *Uruguay*, Doc. A/35/40, p. 107, *Selected Decisions of the Human Rights Committee*, p. 43; *Lanza and Perdoma* v. *Uruguay*, Doc. A/35/40, p. 111, *Selected Decisions of the Human Rights Committee*, p. 45.

[74] Communication 74/92, *Commission Nationale des Droits de l'Homme et des Libertés* v. *Chad*, Ninth Activity Report 1995–1996, Annex VIII, paras. 19 and 24 (*Documents of the African Commission*, p. 449). This was reaffirmed in Communications 27/89, 46/91, 49/91 and 99/93, *Organisation Mondiale Contre la Torture and Association Internationale des Juristes Democrates, Commission Internationale des Juristes (CIJ), Union Interafricaine des Droits de l'Homme* v. *Rwanda*, Tenth Activity Report 1996–1997, Annex X, para. 20 (*Documents of the African Commission*, p. 346). See also Communications 143/95 and 150/96, *Constitutional Rights Project and Civil Liberties Organisation* v. *Nigeria*, Thirteenth Activity Report 1999–2000, Annex V, at para. 28.

respond in a 'convincing manner'[75] and 'submit specific responses and evidence refuting the allegations', and that 'a rejection of the allegations by a State is not enough'.[76] So in one case the Commission noted that 'although the present government contends that there were "irregularities" in the elections, it fails to explain what these were'.[77] Similarly, in its recent decision on cases against Sudan, the government had contested allegations that soldiers who were subsequently executed were given no legal representation during their trial. The Commission held:

> while there is a simple contradiction of testimony between the government and the complainant, the Commission must admit that in the case of the . . . executed army officers basic standards of fair trial have not been met. Indeed, the Sudanese Government has not given the Commission any convincing reply as to the fair nature of the cases that resulted in the execution of twenty-eight officers. It is not sufficient for the government to state that these executions were carried out in conformity with its legislation. The government should provide proof that its laws are in accordance with the provisions of the African Charter and that in the conduct of the trials the accused's right to defence was scrupulously respected.[78]

The Commission found that there was a violation of Article 7 of the African Charter.

Similarly, where the government makes no response at all to the allegations the African Commission has stated on numerous occasions that it will 'take the facts as given' by the complainant:

---

[75] Communications 48/90, 50/91, 52/91 and 89/93, *Amnesty International; Comité Loosli Bachelard; Lawyers' Committee for Human Rights; Association of Members of the Episcopal Conference of East Africa v. Sudan*, Thirteenth Activity Report 1999–2000, Addendum, para. 75.

[76] Information Sheet No. 3, p. 14. In Communications 140/94, 141/94 and 145/95, *Constitutional Rights Project, Civil Liberties Organisation and Media Rights Agenda v. Nigeria*, Thirteenth Activity Report 1999–2000, Annex V, in relation to detentions in violation of Article 6, the government alleged that no one was presently being detained without charge. The Commission held 'this will not excuse past arbitrary detentions. The government has failed to address the specific cases alleged in the communications.' *Ibid.*, para. 51. A violation of Article 6 was found.

[77] Communication 102/93, *Constitutional Rights Project v. Nigeria*, Twelfth Activity Report 1998–1999, Annex V, para. 47 (*Documents of the African Commission*, p. 712). See further below.

[78] Communications 48/90, 50/91, 52/91 and 89/93, *Amnesty International; Comité Loosli Bachelard; Lawyers' Committee for Human Rights; Association of Members of the Episcopal Conference of East Africa v. Sudan*, Thirteenth Activity Report 1999–2000, Addendum, para. 66.

where allegations of human rights abuse go uncontested by the government concerned, even after repeated notifications, the Commission must decide on the facts provided by the complainant and treat those facts as given. This principle conforms with the practice of other international human rights adjudicatory bodies and the Commission's duty to protect human rights. Since the government of Zaire does not wish to participate in a dialogue, the Commission must, regrettably, continue its consideration of the case on the basis of facts and opinions submitted by the complainants alone.[79]

This has been followed in numerous other cases against, for example, Angola[80] and Nigeria.[81] In addition, in cases against Sudan when considering

[79] Communications 137/94, 139/94, 154/96 and 161/97, *International Pen, Constitutional Rights Project, Interights on behalf of Ken Saro-Wiwa Jr and Civil Liberties Organisation v. Nigeria*, Twelfth Activity Report 1998–1999, Annex V, para. 81 (*Documents of the African Commission*, p. 729). Rule 120(1) notes that, after admissibility, the Commission makes its consideration 'in the light of all the information that the individual and State Party concerned have submitted in writing'. There is no further indication in its Rules of Procedure of how the information will be considered.

[80] Communication 159/96, *Union Interafricaine des Droits de l'Homme, Féderation Internationale des Ligues des Droits de l'Homme, Rencontre Africaine des Droits de l'Homme, Organisation Nationale des Droits de l'Homme au Sénégal and Association Malienne des Droits de l'Homme v. Angola*, Eleventh Activity Report 1997–1998, Annex II (*Documents of the African Commission*, p. 615). See also Communications 25/89, 47/90, 56/91 and 100/93 (joined), *Free Legal Assistance Group, Lawyers' Committee for Human Rights, Union Interafricaine des Droits de l'Homme, Les Témoins de Jehovah v. Zaire*, Ninth Activity Report 1995–1996, Annex VIII, para. 40 (*Documents of the African Commission*, p. 444); Communication 59/91, *Embga Mekongo Louis v. Cameroon*, Eighth Activity Report 1994–1995, Annex VI (*Documents of the African Commission*, p. 385); Communication 103/93, *Alhassan Abubakar v. Ghana*, Tenth Activity Report 1996–1997, Annex X, para. 10 (*Documents of the African Commission*, p. 571).

[81] Communications 137/94, 139/94, 154/96 and 161/97, *International Pen, Constitutional Rights Project, Interights on behalf of Ken Saro-Wiwa Jr and Civil Liberties Organisation v. Nigeria*, Twelfth Activity Report 1998–1999, Annex V, para. 101 (*Documents of the African Commission*, p. 729). See also Communications 105/93, 128/94, 130/94 and 152/96, *Media Rights Agenda and Constitutional Rights Project v. Nigeria*, Twelfth Activity Report 1998–1999, Annex V (*Documents of the African Commission*, p. 718); Communication 60/91, *Constitutional Rights Project (in respect of Wahab Akamu, G. Adega and others) v. Nigeria*, Eighth Activity Report 1994–1995, Annex VI (*Documents of the African Commission*, p. 385); Communication 87/93, *Constitutional Rights Project (in respect of Zamani Lakwot and 6 Others) v. Nigeria*, Eighth Activity Report 1994–1995, Annex VI (*Documents of the African Commission*, p. 391); Communication 101/93, *Civil Liberties Organisation in respect of the Nigerian Bar Association v. Nigeria*, Eighth Activity Report 1994–1995, Annex VI (*Documents of the African Commission*, p. 394); Communication 148/96, *Constitutional Rights Project v. Nigeria*, Thirteenth Activity Report 1999–2000, Annex V, paras. 12

allegations of executions contrary to Article 4, the Commission held: 'according to the Commission's long-standing practice, in cases of human rights violations, the burden of proof rests with the government. If the government provides [no] evidence to contradict an allegation of human rights . . . made against it, the Commission will take it as proven, or at the least probable or plausible.'[82]

This approach obscures a difficulty: before even coming to this decision cases are often delayed for years awaiting some response from the State. Although Rule 119(4) of the African Commission's Rules of Procedure holds that 'State Parties from whom explanations or statements are sought within specified times shall be informed that if they fail to comply within those times the Commission will act on the evidence before it', the Commission has extended these limits without hesitation.

The approach is mixed, however, as, while these cases appear to suggest that the Commission does not test the validity or reliability of the complainant's evidence, there have been occasions when it seems to have required something more. In some cases, the Commission has found no violations of the Charter, suggesting that the complainant's evidence alone is not sufficient,[83] and the Special Rapporteur on Extrajudicial Executions has noted in relation to names submitted to him on individuals executed, that 'it is imperative that the inquiries into these executions be made with the greatest seriousness'.[84] Furthermore, the Commission has appeared on

---

and 13; Communication 206/97, *Centre for Free Speech* v. *Nigeria*, Thirteenth Activity Report 1999–2000, Annex V, para. 17; Communication 215/98, *Rights International* v. *Nigeria*, Thirteenth Activity Report 1999–2000, Annex V, para. 31. In Communication 151/96, *Civil Liberties Organisation* v. *Nigeria*, Thirteenth Activity Report 1999–2000, Annex V, para. 24. See also before the UN Human Rights Committee, *J. L. Massera and Others* v. *Uruguay*, Doc. A/34/40, p. 124, *Selected Decisions of the Human Rights Committee*, p. 40. In contrast, see International Court of Justice, *Corfu Channel Case (UK* v. *Albania)*, Merits, ICJ Reports (1949) 4.

[82] It went on to find a violation in this case: see Communications 48/90, 50/91, 52/91 and 89/93, *Amnesty International; Comité Loosli Bachelard; Lawyers' Committee for Human Rights; Association of Members of the Episcopal Conference of East Africa* v. *Sudan*, Thirteenth Activity Report 1999–2000, Addendum.

[83] See below.

[84] Progress of the Report on Extrajudicial, Summary or Arbitrary Executions: Rwanda, Burundi, Tenth Annual Activity Report of the African Commission on Human and Peoples' Rights, 1996–7, ACHPR/RPT/10th, Annex VI (*Documents of the African Commission*, p. 516).

some occasions to require corroboration of evidence,[85] for example by suggesting that there should be 'direct evidence' to support facts alleged,[86] say, from other sources,[87] that violations should be 'many reported',[88] that the evidence should be 'ample',[89] and that the 'veracity' of material should be checked.[90] The Commission has suggested that it is its responsibility to investigate the facts further,[91] although the extent to which it has taken a proactive role is questionable. A more careful approach is evident from other international mechanisms which have required, for example, that the evidence produced by the complainant 'does not lead to a different conclusion',[92] or 'so long as the contrary is not indicated by the record or is not compelled as a matter of law'.[93] As Cerna notes in relation to the Inter-American bodies,[94]

---

[85] See *Velàsquez Rodriguez*, Series C, No. 4, Judgment of 29 July 1988, para. 147(h) and Inter-American Court, *Fairén Garbi and Solís Corrales*, Series C, No. 6, Judgment of 15 March 1989, para. 145 and paras. 158–9; *Akdivar* v. *Turkey*, Reports 1996-IV, 23 EHRR 143, para. 81; International Criminal Tribunal for the Former Yugoslavia, Rules of Procedure and Evidence, IT/32/Rev.17, Rules 94*ter* and 96, and *Furundzija Case*, Judgment of 10 December 1998, IT-95-17/1 at paras. 111–13.

[86] Communications 137/94, 139/94, 154/96 and 161/97, *International Pen, Constitutional Rights Project, Interights on behalf of Ken Saro-Wiwa Jr and Civil Liberties Organisation* v. *Nigeria*, Twelfth Activity Report 1998–1999, Annex V, para. 96 (*Documents of the African Commission*, p. 729).

[87] In cases against Sudan, the Commission stated that alleged executions 'are supported by evidence collected by the UN Special Rapporteur': Communications 48/90, 50/91, 52/91 and 89/93, *Amnesty International; Comité Loosli Bachelard; Lawyers' Committee for Human Rights; Association of Members of the Episcopal Conference of East Africa* v. *Sudan*, Thirteenth Activity Report 1999–2000, Addendum, paras. 8. See also para. 48.

[88] Communications 27/89, 46/91, 49/91 and 99/93, *Organisation Mondiale Contre la Torture and Association Internationale des Juristes Democrates, Commission Internationale des Juristes (CIJ), Union Interafricaine des Droits de l'Homme* v. *Rwanda*, Tenth Activity Report 1996–1997, Annex X (*Documents of the African Commission*, p. 346).

[89] *Ibid.*

[90] '[T]he fact that the complainant's allegations were not contested, or were partially contested by the State does not mean that the Commission will accept their veracity': Information Sheet No. 3, p. 15.

[91] *Ibid.*

[92] Regulations of the Inter-American Commission, Article 42: 'The facts reported in the petition whose pertinent parts have been transmitted to the government of the State in reference shall be presumed to be true if, during the maximum period set by the Commission under the provisions of Article 34 para. 5, the government has not provided the pertinent information, as long as other evidence does not lead to a different conclusion.'

[93] *Velàsquez Rodriguez*, Series C, No. 4, Judgment of 29 July 1988, para. 138; see also Communication 464/91 and 482/91, *Peart and Peart* v. *Jamaica*, Report of Human Rights Committee, 6 May 1999, A/50/40, vol. II.

[94] Cerna, 'The Inter-American Commission', p. 98.

'for the presumption of truth to apply, the petitioner's version of the facts must comply with the criteria of "consistency, specificity and credibility".[95] In this respect, Cerna states, 'the determination of consistency is a matter of the logical/rational comparison of information furnished by the petitioner, to establish that there is no contradiction between the facts and/or the evidence submitted'; furthermore, 'credibility . . . is determined by assessing the version submitted including its consistency and specificity, in evaluating the evidence furnished, taking into account public and well-known facts and any other information the Commission considers pertinent'. Specificity is 'a corollary of those two factors'.[96] There has been some suggestion by the Inter-American bodies that facts which have not been contested by the state which otherwise are corroborated by it, may be accepted in evidence.[97]

While one can sympathise with the Commission's difficulties where the only information before it is that provided by the complainant, some questioning of the validity of that evidence is important not only to give at least the appearance of impartiality[98] but also because such matters are 'of immense practical importance to the functioning' of the body.[99]

The easy acceptance of the complainant's evidence in some cases, and the unwillingness of the Commission to impose time limits on the receipt of information from the individual, despite its ability to do so,[100] could be explained as an attempt by the Commission to take account

---

[95] Report No. 13/96, Case 10.948 (El Salvador), 1 March 1996, Annual Report of the Inter-American Commission on Human Rights 1995, OEA/Ser.L/V/II.91, Doc. 7 rev., 28 February 1996, pp. 101–12; see also the Inter-American Court's *Velàsquez* decision, paras. 20, 143 and 146.

[96] *Ibid.*, para. 20.

[97] See, for example, Report No. 63/99, Case 11.427, *Victor Rosario Congo v. Ecuador*, 13 April 1999, Annual Report of the Inter-American Commission of Human Rights, 1998, vol. I, OEA/Ser.L/V/II.102, Doc. 6 rev., 16 April 1999, para. 33.

[98] As Franck has stated in relation to the International Court of Justice, '[t]he non-appearance of a party thus presents a particular evidentiary challenge to the Court, since the appearing party has no formal competition in presenting evidence. Meeting this challenge is a necessary part of the Court's defence of its credibility.' Franck, *Fairness in International Law*, p. 337.

[99] See McGoldrick, *The Human Rights Committee*, p. 145.

[100] The Commission has a discretion to do so: Rule 119(3). In relation to those for merits, the Commission's Rules of Procedure, Rule 119(2), require that the State submit within three months 'explanations or statements elucidating the issue under consideration and indicating, if possible, measures it was able to take to remedy the situation'.

of the weaker position of the individual, relative to the State.[101] Other international bodies have suggested that this should particularly be the case if the complainant needed the co-operation of the State to obtain the evidence.[102]

However, while the Rules of Procedure appear to be stricter for States, setting a three-month time limit for submission of information,[103] these also are not enforced.[104] Thus, rather than this relaxed attitude being to prevent 'the procedural equilibrium and equality of the parties' being 'seriously affected'[105] it could have more to do with administrative inefficiency or the desire to maintain the goodwill of the State.

Where the government admits to the violations alleged by the complainant, the Commission comes easily to a decision:

> all parties agree that Mr Mazou was held beyond the expiry of his sentence. No judgment was passed to extend his sentence. Therefore the detention is arbitrary.[106]

Similarly, despite being unwilling to make any pronouncements on violations as the result of its mission, in the subsequent decisions against Mauritania adopted several years after the mission report, the government was willing to accept that serious violations occurred and the Commission found numerous violations of the Charter.[107]

---

[101] Also suggested by the Human Rights Committee: see Communication 458/91, Decision of 21 July 1994, *Revue Universalle des Droits de l'Homme* 6 (1994) No. 9(2) 457–63, CCPR/C/51/D/458/1991, 10 August 1994, CCPR/C/51/D/458/1991, Fifty-First Session, before the United Nations Human Rights Committee under the ICCPR.

[102] E.g. *Velàsquez Rodriguez*, Series C, No. 4, Judgment of 29 July 1988, paras. 135–6.

[103] Rules 104 and 117(1) and (4).

[104] The Inter-American Commission does permit evidence to be heard after deadlines have expired, only if there are new facts or legal arguments not previously considered: Regulations of the Inter-American Commission, Article 54(1).

[105] *Godínez Cruz*, Series C, No. 5, Judgment of 20 January 1989, para. 39.

[106] Communication 39/90, *Annette Pagnoulle (on behalf of Abdoulaye Mazou) v. Cameroon*, Eighth Activity Report 1994–1995, Annex VI; Tenth Activity Report 1996–1997, Annex X (*Documents of the African Commission*, pp. 384 and 555). Similarly, Communication 102/93, *Constitutional Rights Project v. Nigeria*, Twelfth Activity Report 1998–1999, Annex V, para. 46 (*Documents of the African Commission*, p. 712): government statements 'accord with the complainant's argument that the question of the election can no longer be the subject of meaningful negotiation'.

[107] Communications 54/91, 61/91, 98/93, 164/97 and 210/98, *Malawi African Association; Amnesty International; Ms Sarr Diop, Union Interafricaine des Droits de l'Homme and RADDHO; Collectif des Veuves et Ayants-droits; Association Mauritanienne des Droits de l'Homme v. Mauritania*, Thirteenth Activity Report 1999–2000, Addendum.

The difficulty has arisen, however, where the government does dispute facts on which the complaint is based. The Special Rapporteur himself has been aware of the difficulties of assessing facts and has thus stated that:

> It is probably that in cases submitted to the attention of the Special Rapporteur, the information provided by governments and other sources will be contradictory. In these cases, after analysis and verification, the Special Rapporteur will present his recommendation to the Commission which will decide what action to take on the case.[108]

The approach of the Commission is mixed. The Commission has had some difficulties in dealing with cases where the government disputes the facts. Communication 40/90, *Bob Ngozi Njoku* v. *Egypt*[109] related to the treatment of Mr Njoku at Cairo airport, although the communication detailed by the Commission did not expressly mention any specific Articles of the Charter alleged to have been violated. The government agreed that he was arrested on the date in question but did not agree with other specific points. These included allegations by the complainant that a suitcase which did not belong to him, and which contained drugs, was assigned to him at the airport. The complainant also said that he had made a statement to this effect in the presence of two Nigerian diplomats, all three signing a written document which was not translated, the government contending that the statement contained the confession for the possession of the drugs. The government also disagreed with the complainant that the lawyer assigned to him was ineffective. It was not clear from the Commission's decision if the government contested the allegations that the complainant was tried *in camera* with no translator. The complainant argued that the laws under which he was sentenced were inapplicable to him; the government argued it was actually applying a less harsh rule than available.

The Commission found no violations of the Charter. It noted that, although 'the rest of the communication contains serious divergences as regards the information provided by the parties', it did not consider that its task was to 'judge the facts. This is the responsibility of the Egyptian courts.' The Commission then affirmed that its role:

> in such a case is to ensure that during the process from the arrest to the conviction of Mr Ngozi Njoku, no provision of the African Charter . . . was

---

[108] Report on Extrajudicial, Summary or Arbitrary Executions.
[109] Communication 40/90, *Bob Ngozi Njoku* v. *Egypt*, Eleventh Activity Report 1997–1998, Annex II (*Documents of the African Commission*, p. 604).

violated. It is also incumbent on it to ensure that the defendant State respected and indeed enforced its own law in total good faith. To all these questions the Commission responded in the affirmative.[110]

The Commission gave no indication of what methods and approach it employed to arrive at this conclusion. The proviso at the end of the decision, that it mandated one of its Commissioners to 'pursue his good offices with the Egyptian Government with a view to obtaining clemency for Mr Njoku on purely humanitarian grounds', suggests a certain amount of sympathy with the complainant's cause. Its finding implies that it did not wish to risk any non-cooperative action from the government by finding a violation but instead pursued this 'amicable resolution' approach and left the case, in effect, open to its scrutiny behind the scenes.

The same approach would appear to have been taken in reports of the Commission's visits to Senegal and Mauritania. In relation to the latter, the Commission was asked to consider allegations of slavery which were disputed by the government, stating that 'to hold, like "SOS-Slavery", that slavery remains a living reality which touches 60 per cent of the population of Mauritania is not credible. One can only admit to the existence of several rare cases in the remote countryside isolated from the competent authorities.'[111] It was willing to conclude, however, that there were 'vestiges of slavery',[112] that measures already taken by the government should be 'amplified and deepened',[113] and that 'in sum, the promotion of women's rights is deficient in the country and merits particular attention'.[114] It did not, however, find any violations of the Charter in the context of its mission report.

In contrast, however, there are several cases where the Commission appears to have been more robust. As seen above, there has been some suggestion from the Commission that, once the State contradicts the complainant, it bears the burden of proof. So in one case against Zambia, the government 'disputes the characterisation of the expulsions as "en masse" by arguing that the deportees were arrested over a two-month period of time, at different places, and served with deportation orders on different dates . . . Zambia,

---

[110] *Ibid.*, para. 61.

[111] There is no indication the Commission visited such areas: see Report of the Mission to Mauritania.

[112] *Ibid.*, p. 20.   [113] Report of the Mission to Mauritania.   [114] *Ibid.*, p. 22.

however, cannot prove that the deportees were given the opportunity to seek appeal against the decision on their deportation'.[115]

A way of explaining these different approaches may rest on the amount of cooperation that is available from the State. The African Commission has stated that the Charter contains a duty on the State to co-operate with it. In a case against Angola alleging the mass expulsion of West African nationals from Angola, the African Commission stated that Article 57[116] of the Charter 'implicitly indicates that the State Party to the said Charter against which the allegation of human rights violations is levelled is required to consider them in good faith and to furnish the Commission with all information at its disposal to enable the latter to come to an equitable decision'.[117] It found in the case that 'in view of the defendant State's refusal to co-operate with the Commission, the latter can only give more weight to the accusations made by the complainants and this on the basis of the evidence furnished by them'.[118] Conversely, where the State has failed to cooperate or take the allegations seriously, the Commission has been more willing to rely on the complainant's evidence. It could, therefore, perhaps be implied that the burden on the complainant is lessened if the State does not co-operate with the Commission. As has been suggested in relation to the UN's Human Rights Committee:

> As for the obligations on the State Party [to supply evidence] it is unfortunate that the Human Rights Committee's approach can for the most part only be gleaned from cases in which the State Party concerned has generally proved uncooperative. Therefore . . . many of the Human Rights Committee's views effectively take the form of a judgment by default and . . . decisions against States which do not co-operate have been a 'one-sided affair'.[119]

Where the State does appear to cooperate, however, the more the burden will be placed on the applicant to prove the allegations, for example by

---

[115] Communication 71/92, *Rencontre Africaine pour la Defense de Droits de l'Homme* v. *Zambia*, Tenth Activity Report 1996–1997, Annex X, para. 27 (*Documents of the African Commission*, p. 563).

[116] This reads: 'Prior to any substantive consideration, all communications shall be brought to the knowledge of the State concerned by the Chairman of the Commission.'

[117] Communication 159/96, *Union Interafricaine des Droits de l'Homme, Féderation International des Ligues des Droits de l'Homme, Rencontre Africaine des Droits de l'Homme, Organisation Nationale des Droits de l'Homme au Sénégal and Association Malienne des Droits de l'Homme* v. *Angola*, Eleventh Activity Report 1997–1998, Annex II (*Documents of the African Commission*, p. 615).

[118] *Ibid.*   [119] McGoldrick, *The Human Rights Committee*, p. 59.

'substantiating' them. In Communication 205/97,[120] the Commission appeared initially, on the one hand, to say that, where allegations of torture and inhuman treatment were not 'substantiated', 'in the absence of specific information on the nature of the acts complained of, the Commission is unable to find a violation'.[121] In this case, however, having considered that the government failed to respond to any request for its reaction, it 'must take the facts as given' and it therefore found a violation of Article 5.[122] Similarly, in Communications 147/95 and 149/96,[123] the Commission noted that the 'burden of proof is on the complainant to furnish the Commission with evidence of his allegations' and that 'concrete proof' was required.[124] It was unwilling to find violations of Articles 4 and 5.

One should be wary of coming to any firm conclusions on this basis about the approach of the Commission given the lack of detail provided by the cases. Thus, in Communication 71/92 the government contested the allegations that deportees were arrested and assembled in order to be expelled, arguing it was done in order to verify their nationality and give them time to contact their lawyers. The Commission held in favour of the complainants but without a clear indication of how it arrived at this conclusion.[125] Similarly, in Communication 103/93, where there was a dispute over whether escaped prisoners returning to Ghana would face arrest and imprisonment, the Commission held 'the facts provided are insufficient to find that the complainant's right to return to his country has been violated', with no further reasoning.[126]

STANDARD OF PROOF

While the applicant has to provide a *prima facie* case for the purposes of admissibility, as seen above, it is not clear if this is all that is required for

---

[120] Communication 205/97, *Kazeem Aminu* v. *Nigeria*, Thirteenth Activity Report 1999–2000, Annex V.

[121] *Ibid.*, para. 16.　　[122] *Ibid.*, paras. 24–6.

[123] Communications 147/95 and 149/96, *Sir Dawda K. Jawara* v. *The Gambia*, Thirteenth Activity Report 1999–2000, Annex V.

[124] *Ibid.*, paras. 53 and 56.

[125] Communication 71/92, *Rencontre Africaine pour la Defense de Droits de l'Homme* v. *Zambia*, Tenth Activity Report 1996–1997, Annex X (*Documents of the African Commission*, p. 563).

[126] Communication 103/93, *Alhassan Abubakar* v. *Ghana*, Tenth Activity Report 1996–1997, Annex X (*Documents of the African Commission*, p. 571).

the Commission to find a case on the merits in his or her favour. What constitutes a *prima facie* case is not clear, although the Commission has said that an 'allegation in a general manner is not enough'[127] and:

> the communication should invoke the provisions of the African Charter alleged to have been violated and/or principles enshrined in the OAU Charter. A communication which does not indicate a *prima facie* violation of the Banjul Charter or some of the basic principles of the OAU Charter such as 'freedom, equality, justice and dignity', will not be examined.[128]

Cases have been held inadmissible on this basis for failing to state the violations suffered,[129] for being 'vague'[130] or 'incoherent',[131] and for failing to provide a certain degree of specificity.[132] For example, in one case a report was submitted relating to violations in a number of countries. The Commission held that it did not give specific places, dates and times of alleged incidents sufficient to permit the Commission to intervene or investigate. In some cases, incidents are cited without given [*sic*] the names of the aggrieved parties.[133]

Beyond this *prima facie* hurdle, it would appear that, if the government provides a response to the allegations and therefore the burden shifts back to the complainant to prove the case,[134] the Commission has mentioned

---

[127] See Communication 57/91, *Tanko Bariga* v. *Nigeria*, Seventh Activity Report 1993–1994, Annex IX (*Documents of the African Commission*, p. 346); and Communication 1/88, *Frederick Korvah* v. *Liberia*, Seventh Activity Report 1993–1994, Annex IX, p. 8 (*Documents of the African Commission*, p. 337); and Communication 63/92, *Congress for the Second Republic of Malawi* v. *Malawi*, Seventh Activity Report 1993–1994, Annex IX (*Documents of the African Commission*, p. 346).

[128] Information Sheet No. 3, p. 8.

[129] Communication 13/88, *Hadjali Mohamad* v. *Algeria*, Seventh Activity Report 1993–1994, Annex IX (*Documents of the African Commission*, p. 340).

[130] Communication 35/89, *Seyoum Ayele* v. *Togo*, Seventh Activity Report 1993–1994, Annex IX (*Documents of the African Commission*, p. 343).

[131] Communication 57/91, *Tanko Bariga* v. *Nigeria*, Seventh Activity Report 1993–1994, Annex IX (*Documents of the African Commission*, p. 346); Communication 142/94, *Muthuthirin Njoka* v. *Kenya*, Eighth Activity Report 1994–1995, Annex VI (*Documents of the African Commission*, p. 398).

[132] Communication 65/92, *Ligue Camerounaise des Droits de l'Homme* v. *Cameroon*, Tenth Activity Report 1996–1997, Annex X (*Documents of the African Commission*, p. 562).

[133] Communications 104/93 and 109–126/94, *Centre for Independence of Judges and Lawyers* v. *Algeria and others*, Eighth Activity Report 1994–1995, Annex VI (*Documents of the African Commission*, pp. 349 and 396). See Chapter 3 for further discussion.

[134] See above.

a variety of standards of proof. These have included, for example, that allegations be 'valid and logical',[135] that there is 'concrete'[136] or 'compelling'[137] evidence, that there is evidence 'from all appearances',[138] or that the facts are 'pertinent',[139] or, even further, that the position must be accepted 'in its entirety'.[140]

In one case, the Commission appeared to require several different standards: 'elements likely to reasonably lead to such a conclusion',[141] as well as 'to clearly establish' a violation[142] and a 'clear and precise understanding of the case before it'. The communication was declared admissible, implying that the evidence did amount to at least a *prima facie* case. However, in its consideration of the merits, the Commission found no violations. Although this may suggest that something more is required than a *prima facie* case, this is not a clear cut conclusion, as there were facts in the case which do not appear to have been dealt with by the Commission, such as allegations relating to Article 20(1), which, on the face of the information provided in the decision, were not contested. The outcome of the case may, therefore, have more to do with the fact that the parties did not appear to co-operate with the Commission in its request for information and its unwillingness to deal with the case further as a result:

> the Commission deplores the silence maintained by the parties in spite of its repeated request for information relating to the exhaustion of local remedies and other procedural aspects of the case. It is of the view that such lack

---

[135] Communication 44/90, *Peoples' Democratic Organisation for Independence and Socialism* v. *The Gambia*, Tenth Activity Report 1996–1997, Annex X, para. 16 (*Documents of the African Commission*, p. 559), although this term was one initially employed by the government.

[136] Communication 75/92, *Katangese Peoples' Congress* v. *Zaire*, Eighth Activity Report 1994–1995, Annex VI (*Documents of the African Commission*, p. 388); Communication 198/97, *SOS-Esclaves* v. *Mauritania*, Twelfth Activity Report 1998–1999, Annex V (*Documents of the African Commission*, p. 742).

[137] Communication 212/98, *Amnesty International* v. *Zambia*, Twelfth Activity Report 1998–1999, Annex V (*Documents of the African Commission*, p. 745), para. 37.

[138] Communication 198/97, *SOS-Esclaves* v. *Mauritania*, Twelfth Activity Report 1998–1999, Annex V (*Documents of the African Commission*, p. 742), para. 15.

[139] Report of the Mission of Good Offices to Senegal, p. 13.

[140] *Ibid.*

[141] Communication 144/95, *William Courson (acting on behalf of Severo Moto)* v. *Equatorial Guinea*, Eleventh Activity Report 1997–1998, Annex II (*Documents of the African Commission*, p. 609).

[142] *Ibid.*

of co-operation does not help the Commission to have a clear and precise understanding of the case before it.[143]

What this variety of approaches seems to indicate is that the African Commission may adopt a number of different standards. The Inter-American Commission has referred to standards of 'convincing proof',[144] 'enough proof to ascertain',[145] a 'tend[ency] to show',[146] 'sufficient to overcome the weight of evidence offered' by the complainant,[147] or even 'absolute certainty'.[148] The European Court of Human Rights has required a higher standard of 'beyond reasonable doubt' in some inter-State cases[149] and the UN Human Rights Committee 'has not made any general comment on the matter of the standard of proof other than that of a *prima facie* requirement at the admissibility stage . . . However, the general approach of the [Committee] would suggest that it is applying something approximating to proof on a "balance of probabilities" rather than a "beyond reasonable doubt" standard'.[150]

A variation in standard could be explained by the differing circumstances of the particular case. The International Court of Justice, for example, has suggested that the more serious the allegations, the higher the 'degree of certainty' required and thus the more the facts will be considered.[151] Similarly, in relation to disappearances, before the Inter-American organs, if there is 'sufficient evidence that the arrest was carried out by State agents acting within the general framework of an official policy of disappearances,

---

[143] *Ibid.* This is something which is supported by the Inter-American Court: see, for example, Inter-American Court, *Fairén Garbi and Solís Corrales*, Series C, No. 6, Judgment of 15 March 1989, para. 160.

[144] *Velàsquez Rodriguez*, Series C, No. 4, Judgment of 29 July 1988, para. 10, noting the Resolution 22/86 of the Commission, 18 April 1986.

[145] *Ibid.*, para. 39, although this was in relation to provisional measures.

[146] *Godínez Cruz*, Series C, No. 5, Judgment of 20 January 1989, para. 125.

[147] *Fairén Garbi*, Series C, No. 5, Judgment of 20 January 1989, para. 101.

[148] *Godínez Cruz*, Series C, No. 5, Judgment of 20 January 1989, para. 11, but also that it was 'impossible to identify the persons allegedly responsible'.

[149] *Denmark, Norway, Sweden and The Netherlands v. Greece*, Yearbook of the Convention (1969), p. 196, para. 30.

[150] McGoldrick, *The Human Rights Committee*, p. 150. Before international criminal tribunals, where one would expect the standard to be higher given the criminal nature of the procedure, the standard of proof applied was that of beyond reasonable doubt: *Furundzija Case*, Judgment of 10 December 1998, IT-95-17/1, para. 120.

[151] *Corfu Channel Case (UK v. Albania)*, Merits, ICJ Reports (1949) 4.

it shall be presumed that the victim's disappearance was brought about by acts of . . . State agents, unless that State gives proof to the contrary'.[152] In this respect, one could discern a particular standard from the wording of Article 58 of the African Charter relating to serious or massive violations.[153] This suggests the appropriate standard is as implied by the terms '*when it appears*', after the Commission has deliberated, that one or more communications '*apparently relate to* special cases which *reveal the existence of* a series of serious or massive violations'.[154]

The Inter-American Court has suggested that the standard may vary depending on the right being violated, noting the 'special seriousness' of finding a State liable for a practice of violations, which 'requires the Court to apply a standard of proof which considers the seriousness of the charge and which, notwithstanding what has already been said, is capable of establishing the truth of the allegation in a convincing manner'.[155] There is, however, no similar pattern in the case law of the African Commission. Its comment that 'the responsibility of the government is heightened in cases where the individual is in its custody and therefore someone whose integrity and well-being is completely dependent on the activities of the

---

[152] Report No. 52/99: Case 10.544, *Raúl Zevallos Loayza, Víctor Padilla Lujàn and Nazario Taype Huamani*; Case 10.745, *Modesto Huamani Cosigna*; Case 11.098 *Rubén Aparicio Villaneuva v. Peru*, 13 April 1999, Annual Report of the Inter-American Commission on Human Rights, 1998, vol. II, OEA/Ser.L/V/II.102, Doc. 6, rev., 16 April 1999, para. 64.

[153] No other indication is given in the Charter of how communications which do not amount to serious or massive violations should be assessed.

[154] See Communications 27/89, 46/91, 49/91 and 99/93, *Organisation Mondiale Contre la Torture and Association Internationale des Juristes Democrates, Commission Internationale des Juristes (CIJ), Union Interafricaine des Droits de l'Homme v. Rwanda*, Tenth Activity Report 1996–1997, Annex X (*Documents of the African Commission*, p. 346), para. 15. See also Communications 25/89, 47/90, 56/91 and 100/93 (joined), *Free Legal Assistance Group, Lawyers' Committee for Human Rights, Union Interafricaine des Droits de l'Homme, Les Témoins de Jehovah v. Zaire*, Ninth Activity Report 1995–1996, Annex VIII (*Documents of the African Commission*, p. 444), para. 35.

[155] Inter-American Court, *Fairén Garbi and Solís Corrales*, Series C, No. 6, Judgment of 15 March 1989, paras. 123 and 131; see also *Velàsquez Rodriguez*, Series C, No. 4, Judgment of 29 July 1988, para. 129. See also M. Shaw, *International Law* (Grotius, 1997), p. 764, citing the dissenting opinion of Judge Shahabuddeen in *Qatar v. Bahrain*, ICJ Reports (1995) 6 at 63. In relation to the UN Human Rights Committee, 'there may be some flexibility within this standard depending on the seriousness of the allegations involved', citing *Ireland v. UK* (1978) Series A, vol. 25, 2 EHRR 25, ECHR, McGoldrick, *The Human Rights Committee*, p. 150.

authorities'[156] could suggest that such situations may affect the standard of proof. As the European Commission on Human Rights held: 'taking into account the applicant's particular vulnerability while he was unlawfully held in police custody, the Commission declared itself fully satisfied that he had been subjected to physical violence which amounted to inhuman and degrading treatment.'[157]

ADMISSIBILITY AND ISSUES OF WEIGHT

The Commission has, as seen, faced difficulties where the alleged facts are disputed by the government. At the domestic level, weighing up the facts is usually a task for the jury, with issues of admissibility of particular types of evidence being a matter for the judge.[158] Where the judicial or quasi-judicial body is acting as both decider of facts and law, as is the case with the African Commission and other international human rights bodies, the two elements may overlap.[159]

In cases where the facts have been considered by the national courts, the approach of the African Commission has been that it will not substitute its judgment for that of the domestic tribunal.[160] The Commission has said that it is not a 'court of fourth appeal' from national bodies and, therefore, cannot:

> in any way, substitute [its view for that of] the police and judicial organs of the concerned country, nor play the role of detective, [although] it nevertheless remains that [the Commission] must evaluate the adequacy of the means of inquiry made by national organs and the credibility of the conclusions adopted by national investigative organs.[161]

---

[156] Communications 105/93, 128/94, 130/94 and 152/96, *Media Rights Agenda and Constitutional Rights Project v. Nigeria*, Twelfth Activity Report 1998–1999, Annex V (*Documents of the African Commission*, p. 718), para. 91.

[157] *Ribitsch v. Austria*, Series A, No. 336, 21 EHRR 253, para. 36.

[158] C. Tapper, *Cross and Tapper on Evidence* (London: 1999).

[159] In fact, even where different entities are carrying out the functions, the dividing line between weight and admissibility is not always clear-cut: see Franck, *Fairness in International Law and Institutions*, p. 335: 'the ICJ is a court of both first and last resort. As the former it must weigh evidence, may hear witnesses, and establishes a probable factual scenario. As the latter, it weighs and refines legal principles and seeks consistency.'

[160] Communication 40/90, *Bob Ngozi Njoku v. Egypt*, Eleventh Activity Report 1997–1998, Annex II (*Documents of the African Commission*, p. 604).

[161] Report of the Special Rapporteur on Extrajudicial Executions. In Communication 212/98, *Amnesty International v. Zambia*, Twelfth Activity Report 1998–1999, Annex V (*Documents*

The task of the Commission, therefore, is to examine the case in the light of human rights principles under the relevant instrument.[162] The Special Rapporteur has asserted that his main aim is to 'verify the facts contained therein, using facts provided to him by the responses of States, with the object of identifying those responsible for the extrajudicial execution and to determine the degree of implication of the authors or initiators of such acts'.[163] The Commission itself, in examining communications, has stressed, following the approach of other international organs, that its task is to apply the standards of the instrument to the case, not to deal with issues of fact:[164]

> After studying the arguments presented by both parties, and bearing in mind the principles of international human rights law which is basically aimed at protecting the individuals from State's encroachment, the Commission may then make a decision . . . [A] decision on the merits is an application of the international human rights law and an interpretation of the Charter *vis-à-vis* the allegations alleged by the victim. It is an examination of these allegations and all the arguments submitted by the parties within the context of the African Charter in particular and international human rights law in general . . . .[165]

This accords with other international bodies which appear to accept the findings of the national courts unless there are 'cogent' or other reasons to reject them.[166] The international bodies are not, however, bound by the findings of the national courts.[167] Domestic law is also taken as a matter of fact.

Several of the other international bodies have made the distinction between the roles of their Commission as opposed to their Court, with the latter being the arbiter of the law.[168] This may be a consideration for the

---

of the African Commission, p. 745), para. 32, the Commission held that it 'was not competent to substitute the judgments of the Zambian courts, especially on matters of fact'.

[162] For example, Communications 105/93, 128/94, 130/94 and 152/96, *Media Rights Agenda and Constitutional Rights Project v. Nigeria*, Twelfth Activity Report 1998–1999, Annex V (*Documents of the African Commission*, p. 718).

[163] Report of the Special Rapporteur on Extrajudicial Executions, p. 3.

[164] See, for example, *Nicaragua Case* (Merits), ICJ Reports (1986) 14 at 110; *Nuclear Tests cases*, ICJ Reports (1974) 253 and 457 at 466–7.

[165] Information Sheet No. 3, pp. 12 and 15.

[166] *Ribitsch v. Austria*, Series A, No. 336, 21 EHRR 253, para. 112.

[167] *Ibid.*

[168] See A. Trindade, 'The Operation of the Inter-American Court of Human Rights', in D. Harris and S. Livingstone (eds.), *The Inter-American System of Human Rights* (Oxford:

African Commission in the future with the coming into operation of the African Court on Human and Peoples' Rights,[169] but at present, as is the case with the UN Human Rights Committee, the African Commission must undertake both tasks.

It is for the international body to decide issues of admissibility of evidence.[170] Although there is no indication that the African Commission has rejected evidence, certain criteria seem to apply. It has indicated in some cases that sources should be independent[171] and its Special Rapporteur on Extrajudicial Executions has suggested that evidence be 'well founded'.[172] He has also taken into account the 'credibility of sources of information' which require allegations to be 'based on unquestionable criteria'.[173] In assessing the information provided by the government,[174] a number of elements must be taken into account, including the 'character of inquiry ... and its objectivity ... [and] applicable procedures, particularly those which concern the collection and evolution of elements of proof'. Whether some types of evidence have more value than others has been an issue in a recent case before the African Commission. While it has so far not questioned objections by one party to the other's witnesses,[175] it has considered the 'validity' or

---

1998), pp. 133–51 at pp. 148–9, in relation to the Inter-American bodies. See also *Akdivar v. UK*, Reports 1996-IV, 23 EHRR 143, para. 99; *McCann and Others* v. *United Kingdom*, Judgment of 27 September 1995, Series A, No. 324, p. 50, para. 168; *Ribitsch* v. *Austria*, Series A, No. 336, 21 EHRR 253.

[169] See the later discussion on the Court in Chapter 10 below.

[170] *Velàsquez Rodriguez*, Series C, No. 4, Judgment of 29 July 1988, para. 24. The term 'admissibility' should not be confused with considerations under Article 56 of the Charter. Such issues are dealt with in Chapter 3.

[171] Communication 67/91, *Civil Liberties Organisation* v. *Nigeria*, Seventh Activity Report 1993–1994, Annex IX (*Documents of the African Commission*, p. 346).

[172] '[T]he success of the mission of the Special Rapporteur ... can be significant only if he is able, thanks to specific information, to convince States that the cases he submits are well-founded.' Report on Extrajudicial, Summary or Arbitrary Executions.

[173] *Ibid.*   [174] *Ibid.*

[175] *Nicaragua Case* (Merits), ICJ Reports (1986) 14. The Inter-American Court has not permitted the argument of the government to succeed that witnesses testifying against the government were therefore disloyal to the State, and this was particularly the case in the context of human rights law: Inter-American Court, *Fairén Garbi and Solís Corrales*, Series C, No. 6, Judgment of 15 March 1989, paras. 139–45, or that those witnesses who were related to the victims had an interest in the case to justify their not being heard, *Velàsquez Rodriguez*, Series C, No. 4, Judgment of 29 July 1988, para. 111. See also *Prosecutor* v. *Tadic*, Case No. IT-94-1, Trial Chamber II, paras. 540–1, where the Trial Chamber rejected the argument that witnesses who are members of the conflict are unreliable.

authenticity of documents.[176] In Communications 147/95 and 149/96,[177] the Commission considered allegations of extrajudicial executions. In relation to the post-mortem reports submitted by the government the Commission held that:

> it is not for the Commission to verify the authenticity of the post-mortem reports or the truth of the government's defence. The burden is on the complainant to furnish the Commission with evidence of his allegations. In the absence of concrete proof, the Commission cannot hold the latter to be in violation of Article 4 of the Charter.[178]

This would suggest that there may be a presumption of the veracity of such documents until the complainant can prove otherwise.

In general, the Commission does not appear willing to consider the probative value of each statement, unlike the International Court of Justice, for example, which 'is prepared to attach particular probative value to statements from high-ranking official political figures "when they acknowledge facts or conduct unfavourable to the State represented by the person making them"'.[179] There is some suggestion, however, that comments by States Parties, on the other hand, may be subject to some scrutiny; for example, in Communication 209/97, *Africa Legal Aid* v. *The Gambia*, the Commission requested its Secretariat to 'inquire as to the veracity of the statement of the State Party'.[180] The Commission has, however, included the contents of delegate's speeches, albeit positive to the State, in its decisions.[181]

There does not yet appear to have been a situation where the Commission

---

[176] See Inter-American Court, *Velàsquez Rodriguez*, Series C, No. 4, Judgment of 29 July 1988, para. 140; and *Nicaragua Case* (Merits), ICJ Reports (1986) 14.

[177] Communications 147/95 and 149/96, *Sir Dawda K. Jawara* v. *The Gambia*, Thirteenth Activity Report 1999–2000, Annex V.

[178] *Ibid.*, para. 53.

[179] See Shaw, *International Law*, p. 764, *Nicaragua Case* (Merits), ICJ Reports (1986) 14 at 41, which further states '*affidavits* and sworn *statements* made by members of a Government, the Court considers that it can certainly retain such parts of this evidence as may be regarded as contrary to the interests or contentions of the State to which the witness has allegiance; for the rest such evidence has to be treated with great reserve'.

[180] Communication 209/97, *Africa Legal Aid* v. *The Gambia*, Thirteenth Activity Report 1999–2000, Annex V, para. 10.

[181] In Communications 105/93, 128/94, 130/94 and 152/96, *Media Rights Agenda and Constitutional Rights Project* v. *Nigeria*, Twelfth Activity Report 1998–1999, Annex V (*Documents of the African Commission*, p. 718), paras. 78–82, the government raised a defence in its oral statement that 'it is in the nature of military regimes to provide for ouster clauses', without which the amount of litigation 'would make it too cumbersome for the government to do what it wants to do'. The Commission rejected this and held a violation of Article 7(1) of the Charter.

has had to deal with evidence that has been improperly obtained. Other international bodies have been confronted with the issue.[182]

As to incapacity of parties, in Communication 65/92, *Ligue Camerounaise des Droits de l'Homme* v. *Cameroon*,[183] the Commission was required to consider an allegation by the government that aspects of the case submitted by Mr Vitine relating to his claims of persecution by former police colleagues, should be declared inadmissible 'because the author did not appear to be in possession of his full mental faculties'.[184] The Commission does not appear to have considered this issue directly, instead finding the complaint inadmissible for failing to satisfy a *prima facie* case. Similarly, in Communication 142/94, *Muthuthirin Njoka* v. *Kenya*,[185] the allegations related to the illegal admission of the individual to mental hospital, torture, imprisonment of his sons and family and confiscation of property. The Commission declared the complaint to be 'incoherent', 'vague' and inadmissible, noting that 'the author alleges . . . that his suits have been pending in court for nine years. One was against Kenya claiming the sum of 7.5 billion Kenyan shillings for the wrongful implementation of colonial statutes and . . . for wrongfully passing those legislations' and there was correspondence to the World Health Organization seeking the definition of mental capacity, and to the OAU requesting that 'sentences imposed on my sons' be quashed and they be released.

There has been some indication by the African Commission that circumstantial evidence may not be accepted. In Communication 144/95, it held that:

> the information relating to the arrest of another opposition leader contained in the complainant's submission is rather circumstantial and does not enable the Commission to clearly establish that Mr Moto was arrested because of his political opposition to the government of the day. The information does not

---

[182] See, for example, *Corfu Channel Case (UK* v. *Albania)*, Merits, ICJ Reports (1949) 4 at 32–6. Note also the Rules of Procedure and Evidence of the Yugoslavia Tribunal, Rule 95: 'No evidence shall be admissible if obtained by methods which cast substantial doubt on its reliability or its admission is antithetical to, and would seriously damage, the integrity of the proceedings.'

[183] Communication 65/92, *Ligue Camerounaise des Droits de l'Homme* v. *Cameroon*, Tenth Activity Report 1996–1997, Annex X (*Documents of the African Commission*, p. 562).

[184] *Ibid*. These aspects were then submitted as a separate case: Communication 106/93, *Amuh Joseph Vitine* v. *Cameroon*, Seventh Activity Report 1993–1994, Annex IX (*Documents of the African Commission*, p. 350).

[185] Communication 142/94, *Muthuthirin Njoka* v. *Kenya*, Eighth Activity Report 1994–1995, Annex VI (*Documents of the African Commission*, p. 398), previously Communication 56/91.

also indicate how Mr Moto allegedly tried to express his political opinions or set up associations with other persons. In view of the foregoing, the Commission is of the view that the violation of the above-mentioned provisions of the Charter has not been established.[186]

This is contrary to the Inter-American Court which has appeared to suggest that different types of evidence may be more appropriate for different allegations and that circumstantial evidence may thus be admissible in some situations, 'so long as they lead to conclusions consistent with the facts'.[187] So, for example, when there are disappearances and 'an attempt to suppress all information about the kidnapping or the whereabouts and fate of the victim'[188] or 'when human rights violations imply the use of State power for the destruction of direct evidence', it would admit circumstantial evidence as this may 'be the only means available'.[189] The African Commission has said nothing expressly about hearsay.[190]

Aims of the communication procedure

One could argue that the approach of the Commission to analysing the information provided to it in communications is *ad hoc* and incoherent. It is possible, however, that its approach can be better understood by considering the aims of the communication procedure as a whole. To determine the aim of the communication procedure is central to an assessment of how international bodies deal with evidence:

> the decision-makers should ideally determine the purposes for the information and the forum in which it is to be used (e.g. criminal trial vs. investigatory commission) before investigators are given the task of developing evidence.[191]

---

[186] Communication 144/95, *William Courson (acting on behalf of Severo Moto)* v. *Equatorial Guinea*, Eleventh Activity Report 1997–1998, Annex II (*Documents of the African Commission*, p. 609).

[187] *Velàsquez Rodriguez*, Series C, No. 4, Judgment of 29 July 1988, paras. 130–1. See also Inter-American Court, *Fairén Garbi and Solís Corrales*, Series C, No. 6, Judgment of 15 March 1989, para. 133.

[188] *Ibid.*

[189] *Godínez Cruz*, Series C, No. 5, Judgment of 20 January 1989, para. 155.

[190] See Inter-American Court, *Velàsquez Rodriguez*, Series C, No. 4, Judgment of 29 July 1988, para. 65; see also Decision on Defence Motion on Hearsay by International Criminal Tribunal for the Former Yugoslavia, *Prosecutor* v. *Tadic*, Case No. IT-94-1, Trial Chamber II, 5 August 1996.

[191] Ratner and Abrams, *Accounting for Human Rights Atrocities*, p. 218.

Despite the fact that the African Commission is not a prosecutorial body, and therefore 'less stringent evidentiary rules and requirements of these processes inevitably render the evidence gathering task somewhat easier',[192] the:

> credibility and success will still depend on careful and prudent investigatory techniques. The major challenge in evidence-gathering for non-prosecutorial processes is to ensure that investigators carry it out with sufficient regard for the possibility of subsequent prosecutions, so that their activities do not taint important evidence and jeopardise the success of those prosecutions.[193]

At times the Commission appears to have had difficulty with defining the aim of its communication procedure. It has said that its 'main goal . . . is to initiate a positive dialogue, resulting in an amicable resolution between the complainant and the State concerned, which remedies the prejudice complained of',[194] and it is clear that neither the Commission nor other international human rights procedures intend to find the 'guilt' of the State as such.[195] There does appear, however, to be a tension between the finding of a violation and the provision of a remedy to the victim on the one hand, and the need to maintain a dialogue with the State on the other. There has been only one occasion where the Commission has said that, 'given that the process of arriving at an amicable resolution can take a substantial period of time, the Commission believes it is important to make a statement on the question of law raised by the communication', going on to find violations of the Charter.[196] Other jurisprudence of the Commission implies an either/or approach, for example with the outcome of the communication being an 'amicable resolution' in which no

---

[192] *Ibid.*, p. 220. [193] *Ibid.*

[194] E.g. Communications 25/89, 47/90, 56/91 and 100/93 (joined), *Free Legal Assistance Group, Lawyers' Committee for Human Rights, Union Interafricaine des Droits de l'Homme, Les Témoins de Jehovah* v. *Zaire*, Ninth Activity Report 1995–1996, Annex VIII (*Documents of the African Commission*, p. 444), para. 39. See also Information Sheet No. 3, p. 13: 'once a communication has been declared admissible, the Commission puts itself at the disposal of the parties in a bid to secure a friendly settlement of the dispute. The Commission offers its good offices for friendly settlement at any stage of the proceedings.'

[195] Inter-American Court, *Fairén Garbi and Solís Corrales*, Series C, No. 6, Judgment of 15 March 1989, paras. 135–6; cited also in Inter-American Court, *Velàsquez Rodriguez*, Series C, No. 4, Judgment of 29 July 1988, at paras. 132–3. See also *Ribitsch* v. *Austria*, Series A, No. 336, 21 EHRR 253, para. 111.

[196] Communication 71/92, *Rencontre Africaine pour la Defense de Droits de l'Homme* v. *Zambia*, Tenth Activity Report 1996–1997, Annex X (*Documents of the African Commission*, p. 563), para. 18.

decision is made as to whether any Articles of the Charter were actually violated.[197]

Whether the case is declared to be amicably resolved may appear to be academic, but it has practical implications. There does seem to be some indication that the ability of, in particular, the investigative missions to collect and use information has been sacrificed by a desire not to upset the State. The stated aims of the missions have been 'fact-finding . . . in order to try and settle matters amicably',[198] 'to bring an end to the situation'[199] and 'not to decide whether what was encountered was wrong or right, but above all, to listen to all sides with the objective of bringing clarification to the Commission in its contribution to the search for an equitable solution through dialogue'.[200] However, while the missions were undertaken in response to communications, none of the mission reports found violations of the Charter, leaving the cases to be settled, if at all, when the communications were decided years later.[201] Furthermore, in the subsequent decisions, as has been seen, the Commission was careful to state that the mission was not part of the communication procedure.[202]

Recently, the Commission has appeared more careful in ensuring that an amicable resolution is satisfactory to both parties. In Communication 133/94[203] the Commission noted that 'for its part, the respondent State transmitted to the Commission documents strongly suggesting that arrangements made to obtain a lasting settlement of the demands of the victims of the violations blamed on the armed forces had been established and consequently calls on the Commission to declare the case inadmissible'.[204] The Commission met with the complainant and clarified that a settlement had been reached.

Similarly, in the cases against Mauritania, although the government had admitted that there had been violations, the government claimed that it had

---

[197] See Communication 40/90, *Bob Ngozi Njoku* v. *Egypt*, Eleventh Activity Report 1997–1998, Annex II (*Documents of the African Commission*, p. 604), discussed fully above.

[198] Mauritius Plan of Action, 1996–2001, para. 38 (*Documents of the African Commission*, p. 579).

[199] Report of the Mission to Mauritania, p. 4.   [200] *Ibid.*, p. 6.

[201] For a detailed analysis of the missions, see Murray, 'On-Site Visits'.

[202] See above.

[203] Communication 133/94, *Association pour la Défense des Droits de l'Homme et des Libertés* v. *Djibouti*, Thirteenth Activity Report 1999–2000, Annex V.

[204] *Ibid.*, para. 16.

resolved many issues and others were in the process of being settled. The Commission held that:

> though the . . . declaration by the government representative could have constituted a basis for an amicable settlement, such a solution could only take place with the agreement of both parties. However, at least one of the complainants has clearly indicated that a resolution can only be reached on the basis of some specific conditions, of which none has so far been met to its satisfaction. While it appreciates the government's good will . . . the Commission has an obligation to adjudge on the clearly stated facts contained in the various communications.[205]

In relation to its search for information relating to communications, one might expect that an amicable resolution would require less stringent consideration of the evidence provided than a finding of a violation of the Charter. One is therefore left with the impression that, certainly in the earlier cases, an amicable resolution was an easy solution to a situation where there were difficulties with the evidence. It is therefore essential that the Commission is clear about the reasons for collecting information, its relationship to communications and the eventual outcome of these communications.

Conclusion

One should be wary of applying the criticisms, such as the lack of formality, often directed at the African Commission, in an area such as this where flexibility is a feature of international mechanisms. One could argue that a greater degree of discretion should be permitted to individuals in their submission of communications on the basis that they are carrying out a function which has wider implications than just the outcome of their particular case and where they could be seen as agents of the public interest.[206]

It is clear that the African Commission now takes its role more seriously in its consideration of communications. However, in cases where there is conflicting evidence, there is some suspicion that the Commission's willingness to find violations, or otherwise, seems to depend on the co-operation

---

[205] Communications 54/91, 61/91, 98/93, 164/97 and 210/98, *Malawi African Association; Amnesty International; Ms Sarr Diop, Union Interafricaine des Droits de l'Homme and RADDHO; Collectif des Veuves et Ayants-droits; Association Mauritanienne des Droits de l'Homme* v. *Mauritania*, Thirteenth Activity Report 1999–2000, Addendum, para. 89.

[206] J. Kokott, *The Burden of Proof*, p. 210, and the reference therein.

of the State. While its attempts to ensure its good relationship with States are essential to the success of the communication procedure, the Commission must ensure that it deals with the allegations adequately. This can be achieved through, for example, more detailed reasoning and a willingness to be open to examining the facts on which the allegations are made. To do so is necessary if it is to maintain its credibility and thereby avoid the appearance that it is bowing to government pressure.

5

CIVIL AND POLITICAL RIGHTS IN THE AFRICAN CHARTER

CHRISTOF HEYNS

Introduction

In considering the African Charter, one's attention is easily captured by its more unusual aspects: the concepts of 'peoples' rights' and individual and State 'duties', and the inclusion of all three 'generations' of rights in the same supranational human rights instrument are such intriguing notions that they are hard to ignore.[1] It is important to note, however, that behind these more exotic features of the Charter lie the more 'traditional' civil and political rights which constitute the daily staple of regional, and indeed domestic, human rights mechanisms. Whereas academic writers tend to focus more on the unusual aspects of the Charter, the civil and political rights of individuals have thus far attracted the lion's share of the attention of the African Commission, and it is likely in future that the main thrust of the attention of the Court will have a similar focus.

This is not to say that civil and political rights are more important than others, especially in the African context.[2] Civil and political rights do lend themselves more easily, however, to supranational enforcement: their content is more clearly defined, and when an international body demands the rectification of a violation of a civil and political right this usually involves

---

[1] For an overview, see F. Viljoen, 'Review of the African Commission on Human and Peoples' Rights', in C. H. Heyns (ed.), *Human Rights Law in Africa 1997* (The Hague: Kluwer, 1999), p. 47.

[2] However, the preamble of the Charter seems to overstate the case for socio-economic rights where it says 'the satisfaction of economic, social and cultural rights is a guarantee for the enjoyment of civil and political rights'. The realisation of the one set of rights is a necessary, but not sufficient, condition for the satisfaction of the other set of rights.

less of an infringement of the cherished concept of State sovereignty, than is the case in respect of socio-economic or peoples' rights.[3]

This chapter will first consider the general provisions of the Charter that affect civil and political rights, and, thereafter, examine the different civil and political rights recognised in the Charter.

General provisions

Article 1 describes the obligations of States in respect of the rights recognised in the African Charter as follows:

> The Member States of the Organization of African Unity parties to the present Charter shall recognise the rights, duties and freedoms enshrined in this Charter and shall undertake to adopt legislative or other measures to give effect to them.

This should be read together with the first part of Article 2 of the Charter:

> Every individual shall be entitled to the enjoyment of the rights and freedoms recognised and guaranteed in the present Charter . . .

The primary duty created by the Charter is consequently the obligation placed on States Parties to *recognise* and *give effect to* the rights in the Charter; individuals on the other hand are entitled to *enjoy* these rights.[4] The obligation placed on the State by a human rights instrument such as the Charter is normally considered to have four components, namely, to respect, to protect, to promote and to fulfil the rights recognised.[5] First, 'respect' refers to the negative obligation on the State not to interfere with the right itself. An example of a violation would be a breach of freedom of expression through the arbitrary closure of newspaper offices by agents of the State. To 'protect' refers to the positive duty on the State to ensure that other individuals do not violate one's rights. The African Commission has held in this regard that 'if a State neglects to ensure the rights in the African Charter, this can constitute

---

[3] The concept of a supranational court enforcing socio-economic rights is certainly novel, and it remains to be seen how active the African Court on Human Rights will be in this regard.

[4] See Communications 48/90, 50/91, 52/91 and 89/93, *Amnesty International; Comité Loosli Bachelard Lawyers Committee for Human Rights Association of Members of the Episcopal Conference of East Africa* v. *Sudan*, Thirteenth Activity Report 1999–2000, Annex V, para. 42.

[5] See H. Shue, *Basic Rights: Subsistence, Affluence and US Foreign Policy* (Princeton University Press, 1980), p. 5.

a violation, even if the State or its agents are not the immediate cause of the violation'.[6] 'Promote' refers to the positive obligation on the State to advance a culture of human rights.[7] Lastly, 'fulfil' relates to a positive obligation on the State to create an environment in which people actually have access to the social goods in question. A failure by the State to establish independent and well-functioning courts, necessary to ensure a fair trial, would be an example of a breach of this obligation.

It is recognised that, although some rights may be absolute, others may be subject to limitations by States in particular circumstances. These limitations, however, must meet certain standards in order for human rights norms to retain their meaning. There are, so to speak, limits to the limitations, and human rights instruments should spell out these standards to ensure that restrictions are only exercised in a responsible fashion.

It can, thus, be seen as a weakness of the African Charter that it does not contain an explicit derogation clause setting out the procedures to be followed during times of war or national disasters. The absence of such a provision, it could be argued, would not prevent governments declaring states of emergency, but, rather, would result in the Charter being ignored at such times. However, in several cases, the Commission has held that the lack of a derogation clause means that States cannot derogate from the rights in the Charter at any time, whether during war, situations of emergency or peace.[8]

However, the Charter does limit rights in other ways. First, Article 27(2) could play the role of a general limitation clause in respect of all the rights; and, secondly, some of the provisions recognising civil and political rights contain internal limitations. Under the heading 'Duties', Article 27(2) reads:

> The rights and freedoms of each individual shall be exercised with due regard to the rights of others, collective security, morality and common interest.

---

[6] Communication 74/92, *Commission Nationale des Droits de l'Homme et des Libertés* v. *Chad*, Ninth Activity Report 1995–1996, Annex VIII, para. 20; R. Murray and M. Evans (eds.), *Documents of the African Commission on Human and Peoples' Rights* (Oxford: Hart Publishing, 2001) (hereinafter *Documents of the African Commission*) p. 449.

[7] Article 25 provides that: 'States Parties to the present Charter shall have the duty to promote and ensure through teaching, education and publication, the respect of the rights and freedoms contained in the present Charter and to see to it that these freedoms and rights as well as corresponding obligations and duties are understood.'

[8] Communication 74/92, *Commission Nationale des Droits de l'Homme et des Libertés* v. *Chad*, Ninth Activity Report 1995–1996, Annex VIII (*Documents of the African Commission*, p. 449).

Traditionally, international treaties bind only States. The African Charter, however, also imposes duties on individuals.[9] These duties have the potential to limit the rights recognised in the Charter.[10]

Although there is little jurisprudence from the African Commission on this point, it is likely that Article 27(2) will increasingly be used by States as a general limitation clause. The Commission has stated that 'the only legitimate reasons for limitations to the rights and freedoms of the African Charter are to be found in Article 27(2)'[11] and that the onus is on the State to provide the justification for limiting rights.[12] Consequently, it seems that the Commission is moving in the direction of following a two-stage limitation approach, according to which the onus is first on the complainant to show that a protected right had been infringed, and secondly on the respondent State to show that the limitation had been justified. In addition,

---

[9] These are secondary as their existence depends upon the State having assumed the primary duty to be bound by the treaty.

[10] The fact that Article 27(2) appears under the heading 'Duties' reinforces the idea that duties and limitations are interchangeable concepts. It is stated in the Preamble to the African Charter that 'the enjoyment of rights and freedoms also implies the performance of duties on the part of everyone'. Two interpretations of this statement seem to be possible: the performance of duties could be seen as a precondition for attaining rights; or the approach could be that rights are naturally limited by duties. The latter would appear to be more appropriate. For example, the duties of solidarity imposed by Article 29 could be used to justify certain forms of community service that could otherwise have constituted violations of civil and political rights, such as freedom of association or movement. See C. H. Heyns, 'Extended Medical Training and the Constitution: Balancing Civil and Political Rights and Socio-Economic Rights', *De Jure* 30 (1997) 1–17.

[11] Communications 105/93, 128/94, 130/94 and 152/96, *Media Rights Agenda and Constitutional Rights Project* v. *Nigeria*, Twelfth Activity Report 1998–1999, Annex V (*Documents of the African Commission*, p. 712), para. 68. See also Communications 140/94, 141/94 and 145/95, *Constitutional Rights Project, Civil Liberties Organisation and Media Rights Agenda* v. *Nigeria* Thirteenth Activity Report 1999–2000, Annex V, para. 4. The word 'only' appears to be too strong, in view of the role played by the internal limitations. In view of the general reach of Article 27(2), the distinction made in U. O. Umozurike, *The African Charter on Human and Peoples' Rights* (The Hague: Martinus Nijhoff, 1997) between 'unrestricted rights' and 'rights that may be restricted' cannot be supported. All limitations that are acceptable under international human rights law may also be applied in respect of all the rights in the Charter. There can consequently not be a category of 'unrestricted rights', although in terms of international standards a right such as the right against torture may possibly not be subject to limitations.

[12] See Communications 105/93, 128/94, 130/94 and 152/96, *Media Rights Agenda and Constitutional Rights Project* v. *Nigeria*, Twelfth Activity Report 1998–1999, Annex V (*Documents of the African Commission*, p. 712), paras. 73 and 77.

the Commission appears to have required limitations to be 'necessary' (and not, for example, just 'reasonable'):[13]

> The reasons for possible limitations must be founded in a legitimate State interest and the evils of limitations of rights must be strictly proportionate with and absolutely necessary for the advantages which are to be obtained. Even more important, a limitation may never have as a consequence that the right becomes illusory.[14]

In addition to this general restriction, some provisions that recognise civil and political rights also contain internal qualifications that limit the scope of that particular right. In principle there is nothing unusual about having such internal limitations in a human rights instrument, but the way in which it is done in some of the Articles in the African Charter is potentially problematic. Different categories of internal limitations in the African Charter may be distinguished. First, some provisions require infringements to meet both formal and substantive standards.[15] For example, Article 11 of the African Charter recognises the right of freedom of assembly, and then states that this right may be limited only by law (the formal requirement) where it is necessary in the interests of, among others, national security and safety (the substantive standards).

In other Articles internal limitations require only a substantive standard for infringements. Article 8, for example, provides that freedom of conscience and religion shall be guaranteed. This right may be limited only in the interests of the protection of law and order. No formal requirements concerning the method of limitation, namely, that it has to be done through law, are imposed explicitly.

The real difficulty lies with the third category of internal limitations, where only a formal requirement is explicitly posed for the limitation of rights, that is, where the provision in question appears to allow *any* limitation, as long

---

[13] *Ibid.*, para. 69 and 70. See also Communications 140/94 and 141/95, *Constitutional Rights Project, Civil Liberties Organisation and Media Rights Agenda* v. *Nigeria*, Thirteenth Activity Report 1999–2000, Annex V, para. 42.

[14] The word 'absolutely' in this sentence also appears to be too strong. Necessity is already a high hurdle to cross – absolute necessity is not feasible. The words 'not more than necessary' used elsewhere in the same decision seem to capture the test better. It is also debatable whether limitations are necessarily 'evil' – especially if they are required to protect other rights.

[15] This model is followed in Articles 8–11 of the European Convention on Human Rights.

as it is done 'by law'. These are the classical so-called 'clawback' clauses and Article 9(2) provides a good example: 'Every individual shall have the right to express and disseminate his opinions within the law.' No substantive standard which the infringement must meet, is imposed.

The presence of the clawback clauses[16] has been seen as perhaps the most serious flaw in the Charter[17] if one interprets 'law' as *domestic law*. This renders the right in question to be recognised only in so far as it does not conflict with domestic law, whether or not the domestic law in question conforms with substantive human rights norms. If that were indeed the intended effect of the clawback clauses, the status of the Charter as an instrument of international supervision would have been under serious threat. Each clawback clause would have functioned like a virus that destroys its own environment from the inside, and ultimately the organism as a whole.

Fortunately, the Commission has not followed this literal (and indeed obvious) interpretation, and it is now settled that the phrase 'subject to law', when used as part of a clawback clause could be understood to refer not to domestic, but instead to *international law*:

> In regulating the use of this right [freedom of association, under Article 10], the competent authorities should not enact provisions which would limit the exercise of this freedom. The competent authorities should not override constitutional provisions or undermine fundamental rights guaranteed by the constitution and international human rights standards.[18]

The Commission has cited this finding and elaborated upon it in subsequent cases:

> With these words the Commission states a general principle that applies to all rights, not only freedom of association. Government should avoid restricting rights, and take special care with regard to those rights protected by constitutional or international human rights law. No situation justifies the wholesale violation of human rights. In fact, general restrictions on rights diminish public confidence in the rule of law and are often counterproductive.[19]

---

[16] Only civil and political rights are subjected to clawback clauses.

[17] See, for example, E. A. Ankumah, *The African Commission on Human and Peoples' Rights* (The Hague: Martinus Nijhoff, 1996), p. 176.

[18] Communication 101/93, *Civil Liberties Organisation in respect of the Nigerian Bar Association* v. *Nigeria,* Eighth Activity Report 1994–1995, Annex VI (*Documents of the African Commission,* p. 394), para. 16.

[19] Communication 102/93, *Constitutional Rights Project* v. *Nigeria,* Twelfth Activity Report 1998–1999, Annex V (*Documents of the African Commission,* p. 712), paras. 57 and 58.

A strong exposition of the Commission's approach (see also the discussion of Article 9 below) is to be found in Communications 105/93, 128/94, 130/94 and 152/96, *Media Rights Agenda, Constitutional Rights Project, Media Rights Agenda and Constitutional Rights Project* v. *Nigeria:*[20]

> According to Article 9(2) of the Charter, dissemination of opinions may be restricted by law. This does not mean that national law can set aside the right to express and disseminate one's opinions; this would make the protection of the right to express one's opinions ineffective. To allow national law to have precedent over the international law of the Charter would defeat the purpose of the rights and freedoms enshrined in the Charter. *International human rights standards must always prevail over contradictory national law.* Any limitation on the rights of the Charter must be in conformity with the provisions of the Charter.

In Communication 212/98, *Amnesty International* v. *Zambia,*[21] the Commission referred to the internal limitation in Article 12(2) as follows, stressing that the burden was on the State to justify use of the limitation:

> The Commission is of the view that the 'clawback' clauses must not be interpreted against the principles of the Charter. Recourse to these should not be used as a means of giving credence to violations of the express provisions of the Charter . . . It is important for the Commission to caution against a too easy resort to the limitation clauses in the African Charter. The onus is on the State to prove that it is justified to resort to the limitation clause. The Commission should act bearing in mind the provisions of Articles 61 and 62 of the Charter.[22]

The Commission was able to neutralise the clawback clauses by referring to its duty to interpret the Charter in light of international human rights jurisprudence as required by Articles 60 and 61. It is submitted that in future the Commission is likely to follow the approach – if not explicitly, then implicitly – that all rights in the Charter may be limited if the limitation is justifiable in terms of international practice. Such practice requires that

---

[20] Twelfth Activity Report 1998–1999, Annex V (*Documents of the African Commission,* p. 718), para. 66 (emphasis added).

[21] Communication 212/98, *Amnesty International* v. *Zambia,* Twelfth Activity Report 1998–1999, Annex V (*Documents of the African Commission,* p. 745), para. 50.

[22] Although the sentiment expressed is to be welcomed, it may be doubted whether it is correct to refer to Article 12(2) as a 'clawback' clause, since the substantive standards which limitations must meet are defined.

any limitation of the right must be set down in domestic law;[23] the State will have to show that the limitation was necessary to protect an internationally recognised interest,[24] and the measures taken should be proportionate to the interest being protected.

It should also be noted that the presence of socio-economic rights in a human rights instrument such as the Charter could potentially limit the scope of the civil and political rights recognised in that instrument.[25] For example, the inclusion of a 'right to receive medical attention [when one is] sick'[26] could serve to outweigh the claims by a medical graduate who is required to do community service that this constitutes a violation of his or her freedom not to be discriminated against, if members of other professions are not required to do the same.

Specific rights

THE RIGHT AGAINST DISCRIMINATION

Article 2 provides:

> Every individual shall be entitled to the enjoyment of the rights and freedoms recognised and guaranteed in the present Charter without distinction of any kind such as race, ethnic group, colour, sex, language, religion, political or any other opinion, national and social origin, fortune, birth or other status.

---

[23] A strong case could be made out that it should be by means of a law of general application. The Commission has ruled that bills of attainder or *ad hominem* legislation – the opposite of laws of general application – are not acceptable: Communications 105/93, 128/94, 130/94 and 152/96, *Media Rights Agenda and Constitutional Rights Project v. Nigeria*, Twelfth Activity Report 1998–1999, Annex V (*Documents of the African Commission*, p. 718), para. 71. The same finding was made in Communication 102/93, *Constitutional Rights Project v. Nigeria*, Twelfth Activity Report 1998–1999, Annex V (*Documents of the African Commission*, p. 712), para. 59. In Communications 140/94, 141/94 and 145/95, *Constitutional Rights Project, Civil Liberties Organisation and Media Rights Agenda v. Nigeria*, Thirteenth Activity Report 1999–2000, Annex V, para. 44, the Commission said the following: 'For the government to proscribe a particular publication, by name, is thus disproportionate and not necessary. Laws made to apply specifically to one individual or legal personality raise the serious danger of discrimination and lack of equal treatment before the law, guaranteed by Article 3. The proscription of these publications cannot therefore be said to be "within the law" and constitutes a violation of Article 9(2).'

[24] This will include interests recognised explicitly in the internal limitations – such as health or public security – but it is not confined to these.

[25] See C. H. Heyns, 'Extended Medical Training and the Constitution'.

[26] Article 16(2).

This provision mirrors Article 2 of the International Covenant on Civil and Political Rights (ICCPR) almost word for word and, as a result, the interpretation given to that Article by the Human Rights Committee (HRC) should carry substantive weight when the African Commission has to interpret the African Charter's version of Article 2.[27]

A number of aspects of the above right are striking. Non-discrimination is the first substantive right listed in the Charter, even before life.[28] This emphasises the importance that must have been attached to this right at the time when the Charter was drafted – a time when colonisation was still vividly remembered and apartheid was alive and well. Secondly, the reach of the Article is quite wide. The grounds on which discrimination is prohibited are not exhaustive: '[D]istinction of any kind' is prohibited, and the grounds listed serve merely as examples of the kinds of distinctions that are envisaged. The open-ended nature of the list is reinforced by the words 'or other status' at the end of the Article. The following grounds are, for example, not explicitly listed: gender, age, disability and sexual orientation; while the unusual ground of 'fortune' (as opposed to 'property' in the ICCPR) is included. The width of the Article is also reinforced by the fact that it does not attempt to define types of differentiation, such as 'unfair discrimination'.

It is not only Article 2 that relates to non-discrimination, but also Article 3, and discrimination in the context of expulsion of foreigners is covered explicitly in Article 12(4) and (5). The Commission has found in two cases, one involving Zambia and the other Angola, that mass expulsion of foreigners without access to the courts constituted a violation (*inter alia*) of Articles 2 and 12(4) and (5).[29] Violations of the same Articles

---

[27] See D. McGoldrick, *The Human Rights Committee. Its Role in the Development of the International Covenant on Civil and Political Rights* (Oxford University Press, 1996), p. 269.

[28] As far as peoples' rights are concerned, equality and non-discrimination (Article 19) are also listed before the right of peoples to existence (Article 20).

[29] In Communication 71/92, *Rencontre Africaine pour la Defense de Droits de l'Homme* v. *Zambia*, Tenth Activity Report 1996–1997, Annex X (*Documents of the African Commission*, p. 563), over 500 West Africans were expelled *en masse*, without recourse to lawyers, from Zambia. In Communication 159/96, *Union Interafricaine des Droits de l'Homme, Féderation International des Ligues des Droits de l'Homme, Rencontre Africaine des Droits de l'Homme, Organisation Nationale des Droits de l'Homme au Sénégal and Association Malienne des Droits de l'Homme* v. *Angola*, Eleventh Activity Report 1997–1998, Annex II (*Documents of the African Commission*, p. 615), an unspecified number of West Africans were also expelled from Angola in similar circumstances.

was found where numerous rights were denied to Burundian nationals and Tutsis, on the basis of their nationality and ethnicity.[30] Expulsion of politicians due to their political or other opinion has also been found to violate Article 2.[31]

Article 18 proscribes discrimination against women, children, the aged and the disabled. Article 18 also makes provision for 'special measures' of protection in respect of the aged and the disabled. These are the only groups in respect of which affirmative action is explicitly endorsed and indeed required by the Charter.

Article 28 applies to relations on the horizontal plane and deals with discrimination between individuals. It holds:

> Every individual shall have the duty to respect and consider his fellow beings without discrimination, and to maintain relations aimed at promoting, safeguarding and reinforcing mutual respect and tolerance.

This duty clearly has the potential to limit rights such as freedom of expression.

The Commission has ruled that *Shari'a* law in Sudan cannot be imposed on non-Muslims.[32] In respect of discrimination against black Mauritanians, the Commission has held that:

> [f]or a country to subject its own indigenes to discriminatory treatment only because of the colour of their skin is an unacceptable discriminatory attitude and a violation of the very spirit of the African Charter and of the letter of its Article 2.[33]

---

[30] Communications 27/89, 46/91, 49/91 and 99/93, *Organisation Mondiale Contre la Torture and Association Internationale des Juristes Democrates, Commission Internationale des Juristes (CIJ), Union Interafricaine des Droits de l'Homme* v. *Rwanda*, Tenth Activity Report 1996–1997, Annex X (*Documents of the African Commission*, p. 551), paras. 22, 28 and 30, although Article 2 is not cited in the list of Articles violated that is contained in the eventual holding of the Commission.

[31] Communication 212/98, *Amnesty International* v. *Zambia*, Twelfth Activity Report 1998–1999, Annex V (*Documents of the African Commission*, p. 745), para. 52. The statement in the same paragraph that '[b]y forcibly expelling the two victims from Zambia, the State has violated their right to enjoyment of *all* the rights enshrined in the African Charter' (emphasis added) must be a mistake.

[32] See the discussion of Article 8 below.

[33] Communications 54/91, 61/91, 98/93, 164/97–196/97 and 210/98, *Malawi African Association, Amnesty International, Ms Sarr Diop, Union Interafricaine des Droits de l'Homme and RADDHO, Collectif des Veuves et Ayants-droit, Association Mauritanienne des Droits de l'Homme* v. *Mauritania*, Thirteenth Activity Report 1999–2000, Annex V, para. 131.

THE RIGHT TO EQUALITY

Article 3 provides:

1. Every individual shall be equal before the law.
2. Every individual shall be entitled to equal protection of the law.

Article 13(2) and (3) also require equality of all persons in respect of access to public property and services. It should be noted that Article 3 supplements Article 2 by providing a general equality requirement. Like the ICCPR, the African Charter consequently represents an advance on the European Convention on Human Rights which only prohibits discrimination in the enjoyment of the rights and freedoms set out in that Convention.[34]

The Commission has held that the 'rampant arrest' of an individual violated this Article.[35] He had been arrested 'on several occasions' during a two-year period.

THE RIGHT TO BODILY INTEGRITY AND THE RIGHT TO LIFE

Article 4 provides:

> Human beings are inviolable. Every human being shall be entitled to respect for his life and the integrity of his person. No one may be arbitrarily deprived of this right.

The provision that no one may be 'arbitrarily deprived' of the right to life and personal integrity could probably be traced to Article 6 of the ICCPR. A substantial jurisprudence around this right has been developed by the HRC.[36] The African Commission has made a number of findings of serious or massive violations in terms of Article 58, in all of which findings of violations of the right to life contributed towards this eventual result. It is difficult to imagine that findings of serious or massive violations will not involve breaches of this right. In the cases against Malawi[37] it appears

---

[34] Article 14. When Protocol 12 enters into force, this will become a stand-alone provision.

[35] Communication 205/97, *Kazeem Aminu* v. *Nigeria*, Thirteenth Activity Report 1999–2000, Annex V, paras. 14–15.

[36] See McGoldrick, *The Human Rights Committee*, p. 328.

[37] Communications 64/92, 68/92 and 78/92, *Krischna Achuthan, Amnesty International, Amnesty International* v. *Malawi*, Seventh Activity Report 1993–1994, Annex IX; Eighth Activity Report 1994–1995, Annex VI (*Documents of the African Commission*, pp. 347 and 387), para. 4.

that the violation occurred when 'peacefully striking workers were shot and killed by the police'.[38] In another case[39] extrajudicial killings were held to have constituted a violation of Article 4, although it was not clear from the record who were the perpetrators. While the Commission did not make an explicit finding in this case that the government could be held accountable for failure to act in respect of violations by private parties, it has reached this conclusion elsewhere.

In a decision against Chad the Commission held that, even if State agents did not commit the violations, the actions could still be imputed to the State, it being responsible for ensuring the protection of the rights of those on its territory.[40] In this case, the Commission held, on the basis of several accounts of killings (and seemingly also disappearances), as well as an assassination by unknown people, which the government did not attempt to prevent or investigate afterwards, that Article 4 had been violated. It was thus established that the State's failure to 'protect'[41] individuals under its jurisdiction could also constitute a violation of Article 4.[42] The government of Sudan's 'responsibility to protect all people residing under its jurisdiction' was also emphasised by the Commission in respect of executions in that country. Sudan was held to have violated Article 4, irrespective of whether the executions were committed by government forces.[43]

Where there was a 'massacre of a large number of Rwandan villagers by the Rwandan armed forces and the many reported extrajudicial executions for reasons of their membership of a particular ethnic group' this constituted

[38] The comment in Ankumah, *The African Commission*, p. 115, that the Commission found that Mr Chirwa's right to life had been violated because he died in detention, is not reflected in the decision as reported.

[39] Communications 25/89, 47/90, 56/91 and 100/93, *Free Legal Assistance Group, Lawyers' Committee for Human Rights, Union Interafricaine des Droits de l'Homme, Les Témoins de Jehovah* v. *Zaire*, Ninth Activity Report 1995–1996, Annex VIII (*Documents of the African Commission*, p. 444).

[40] Communication 74/92, *Commission Nationale des Droits de l'Homme et des Libertés* v. *Chad*, Ninth Activity Report 1995–1996, Annex VIII (*Documents of the African Commission*, p. 449).

[41] As discussed above.

[42] See, in the Inter-American system, *Velàsquez Rodríguez*, Series C, No. 4, Judgment of 29 July 1988.

[43] Communications 48/90, 50/91, 52/91 and 89/93, *Amnesty International, Comité Loosli Bachelard, Lawyers Committee for Human Rights, Association of Members of the Episcopal Conference of East Africa* v. *Sudan*, Thirteenth Activity Report 1999–2000, Annex V, paras. 47–52.

a violation of Article 4.[44] In a case against Nigeria the denial of medication to a prisoner to the extent that his life was seriously endangered was also considered to be a violation of the right to life, even though this had not caused his death.[45] While Article 4 itself does not obviously favour any side in the abortion or death penalty debates, it was held that, since the trial itself violated Article 7 of the African Charter, the subsequent death penalty that was imposed in that case was arbitrary and transgressed Article 4 of the Charter.[46] The Commission held in Communication 205/97, *Kazeem Aminu* v. *Nigeria* that a series of arrests and detentions could in themselves constitute a violation of Article 4, even where there was no actual loss of life: 'It would be a narrow interpretation of this right to think that it can only be violated when one is deprived of it. It cannot be said that the right to respect for one's life and the dignity of his person, which this Article guarantees would be protected in a state of constant fear and/or threats, as experienced by [the complainant].'[47]

In addition, the Commission has held that arbitrary and brutal executions in Mauritania constituted violations of Article 4.[48]

In its 'Resolution Urging States to Envisage a Moratorium on the Death Penalty',[49] the African Commission stated that it:

1. Urges all States Parties to the African Charter on Human and Peoples' Rights that still maintain the death penalty to comply fully with their obligations under the treaty and to ensure that persons accused of crimes for which the death penalty is a competent sentence are afforded all the guarantees in the African Charter.

---

[44] Communications 27/89, 46/91, 49/91 and 99/93, *Organisation Mondiale Contre la Torture and Association Internationale des Juristes Democrates, Commission Internationale des Juristes (CIJ), Union Interafricaine des Droits de l'Homme* v. *Rwanda*, Tenth Activity Report 1996–1997, Annex X (*Documents of the African Commission*, p. 551), para. 24 (filed before the 1994 genocide, but decided only in 1997).

[45] Communications 137/94, 139/94, 154/96 and 161/97, *International Pen, Constitutional Rights Project, Interights on behalf of Ken Saro-Wiwa Jr and Civil Liberties Organisation* v. *Nigeria*, Twelfth Activity Report 1998–1999, Annex V (*Documents of the African Commission*, p. 729), para. 104.

[46] *Ibid.*, para. 103.   [47] At para. 18.

[48] Communications 54/91, 61/91, 98/93, 164/97–196/97 and 210/98, *Malawi African Association, Amnesty International, Ms Sarr Diop, Union Interafricaine des Droits de l'Homme and RADDHO, Collectif des Veuves et Ayants-droit, Association Mauritanienne des Droits de l'Homme* v. *Mauritania*, Thirteenth Activity Report 1999–2000, Annex V, para. 119.

[49] Adopted at the 26th Ordinary Session of the African Commission on Human and Peoples' Rights, Kigali, Rwanda, 1–15 November 1999, DOC/OS (XXVI) INF.19.

2. Calls upon all States Parties that still maintain the death penalty to:
   (a) limit the imposition of the death penalty only to the most serious crimes;
   (b) consider establishing a moratorium on executions, especially in cases where there may not have been full compliance with international standards for a fair trial;
   (c) reflect on the possibility of abolishing [the] death penalty.

THE RIGHT TO DIGNITY AND PROHIBITION OF TORTURE AND INHUMAN TREATMENT

Article 5 provides:

> Every individual shall have the right to the respect of the dignity inherent in a human being and to the recognition of his legal status. All forms of exploitation and degradation of man, particularly slavery, slave trade, torture, cruel, inhuman or degrading punishment and treatment shall be prohibited.

This provision essentially protects dignity – the only right in the African Charter described as 'inherent in a human being' – and then lists certain examples of exploitative practices which would constitute violations of this right without pretending to provide a full list. Slavery, torture and cruel, inhuman and degrading punishment are explicitly listed as examples.[50] The usual reference to 'forced or compulsory labour'[51] is not included. It is unusual for dignity and the right against slavery to be dealt with in the same provision and this no doubt reflects the historical consciousness of the drafters of the Charter. As is the case with findings of violations of the right to life, violations of Article 5 constituted an element of all the findings of 'serious or massive violations' that have been made by the Commission.

Aspects of imprisonment have constituted violations of Article 5 such as overcrowding, beatings, torture, excessive solitary confinement, shackling within a cell, 'extremely poor quality food' and denial of access to adequate medical care (presumably also contraventions of the socio-economic

---

[50] In Communication 198/97, *SOS-Esclaves* v. *Mauritania*, Twelfth Activity Report 1998–1999, Annex V (*Documents of the African Commission*, p. 742), para. 15, the Commission eventually did not admit the communication because of non-exhaustion of domestic remedies, but nevertheless expressed its concerns about allegations of slavery.

[51] See e.g. ICCPR Article 8(3), ECHR Article 4(2).

rights provisions of the Charter).[52] Often the Commission finds violations of Article 5 on the basis of torture being practised, but provides no more information of what actions amounted to this.[53]

The Commission has stated that detention which violates the 'physical and psychological integrity' of individuals (in that particular case, women, children and the aged) will amount to a violation of Article 5.[54] In this respect, the Commission held in one case:[55]

> Article 5 prohibits not only torture, but also cruel, inhuman or degrading treatment. This includes not only actions which cause serious physical or psychological suffering, but which humiliate the individual or force him or her to act against his will or conscience.

The Commission accepted the allegations that Ken Saro-Wiwa was:

> kept in leg irons and handcuffs and subjected to ill-treatment including beatings and being held in cells which were airless and dirty, then denied medical attention, during the first days of his arrest. There was no evidence of any violent action on his part or escape attempts that would justify holding him in irons. Part of the complaint alleged that all the victims were manacled in their cells, beaten and chained to the walls in their cells.

[52] Communications 64/92, 68/92 and 78/92, *Krischna Achuthan, Amnesty International, Amnesty International* v. *Malawi*, Seventh Activity Report 1993–1994, Annex IX; Eighth Activity Report 1994–1995, Annex VI (*Documents of the African Commission*, pp. 347, 387), para. 8. Unfortunately, as is the case with several other seemingly brave decisions, the finding of the Commission only came after the Banda regime had been toppled.

[53] Communication 74/92, *Commission Nationale des Droits de l'Homme et des Libertés* v. *Chad*, Ninth Activity Report 1995–1996, Annex VIII (*Documents of the African Commission*, p. 449); See Communications 25/89, 47/90, 56/91 and 100/93, *Free Legal Assistance Group, Lawyers' Committee for Human Rights, Union Interafricaine des Droits de l'Homme, Les Témoins de Jehovah* v. *Zaire*, Ninth Activity Report 1995–1996, Annex VIII (*Documents of the African Commission*, p. 444), where there was torture of fifteen people by a military unit.

[54] Communications 27/89, 46/91, 49/91 and 99/93, *Organisation Mondiale Contre la Torture and Association Internationale des Juristes Democrates, Commission Internationale des Juristes (CIJ), Union Interafricaine des Droits de l'Homme* v. *Rwanda*, Tenth Activity Report 1996–1997, Annex X (*Documents of the African Commission*, p. 551), para. 26.

[55] Communications 137/94, 139/94, 154/96 and 161/97, *International Pen, Constitutional Rights Project, Interights on behalf of Ken Saro-Wiwa Jr and Civil Liberties Organisation* v. *Nigeria*, Twelfth Activity Report 1998–1999, Annex V (*Documents of the African Commission*, p. 729), paras. 79–80. See also Communications 54/91, 61/91, 98/93, 164/97–196/97 and 210/98, *Malawi African Association, Amnesty International, Ms Sarr Diop, Union Interafricaine des Droits de l'Homme and RADDHO, Collectif des Veuves et Ayants-droit, Association Mauritanienne des Droits de l'Homme* v. *Mauritania*, Thirteenth Activity Report 1999–2000, Annex V, paras. 115 and 132.

The Commission found violations of Article 5.

The Commission has gone further and also held that:

> [b]y forcing [individuals] to live as stateless persons under degrading conditions, the government . . . has deprived them of their family and is depriving their families of the men's support, and this constitutes a violation of the dignity of a human being.[56]

The Commission has held that sending armed gangs to attack human rights activists and destroying their homes violates this provision.[57]

The Commission has held that:

> holding an individual without permitting him or her to have contact with his or her family, and refusing to inform the family if and where the individual is being held, is inhuman treatment of both the detainee and the family concerned.[58]

In a case concerning Mauritania the Commission found that, although slavery had officially been abolished in that country, this was not effectively enforced by the government.[59]

THE RIGHT TO LIBERTY AND SECURITY

Article 6 provides:

> Every individual shall have the right to liberty and to the security of his person. No one may be deprived of his freedom, except for reasons and conditions

---

[56] Communication 212/98, *Amnesty International* v. *Zambia*, Twelfth Activity Report 1998–1999, Annex V (*Documents of the African Commission*, p. 745), para. 58. Strangely, however, no finding of a violation of Article 5 was made at the end of the decision.

[57] Communications 140/94, 141/94 and 145/95, *Constitutional Rights Project, Civil Liberties Organisation and Media Rights Agenda* v. *Nigeria*, Thirteenth Activity Report 1999–2000, Annex V, paras. 49 and 46.

[58] Communications 48/90, 50/91, 52/91 and 89/93, *Amnesty International, Comité Loosli Bachelard, Lawyers Committee for Human Rights, Association of Members of the Episcopal Conference of East Africa* v. *Sudan*, Thirteenth Activity Report 1999–2000, Annex V, para. 54.

[59] 'The Commission deems that there was a violation of Article 5 of the Charter due to practices analogous to slavery, and emphasises that unremunerated work is tantamount to a violation of the right to respect for the dignity inherent in the human being.' Communications 54/91, 61/91, 98/93, 164/97–196/97 and 210/98, *Malawi African Association, Amnesty International, Ms Sarr Diop, Union Interafricaine des Droits de l'Homme and RADDHO, Collectif des Veuves et Ayants-droit, Association Mauritanienne des Droits de l'Homme* v. *Mauritania*, Thirteenth Activity Report 1999–2000, Annex V, para. 135.

previously laid down by law. In particular, no one may be arbitrarily arrested or detained.

This right is aimed against arbitrary arrest and detention on the basis of recognition of the right to security of the person. To the extent that infringements are justified, they may also be done only in terms of legal rules established in advance.

The cursory manner in which the right is formulated leaves most of the crucial aspects of pre-trial detention untouched. The formulation of the right seems to draw heavily on Article 9(1) of the ICCPR, but the other subsections of that Article that relate to arrest and detention have no equivalent in the African Charter. The Commission has, however, clarified some of these issues in a number of cases. When considering the length of detention without trial, the Commission held, unsurprisingly, that imprisonment of over twelve years without trial, without the possibility of challenging this in court, constituted a violation of Article 6.[60] Three years' detention without trial[61] or even three months' may be sufficient to violate Article 6.[62] Similarly, holding individuals indefinitely will also breach the Article.[63]

In Communication 39/90, *Annette Pagnoulle (on behalf of Abdoulaye Mazou) v. Cameroon*[64] the Commission stated that holding an individual after he has served his sentence will also violate Article 6. In this case, since Cameroon ratified the African Charter after the sentence had expired, the Commission could not rule on the original imprisonment, only on its subsequent extension.

In other cases it was not so much the duration, but the grounds and manner of the detention that constituted the violation. In a case against

---

[60] See Communications 64/92, 68/92 and 78/92, *Krischna Achuthan, Amnesty International, Amnesty International v. Malawi*, Seventh Activity Report 1993–1994, Annex IX; Eighth Activity Report 1994–1995, Annex VI (*Documents of the African Commission*, pp. 347 and 387).

[61] Communication 102/93, *Constitutional Rights Project v. Nigeria*, Twelfth Activity Report 1998–1999, Annex V (*Documents of the African Commission*, p. 712).

[62] Communications 137/94, 139/94, 154/96 and 161/97, *International Pen, Constitutional Rights Project, Interights on behalf of Ken Saro-Wiwa Jr and Civil Liberties Organisation v. Nigeria*, Twelfth Activity Report 1998–1999, Annex V (*Documents of the African Commission*, p. 729), para. 83.

[63] See Communications 25/89, 47/90, 56/91 and 100/93, *Free Legal Assistance Group, Lawyers' Committee for Human Rights, Union Interafricaine des Droits de l'Homme, Les Témoins de Jehovah v. Zaire*, Ninth Activity Report 1995–1996, Annex VIII (*Documents of the African Commission*, p. 444).

[64] Eighth Activity Report 1994–1995, Annex VI; Tenth Activity Report 1996–1997, Annex X (*Documents of the African Commission*, pp. 384 and 555).

Chad[65] the Commission held that there was a violation of Article 6, presumably in the form of arbitrary arrests by the government, among others, of members of the opposition party. In another case[66] a violation of Article 6 was found on the basis of 'arrests and detentions of [presumably 'by'] the Rwandan Government' of thousands of people 'based on grounds of ethnic origin alone, in light of Article 2 in particular'.[67] Similarly, arrest and detention on the basis of one's political opinion will also contravene Article 6. In Communication 103/93[68] a political dissident had been detained without trial, before he escaped from prison. The Commission held that his detention had constituted a violation of Article 6.[69]

Depriving the courts of their ability to consider the legality of any detention will constitute a violation of Article 6. As the Commission noted in relation to the laws in Nigeria:

> All the victims were arrested and kept in detention for a lengthy period under the State Security (Detention of Persons) Act of 1984 and State Security (Detention of Persons) Amended Decree No. 14 (1994), that stipulates that the government can detain people without charge for as long as three months in the first instance. The decree also states that the courts cannot question any such detention or in any other way intervene on behalf of the detainees. This decree allows the government to arbitrarily hold people critical of the government for up to three months without having to explain themselves and without any opportunity for the complainant to challenge the arrest and detention before a court of law. The decree therefore *prima facie* violates the right not to be arbitrarily arrested or detained protected in Article 6.[70]

---

[65] See Communication 74/92, *Commission Nationale des Droits de l'Homme et des Libertés* v. *Chad*, Ninth Activity Report 1995–1996, Annex VIII (*Documents of the African Commission*, p. 449).

[66] Communications 27/89, 46/91, 49/91 and 99/93, *Organisation Mondiale Contre la Torture and Association Internationale des Juristes Democrates, Commission Internationale des Juristes (CIJ), Union Interafricaine des Droits de l'Homme* v. *Rwanda*, Tenth Activity Report 1996–1997, Annex X (*Documents of the African Commission*, p. 551).

[67] *Ibid.*, para. 28.

[68] Communication 103/93, *Alhassan Abubakar* v. *Ghana*, Tenth Activity Report 1996–1997, Annex X (*Documents of the African Commission*, p. 571).

[69] The Commission did not comment on the chilling evidence before it that the complainant's sister and his wife were detained in an attempt to get information on his whereabouts after his escape. See also Communications 140/94, 141/94 and 145/95, *Constitutional Rights Project, Civil Liberties Organisation and Media Rights Agenda* v. *Nigeria*, Thirteenth Activity Report 1999–2000, Annex V.

[70] Communications 137/94, 139/94, 154/96 and 161/97, *International Pen, Constitutional Rights Project, Interights on behalf of Ken Saro-Wiwa Jr and Civil Liberties Organisation* v.

The Commission has held that the words 'previously laid down by law' in Article 6 require a State that seeks to limit the right to liberty and security to show that such limitation is consistent with the Charter.[71] This seems to imply that the phrase in question is not only a temporal but also a substantive standard.

In Communications 143/95 and 150/96, *Constitutional Rights Project and Civil Liberties Organisation* v. *Nigeria* the Commission considered a Nigerian decree that provided for a person to be detained for a period of three months, and another decree that prohibited the writ of *habeas corpus*. The Commission found that there was a violation of Article 6.[72]

THE RIGHT TO A FAIR TRIAL

Article 7(1) provides as follows:

> Every individual shall have the right to have his cause heard. This comprises:
>
> (a) the right to an appeal to competent national organs against acts violating his fundamental rights as recognised and guaranteed by conventions, laws, regulations and customs in force;
> (b) the right to be presumed innocent until proved guilty by a competent court or tribunal;
> (c) the right to defence, including the right to be defended by counsel of his choice;
> (d) the right to be tried within a reasonable time by an impartial court or tribunal.

Although detention and trial are often the areas where systematic violations of civil and political rights occur, the African Charter deals with both the issues in an inadequate manner. The formulation of the rights in Article 7(1), as was noted in respect of Article 6 above, appears to be inadequate. Compared to, for example, Article 14 of the ICCPR, the African Charter leaves the answer to the question whether many of the crucial aspects of a fair trial need to be observed up to the creative interpretation of the Commissioners. This includes the right to a public hearing, the right to interpretation, the right against self-incrimination and the right against double jeopardy.

Nigeria, Twelfth Activity Report 1998–1999, Annex V (*Documents of the African Commission*, p. 729), para. 83.

[71] Communications 147/95 and 149/96, *Sir Dawda K. Jawara* v. *The Gambia*, Thirteenth Activity Report 1999–2000, Annex V, paras. 58 and 59.

[72] Thirteenth Activity Report 1999–2000, Annex v. paras. 22–34.

The Commission has, indeed, interpreted the Charter to include certain of these elements. There is also a suggestion that the trial should be fair as a whole: in Communication 25/89, *Free Legal Assistance Group* v. *Zaire* it was held that certain 'unfair trials' constituted a violation of Article 7, although the record does not disclose the nature of these trials.

The word 'appeal' in Article 7(1)(a) seems to refer primarily to the general right to seek a judicial remedy. In communications against Rwanda[73] the Commission held that the mass expulsion of refugees without granting them the opportunity to have their cases heard violated Article 7(1). The same conclusion was reached in Communication 71/92, *Rencontre Africaine pour la Defense des Droits de l'Homme* v. *Zambia*[74] and Communication 159/96.[75]

Communication 129/94[76] concerned decrees by the military government in Nigeria. The decrees had not only suspended the Constitution, dissolved political parties and nullified the domestic effect of the African Charter, but had also ousted the jurisdiction of the courts to examine any decree issued during the preceding ten years. The Commission held that Article 7 had been violated, commenting as follows:[77]

> The ousting of jurisdiction of the courts of Nigeria over any decree enacted in the past ten years, and those to be subsequently enacted, constitutes an attack of incalculable proportions on Article 7. The complaint refers to a few examples of decrees which violate human rights but which are now beyond review by the courts. An attack of this sort on the jurisdiction of the courts is especially invidious, because while it is a violation of human rights in itself, it permits other violations of rights to go unredressed.

---

[73] Communications 27/89, 46/91, 49/91 and 99/93, *Organisation Mondiale Contre la Torture and Association Internationale des Juristes Democrates, Commission Internationale des Juristes (CIJ), Union Interafricaine des Droits de l'Homme* v. *Rwanda*, Tenth Activity Report 1996–1997, Annex X (*Documents of the African Commission*, p. 551).

[74] Tenth Activity Report 1996–1997, Annex X (*Documents of the African Commission*, p. 563).

[75] Communication 159/96, *Union Interafricaine des Droits de l'Homme, Féderation International des Ligues des Droits de l'Homme, Rencontre Africaine des Droits de l'Homme, Organisation Nationale des Droits de l'Homme au Sénégal and Association Malienne des Droits de l'Homme* v. *Angola*, Eleventh Activity Report 1997–1998, Annex II (*Documents of the African Commission*, p. 615).

[76] Communication 129/94, *Civil Liberties Organisation* v. *Nigeria*, Ninth Activity Report 1995–1996, Annex VIII (*Documents of the African Commission*, p. 452).

[77] *Ibid.*, para. 14.

In the same case the Commission held that Article 26[78] had also been breached. It explained the relationship between Articles 7 and 26 as follows:[79]

> Article 26 of the African Charter reiterates the right enshrined in Article 7 but is even more explicit about States Parties' obligations to guarantee the independence of the Courts and allow the establishment and improvement of appropriate national institutions entrusted with the promotion and protection of the rights and freedoms guaranteed by the present Charter. While Article 7 focuses on the individual's right to be heard, Article 26 speaks of the institutions which are essential to give meaning and content to that right. This Article clearly envisions the protection of the courts which have traditionally been the bastion of protection of the individual's rights against the abuses of State power.

In relation to Article 7(1)(a) the Commission has held that the nullification of suits in progress against the government by executive decree in Nigeria constituted a violation of this provision.[80] In addition, Article 7(1)(a) could also be interpreted to encompass the right to approach a higher court to reconsider the findings of a lower court.[81] In Communication 87/93 against Nigeria[82] the Commission ruled that a decree that created a special criminal tribunal and ousted the ability of the regular courts to 'inquire' into the actions of the tribunal, violated Article 7(1)(a).[83]

---

[78] Article 26 reads: 'States Parties to the present Charter shall have the duty to guarantee the independence of the Courts and shall allow the establishment and improvement of appropriate national institutions entrusted with the promotion and protection of the rights and freedoms guaranteed by the present Charter.' According to Umozurike, *The African Charter*, p. 40 the 'institutions' referred to would include a judicial services commission to appoint judges.

[79] Communication 129/94, *Civil Liberties Organisation* v. *Nigeria*, Ninth Activity Report 1995–1996, Annex VIII (*Documents of the African Commission*, p. 452), para. 15.

[80] Communications 140/94, 141/94 and 145/95, *Constitutional Rights Project, Civil Liberties Organisation and Media Rights Agenda* v. *Nigeria*, Thirteenth Activity Report 1999–2000, Annex V, para. 33.

[81] See Ankumah, *The African Commission*, p. 124.

[82] Communication 87/93, *Constitutional Rights Project (in respect of Zamani Lakwot and 6 Others)* v. *Nigeria*, Eighth Activity Report 1994–1995, Annex VI (*Documents of the African Commission*, p. 391).

[83] *Ibid.*, para. 11. See also Communications 137/94, 139/94, 154/96 and 161/97, *International Pen, Constitutional Rights Project, Interights on behalf of Ken Saro-Wiwa Jr and Civil Liberties Organisation* v. *Nigeria*, Twelfth Activity Report 1998–1999, Annex V (*Documents of the African Commission*, p. 729), para. 93; and Communication 212/98, *Amnesty International* v. *Zambia*, Twelfth Activity Report 1998–1999, Annex V (*Documents of the African Commission*, p. 745), paras. 60 and 61.

In relation to the presumption of innocence guaranteed under Article 7(1)(b), this provision was found to have been violated in a number of cases.[84] In *Annette Pagnoulle v. Cameroon*[85] the Commission held that the detention of the complainant for two years after he had served his sentence of imprisonment on the suspicion that he 'may cause problems' was a violation of his right to be presumed innocent.

Trial without being defended was held to be a violation of Article 7(1)(c).[86] The guarantee in Article 7(1)(c) of a right to be defended by 'counsel' of one's choice is problematic, if 'counsel' is understood to mean a fully qualified and admitted lawyer.[87] It is submitted that such an interpretation should consequently be avoided, and counsel should be understood to mean 'a legal representative'. Harassment of defence counsel during a trial (although it is not clear from the record who did the harassment) to the point where the counsel withdrew from the case, was held to be a violation of Article 7(1)(c) in Communication 87/93.[88] In another case against Nigeria[89] a similar finding was made, *inter alia* on the basis of assault of the defence lawyers by soldiers.[90] It has also been held that the right to be defended by counsel of one's choice under Article 7(1)(c) implies that one has the right of access to a lawyer when being detained without trial.[91]

---

[84] Communications 137/94, 139/94, 154/96 and 161/97, *International Pen, Constitutional Rights Project, Interights on behalf of Ken Saro-Wiwa Jr and Civil Liberties Organisation v. Nigeria,* Twelfth Activity Report 1998–1999, Annex V (*Documents of the African Commission,* p. 729), para. 96.

[85] Communication 39/90, *Annette Pagnoulle (on behalf of Abdoulaye Mazou) v. Cameroon,* Eighth Activity Report 1994–1995, Annex VI; Tenth Activity Report 1996–1997, Annex X (*Documents of the African Commission,* pp. 384 and 565).

[86] Communications 64/92, 68/92 and 78/92, *Krischna Achuthan, Amnesty International, Amnesty International v. Malawi,* Seventh Activity Report 1993–1994, Annex IX; Eighth Activity Report 1994–1995, Annex VI (*Documents of the African Commission,* pp. 347 and 387).

[87] See e.g. Ankumah *The African Commission,* p. 126.

[88] Communication 87/93, *Constitutional Rights Project (in respect of Zamani Lakwot and 6 Others) v. Nigeria,* Eighth Activity Report 1994–1995, Annex VI (*Documents of the African Commission,* p. 391), para. 12.

[89] Communications 137/94, 139/94, 154/96 and 161/97, *International Pen, Constitutional Rights Project, Interights on behalf of Ken Saro-Wiwa Jr and Civil Liberties Organisation v. Nigeria,* Twelfth Activity Report 1998–1999, Annex V (*Documents of the African Commission,* p. 729).

[90] *Ibid.,* para. 97.

[91] Communications 105/93, 128/94, 130/94 and 152/96, *Media Rights Agenda and Constitutional Rights Project v. Nigeria,* Twelfth Activity Report 1998–1999, Annex V (*Documents of the African Commission,* p. 718).

In a number of cases detention without trial within a reasonable time was condemned as a violation of Article 7, and in some instances specifically the reasonable time provisions of Article 7(1)(d).[92] In Communication 103/93[93] the Commission held that seven years' detention without trial did not meet with the norm of trial 'within a reasonable time' in Article 7(1)(d). Similarly, detention without any trial was condemned as a violation of Article 7 in a case against Chad.[94]

The impartiality of the court as guaranteed in Article 7(1)(d) was dealt with by the Commission in *Constitutional Rights Project (Akamu) v. Nigeria*[95] in relation to the special tribunals that had been created to deal with cases involving robbery and firearms. The Commission held as follows:

> The Robbery and Firearms (Special Provision) Act, Section 8(1), describes the constitution of the tribunals, which shall consist of three persons: one Judge, one officer of the Army, Navy or Air Force and one officer of the Police Force. Jurisdiction has thus been transferred from the normal courts to a tribunal chiefly composed of persons belonging to the executive branch of government, the same branch that passed the Robbery and Firearms Decree, whose members do not necessarily possess any legal expertise. Article 7(1)(d) of the African Charter requires the court or tribunal to be impartial. Regardless of the character of the individual members of such tribunals, its composition alone creates the appearance of, if not actual, lack of impartiality. It thus violates Article 7(1)(d).

Appearance of partiality is consequently enough to constitute a violation. The Commission has held similarly in subsequent cases.[96]

---

[92] Communications 64/92, 68/92 and 78/92, *Krischna Achuthan, Amnesty International, Amnesty International v. Malawi,* Seventh Activity Report 1993–1994, Annex IX; Eighth Activity Report 1994–1995, Annex VI (*Documents of the African Commission,* pp. 347 and 387). The basis of the finding of a violation of Article 7 in Communication 59/91, *Embga Mekongo Louis v. Cameroon,* Eighth Activity Report 1994–1995, Annex VI (*Documents of the African Commission,* pp. 000–0), the first recorded finding of a violation by the Commission, is unclear from the record.

[93] Communication 103/93, *Alhassan Abubakar v. Ghana,* Tenth Activity Report 1996–1997, Annex X (*Documents of the African Commission,* p. 571), para. 12.

[94] See Communication 74/92, *Commission Nationale des Droits de l'Homme et des Libertés v. Chad,* Ninth Activity Report 1995–1996, Annex VIII (*Documents of the African Commission,* p. 449).

[95] Communication 60/91, *Constitutional Rights Project (in respect of Sehab Akamu, G. Adega and others) v. Nigeria,* Eighth Activity Report 1994–1995, Annex VI (*Documents of the African Commission,* p. 385).

[96] Communication 87/93, *Constitutional Rights Project (in respect of Zamani Lakwot and 6 Others) v. Nigeria,* Eighth Activity Report 1994–1995, Annex VI (*Documents of the African*

Article 7(2) adds to the protection afforded in Article 6 against retrospective laws, and provides as follows:

No one may be condemned for an act or omission which did not constitute a legally punishable offence at the time it was committed. No penalty may be inflicted for an offence for which no provision was made at the time it was committed. Punishment is personal and can be imposed only on the offender.

Retroactivity of laws was considered in a number of cases.[97] In *Media Rights Agenda* v. *Nigeria*[98] the Commission ruled that a retroactive decree violated Article 7(2) and condemned a situation where decisions of the courts were not followed as a violation of Article 7(1):

Article 7(2) must be read to prohibit not only condemnation and infliction of punishment for acts which did not constitute crimes at the time they were committed, but retroactivity itself. It is expected that citizens must take the laws seriously. If laws change with retroactive effect, the rule of law is undermined since individuals cannot know at any moment if their actions are legal. For a law-abiding citizen, this is a terrible uncertainty, regardless of the likelihood of eventual punishment.

Furthermore, the Commission unfortunately cannot rest total confidence in the assurance that no one and no newspaper has yet suffered under the retroactivity of Decree No. 43. Potential prosecution is a serious threat. An unjust but unenforced law undermines, as above, the sanctity in which the law should be held. The Commission must thus hold that Decree No. 43 violates Article 7(2). Communication 152/96 states that two different courts have declared Decree No. 43 null and void, without any result. This shows not only a shocking disrespect by the Nigerian Government for the judgments of the courts, it is also a violation of Article 7(1). The right to have one's cause heard by competent and independent courts must naturally

---

Commission, p. 391), para. 14; Communications 137/94, 139/94, 154/96 and 161/97, *International Pen, Constitutional Rights Project, Interights on behalf of Ken Saro-Wiwa Jr and Civil Liberties Organisation* v. *Nigeria,* Twelfth Activity Report 1998–1999, Annex V (*Documents of the African Commission,* p. 729), para. 95, where it was found that Article 26 had also been violated.

[97] See Communication 101/93, *Civil Liberties Organisation in respect of the Nigerian Bar Association* v. *Nigeria,* Eighth Activity Report 1994–1995, Annex VI (*Documents of the African Commission,* p. 394).

[98] Communications 105/93, 128/94, 130/94 and 152/96, *Media Rights Agenda and Constitutional Rights Project* v. *Nigeria,* Twelfth Activity Report 1998–1999, Annex V (*Documents of the African Commission,* p. 718). See also Communication 212/98, *Amnesty International* v. *Zambia,* Twelfth Activity Report 1998–1999, Annex V (*Documents of the African Commission,* p. 745), para. 44.

comprise the duty of everyone, including the State, to respect and follow these judgments.[99]

In its 'Resolution on the Right to Recourse Procedure and Fair Trial',[100] the Commission stated the following:[101]

> the right to fair trial includes, among other things, the following:
>
> . . .
>
> (2) persons who are arrested shall be informed at the time of the arrest, in a language which they understand of the reason for their arrest and shall be informed promptly of any charges against them;
>
> . . .
>
> (5) the determination of charges against individuals; the individual shall be entitled in particular to . . . (i) have adequate time and facilities for the presentation of their defence and to communicate in confidence with counsel of their choice.

The Commission stated the following in its Dakar Declaration and Recommendations:[102]

> In many African countries Military Courts and Special Tribunals exist alongside regular judicial institutions. The purpose of Military Courts is to determine offences of a pure military nature committed by military personnel. While exercising this function, Military Courts are required to respect fair trial standards. They should in no circumstances whatsoever have jurisdiction over civilians. Similarly, Special Tribunals should not try offences which fall within the jurisdiction of regular courts.

In respect of military tribunals, the Commission said:

> Independent of the qualities of the persons sitting in such jurisdictions, their very existence constitutes a violation of the principles of impartiality and independence of the judiciary and, thereby, of Article 7(1)(d).[103]

---

[99] *Ibid.*, paras. 59, 60, 61 and 62.

[100] Resolution on the Right to Recourse Procedure and Fair Trial, Fifth Annual Activity Report of the African Commission on Human and Peoples' Rights, 1991–1992, ACHPR/RPT/5th, Annex VI (*Documents of the African Commission*, p. 224).

[101] This was confirmed in Communication 206/97, *Centre for Free Speech* v. *Nigeria*, Thirteenth Activity Report 1999–2000, Annex V, para. 14 and Communication 215/98, *Rights International* v. *Nigeria*, Thirteenth Activity Report 1999–2000, Annex V, para. 29.

[102] Further to the Declaration on the Right to a Fair Trial and Legal Assistance in Africa, DOC/OS (XXVI) INF.19.

[103] Para. 98.

In this respect a couple of examples are worth mentioning. Thus, in a case concerning Sudan, the Commission found that:

> The government confirms the situation alleged by the complainants in respect of the composition of the Special Courts. National legislation permits the President, his deputies and senior military officers to appoint these courts to consist of 'three military officers or any other persons of integrity and competence'.
>
> The composition alone creates the impression, if not the reality, of lack of impartiality and as a consequence, violates Article 7(1)(d). The government has a duty to provide the structures necessary for the exercise of this right. By providing for courts whose impartiality is not guaranteed, it has violated Article 26.
>
> The dismissal of over one hundred judges who were opposed to the formation of special courts and military tribunals is not contested by the government. To deprive courts of the personnel qualified to ensure that they operate impartially thus denies the right to individuals to have their case heard by such bodies. Such actions by the government against the judiciary constitute violations of Articles 7(1)(d) and 26 of the Charter.[104]

Further, the Commission ruled in respect of Mauritania that:

> The State Security Section of the Special Tribunal does not provide for any appeal procedure. [In] two specific cases mentioned in the communications . . . no appeals were authorised. One of the trials ended in the execution of 3 army lieutenants.
>
> Furthermore, even when an appeal was allowed . . . the Court of Appeal confirmed the verdicts, even though the accused had contested the procedure of the initial trial and the Public Prosecutor's office did not contest the complaints of the accused. From all indications, the Court of Appeal simply confirmed the sentences without considering all the elements of fact and law. Such a practice cannot be considered a genuine appeal procedure. For an appeal to be effective, the appellate jurisdiction must, objectively and impartially, consider both the elements of fact and of law that are brought before it. Since this approach was not followed in the cases under consideration, the Commission considers, consequently, that there was a violation of Article 7(1)(a) of the Charter.
>
> In [another judgment] the presiding judge declared that the refusal of the accused persons to defend themselves was tantamount to an admission of guilt. In addition, the tribunal based itself, in reaching the verdicts it handed

---

[104] Communications 48/90, 50/91, 52/91 and 89/93, *Amnesty International, Comité Loosli Bachelard, Lawyers Committee for Human Rights, Association of Members of the Episcopal Conference of East Africa* v. *Sudan*, Thirteenth Activity Report 1999–2000, Annex V, paras. 68–9.

down, on the statements made by the accused during their detention in police cells, which statements were obtained from them by force. This constitutes a violation of Article 7(1)(b).

In most of the cases . . . the accused either had no access or had restricted access to lawyers, and the latter had insufficient time to prepare the defence of their clients. This constitutes a violation of Article 7(1)(c) on the right to defence.

The right to defence should also be interpreted as including the right to understand the charges being brought against oneself. In the trial on the September Manifesto (para. 3), only 3 of the 21 accused persons spoke Arabic fluently, and this was the language used during the trial. This means that the 18 others did not have the right to defend themselves; this also constitutes a violation of Article 7(1)(c).[105]

FREEDOM OF CONSCIENCE

Article 8 provides as follows:

> Freedom of conscience, the profession and free practice of religion shall be guaranteed. No one may, subject to law and order, be submitted to measures restricting the exercise of these freedoms.

The provision 'subject to law and order' defines a substantive norm against which limitation of the right may be tested and as such does not constitute a classical 'clawback clause' as defined above. In accordance with international standards in this regard, freedom of conscience and religion must also encompass a right to change one's religion. In a case against Zaire,[106] the Commission found that the harassment of Jehovah's Witnesses through arbitrary arrests, appropriation of church property and exclusion from access to education (also a socio-economic right) constituted a violation of Article 8. Similarly, in *Amnesty International v. Zambia*[107] the Commission appeared to hold that the deportation of political opponents, in addition

---

[105] Communications 54/91, 61/91, 98/93, 164/97–196/97 and 210/98, *Malawi African Association, Amnesty International, Ms Sarr Diop, Union Interafricaine des Droits de l'Homme and RADDHO, Collectif des Veuves et Ayants-droit, Association Mauritanienne des Droits de l'Homme v. Mauritania*, Thirteenth Activity Report 1999–2000, Annex V, paras. 93–7.

[106] Communications 25/89, 47/90, 56/91 and 100/93, *Free Legal Assistance Group, Lawyers' Committee for Human Rights, Union Interafricaine des Droits de l'Homme, Les Témoins de Jehovah v. Zaire*, Ninth Activity Report 1995–1996, Annex VIII (*Documents of the African Commission*, p. 444).

[107] Communication 212/98, *Amnesty International v. Zambia*, Twelfth Activity Report 1998–1999, Annex V (*Documents of the African Commission*, p. 745), para. 54, read with the holding at the end of the decision.

to constituting transgressions of other Articles of the Charter, constituted a violation of their freedom of conscience.

In dealing with a case against Sudan, the Commission has held that freedom of religion – in that case, the freedom to apply *Shari'a* law – has to be exercised in a way that does not violate the equal protection of the laws, as guaranteed by the African Charter. *Shari'a* trials may not be imposed, and everyone should have the right to be tried by a secular court if they wish.[108]

THE RIGHT TO INFORMATION AND FREEDOM OF EXPRESSION

Article 9 provides:

1. Every individual shall have the right to receive information.
2. Every individual shall have the right to express and disseminate his opinions within the law.

The right to receive information as provided by Article 9(1) was dealt with in *Amnesty International* v. *Zambia*,[109] where the Commission said that the failure of the government to provide two deportees with reasons for the action taken against them 'means that the right to receive information was denied to them'.[110]

Freedom of expression as defined in Article 9(2) is not subjected to special duties, as is the case in the ICCPR[111] or the European Convention,[112] and does not contain explicit exceptions in respect of hate speech.[113] However, it is subject to a clawback clause and could consequently easily be made subjected to these.

---

[108] Communications 48/90, 50/91, 52/91 and 89/93, *Amnesty International, Comité Loosli Bachelard, Lawyers Committee for Human Rights, Association of Members of the Episcopal Conference of East Africa* v. *Sudan*, Thirteenth Activity Report 1999–2000, Annex V, para. 73.

[109] Communication 212/98, *Amnesty International* v. *Zambia*, Twelfth Activity Report 1998–1999, Annex V (*Documents of the African Commission*, p. 745).

[110] However, the Commission at the end of the decision did not hold that there was a violation of Article 9(1). In the same case the Commission's position in respect of freedom of expression under Article 9(2) was even more confusing, since it found a violation after making the following statement: 'The Commission has to determine whether the "deportations", being politically motivated, violate the provisions of Article 9(2) of the African Charter as the two victims were denied the right to freedom of conscience as stipulated in Article 8 of the Charter'. Communication 212/98, *Amnesty International* v. *Zambia*, Twelfth Activity Report 1998–1999, Annex V (*Documents of the African Commission*, p. 745).

[111] Article 19.   [112] Article 10(2).   [113] See Article 20 of the ICCPR.

In *Media Rights Agenda* v. *Nigeria*,[114] the Abachan military government in Nigeria had proscribed by decree the publication of two magazines and ten newspapers. The Newspapers Registration Board was also given an absolute and unchallengeable discretion as to whether newspapers could be registered, and publication without registration was a criminal offence. This decree applied retroactively. Journalists were detained. The Commission held that Article 9 had been violated, and that the violation was not permitted by the clawback clause in that Article.[115] The Commission also advanced the position, which is in line with international jurisprudence in this regard, but nevertheless significant in the African context, that those in public life should expect less protection from free expression than other people:[116]

> The only person whose reputation was perhaps tarnished by the article was the head of State. However, in the [absence] of evidence to the contrary, it should be assumed that criticism of the government does not constitute an attack on the personal reputation of the head of State. People who assume highly visible public roles must necessarily face a higher degree of criticism than private citizens; otherwise public debate may be stifled altogether.
>
> It is important for the conduct of public affairs that opinions critical of the government be judged according to whether they represent a real danger to national security. If the government thought that this particular article represented merely an insult towards it or the head of State, a libel action would have been more appropriate than the seizure of the whole edition of the magazine before publication. The seizure of the TELL therefore amounts to a violation of Article 9(2).

It appears from the above that the Commission uses the test of whether an expression poses a 'real danger' before it permits it to be curtailed. In another case against Nigeria[117] the Commission agreed with the proposition advanced on behalf of the complainants that they were 'expressing' themselves peacefully through their association with a political grouping and through the rally that they had organised. Holding that '[t]here is a close

---

[114] Communications 105/93, 128/94, 130/94 and 152/96, *Media Rights Agenda and Constitutional Rights Project* v. *Nigeria*, Twelfth Activity Report 1998–1999, Annex V (*Documents of the African Commission*, p. 718).

[115] *Ibid.*, paras. 66 and 71.   [116] *Ibid.*, paras. 74 and 75.

[117] Communications 137/94, 139/94, 154/96 and 161/97, *International Pen, Constitutional Rights Project, Interights on behalf of Ken Saro-Wiwa Jr and Civil Liberties Organisation* v. *Nigeria*, Twelfth Activity Report 1998–1999, Annex V (*Documents of the African Commission*, p. 729).

relationship between the rights expressed in Articles 9(2), 10(1) and 11',[118] the Commission found that Article 9 had also been violated, in addition to the other violations, because the eventual murder trial was aimed against the political rallies that Saro-Wiwa and his associates had organised.[119]

In *Constitutional Rights Project, Civil Liberties Organisation and Media Rights Agenda* v. *Nigeria*,[120] the Commission dealt with the proscription of newspapers through executive decree by the military government in Nigeria, as part of its broader clampdown on opposition. The Commission held that:[121]

> Freedom of expression is a basic human right, vital to an individual's personal development and political consciousness, and participation in the conduct of public affairs in his country. Under the African Charter, this right comprises the right to receive information and express opinion.

The Commission continued:[122]

> The proscription of specific newspapers by name and the sealing of their premises, without a hearing at which they could defend themselves, or any accusation of wrongdoing, legal or otherwise, amounts to harassment of the press. Such actions not only have the effect of hindering the directly affected persons in disseminating their opinions, but also pose an immediate risk that journalists and newspapers not yet affected by . . . the Decree will subject themselves to self-censorship in order to be allowed to carry on their work.

Moreover:[123]

> Decrees like these pose a serious threat to the public of the right to receive information not in accordance with what the government would like the public to know. The right to receive information is important: Article 9 does not seem to permit derogation, no matter what the subject of the information or opinions and no matter the political situation of a country. Therefore, the Commission finds that the proscription of the newspapers is a violation of Article 9(1).

---

[118] *Ibid.*, para. 110.

[119] *Ibid.*, para. 110. Somewhat enigmatically, the Commission stated that '[t]he Government's action is inconsistent with Article 9(2) implicit when it violated Articles 10(1) and 11'.

[120] Communications 140/94, 141/94 and 145/95, Thirteenth Activity Report 1999–2000, Annex V.

[121] *Ibid.*, para. 36.   [122] *Ibid.*, para. 37.   [123] *Ibid.*, para. 38.

In relation to Article 9(2) the Commission said:[124]

> According to Article 9(2) of the Charter, dissemination of opinions may be restricted by law. This does not, however, mean that national law can set aside the right to express and disseminate one's opinions guaranteed at the international level; this would make the protection of the right to express one's opinion ineffective. To permit national law to take precedence over international law would defeat the purpose of codifying certain rights in international law and indeed, the whole essence of treaty making.

Thus, in respect of the coup government of The Gambia, the Commission held:

> The intimidation and arrest or detention of journalists for articles published and questions asked deprives not only the journalists of their rights to freely express and disseminate their opinions, but also the public, of the right to information. This action is clearly a breach of the provisions of Article 9 of the Charter.[125]

Similarly, in respect of Sudan the Commission has found as follows:[126]

> The Commission has established the principle that where it is necessary to restrict rights, the restriction should be as minimal as possible and not undermine fundamental rights guaranteed under international law. Any restrictions on rights should be the exception. The Government here has imposed a blanket restriction on the freedom of expression. This constitutes a violation of the spirit of Article 9(2).

In a case against Mauritania the Commission stated that, since a document that was distributed to protest about racial discrimination did not contain any incitement to violence, it should be protected.[127]

---

[124] *Ibid.*, para. 40.

[125] Communications 147/95 and 149/96, *Sir Dawda K. Jawara v. The Gambia*, Thirteenth Activity Report 1999–2000, Annex V, para. 65.

[126] Communications 48/90, 50/91, 52/91 and 89/93, *Amnesty International, Comité Loosli Bachelard, Lawyers Committee for Human Rights, Association of Members of the Episcopal Conference of East Africa v. Sudan*, Thirteenth Activity Report 1999–2000, Annex V, para. 80.

[127] Communications 54/91, 61/91, 98/93, 164/97–196/97 and 210/98, *Malawi African Association, Amnesty International, Ms Sarr Diop, Union Interafricaine des Droits de l'Homme and RADDHO, Collectif des Veuves et Ayants-droit, Association Mauritanienne des Droits de l'Homme v. Mauritania*, Thirteenth Activity Report 1999–2000, Annex V, para. 102.

FREEDOM OF ASSOCIATION

Article 10 provides as follows:

1. Every individual shall have the right to free association provided that he abides by the law.
2. Subject to the obligation of solidarity provided for in Article 29, no one may be compelled to join an association.

This right traditionally encompasses the right to join or form trade unions and political parties. Article 10(1), contains a clawback clause, but in respect of the right against forced association this is supplemented by Article 10(2), which sets out the substantive requirement that must be met before limitations of the right are acceptable, with reference to Article 29. Article 29 provides as follows:

The individual shall also have the duty:

1. to preserve the harmonious development of the family and to work for the cohesion and respect of the family, to respect his parents at all times, to maintain them in case of need;
2. to serve his national community by placing his physical and intellectual abilities at its service;
3. not to compromise the security of the State whose national or resident he is;
4. to preserve and strengthen social and national solidarity, particularly when the latter is threatened;
5. to preserve and strengthen the national independence and the territorial integrity of his country and to contribute to its defence in accordance with the law;
6. to work to the best of his abilities and competence, and to pay taxes imposed by law in the interest of the society;
7. to preserve and strengthen positive African cultural values in his relations with other members of the society, in the spirit of tolerance, dialogue and consultation and, in general, to contribute to the promotion of the moral well-being of society;
8. to contribute to the best of his abilities, at all times and at all levels, to the promotion and achievement of African unity.

The question arises, to what does the phrase 'obligation of solidarity provided for in Article 29' in Article 10(2) refer? Does it refer to Article 29(4) only, since the word 'solidarity' is used only in that paragraph of Article 29, or does it refer to other duties contained in Article 29 which also have a component of solidarity, such as Article 29(8), since the drafters could easily have stated that they had Article 29(4) in mind if that was their intention? It is submitted that Article 10(2) refers to Article 29(4), in view of the explicit use of the word 'solidarity' in Articles 10(2) and 29(4) and the fact that reference is made to the 'obligation of solidarity' in the singular form in Article 10(2).[128] Be that as it may, this provides a good illustration of how a duty can limit a right, in that forced association could be justified at least in order to strengthen social and national solidarity.

Communication 101/93, *Civil Liberties Organisation in Respect of the Nigerian Bar Association* v. *Nigeria*[129] involved a decree which created a new governing body for the Nigerian Bar Association, called the 'Body of Benchers'. It seems that membership of this body by legal practitioners was compulsory. The Body of Benchers was controlled by the government, and had the power to levy fees and discipline legal practitioners. In spite of the clawback clause in Article 10, the Commission found that the Charter had been violated because international standards in respect of freedom of association had been violated.[130] The Commission in effect found that the right to association also implied a right of dissociation, which had been violated.[131] In making this finding, the Commission also referred to its own resolution on the 'Right to Freedom of Association'.[132]

In another case[133] the Commission found that the tribunal which had convicted Saro-Wiwa and his fellow accused of murder did so because of their membership of a political grouping. This constituted guilt by association, and in the process their freedom of association, as expressed through their membership of that grouping, was violated.[134]

---

[128] However, in order to give meaning to Article 29(4) it might be necessary to make reference to the other paragraphs, and they are consequently indirectly referred to.

[129] Eighth Activity Report 1994–1995, Annex VI (*Documents of the African Commission*, p. 394).

[130] See above.

[131] Communication 101/93, *Civil Liberties Organisation in respect of the Nigerian Bar Association* v. *Nigeria*, Eighth Activity Report 1994–1995, Annex VI (*Documents of the African Commission*, p. 394), para. 17.

[132] Resolution on the Right to Freedom of Association, adopted by the African Commission on Human and Peoples' Rights, at its 11th Ordinary Session (*Documents of the African Commission*, p. 225).

[133] Communications 137/94, 139/94, 154/96 and 161/97, *International Pen, Constitutional Rights Project, Interights on behalf of Ken Saro-Wiwa Jr and Civil Liberties Organisation* v. *Nigeria*, Twelfth Activity Report 1998–1999, Annex V (*Documents of the African Commission*, p. 729).

[134] *Ibid.*, para. 108. See also Communication 212/98, *Amnesty International* v. *Zambia*, Twelfth Activity Report 1998–1999, Annex V (*Documents of the African Commission*, p. 745), para. 57.

The Commission has also found that banning political parties violates Article 10,[135] as is the case where a complainant is sought by the police as a result of his political belief,[136] and where 'any assembly for a political purpose in a private or a public place' is prohibited.[137] In this respect, the Commission has held that:

> any law on associations should include an objective description that makes it possible to determine the criminal nature of a fact or organisation.[138]

THE RIGHT TO ASSEMBLE FREELY WITH OTHERS

Article 11 provides:

> Every individual shall have the right to assemble freely with others. The exercise of this right shall be subject only to necessary restrictions provided for by law, in particular those enacted in the interest of national security, the safety, health, ethics and rights and freedoms of others.

Although the usual requirement, that the assembly must be peaceful, is absent, the presence of such a requirement could be inferred from the limitation in the Article according to which only legal provisions with objectives of a certain kind (including national security) can restrict the right.

Thus, in Communications 147/95 and 149/96, *Sir Dawda K. Jawara v. The Gambia*, it was held that a ban on political parties violates the right to assemble freely with others.[139]

---

[135] Communications 147/95 and 149/96, *Sir Dawda K. Jawara v. The Gambia*, Thirteenth Activity Report 1999–2000, Annex V, para. 68.

[136] Communication 205/97, *Kazeem Aminu v. Nigeria*, Thirteenth Activity Report 1999–2000, Annex V, para. 22.

[137] Communications 48/90, 50/91, 52/91 and 89/93, *Amnesty International, Comité Loosli Bachelard, Lawyers Committee for Human Rights, Association of Members of the Episcopal Conference of East Africa v. Sudan*, Thirteenth Activity Report 1999–2000, Annex V, para. 82.

[138] Communications 54/91, 61/91, 98/93, 164/97–196/97 and 210/98, *Malawi African Association, Amnesty International, Ms Sarr Diop, Union Interafricaine des Droits de l'Homme and RADDHO, Collectif des Veuves et Ayants-droit, Association Mauritanienne des Droits de l'Homme v. Mauritania*, Thirteenth Activity Report 1999–2000, Annex V, para. 107.

[139] *Ibid.*, para. 69. Also see Communications 54/91, 98/93, 164/97–196/97 and 210/98, *Malawi African Association, Amnesty International, Ms Sarr Diop, Union Interafricaine des Droits de l'Homme and RADDHO, Collectif des Veuves et Ayants-droit, Association Mauritanienne des Droits de l'Homme v. Mauritania*, Thirteenth Activity Report 1999–2000, Annex V, paras. 108–11.

In a very loosely worded paragraph in Communication 137/94, the Commission appears to have made the finding that Ken Saro-Wiwa and his fellow accused were convicted of murder because they organised a meeting at which four chiefs were murdered and that Article 11 had as a consequence been violated.[140]

FREEDOM OF MOVEMENT

Article 12 provides:

1. Every individual shall have the right to freedom of movement and residence within the borders of a State provided he abides by the law.
2. Every individual shall have the right to leave any country including his own, and to return to his country. This right may only be subject to restrictions, provided for by law for the protection of national security, law and order, public health or morality.
3. Every individual shall have the right, when persecuted, to seek and obtain asylum in other countries in accordance with the laws of those countries and international conventions.
4. A non-national legally admitted in a territory of a State Party to the present Charter, may only be expelled from it by virtue of a decision taken in accordance with the law.
5. The mass expulsion of non-nationals shall be prohibited. Mass expulsion shall be that which is aimed at national, racial, ethnic or religious groups.

Articles 12(1) and (2) are based largely on the similarly numbered provision in the ICCPR. Article 12(3) is unusual in the sense that it provides that one has the right not only to seek but also to obtain asylum.

The Commission has ruled that Nigeria violated Article 12, where a complainant had fled his country due to abductions and threats.[141] Travel restrictions on former politicians also violate this Article.[142] The same applies to evictions from homes and the deprivation of citizenship.[143]

---

[140] Communications 137/94, 139/94, 154/96 and 161/97, *International Pen, Constitutional Rights Project, Interights on behalf of Ken Saro-Wiwa Jr and Civil Liberties Organisation* v. *Nigeria*, Twelfth Activity Report 1998–1999, Annex V (*Documents of the African Commission*, p. 729), para. 106.

[141] Communication 215/98, *Rights International* v. *Nigeria*, Thirteenth Activity Report 1999–2000, Annex V, para. 30.

[142] Communications 147/95 and 149/96, *Sir Dawda K. Jawara* v. *The Gambia*, Thirteenth Activity Report 1999–2000, Annex V, para. 70.

[143] Communications 54/91, 61/91, 98/93, 164/97–196/97 and 210/98, *Malawi African Association, Amnesty International, Ms Sarr Diop, Union Interafricaine des Droits de l'Homme*

THE RIGHT OF POLITICAL PARTICIPATION

Article 13(1) provides:

> Every citizen shall have the right to participate freely in the government of his country, either directly or through freely chosen representatives in accordance with the provisions of the law.

It becomes clear how limited the scope and reach of this provision is when it is compared to the comparable provisions of the ICCPR, contained in Article 25:

> Every citizen shall have the right and the opportunity, without any of the distinctions mentioned in Article 2 and without unreasonable restrictions:
>
> (a) to take part in the conduct of public affairs, directly or through freely chosen representatives;
> (b) to vote and to be elected at genuine periodic elections which shall be by universal and equal suffrage and shall be held by secret ballot, guaranteeing the free expression of the will of the electors . . .

Although Article 13(1) of the African Charter appears to be based on Article 25(a) of the ICCPR, Article 25(b) of the ICCPR has no explicit equivalent in the African Charter. The omission could not have been accidental, but will have to be rectified through creative interpretation or an amendment to the Charter.[144]

Article 13(1) should be read with Article 20(1), which recognises the right of peoples to self-determination in the following terms:

> All peoples shall have the right to existence. They shall have the unquestionable and inalienable right to self-determination. They shall freely determine their political status and shall pursue their economic and social development according to the policy they have freely chosen.

Article 13(1) was referred to by the Commission in passing in a case concerning peoples' rights in the context of the attempted secession from Zaire by

and RADDHO, *Collectif des Veuves et Ayants-droit, Association Mauritanienne des Droits de l'Homme* v. *Mauritania*, Thirteenth Activity Report 1999–2000, Annex V, para. 126.

[144] Article 10(1), which recognises the right of freedom of association, seems to support the idea that one cannot be compelled to belong to (and perhaps also to vote for) a particular political party – provided Article 10(2) is not used to undermine this approach. See Umozurike, *The African Charter*, p. 39.

Katanga.[145] In that case the Commission declared that there was no violation of Article 20. The Commission determined that:

> In the absence of concrete evidence of violations of human rights to the point that the territorial integrity of Zaire should be called into question and in the absence of evidence that the people of Katanga are denied the right to participate in government as guaranteed by Article 13(1) of the African Charter, the Commission holds the view that Katanga is obliged to exercise a variant of self-determination that is compatible with the sovereignty and territorial integrity of Zaire.[146]

The implication appears to be that massive human rights violations as well as the denial of the right of political participation under Article 13(1) could constitute transgressions of the Charter on such a scale that it would justify secession.[147]

In *Constitutional Rights Project* v. *Nigeria*[148] the Commission found that Nigeria had violated Article 13(1) when it annulled national elections, holding:[149]

> To participate freely in government entails, among other things, the right to vote for the representative of one's choice. An inevitable corollary of this right is that the results of free expression of the will of the voters are respected; otherwise, the right to vote freely is meaningless. In light of this, the annulment of the election results, which reflected the free choice of the voters, is in violation of Article 13(1).

According to Article 13(2) 'Every citizen shall have the right of equal access to the public service of his country.' Articles 13(1) and (2) are the only rights which are granted exclusively to citizens. Article 13(3) provides as follows:

> Every individual shall have the right of access to public property and services in strict equality of all persons before the law.

---

[145] Communication 75/92, *Katangese Peoples' Congress* v. *Zaire*, Eighth Activity Report 1994–1995, Annex VI (*Documents of the African Commission*, p. 388).

[146] *Ibid.*, para. 6.

[147] The following statement in Communications 105/93, 128/94, 130/94 and 152/96, *Media Rights Agenda and Constitutional Rights Project* v. *Nigeria*, Twelfth Activity Report 1998–1999, Annex V (*Documents of the African Commission*, p. 718), para. 80, although reference is made to a 'peoples' right', is also relevant in this context: 'Government by force is in principle not compatible with the rights of peoples freely to determine their political future.' This is a very weak condemnation of military rule.

[148] Communication 102/93, *Constitutional Rights Project* v. *Nigeria*, Twelfth Activity Report 1998–1999, Annex V (*Documents of the African Commission*, p. 712).

[149] *Ibid.*, para. 50.

According to Ankumah paragraph (3) is included in Article 13, which deals with the right to political participation, because it is meant to counter a system of political patronage, whereby access to public property is restricted to those in favour with those in power.[150] Presumably, these provisions will not be read as blanket prohibitions on affirmative action.

In Communications 147/95 and 149/96, *Sir Dawda K. Jawara* v. *The Gambia*, the Commission found that a ban on members of the former government and parliament after a coup in The Gambia was a violation of their Article 13(1) rights.[151] The coup itself was held to be a violation of Article 20(1):

> The military coup was therefore a grave violation of the right of [the] Gambian people to freely choose their government as entrenched in Article 20(1) of the Charter.[152]

THE RIGHT TO PROPERTY

Article 14 provides:

> The right to property shall be guaranteed. It may only be encroached upon in the interest of public need or in the general interest of the community and in accordance with the provisions of appropriate laws.

The objectives of legitimate limitations are set out in this provision and it is required that these limitations are imposed in accordance with law. It should be noted that no explicit reference is made to a need for compensation in any form. The case of mass expulsion of West Africans from Angola referred to above[153] also entailed the loss of property by those expelled. The Commission held that this constituted a violation of their right to property. In one case against Nigeria[154] the Commission found a violation

---

[150] Ankumah, *The African Commission*, p. 141.

[151] Thirteenth Activity Report 1999–2000, Annex V, para. 67.

[152] *Ibid.*, para. 73.

[153] Communication 159/96, *Union Interafricaine des Droits de l'Homme, Féderation International des Ligues des Droits de l'Homme, Rencontre Africaine des Droits de l'Homme, Organisation Nationale des Droits de l'Homme au Sénégal and Association Malienne des Droits de l'Homme* v. *Angola*, Eleventh Activity Report 1997–1998, Annex II (*Documents of the African Commission*, p. 615).

[154] Communications 105/93, 128/94, 130/94 and 152/96, *Media Rights Agenda and Constitutional Rights Project* v. *Nigeria*, Twelfth Activity Report 1998–1999, Annex V (*Documents of the African Commission*, p. 718).

of Article 14, based on the government's sealing up of the premises of a number of publications, and defined the right as follows:

> The right to property necessarily includes a right to have access to property of one's own and the right that one's property not be removed. The decrees which enabled these premises to be sealed up and for publications to be seized cannot be said to be 'appropriate' or in the interest of the public or the community in general. The Commission holds a violation of Article 14. In addition, the seizure of the magazines for reasons that have not been shown to be in the public need or interest also violates the right to property.[155]

In Communications 140/94, 141/94 and 145/95, *Constitutional Rights Project, Civil Liberties Organisation and Media Rights Agenda v. Nigeria*, which also concerned the sealing up of the premises of publications, the Commission held:

> The government did not offer any explanation for the sealing up of the premises of many publications, but maintained the seizure in violation of direct court orders. Those affected were not previously accused or convicted in court of any wrongdoing. The right to property necessarily includes a right to have access to one's property and the right not to have one's property invaded or encroached upon. The Decrees which permitted the newspapers' premises to be sealed up and publications to be seized cannot be said to be 'appropriate' or in the interest of the public or the community in general. The Commission finds a violation of Article 14.[156]

The confiscation and looting of the property of black Mauritanians has been held to violate Article 14.[157]

OTHER RIGHTS

To the extent that family rights are to be considered as civil and political rights reference should be made to Article 18:

> 1. The family shall be the natural unit and basis of society. It shall be protected by the State which shall take care of its physical health and moral [*sic*].

---

[155] *Ibid.*, para. 77.   [156] Thirteenth Activity Report 1999–2000, Annex V, para. 54.
[157] Communications 54/91, 61/91, 98/93, 164/97–196/97 and 210/98, *Malawi African Association, Amnesty International, Ms Sarr Diop, Union Interafricaine des Droits de l'Homme and RADDHO, Collectif des Veuves et Ayants-droit, Association Mauritanienne des Droits de l'Homme v. Mauritania*, Thirteenth Activity Report 1999–2000, Annex V, paras. 127–8.

2. The State shall have the duty to assist the family which is the custodian of morals and traditional values recognised by the community.

In Communication 143/95 and 150/96, *Constitutional Rights Project and Civil Liberties Organisation* v. *Nigeria*, it was held that it is a violation of Article 18 to prevent a detainee from communicating with his family.[158] The Commission has also held that:

Holding people in solitary confinement both before and during the trial, and during such detention, which is, on top of it all, arbitrary (paras. 5, 8, 10, 11 and 12), depriving them their right to a family life constitutes a violation of Article 18(1).[159]

Conclusion

It appears that the civil and political rights jurisprudence of the Commission, although it constitutes the main activity of the Commission in respect of individual communications, is still in embryonic stage. The Commission is faced with the difficult task of overcoming the shortcomings in the way in which the Charter has been drafted, and it has shown some willingness to be creative in this regard. However, at the moment the Commission's creativity does not reach far beyond simply reading internationally accepted principles into the Charter. This is done, ironically it should be added, without explicitly recognising the largely European sources on which they mostly appear to rely. Perhaps the best one could call for at the moment is indeed that the Charter be given a modern interpretation by applying international standards. However, the Commission should at least cast its net beyond the relatively tranquil waters of Europe, and start looking at, for example, the Inter-American system.[160]

Ultimately, one would hope that Africa, through the Commission and the Court, will be bold enough to make a unique contribution towards international human rights jurisprudence – not only by coining phrases

---

[158] Thirteenth Activity Report 1999–2000, Annex V, para. 29.

[159] Communications 54/91, 61/91, 98/93, 164/97–196/97 and 210/98, *Malawi African Association, Amnesty International, Ms Sarr Diop, Union Interafricaine des Droits de l'Homme and RADDHO, Collectif des Veuves et Ayants-droit, Association Mauritanienne des Droits de l'Homme* v. *Mauritania*, Thirteenth Activity Report 1999–2000, Annex V, para. 124.

[160] See F. Viljoen, 'The Relevance of the Inter-American Human Rights System for Africa', *African Journal of International and Comparative Law* 11 (1999) 659.

such as 'peoples' rights' which keep philosophers busy, but in developing a distinct African jurisprudence which influences the way in which courts, lawyers, politicians and ordinary people on the continent act in everyday cases.[161]

The Commission has had to invent its own monitoring capacities;[162] it now has to focus on making the substantive rights workable.

[161] See C. H. Heyns, 'African Human Rights Law and the European Convention', *South African Journal of Human Rights* 11 (1995) 252–63.
[162] Neither the individual communications nor the reporting capacities of the Commission were clearly provided for in the African Charter.

6

IMPLEMENTING ECONOMIC, SOCIAL AND CULTURAL RIGHTS UNDER THE AFRICAN CHARTER ON HUMAN AND PEOPLES' RIGHTS

CHIDI ANSELM ODINKALU[*]

Introduction

Any meaningful discussion of economic, social and cultural rights under the African Charter on Human and Peoples' Rights[1] must overcome the triple barrier of pessimism, history and ideology. The perception of the African regional human rights systems generally has to some degree been shaped by and filtered through a pessimism about Africa that often consigns the continent to a fate worse than making peace with both mediocrity and despondency.[2] The treaty framework and institutional arrangements of

---

[*] I gratefully acknowledge the helpful research assistance and insights of Susi Crawford, LLM Class, 1999/2000, University College London, and Ibrahima Kane, Legal Officer, Interights. Nobuntu Mbelle of the Board of Directors of the Human Rights Committee of South Africa (an NGO) and Emma Playfair, Executive Director of Interights, proffered a most helpful critique of an early draft of this chapter. Fola Adamolekun, JD Class, 2002, Columbia University, assisted in researching economic, social and cultural rights provisions in the national constitutions of African States. The views expressed here are the author's alone and do not necessarily reflect the opinions or policies of Interights or any of the above-named persons. This chapter was mostly written in the hilarious company of my no-longer-so-little friend and son Dilim. It is dedicated to the survival of his generation of Africans.

[1] African Charter on Human and Peoples' Rights, adopted 27 June 1981, OAU Doc. CAB/LEG/67/3.Rev.5, entered into force on 21 October 1986, reprinted in ILM 21 (1982) 59 (hereinafter the 'African Charter' or the 'Charter').

[2] Paraphrasing James Baldwin, 'My Dungeon Shook: Letter to My Nephew on the One Hundredth Anniversary of the Emancipation', in J. Baldwin, *The Fire Next Time* (Penguin Books in association with Michael Joseph, 1963), p. 16. 'You were not expected to aspire to excellence: you were expected to make peace with mediocrity': *ibid*. This pessimism is symbolised by the *Economist* of 21 May 2000, which carried the cover 'Hopeless Africa', under which it wrote: 'Does Africa have some inherent character flaw that keeps it backward and incapable of development? Some think so. They believe Africa's wars, corruption and tribalism are "just the way Africa is", and that African societies are unable to sustain viable

the African Charter in particular have thus been beset from their inception with doubts about their credibility, efficacy and relevance to the continent.[3] Some early writers and commentators doubted 'whether the Charter will ever come into force'.[4] Latterly, others have questioned whether the African Commission on Human and Peoples' Rights,[5] the oversight and implementation mechanism created by the Charter, has the 'power, resources and willingness' to fulfil its functions.[6] The power of the Commission to consider petitions alleging individual violations of human and peoples' rights,[7] to provide a remedy for such violations,[8] and to monitor through a public examination of periodic reports States Parties' compliance with Charter obligations,[9] have all at different times similarly been called into question. The perception of the African regional system that is often conveyed in much of the available literature is something of a juridical misfit with a treaty basis that is dangerously inadequate and an institutional mechanism liable, ironically, to be slated as errant when it pushes the envelope of interpretation positively.

Pessimism and history come together in the opinion of a leading African scholar who once dismissed the entire Charter as 'a façade, a yoke that African leaders have put around our necks',[10] and called on like-minded

States. In the past, outsiders would have described Africa's failure in racial terms. Some still do. They are wrong, but social and cultural factors cannot be discounted.' See 'The Heart of the Matter', www.economist.com/editorial/freeforall/current/sf3364.html, visited 18 May 2000.

[3] Victor Dankwa, the former Chairman of the African Commission on Human and Peoples' Rights, recalls that 'serious violations of civil and political rights . . . led all the commentators to the erroneous conclusion that human rights was not a major concern of African States'. See V. Dankwa, 'The African Charter on Human and Peoples' Rights: Hopes and Fears', in *The African Charter on Human and Peoples' Rights: Development, Context, Significance* (Marburg: African Law Association, 1990), p. 1 at pp. 4–5.

[4] O. Ojo and A. Sesay, 'The OAU and Human Rights: Prospects for the 1980s and Beyond', *Human Rights Quarterly* 8 (1989) 101.

[5] Hereinafter the 'Commission'.

[6] C. E. Welch Jr, 'The African Charter and Freedom of Expression in Africa', *Buffalo Human Rights Law Review* 4 (1998) 103 at 115.

[7] R. Murray, 'Decisions by the African Commission on Human and Peoples' Rights on Individual Communications under the African Charter on Human and Peoples' Rights', *International and Comparative Law Quarterly* 46 (1997) 412 at 413.

[8] W. Benedek, 'The African Charter and Commission on Human and Peoples' Rights: How to Make it More Effective', NQHR 11 (1993) 25 at 31.

[9] Welch, 'The African Charter', p. 115.

[10] M. wa Mutua, 'The African Human Rights System in Comparative Perspective', *Review of the African Commission on Human and Peoples' Rights* 3 (1993) 5 at 10.

peoples and interests to 'cast it off and reconstruct a system that we [Africans] can proudly proclaim as ours'.[11] This view was no doubt influenced by the peculiar circumstances of the adoption of the Charter, which happened during an era of particularly egregious human rights violations around Africa.[12] Although it declared the pursuit of 'freedom, equality, justice and dignity' to be the 'legitimate aspirations of African peoples', the Charter of the Organization of African Unity (OAU) placed a particular premium on the preservation of the independence and sovereign integrity of African States, and the corollary principle of non-interference in the affairs of these States[13] at the expense of protection of the citizens of the continent. As dictators in single party States or of the military kind – and in some cases of both hues[14] – hardly any of the African leaders who participated in the negotiation and adoption of the Charter in Nairobi in 1981 could claim a democratic mandate. With a few exceptions such as the late Julius Nyerere of Tanzania and former President Kenneth Kaunda of Zambia who did not enrich themselves through high political office, most of these rulers were also widely suspected of impoverishing their own peoples through a combination of wrong-headed policies and brazen corruption at a time when the priority of the leadership of the continent was not the protection of the individual but the preservation of their own personal power and influence in the territories inherited from the then recently departed metropolitan colonial powers.[15] The combined legacy of its chequered colonial and post-colonial history

[11] *Ibid.*

[12] For an account of the political background to the Charter, see E. Kannyo, 'The Banjul Charter on Human and Peoples' Rights: Genesis and Political Background', in C. E. Welch Jr and R. I. Meltzer (eds.), *Human Rights and Development in Africa* (Albany: State University of New York Press, 1984), p. 128; R. Gittleman, 'The African Charter on Human and Peoples' Rights: A Legal Analysis', *Virginia Journal of International Law* 22 (1982) 667.

[13] Charter of the Organization of African Unity (OAU), reprinted in ILM 2 (1963) 766, Preamble and Articles II and III.

[14] Presidents Kerekou and Eyadema, of Benin Republic and Togo respectively, were just two examples at the time of military rulers of single party States.

[15] J. Oloka-Onyango, 'Beyond the Rhetoric: Reinvigorating the Struggle for Economic and Social Rights in Africa', *California Western International Law Journal* 26 (1995) 1 at 42–3; C. M. Peter, *Human Rights in Africa: A Comparative Study of the African Human and Peoples' Rights Charter and the New Tanzanian Bill of Rights* (Greenwood Press, 1990), pp. 7–10; R. Howard, 'The Full Belly Thesis: Should Economic Rights Take Priority Over Civil and Political Rights? Evidence from Sub-Saharan Africa', *Human Rights Quarterly* 9 (1987) 467; A. N. M. Abdullahi, 'Human Rights Protection in Africa: Towards Effective Mechanisms', *East Africa Journal of Peace and Human Rights* 3 (1997) 1.

continues today to haunt Africa through the unacceptably rampant incidence of mass impoverishment, disease, unemployment, under-development, political instability, conflict, and cyclic, gross and massive violations of human rights.[16]

Notwithstanding the early affirmation of the indivisibility of human rights in the Proclamation of Tehran in 1968,[17] the negotiation of the African Charter over a decade later would be riven with the traditional ideological disputes as to the status of economic, social and cultural rights.[18] The African Charter was the product of the ideological cleavages of the Cold War and reflects a compromise between the ideological and belief systems represented at its negotiation. These diverse interests were described by one author as including 'atheists, animists, Christians, Hindus, Jews and Muslims; and . . . over fifty countries and islands with Marxist-Leninist, capitalist, socialist, military, one-party and democratic regimes'.[19] Before the adoption of the Charter, these ideological disputes had undermined the realisation of the integrated vision of human rights articulated in the Universal Declaration of Human Rights,[20] resulting in the bifurcation of the international human rights treaty regimes when the international human rights covenants were unveiled in 1966.[21] In the somewhat hierarchical templates for analysing human rights that have since ensued, a substantial body of opinion consigned – and continues to consign – economic, social and cultural rights to a 'second-rate

---

[16] Twenty-four of the twenty-five poorest States in the world and thirty-eight of the fifty poorest States on the basis of the most current Human Development Index are parties to the African Charter. See United Nations Development Programme, *Human Development Report* (2000), pp. 157–60.

[17] Proclamation of Tehran, UN Sales No. E.68.XIV.2 (1968), Article 13; reaffirmed and updated in the Vienna Declaration and Programme of Action, UN World Conference on Human Rights, 14–25 June 1993, UN Doc. A/CONF.157/24 (Part 1), Article 5.

[18] Acknowledging this ideological dispute, the South African Constitutional Court stated as recently as 1996 that economic, social and cultural rights were 'not universally accepted fundamental rights'. See *Re Certification of the Constitution of the Republic of South Africa*, Butterworths Constitutional Law Reports *(CC)* 10 (1996) 1253 at 1290 (hereinafter referred to as 'the *South African Constitution Certification* case').

[19] Dankwa, 'The African Charter', p. 8.

[20] The Universal Declaration of Human Rights, 10 December 1948, GA Res. 217A, UN GAOR, 3rd Session, Part 1, Resolutions, p. 71, UN Doc. A/810 (1948) (hereinafter 'the UDHR').

[21] See C. Scott, 'Reaching Beyond (Without Abandoning) the Category of Economic, Social and Cultural Rights', *Human Rights Quarterly* 21 (1999) 633 at 634, where the author calls for 'a return to the original promise of the UDHR: human dignity should be pursued in the light of both the overarching purposes and the underlying values of human rights protection, rather than under the constraint of false dichotomies'.

status',[22] in some cases denying their intrinsic character as rights or their capacity to create obligations binding on States in international law.[23]

Another reflection of the ideological cleavages that afflict this field is what appears to be a recent tendency among activists as well as academics and researchers to excise 'cultural' from 'economic, social and cultural rights'. This results in a disavowal of culture both as a human right and as a context that determines the enjoyment of all other rights. This effect is achieved by a fashionable fission of economic, social and cultural rights, yielding a palatable category of 'economic and social rights' on the one hand, and a deniable (and therefore emasculated) category of 'cultural rights' on the other. Underlying this is an often unstated explanation that culture and cultural rights are the preoccupation of the political/ideological right. Alternatively, it reflects the discomfort of some northern or mostly neo-liberal constituencies unable to shake off a hangover from the colonial project, with its ill-concealed bias for Western interpretations of Christian cultures. This exercise introduces additional layers of complication, privilege and exclusion into the already bizarrely exclusionary 'categories' of human rights norms. Far from being a neutral position, this tendency is itself culturally and politically biased. It cedes strategic political ground to opposing ideological camps in shaping the content of culture as an evolving human experience. The increasing tendency to exclude culture from references to human rights reinforces the marginalisation of the poor, the underprivileged, rural dwellers generally, and rural women in particular, all victims of the negative interpretations of culture as an assertion of dominant power. These people are ironically the theoretical beneficiaries of what is otherwise portrayed as a progressive ideological position on culture. Moreover, implicit in this tendency also is the assumption, entirely unfounded in experience or theory, that culture or the rights asserted in its name or flowing from its assertion, can be severed from the universe of human rights.[24] Racism, sexism, slavery and religious

[22] G. J. H. van Hoof, 'The Legal Nature of Economic, Social and Cultural Rights: A Rebuttal of Some Traditional Views', in P. Alston and K. Tomasevski (eds.), *The Right to Food* (Utrecht: Stichting studie- en Informatiecentrum mensenrechten, 1984).

[23] For an excellent discussion and rebuttal of these views, see *ibid.*, pp. 98–102; and C. Scott and P. Macklem, 'Constitutional Ropes of Sand or Justiciable Guarantees? Social Rights in a New South African Constitution', *University of Pennsylvania Law Review* 141 (1992) 1 at 43–75.

[24] Thus while language, for instance, is an expression of culture, and language-related rights are, therefore, cultural rights, the use of language is central to the right to freedom of expression. Access to language is often a matter of the economic capacity of the different people which is related to political rights and social status. These relationships between the different

discrimination are only four examples of exclusion and human rights violations that are founded in and justified by reference to culture. It remains true that, while the values that underlie human rights are unarguably universal, the effective implementation of these rights is necessarily culturally mediated.[25] For these reasons, the nomenclature of economic, social and cultural rights is preserved and used in this chapter.

Contemporary work on economic, social and cultural rights is a prisoner of sorts to the muddled normative framework created by the International Covenant on Economic, Social and Cultural Rights (ICESCR),[26] as the international human rights instrument created by the initial fission of the human rights family. It is equally beholden to the ideological disputes on the nature of economic, social and cultural rights, itself the product of a deeper philosophical controversy regarding the nature of human autonomy and the role of the State and government in our lives.[27] In a formulation that defies both comprehension and interpretation, the Covenant requires States Parties in Article 2(1) 'to take steps, individually and through international assistance and co-operation, especially economic and technical, to the maximum of its available resources, with a view to achieving progressively the full realisation of the rights recognised in the present Covenant by all appropriate means, including particularly the adoption of legislative measures'.[28] Evidencing the intellectual and policy constipation that is induced by this formulation, one writer has described Article 2(1) of the ICESCR as 'a difficult phrase – two warring adjectives describing an undefined noun',[29] while

dimensions of language-related rights are not easily disentangled. For a study on the multiple relationships of free expression to culture, politics and economics, see S. Fish, *There's No Such Thing as Free Speech and It's a Good Thing Too* (Oxford University Press, 1994).

[25] See A. An-Na'im, 'The Cultural Mediation of Human Rights: The Al-Arqam Case in Malaysia', in J. E. Bauer and D. A. Bell (eds.), *The East Asian Challenge for Human Rights* (Cambridge and New York: 1999), p. 147.

[26] The International Covenant on Economic, Social and Cultural Rights, UN GA Res. 2200 (XXI), UN GAOR, 21st Session, Supp. No. 16, UN Doc. A/6316, adopted 16 December 1966, entered into force 3 January 1976, 993 UNTS 3 (hereinafter 'ICESCR' or the 'Covenant').

[27] I. Berlin, 'Two Concepts of Liberty', in I. Berlin, *Four Essays on Liberty* (Oxford Paperbacks, 1969), p. 118.

[28] ICESCR, Article 2(1). The Committee on Economic, Social and Cultural Rights articulated and published its interpretation of this provision in its 'General Comment No. 3 on Article 2 para. 1: The Nature of States Parties Obligations', adopted by the Committee on Economic, Social and Cultural Rights, 14 December 1990, UN Doc. E/1991/23.

[29] R. E. Robertson, 'Measuring State Compliance with the Obligation to Devote "Maximum Available Resources" to Realizing Economic, Social and Cultural Rights', *Human Rights Quarterly* 16 (1994) 694 at 713.

another dismisses the rights endorsed by the Covenant as 'of such a nature as to be legally negligible'.[30] Although this text was the result of a peculiar Cold War compromise,[31] it continues to dominate and overshadow the understanding of economic, social and cultural rights as one of those monuments that ensure that the Cold War will never quite be consigned to the cemetery of mere memory.

In reflecting on the implementation of economic, social and cultural rights under the African Charter, it is important to bear this baggage in mind without necessarily, however, dwelling on them. It is also useful to recall that the African regional human rights system was preceded by the two regional human rights systems of the Americas and Europe. The European Convention on the Protection of Human Rights and Fundamental Freedoms[32] avoided economic, social and cultural rights as such although the European Court on Human Rights increasingly finds itself saddled with petitions alleging violations of economic, social and cultural rights.[33] The articulation of these rights in Europe was left to the less judicial mechanisms of the European Social Charter,[34] and, to a lesser extent, to the so-called human dimension of the Organization for Security and Cooperation in Europe (OSCE).[35]

[30] E. Vierdag, 'The Legal Nature of the Rights Granted by the International Covenant on Economic, Social and Cultural Rights', *Netherlands Yearbook of International Law* 9 (1978) 69.

[31] For some of the drafting history of this Article, see P. Alston and G. Quinn, 'The Nature and Scope of States Parties' Obligations Under the International Covenant on Economic, Social and Cultural Rights', *Human Rights Quarterly* 9 (1987) 156. The analysis of these authors is reflected in the General Comment 3 of the Committee on Economic, Social and Cultural Rights on the Nature of States Parties' Obligations, paras. 1–2.

[32] The European Convention on the Protection of Human Rights and Fundamental Freedoms, 4 November 1950, 213 UNTS 221 (hereinafter the 'European Convention').

[33] See, for instance, *Akdivar and Others* v. *Turkey, Butterworths Human Rights Cases* 1 (1996) 137 in which the European Court of Human Rights addressed claims involving forced evictions as a violation of the right to privacy in Article 8 of the European Convention. For an insight into how the mechanisms of the Convention are adjusting to the challenge of addressing very basic violations of economic, social and cultural rights in the Council of Europe countries, see A. Reidy, F. Hampson and K. Boyle, 'Gross Violations of Human Rights: Invoking the European Convention on Human Rights in the Case of Turkey', *Netherlands Quarterly on Human Rights* 15 (1997) 161.

[34] The European Social Charter, 18 October 1961, 529 UNTS 89, entered into force 26 February 1965.

[35] See A. Bloed, 'The Human Dimension of the OSCE: Past, Present and Prospects', *OSCE Office for Democratic Institutions and Human Rights (ODIHR) Bulletin* 3 (1995) 16; A. Bloed (ed.), *From Helsinki to Vienna: Basic Documents of the Helsinki Process* (The Hague: Martinus

In the Americas, the American Declaration of the Rights and Duties of Man[36] contained elaborate provisions on economic, social and cultural rights which were, however, not repeated as such when the Inter-American regional human rights system was given a treaty basis in the Inter-American Convention on Human Rights in 1969.[37] Adopting an even more curious variant of the 'progressive realisation' formulation in the ICESCR, Article 26 of the Inter-American Convention merely required the States Parties thereto:

> to adopt measures both internally and through international co-operation, especially those of an economic and technical nature, with a view to achieving progressively, by legislation or other appropriate means, the full realisation of the rights *implicit in* the economic, social, educational, scientific, and cultural standards set forth in the Charter [of the Organization of American States].[38]

In 1988, the General Assembly of the Organization of American States (OAS) eventually adopted a Protocol on Economic, Social and Cultural Rights (the San Salvador Protocol) which reduced into due treaty form, economic, social and cultural rights recognised in the Inter-American human rights system. This Protocol took eleven years to attain trigger ratification, only entering into force at the end of 1999.[39] It enumerates several rights as economic, social and cultural rights and provides for a reporting obligation as the principal implementation and monitoring mechanism for the rights enumerated.[40] The responsibility for this monitoring rests not with the core

---

Nijhoff, 1990). The OSCE replaced and succeeded the former Conference on Security and Cooperation in Europe (CSCE) in 1995. For an understanding of the evolution from the CSCE to the OSCE, see 'The Budapest Summit Declaration: Towards a Genuine Partnership in a New Era, 6 December 1994', *Human Rights Law Journal* 15 (1994) 449.

[36] Res. XXX, 9th International Conference of American States, Bogota, Colombia, 30 March to 2 May 1948, Final Act, p. 38.

[37] Inter-American Convention on Human Rights (the Pact of San José), 22 November 1969, OAS Off. Rec., OEA. Ser.L/V/IL.23, Doc. 21 rev.6 (1979), entered into force 18 July 1978 (hereinafter the 'Inter-American Convention').

[38] *Ibid.*, Article 26 (emphasis added). For a discussion of the evolution of economic, social and cultural rights in the Inter-American human rights system, see M. Craven, 'The Protection of Economic, Social and Cultural Rights Under the Inter-American System of Human Rights', in D. Harris and S. Livingstone (eds.), *The Inter-American System of Human Rights* (Oxford University Press, 1998), p. 289.

[39] Additional Protocol to the Inter-American Convention on Human Rights in the Area of Economic, Social and Cultural Rights (the Protocol of San Salvador), adopted on 14 November 1988, entered into force 16 November 1999, reprinted in I. Brownlie (ed.), *Basic Documents on Human Rights* (3rd edn, Oxford University Press, 1992), p. 521.

[40] *Ibid.*, Article 19(1).

institutions of the Inter-American human rights system – the Court and the Commission – but with the Inter-American Economic and Social Council and the Inter-American Council for Education, Science and Culture.[41] Under the San Salvador Protocol, the case and complaints procedures of the Inter-American Commission and Court of Human Rights are available solely for the protection of trade union rights and the right to education.[42]

The concept and vision of economic, social and cultural rights that emerges from these standards is both outdated and clearly polluted by ideology no longer relevant to our post-ideological world. Quite apart from refusing to recognise the indivisibility of human rights as human experience, these standards currently limit *a priori* the options for implementing economic, social and cultural rights and, in so doing, deny that the implementation of human rights is a dynamic project that is and must be enriched by the experience of succeeding generations. Against this background, this chapter seeks to demonstrate that the African Charter on Human and Peoples' Rights represents a significantly new and challenging normative framework for the implementation of economic, social and cultural rights, placing the implementing institutions of the Charter and human rights advocates working in or on Africa in a position to pioneer imaginative approaches to the realisation of these rights. The chapter begins with an examination of the scope and essential features of these rights under the Charter. Thereafter, I proceed to describe and analyse how the African Commission has protected or elaborated these rights or, more appropriately, sought to do so through the implementation options – State reporting, case-based and advisory – conferred on the Commission by the Charter. This section will show an integrated approach to the interpretation and implementation of these rights in the emerging jurisprudence of the Commission that is commended to other international and regional human rights mechanisms as well as to national courts and human rights institutions. I will conclude with comments on the prospects for the advancement of economic, social and cultural rights in Africa, addressing the respective roles of the States Parties, civil society and non-governmental actors, and the Commission in this process.

The focus on economic, social and cultural rights in this chapter is only a convenient tool of presentation and analysis rather than an acceptance of the implicit premise that there are different categories or hierarchies of rights. The analytical framework deployed here takes its bearing from

---

[41] *Ibid.*, Article 19(2).   [42] *Ibid.*, Article 19(6).

the affirmation in the Vienna Declaration and Plan of Action that all human rights are 'indivisible, and interrelated, and interdependent'.[43] In effect, each right, however formulated, is at once civil, political, economic, social and cultural, all of which aspects together define its essential character and content.[44] Economic, social and cultural rights are, as a result, not just normative standards embodying legal obligations in and of themselves, but also have implications for the methodology and philosophy that we deploy in interpreting, explaining or communicating all rights including those that are traditionally regarded as civil and political in the literature. In addition, therefore, to examining those rights regarded traditionally as economic, social and cultural, I also explore here the ways in which the African regional system has operationalised the economic, social and cultural aspects of those rights traditionally – but erroneously – regarded as exclusively civil and political. Primary reliance will be placed on the Charter and on the work or records of the work of the African Commission on Human and Peoples' Rights including its resolutions, decisions, recommendations, communiqués and publications available as at the end of the first half of 2000. As secondary sources, I also rely on relevant comparative and international standards and case materials as appropriate.[45]

The normative framework for economic, social and cultural rights in the African charter

Leopold Sedar Senghor, then President of Senegal and a driving force behind the adoption of the Charter, set the parameters for economic, social and cultural rights in the Charter when he requested the experts who met to draft the Charter in Dakar, the capital of Senegal in 1979, to 'keep constantly in mind our values of civilisation *and the real needs of Africa*'.[46] The document which

---

[43] See note 17 above. The Final Declaration adopted by the African Regional Preparatory Meeting of the World Conference on Human Rights went further in asserting that: 'The principle of the indivisibility of human rights is sacrosanct. Civil and political rights cannot be dissociated from economic, social and cultural rights. None of these rights takes precedence over the others.' Report of the Regional Meeting for Africa of the World Conference on Human Rights, Tunis, 2–6 November 1992, A/CONF.157/PC57 A/CONF. 157/AFRM/14, 24 November 1992, para. 6.

[44] M. Delmas Marty, *Trois defis pour un droit mondial* (Paris: 1998), pp. 44–60.

[45] Cf. African Charter, Articles 60 and 61.

[46] Address of President Leopold Senghor to the Dakar Meeting of Experts Preparing the Draft African Charter on Human and Peoples' Rights, OAU Doc. CAB/LEG/67/X, reprinted

resulted at the end of the drafting process contains unique characteristics that departed significantly from the orthodoxies of the era.[47] The preamble to the Charter lays down the marker in expressing the conviction that:

> it is henceforth essential to pay a particular attention to the right to development and that civil and political rights cannot be disassociated from economic, social and cultural rights in their conception as well as universality and that the satisfaction of economic, social and cultural rights is a guarantee for the enjoyment of civil and political rights.[48]

This formulation went much further than was implied in the principles of universality, indivisibility and interdependence of human rights that were acknowledged in varying degrees in the Charter's preamble, and appeared to suggest that the Charter would accord priority to economic, social and cultural rights over the so-called civil and political rights.[49] An early writer on the Charter indeed feared that this result would 'undoubtedly grant a State great latitude',[50] presumably to restrict or violate civil and political rights. This sentiment was clearly unduly alarmist as the governments then in power in Africa hardly needed to appeal to an unknown regional instrument to justify their well-publicised excesses in power. This sentiment nevertheless reflected the prevalent misunderstanding and suspicion of the nature of economic, social and cultural rights and their place in the human rights universe.

Building on the principle of indivisibility and interdependence of human rights, the African Charter in its main text addresses economic, social and cultural rights at four levels.

CROSS-CUTTING RIGHT

First, the Charter guarantees cross-cutting rights which straddle, underlie or facilitate the exercise of both civil and political rights and economic, social

---

in P. Kunig, W. Benedek and C. R. Mahalu (eds.), *Regional Protection of Human Rights by International Law: The Emerging African System* (Baden-Baden: Nomos Verlagsgesellschaft, 1985), p. 121 (emphasis added).

[47] R. M. D'Sa, '"Human and Peoples"' Rights: Distinctive Features of the African Charter', *Journal of African Law* 29 (1985) 72.

[48] Preamble to the African Charter, para. 8.

[49] *Ibid.*, especially the clause about the satisfaction of economic, social and cultural rights being a *guarantee* for the enjoyment of civil and political rights.

[50] Gittleman, 'The African Charter', p. 687.

and cultural rights. These include the prohibition against discrimination,[51] as well as the rights to equality before the law,[52] life[53] and human dignity.[54] About this right, Arthur Chaskalson, the current President of the South African Constitutional Court, has described the right to human dignity as 'a foundational value of the constitutional order'[55] and 'a value implicit in almost all the rights enumerated in the Universal Declaration',[56] arguing that human rights can only be protected in a State in which 'there is not only equality of rights but also equality of dignity'.[57] There cannot be dignity in life without food, housing, work and livelihood.[58] The

[51] African Charter, Article 2. See Communication 422/90 etc., *Aduayom and Others* v. *Togo, Butterworths Human Rights Cases* 1 (1996) 653 at 658 (Human Rights Committee).

[52] African Charter, Article 3. In the Canadian case of *Canada* v. *Schachter*, No. 21889, cited in Scott and Macklem, 'Constitutional Ropes of Sand or Justiciable Guarantees?', p. 67, the Supreme Court describes 'the equality right' as 'a hybrid of sorts since it is neither purely positive nor purely negative. In some cases, it will be proper to characterise (it) as providing positive rights.'

[53] African Charter, Article 4. In the case of *Mohini Jain* v. *State of Karnataka* [1992] 3 SCR 658 at 669 *per* Kuldip Singh J, the Indian Supreme Court founded a constitutionally protected right to education in the right to life and held, for instance, that the ' "[r]ight to life" is the compendious expression for all those rights which the courts must enforce because they are basic to the dignified enjoyment of life. It extends to the full range of conduct which the individual is free to pursue. The right to education flows directly from the right to life. The right to life under Article 21 [of the Constitution of India] and the dignity of an individual cannot be assured unless it is accompanied by the right to education. The State government is under an obligation to make endeavour to provide educational facilities at all levels to its citizens.' See also *Olga Tellis* v. *Bombay Municipal Corp.* [1987] LRC 351 at 368–9, in which the Indian Supreme Court derived a right to livelihood from the right to life; and *Shantisar Builder* v. *Totame* [1990] AIR (SC) 630, finding a right to shelter in the right to life.

[54] African Charter, Article 5.

[55] A. Chaskalson, 'Human Dignity as a Foundational Value of the Constitutional Order', 3rd Bram Fischer Memorial Lecture, Johannesburg, May 2000.

[56] *Ibid.*, p. 12.   [57] *Ibid.*, p. 28.

[58] *Ibid.* See also E. Harvey, 'A Mockery of our Constitution', *Mail and Guardian* (South Africa), 15–22 July 2000. In *Bandhua Mukti Morcha* v. *Union of India and Others* [1984] 2 SCR 67, the Indian Supreme Court held that 'the right to live with human dignity . . . must include protection of the health and strength of workers, men and women, and of the tender age of children against abuse, opportunities and facilities for children to develop in a healthy manner and in conditions of freedom and dignity, educational facilities, just and humane conditions of work and maternity relief'.

Charter also prohibits slavery,[59] including 'practices analogous to slavery',[60] and requires fair trial and due process.[61] The African Commission has, thus, declared the right to fair trial to be 'a fundamental right, the non-observance of which undermines all other human rights'.[62] Other rights in this category include freedom of expression,[63] and the right to freedom of information,[64] described by the United Nations Human Rights Committee as 'the cornerstones in any free and democratic society',[65] and the freedom of association and assembly, which is the basis of trade union rights.[66]

'NEW' RIGHTS

Next, the Charter recognises new rights of mostly economic, social or cultural import, which are not covered by other international human rights regimes to which African States are party. These rights, found in Articles 13 and 14 of the Charter, include the rights to participate in the government

---

[59] African Charter, Article 5.

[60] Communications 54/91, 61/91, 98/93, 164/97, 196/97 and 210/98, *Malawi African Association, Amnesty International, Ms Sarr Diop, Union InterAfricaine des Droits de l'Homme, RADDHO, Collectif des Veuves et Ayants-droit & Association Mauritanienne des Droits de l'Homme* v. *Mauritania* (Merits), Thirteenth Annual Activity Report 1999–2000, AHG/222 (XXXVI) Addendum 136, 158 (July 2000) (hereinafter the '*Mauritania* cases').

[61] African Charter, Article 7. See, for instance, the decisions of the European Court of Human Rights in *Deumeland* v. *Germany*, Series A, No. 120; (1986) 8 EHRR 448, relating to due process guarantees in the determination of entitlement to social security. See also A. W. Bradley, 'Social Security and the Right to Fair Hearing: The Strasbourg Perspective' (1987) *Public Law* 3. In *Gideon* v. *Wainwright*, 372 US 335, the United States Supreme Court affirmed the existence of a constitutional right to legal assistance for indigent criminal defendants.

[62] Resolution on the Right to A Fair Trial and Legal Assistance in Africa, adopting the Dakar Declaration on the Right to a Fair Trial in Africa, DOC/OS(XXVI)INF.19.

[63] African Charter, Article 9(2). [64] *Ibid.*, Article 9(1).

[65] Communication 422/90 etc., *Aduayom and Others* v. *Togo, Butterworths Human Rights Cases* 1 (1996) 653 at 658 (Human Rights Committee). See also the *South African Constitution Certification* case, p. 1291, affirming that access to information not only facilitates the exercise of other rights but also 'ensure[s] that there is open and accountable administration at all levels of government'.

[66] African Charter, Articles 10 and 11. The African Commission has held that there is a close relationship between the rights to free expression, freedom of association and freedom of assembly under Articles 9, 10 and 11 of the Charter. See Communications 137/94, 139/94, 154/96 and 161/97, *International Pen, Constitutional Rights Project, Interights on behalf of Ken Saro-Wiwa Jr and Civil Liberties Organisation* v. *Nigeria*, Twelfth Activity Report 1998–1999, Annex V, para. 109 (*Documents of the African Commission*, p. 729).

of one's country,[67] of access to the public service of one's country,[68] and of access to public property and services,[69] all of which the Human Rights Committee have held to entail an obligation on the State to avoid discrimination or persecution on grounds of political opinion or expression.[70]

The inclusion of the right to property in Article 14 of the Charter has been criticised as being 'of questionable facility in the African context'[71] because of the complex mix of tenural regimes in post-colonial African societies and the tendency of the protection of property to favour entrenched interests. In response to this, it may be said that Article 14 contains what is undoubtedly the most far-reaching clawback clause in the Charter. This is, however, perhaps the only one of such clauses in the Charter that is justified on the basis of the historical experience of the continent. This is especially true of those societies that experienced settler-colonialism, accompanied as it was by arbitrary and widespread population transfers and deprivation of communal land holdings. Among the permissible grounds for encroaching on the right to property, the Charter recognises the interests of the public need as well as the general interest of the community, without necessarily imposing any express obligations in respect of compensation.[72] A decision as to what is permitted by this provision is clearly open to debate and competing interpretations. It would also be subject to the prevailing political climate in the State that invokes this provision. Dictatorships and democracies alike may easily get away with an oppressive application of the provision in the absence of a active civic advocacy that is both in touch with local communities and prepared to transcend artificial dichotomies between categories of human rights. Any project of land reform that fails to find justification in the provisions of Article 14 will struggle to find legitimacy as just, equitable or desirable.

---

[67] African Charter, Article 13(1). This is reinforced by the guarantee in Article 20 of the Charter of a right to all peoples of the right to 'freely determine their political status . . . according to the policy they have freely chosen'. *Ibid.*, Article 20(1). The African Commission has established that military coups subvert and violate these provisions. See the decision of the Commission in Communication 147/95 and 149/96, *Sir Dawda K. Jawara* v. *The Gambia* (Merits), Thirteenth Annual Activity Report, Annex V, p. 95. Read in the context of the entire Charter, these provisions include a right to commercial participation in the social and economic development of one's country.

[68] *Ibid.*, Article 13(2).   [69] *Ibid.*, Article 13(3).

[70] Communication 422/90 etc., *Aduayom and Others* v. *Togo, Butterworths Human Rights Cases* 1 (1996) 653 at 658 (Human Rights Committee).

[71] Onyango, 'Beyond the Rhetoric', p. 49.

[72] Cf. African Charter, Article 21(2), which imposes a duty to provide 'adequate compensation' in case of spoliation.

CLASSIC ECONOMIC, SOCIAL AND CULTURAL RIGHTS

The African Charter also provides for the classic or traditional economic, social and cultural rights. The distinguishing feature of the Charter in this respect is that it declined to bifurcate human rights at a time when this was the staple of international law. Instead, it articulates a truly indivisible and interdependent normative framework, addressing all rights equally in the same coherent text. Among the classic economic, social and cultural rights guaranteed by the Charter are the right to work under equitable and satisfactory conditions,[73] and to equal pay for equal work.[74] The Charter also protects the right to health, guaranteeing that 'every individual shall have the right to enjoy the best attainable state of physical and mental health'.[75] It obliges States Parties to 'take the necessary measures'[76] to protect the health of their people and ensure that all receive medical attention when they are sick.[77] The specific obligation in Article 16(2) on States Parties to ensure that their people receive medical attention when they are sick supplements the more general obligation in the same provision on States to take the necessary measures to protect the health of their people. It does not exclude primary or prophylactic healthcare. The spectrum of necessary measures that States Parties are obliged to take is indicated in Article 1 of the Charter in which the States Parties undertake, *inter alia*, to adopt legislative and other measures to give effect to the rights guaranteed in the Charter.[78] Article 17 of the Charter deals with the right to education,[79] and the right of individuals to take part in the cultural life of their communities.[80] The Charter contains no express guarantees of the rights to social security, food, an adequate standard of living or housing, or prohibition of forced labour. However, these are not outside the scope of interpretative possibilities open to the instrument and would be well covered by a combined reading of Articles 5 and 15–17 of the Charter.[81]

Joe Oloka-Onyango criticises the Charter provisions on economic, social and cultural rights as 'a significant letdown from the promise of the Preamble'.[82] This criticism fails to take adequate account of the

---

[73] African Charter, Article 15.   [74] *Ibid.*   [75] *Ibid.*, Article 16(1).
[76] *Ibid.*, Article 16(2).   [77] *Ibid.*   [78] African Charter, Article 1.
[79] *Ibid.*, Article 17(1).   [80] *Ibid.*, Article 17(2).
[81] Y. Klerk, 'Forced Labour and the African Charter on Human and Peoples' Rights', in *The African Charter on Human and Peoples' Rights: Development, Context, Significance* (Marburg: African Law Association, 1990), p. 230 at pp. 234 *et seq.*
[82] Onyango, 'Beyond the Rhetoric', p. 51.

interconnectedness and seamlessness of the rights contained in the Charter as well as the implementation and interpretative latitude that the Charter grants to the African Commission.[83] When these are factored into the analysis, the only limitations which will be seen to exist in the horizon of what is achievable in the realm of economic, social and cultural rights under the African Charter would be the imagination, political will and organisational skills of its implementing organ, the African Commission on Human and Peoples' Rights, its personnel and the States Parties.

WOMEN, TRADITION AND CULTURE

Article 18 of the Charter contains provisions that oblige States Parties to protect the family as 'the natural unit and basis of society'.[84] It requires States Parties also to assist the family as the 'custodian of moral and traditional values recognised by the community'.[85] Article 18(3) then requires States Parties to 'ensure the elimination of every discrimination against women and also ensure the protection of the rights of women and the child as stipulated in international declarations and conventions'.[86] Reflecting widespread African communitarian values, the Charter guarantees to the aged and the disabled the right 'to special measures of protection in keeping with their physical and moral needs'.[87] In furtherance of the rights of the aged, the Charter imposes duties on the individual to, among other things, 'respect his parents at all times' and 'maintain them in times of need'.[88]

Article 18 of the Charter has attracted mixed reviews arising from the juxtaposition of women in its provisions with the quite complex and controversial notions of the family, tradition and morality.[89] One view is that

---

[83] See Klerk, 'Forced Labour', p. 85.   [84] African Charter, Article 18(1).

[85] *Ibid.*, Article 18(2). For a comparative analysis of the concept of the family in international human rights law, see T. Nhlapo, 'International Protection of Human Rights and the Family: African Variations on a Common Theme', *International Journal of Law and the Family* 3 (1989) 11.

[86] African Charter, Article 18(3).   [87] *Ibid.*, Article 18(4).

[88] *Ibid.*, Article 29(1). For a study of the influence of African cultures in the framing of the Charter, see M. wa Mutua, 'The Banjul Charter and the African Cultural Fingerprint: An Evaluation of the Language of Duties', *Virginia Journal of International Law* 35 (1995) 339.

[89] See C. Beyani, 'Towards a More Effective Guarantee of Women's Rights in the African Human Rights System', in R. Cook (ed.), *Human Rights of Women: National and International Perspectives* (University of Pennsylvania Press, 1994), p. 285; F. Butegwa, 'Using the African Charter on Human and Peoples' Rights to Secure Women's Access to Land in Africa',

Article 18 consigns the human rights of women in Africa to a 'legal coma'.[90] Another commentator interprets Article 18 as having undertaken the pioneering task in international human rights law of 'collapsing the dichotomy between the private and public spheres'.[91]

Article 18 of the African Charter is further proof of the permeability of human rights. Its place in the Charter clearly excludes a design to consign women to the private cultural sphere or exclude them from the general framework of rights guaranteed by the Charter.[92] On the contrary it is an attempt to address the peculiar historical burdens that this exclusion has imposed on women. Article 18 can only be understood in the context of the entire text of the African Charter which is also remarkable in its use of asexual, gender-neutral language.[93] It is noteworthy in this context that the Charter requires the Commission in interpreting the Charter to take account of 'African practices *consistent with international norms on human and peoples' rights*'.[94]

Article 18 of the Charter dramatises the unique dilemmas confronted by international human rights law in addressing the diverse cultural contexts in which human rights are defined and enjoyed.[95] Although it remains capable of generating impassioned, competing and even contradictory interpretations, Article 18 does not freeze culture in a time capsule and cannot do so.[96] It is thus both possible and desirable to develop progressive interpretations of Article 18 that protect the dignity and human rights of women.[97] For,

in Cook, *ibid.*, p. 495 at pp. 503–4; Onyango, 'Beyond the Rhetoric', p. 47, footnote 294; Nhlapo, 'International Protection of Human Rights'; L. Kois, 'Article 18 of the African Charter on Human and Peoples' Rights: A Progressive Approach to Women's Human Rights', *East Africa Journal of Peace and Human Rights* 3 (1997) 92.

[90] K. Elmadmad, 'The Rights of Women Under the African Charter on Human and Peoples' Rights', in W. Benedek and W. Heinz (eds.), *Regional Systems of Human Rights in Africa, America, and Europe: Proceedings of the Conference* (Friedrich Naumann Stiftung, 1992), p. 17.

[91] Onyango, 'Beyond the Rhetoric', p. 47, footnote 294.   [92] *Ibid.*

[93] African Charter, Article 42(1), which empowers the members of the African Commission to the Commission's 'Chairman and Vice-Chairman'. Article 18 is cited as the inspiration for ongoing work on the drafting of a protocol on the human rights of women additional to the African Charter. See African Commission on Human and Peoples' Rights, Draft Protocol to the African Charter on the Rights of Women in Africa, DOC/OS(XXVII)159b (1999), Preamble, para. 3.

[94] *Ibid.*, Article 61 (emphasis added).

[95] An-Na'im, 'The Cultural Mediation of Human Rights'.

[96] See the sources cited at note 89 above.

[97] Lisa Kois urges advocates for the human rights of women 'to develop interpretations of the African Charter that allow for optimal utilisation of its potential. With the Charter in hand,

otherwise, it is idle to think that the oppressive impact of culture can be wished away simply by ignoring it or pretending that it does not exist. The progressive interpretation of culture is positively mandated by the Charter[98] and by the rules of international law applicable to its interpretation.[99]

The nature of States Parties' obligations regarding economic, social and cultural rights under the African Charter

Unlike the traditional civil and political rights that the Charter mostly circumscribes with clawbacks,[100] the economic, social and cultural rights guaranteed by the Charter are free of both clawbacks and limitations. The Charter does not contain a derogation clause. The African Commission has held this to mean, therefore, that 'limitations on the rights and freedoms enshrined in the Charter cannot be justified by emergencies or special circumstances.'[101]

advocates of the rights of women in Africa have a tool that can prove a useful aid in the battle. It might not quite be a sword, but it acts as an effective shield.' Kois, 'Article 18', p. 92.

[98] African Charter, Article 45.

[99] Vienna Convention on the Law of Treaties, UN Doc. A/CONF.39/27 (1969), 1155 UNTS 331 (entered into force 27 January 1980), Article 31.

[100] A clawback clause is 'one that permits, in normal circumstances, breach of an obligation for a specified number of reasons'. These differ from derogation clauses which 'allow suspension or breach of certain obligations in circumstances of war or public emergency'. See R. Higgins, 'Derogations Under Human Rights Treaties', *British Yearbook of International Law* 48 (1976) 281. The African Commission has sought through its jurisprudence to mitigate and severely constrain the adverse consequences of the clawback clauses in the Charter. In Communication 101/93, *Civil Liberties Organisation (in respect of the Nigerian Bar Association) v. Nigeria*, the Commission held that the clawback clause (in this case in Article 10 of the Charter) did not permit national authorities to limit the exercise of the rights granted by the Charter, Eighth Annual Activity Report 1994–1995, Annex VI (*Documents of the African Commission*, p. 394). In its more recent decision in Communications 105/93, 128/94, 130/94 and 152/96, *Media Rights Agenda and Constitutional Rights Project v. Nigeria*, Twelfth Activity Report 1998–1999, Annex V, para. 63 (*Documents of the African Commission*, p. 718), the Commission lays down that, in order to pass muster, the limitation of Charter rights by national law must be compatible with international law, arguing that 'to allow national law to have precedence over the international law of the Charter would defeat the purpose of the rights and freedoms enshrined in the Charter'.

[101] Communication 105/93 etc., *Media Rights Agenda and Constitutional Rights Project v. Nigeria, ibid.*, para. 64; See also Communication 74/92, *Commission Nationale des Droits de l'Homme et des Libertés v. Chad* (Merits), Ninth Annual Activity Report 1995–1996, Annex VIII (*Documents of the African Commission*, p. 449), p. 12 at p. 15. In Communications 48/90, 50/91, 52/91 and 89/93, *Amnesty International; Comité Loosli Bachelard; Lawyers' Committee for Human Rights; Association of Members of the Episcopal Conference of East Africa v. Sudan*, Thirteenth Activity Report 1999–2000, Addendum, the African

Unlike the ICESCR, the African Charter avoids the incremental language of progressive realisation in guaranteeing these economic, social and cultural rights, except in Article 16(1) which guarantees the *best attainable* state of physical and mental health.[102] Instead, the obligations that States Parties assume with respect to these rights are clearly stated as being of immediate application. Economic, social and cultural rights are placed on the same footing as all other rights in the Charter. This interpretation is accepted by the Commission which, as I show below, firmly applies this philosophy in its jurisprudence. In presenting its 3rd Annual Activity Report to the Assembly of Heads of States and Governments of the OAU in 1990, the Commission acknowledged the difficulty posed by 'the present hostile economic circumstances'[103] but reminded the States Parties that '[o]ur Charter requires that all these rights and more should be implemented now . . . It is a task that must be carried out by every ratifying State'.[104] Other members of the Commission have re-echoed this interpretation at different times as the authoritative interpretation of the nature of the obligation regarding economic, social and cultural rights under the Charter.[105]

States Parties to the Charter undertake a composite of negative, prophylactic and positive obligations to respect, protect and fulfil all the rights in the instrument, including economic, social and cultural rights.[106] The

Commission pointed out that the fact that the Charter contains no derogation clause 'can be seen as an expression of the principle that the restriction of human rights is not a solution to national difficulties: the legitimate exercise of human rights does not pose dangers to a democratic State governed by the rule of law'. Thirteenth Annual Activity Report, Annex V, Addendum, p. 122 at p. 135, para. 79.

[102] African Charter, Article 16(1) (emphasis added).

[103] Presentation of the Third Activity Report by the Chairman of the Commission, Professor U. O. Umozurike to the 26th Session of the Assembly of Heads of State and Government of the Organization of African Unity, 9–11 July 1990, in African Commission on Human and Peoples' Rights, Documentation, 3rd Annual Activity Report of the African Commission on Human and Peoples' Rights of 28 April 1990 covering the 6th and 7th Ordinary Sessions (October/November 1989 and April 1990) as well as Intersession Activities, p. 83 at p. 84 (1990) (*Documents of the African Commission*, p. 201).

[104] *Ibid.*

[105] See Chairman Ibrahima Badawi El-Sheikh's Address to the African Seminar on International Human Rights Standards and the Administration of Justice, Cairo, Egypt, 18–21 July 1991, HR/PUB/6, p. 39. See also N. K. A. Busia Jr and B. G. Mbaye, 'Filing Communications on Economic, Social and Cultural Rights Under the African Charter on Human and Peoples' Rights (the Banjul Charter)', *East Africa Journal of Peace and Human Rights* 3 (1997) 188 at 192–3.

[106] The Maastricht Guidelines on Violations of Economic, Social and Cultural Rights, reprinted in *Human Rights Quarterly* 20 (1998) 691 at 693, para. 6.

obligation to respect imposes a negative obligation on States to refrain from interfering with the exercise or enjoyment of rights.[107] The obligation to protect entails a prophylactic duty to encourage third parties (including non-State actors) to respect these rights or to refrain from violating them. This obligation would be violated, for instance, by the forced eviction of a poor settlement followed by its redevelopment into an up-market enclave unaffordable by the original inhabitants who are then denied alternative set-tlement or compensation to facilitate their resettlement.[108] The obligation to fulfil incurs a duty that 'requires States to take appropriate legislative, administrative, budgetary, judicial and other measures towards the full re-alisation of such rights'.[109]

IMPLICATIONS FOR OVERSIGHT

The formulation of economic, social and cultural rights by the African Charter as obligations of immediate legal import has implications for the methodology or procedures that the African Commission may deploy in implementing or realising them. The format adopted by the African Charter enables the Commission to adopt a violations approach to implementing these rights in a way that would have been unavailable to it had the Charter resorted to the philosophy of 'progressive realisation' found in the ICESCR. As one writer has explained:

> The progressive realisation benchmark assumes that valid expectations and concomitant obligations of States Parties under the Covenant are not uniform or universal, but instead relative to levels of development and available re-sources. This necessitates the development of a multiplicity of performance

---

[107] The South African Constitutional Court asserts that 'at the very minimum, socio-economic rights can be negatively protected from improper invasion'. The *South African Constitution Certification* case, p. 1290. Interpreting the analogous obligation 'to ensure' in the Inter-American Convention, in its *Advisory Opinion on Exceptions to the Exhaustion of Domestic Remedies in Cases of Indigency or Inability to Obtain Legal Representation Because of a Generalised Fear Within the Legal Community*, Advisory Opinion OC-11/90 of 10 August 1990, reprinted in *Human Rights Law Journal* 12 (1991) 20 (hereinafter the *Advisory Opinion on Exceptions to Exhaustion of Domestic Remedies*), the Inter-American Court of Human Rights observed that this required the State 'to take all necessary measures to remove any impediments which might exist that would prevent individuals from enjoying the rights the Convention guarantees'. *Ibid.*, p. 23.

[108] Van Hoof, 'The Legal Nature of Economic, Social and Cultural Rights', p. 107.

[109] Maastricht Guidelines, para. 6.

standards for each enumerated right in relationship to the varied social, developmental, and resources contexts of specific countries.[110]

The task of authoritative data collection, analysis, benchmarking and monitoring that this entails would be well beyond the capacities of any existing international human rights institution[111] and, certainly, of the African Commission. The natural inability of the institution to accomplish this foundational task would in turn limit or stultify the implementation or realisation of Charter obligations through this methodology. By contrast, a violations, case-based approach has the added advantage of creating wider civil society partnerships in monitoring and implementing these rights, enabling the Commission to enlist the assistance of anyone capable of enlightening it in making authoritative determinations on specific allegations of failure by a State Party to fulfil the obligations with respect to these rights.[112] It also renders the pursuit of economic, social and cultural rights both goal-oriented and result-specific, allowing determinations to be made with respect to real-life situations with verifiable outcomes.[113] As will be shown shortly, the African Charter allows the Commission to make such determinations through both its reporting and case-based procedures.

Implementing economic, social and cultural rights in the African Charter

It should be recalled that the African Commission is established under the Charter to promote human rights and ensure their protection in Africa.[114] The mandate of the Commission as elaborated in Article 45 of the Charter includes promotional work through awareness-raising programmes such as conferences, seminars and symposia,[115] and standard-setting involving the formulation of 'principles and rules aimed at solving legal problems

---

[110] A. R. Chapman, 'A "Violations Approach" for Monitoring the International Covenant on Economic, Social and Cultural Rights', *Human Rights Quarterly* 18 (1996) 23 at 31.

[111] Audrey Chapman points out additionally that most States do not have this kind of data or, if they do, would be unwilling to share it with an intergovernmental oversight body. *Ibid.*, p. 34.

[112] African Charter, Article 46.

[113] Cf. Committee on Economic, Social and Cultural Rights, Report on the 7th Session (23 November–11 December 1992), Economic and Social Council Official Records 1993, Supplement No. 2, Annex III, Statement to the World Conference on Human Rights on Behalf of the Committee on Economic, Social and Cultural Rights, Committee on Economic, Social and Cultural Rights, UN Doc. E/1993/22(1993); E/C.12/1992/2 (1992).

[114] African Charter, Article 30.   [115] *Ibid.*, Article 45(1)(a).

relating to human and peoples' rights and fundamental freedoms upon which African Governments may base their legislations'.[116] The protective mandate of the Commission includes considering cases and communications.[117] Cases and communications may be initiated by States[118] or non-State entities.[119] It also extends to special investigative powers with respect to emergency situations or 'special cases which reveal the existence of a series of serious and massive violations' of Charter rights.[120] There is nothing in the Charter to suggest that violations of economic, social and cultural rights on a massive scale would not constitute such an emergency. It is more likely, however, that an emergency situation under Article 58 would entail violations of different categories of Charter rights or particularly egregious violations of a single right.[121] The Commission also has an advisory competence to interpret the Charter 'at the request of a State Party, an institution of the OAU or an African organisation recognised by the OAU'.[122] In addition, there is a State reporting procedure through which the Commission monitors compliance by States Parties with Charter provisions. Under this, it receives and considers periodic reports submitted by the States.[123]

The African Charter further confers three ancillary powers on the Commission relating respectively to evidence and interpretation. With respect to evidence, the Charter empowers the Commission to 'resort to any method of investigation'[124] including hearing from 'the Secretary-General of the Organization of African Unity or any other person capable of enlightening it'.[125] This provision enables the Commission to call on expert governmental,

---

[116] *Ibid.*, Article 45(1)(b).   [117] *Ibid.*, Article 45(2) and Chapter III, Articles 47–59.

[118] *Ibid.*, Articles 47–54. The first and only non-State communication so far registered by the Commission is Communication 227/98, *Democratic Republic of the Congo (DRC) v. Burundi, Rwanda and Uganda*. Initiated in March 1999 by the Government of the Democratic Republic of the Congo, this case alleges multiple violations of both the African Charter and the Geneva Conventions by the respondent States, whom it accuses of invading and levying war on DRC. It was still pending at the time of writing.

[119] African Charter, Articles 55–57.

[120] *Ibid.*, Article 58(1)–(3). For an analysis of Article 58 of the African Charter, see C. A. Odinkalu and R. Mdoe, *Article 58 of the African Charter on Human Rights: A Legal Analysis and Proposals for Implementation* (Interights, 1996); R. Murray, 'Serious and Massive Violations Under the African Charter on Human and Peoples' Rights: A Comparison with the Inter-American and European Mechanisms', *Netherlands Quarterly on Human Rights* 17 (1999) 109.

[121] Odinkalu and Mdoe, *Article 58*, p. 6; Murray, 'Serious and Massive Violations', p. 110 at p. 114.

[122] African Charter, Article 45(3).   [123] *Ibid.*, Article 62.

[124] *Ibid.*, Article 46.   [125] *Ibid.*

non-governmental or intergovernmental testimony or sources as it sees fit in its casework. Concerning its interpretative latitude, the Charter permits the Commission to 'draw inspiration from international law on human and peoples' rights', including other international instruments to which African States are party.[126] It further authorises the Commission to 'take into consideration as subsidiary measures to determine the principles of law'[127] other general or special international conventions, customs generally accepted as law, general principles of law recognised by African States, legal precedents and doctrine as well as African practices consistent with international norms on human and peoples' rights.[128]

In dealing with economic, social and cultural rights in the African Charter, it is thus permissible for the Commission to take due notice of the fact that the ICESCR has been ratified by forty-three of the fifty-three States Parties to the Charter.[129] This fact does not necessarily help the Commission in defining how it implements economic, social and cultural rights in the Charter. There is a significant difference in the thresholds of obligation between the Covenant and the Charter. The latter also offers a potentially more robust implementation machinery for economic, social and cultural rights than does the Covenant. The number of African States ratifying the Covenant could be interpreted as suggesting that most of the African Charter States prefer the 'progressive realisation' standard to the more immediate and peremptory obligation in the African Charter. A better reading of this development would be to regard it as providing the Commission with complementary and cumulative tools of implementation, integrating both the violations and progressive realisation approaches.

While ratification of the Covenant by African States does not necessarily improve in understanding their obligations with respect to economic, social and cultural rights, it is evidence that these States regard these rights as a legitimate subject for supranational human rights oversight. At least as significant is the fact that the constitutions of most African States recognise or guarantee economic, social and cultural rights in different ways as enforceable rights,[130] fundamental objectives and directive principles of

---

[126] *Ibid.*, Article 60.   [127] *Ibid.*, Article 61.   [128] *Ibid.*

[129] The only African Charter States that have yet to sign or ratify the Covenant are Botswana, Burkina Faso, Comoros, Djibouti, Eritrea, Ghana, Mauritania and Swaziland. Liberia, Sao Tomé and Principe and South Africa have signed but not yet ratified the Covenant.

[130] See, for instance, the Constitution of the Republic of South Africa; the Constitution of the Republic of Algeria; the Constitution of the Republic of Uganda; the Constitution

State policy,[131] or as national consensus embodied in preambular constitutional declarations.[132] It would thus be counter-productive for the Commission to interpret the Charter so as to minimise obligations that the States Parties themselves undertake in their own basic law. The remainder of this section examines the record of the African Commission in interpreting and implementing economic, social and cultural rights under the African Charter through, in particular, its State reporting and case-based procedures.

STATE REPORTING

Each State Party to the African Charter undertakes to submit, every two years, 'a report on the legislative or other measures taken with a view to giving effect to the rights and freedoms recognised and guaranteed by the

of the Republic of Cape Verde; the Constitution of the Republic of Mozambique; the Constitution of the Republic of Togo; the Constitution of the Republic of Ghana; the Constitution of the Republic of Namibia; and *La Loi Fondamentale de la Republique de Guinee* 1985.

[131] See, for instance, the Constitution of the Federal Republic of Nigeria 1999; the Constitution of the Republic of Uganda 1995; the Constitution of the Republic of Ghana 1992; and the Constitution of the Republic of Sierra Leone 1991. The courts in Nigeria have held such fundamental objectives and directive principles of State policy to be non-justiciable. See *Archbishop Olubunmi Okogie and Seven Others* v. *Attorney-General of Lagos State*, [1981] 1 NCLR 218. In Ghana and Uganda, however, the courts have given them a quasi-justiciable status, holding that the courts are 'mandated to apply them in their interpretative duty, when they [the fundamental objectives and directive principles of State policy] are read in conjunction with other enforceable parts of the Constitution'. See *New Patriotic Party* v. *Attorney-General* [1996–7] SC Ghana LR 728 at 745 *per* Bamford Addo JSC. See also the decision of the Constitutional Court of Uganda in *Salvatori Abuki and Obuga* v. *Attorney-General, Butterworths Human Rights Cases* 3 (1998) 199. The latter approach is also favoured by the courts in India. See the decision of the Indian Supreme Court in *State of Kerala* v. *Thomas* [1976] SCR 906 at 993; *His Holiness Kesavananda Bharati Sripadagalavaru* v. *State of Kerala* [1973] Supp. SCR 1; *Krishnan* v. *State of Andhra Pradesh* [1993] 4 LRC 250–3. For an analysis of the concept and objective of fundamental objectives and directive principles of State policy, see B. O. Nwabueze, *The Presidential Constitution of Nigeria* (London: C. Hurst and Co., 1982), pp. 18–19.

[132] See, for instance, the Constitution of the Republic of Cameroon. In *Monju* v. *Minister of Economy and Finance, Commonwealth Human Rights Law Digest* 1 (1996) 110, the High Court of Cameroon held that the preambular constitutional declarations protecting human rights, such as, in this case, the prohibition against retroactive laws, were binding on the government and enforceable by the courts.

present Charter'.[133] State reporting in international human rights procedures aims to achieve multiple objectives including:

1. initial review by the implementing or oversight institution by which it is apprised of relevant domestic laws, context, practice and problems;
2. monitoring with a view to addressing systematically associated problems of implementation and compliance;
3. policy formulation which may help the State Party improve its compliance with treaty obligations through appropriate adjustments in domestic policy;
4. ensuring public scrutiny and accountability to both national and international constituencies;
5. benchmarking and evaluation over time of any changes;
6. information exchange; and
7. standard clarification and setting.[134]

To facilitate reporting under Article 62, the African Commission adopted at its Fourth Ordinary Session in Banjul, The Gambia, in October 1988, the 'General Guidelines Relating to the Form and Contents of the Periodic Reports Required Under Article 62'.[135] These Guidelines make it clear that State reporting under the Charter aims to include monitoring of State compliance. It also 'extends to the practices of the courts and administrative organs of the State Party, and other relevant facts'.[136] These Guidelines are divided into seven sections or parts. Section II comprises fifty-nine clauses devoted to general guidelines regarding the form and content of reports on economic and social rights.[137] Section VII consists of nine sets of guidelines regarding the form and content of reports received from States Parties on the elimination of all forms of discrimination against women.[138]

---

[133] African Charter, Article 62.

[134] P. Alston, 'The Purposes of Reporting', in United Nations Manual on Human Rights Reporting Under Six Major International Human Rights Instruments, UN Doc. HR/PUB/91/1 (1991), pp. 13–16.

[135] Guidelines for National Periodic Reports, reprinted in 2nd Annual Activity Report of the African Commission on Human and Peoples' Rights Covering the 4th and 5th Ordinary Sessions (October 1988 and April 1989) and the Extraordinary Session in Banjul in June, as well as Intercession Activities, Annex XII, Documentation No. 1 (1990), pp. 45–69 (hereinafter the 'Reporting Guidelines') (Documents of the African Commission, p. 49).

[136] Ibid., § 1, para. 9.   [137] Ibid., § II.   [138] Ibid., § VII.

The Guidelines also contain interesting glimpses into the Commission's interpretation of economic, social and cultural rights which it defines to include:

> [T]he right to work; right to form and belong to trade unions, right to social security and social insurance, right to protection of family; right to highest attainable standard of physical and mental health, right to education; right to economic development, right to equal pay for equal work; etc.[139]

Notable in these Guidelines is the robustness of the Commission's definition of the scope and content of economic, social and cultural rights in the Charter. It elaborates guidelines for the rights to form and belong to free and independent trade unions,[140] social security and social insurance,[141] rest, leisure and holiday with pay,[142] and an adequate standard of living,[143] none of which are mentioned by name in the Charter. The guidelines concerning the elimination of all forms of discrimination against women support the view that the Commission is inclined to read Article 18 of the Charter progressively rather than restrictively.[144]

An examination of the records of some of the reports that have been considered by the Commission reveals its interpretation of the scope and content of the obligation to protect economic, social and cultural rights in the Charter and the priority that the Commission accords to these rights. For instance, the Commission has interpreted the Charter obligation to protect economic, social and cultural rights to require the inclusion of these rights in the national Constitution,[145] and to prohibit contemporary forms of slavery.[146] It has also addressed through this process the protection of the right to work[147] and trade union rights,[148] including the right to strike.[149]

---

[139] *Ibid.*, § II, para. 1.   [140] *Ibid.*, paras. 10–16.   [141] *Ibid.*, paras. 17–19.
[142] *Ibid.*, para. 9.   [143] *Ibid.*   [144] See note 135 above.
[145] African Commission on Human and Peoples' Rights, Examination of State Reports, 12th Session, October 1992: Gambia, Zimbabwe, Senegal (1993), pp. 17–43 (Examination of the Initial Report of The Gambia).
[146] *Ibid.* Report on the 12th Session of the African Commission on Human and Peoples' Rights held in Banjul, The Gambia, 12–21 October 1992 (African Society of International and Comparative Law, 1992), p. 4 (Examination of the Initial Report of Senegal).
[147] *Ibid.*, pp. 86–8 (Examination of the Initial Report of Zimbabwe); Report on the 13th Session of the African Commission on Human and Peoples' Rights held in Banjul, The Gambia, 29 March–7 April 1993 (African Society of International and Comparative Law, 1993), pp. 16–19 (Examination of the Initial Report of Nigeria).
[148] *Ibid.*, pp. 16–19.
[149] Examination of the Initial Report of Zimbabwe, note 147 above, p. 85.

It also regards this as including an obligation to combat and monitor traditional practices harmful to women.[150] The Commission considers that States have an obligation to bridge the rural/urban divide,[151] declaring in one case that 'we cannot talk about human rights without insisting on the need to emphasise social, economic, and cultural rights to allow a major portion of our population to have minimum living standards'.[152] This extends to a commitment to eliminate poverty and provide access to basic utilities, healthcare and electricity.[153] Recognising the permeability of rights, the Commission has shown a particular interest in access to justice and legal aid as an issue of economic, social and cultural rights.[154] It has thus requested States Parties to report on legal aid and access to judicial and other recourse mechanisms,[155] and to 'allocate adequate resources to judicial and law enforcement institutions'.[156] The Commission has asked States Parties to take immediate measures to ensure better and more effective representation of women in judicial institutions,[157] and to:

> include in their periodic report to the Commission, a special section which addresses the implementation of the right to fair trial including an analysis of the resources provided to judicial institutions as a proportion of the national budget of the State.[158]

The human impact of economic structural adjustment programmes is a priority subject for the Commission in monitoring economic, social and cultural rights under the Charter.[159] The records of examination of periodic reports also reveal how the Commission fulfils the monitoring and information exchange roles in relation to economic, social and cultural

---

[150] Examination of the Initial Report of The Gambia, note 145 above; Examination of the Initial Report of Nigeria, note 147 above, pp. 16–19.

[151] Examination of the Initial Report of Nigeria, note 147 above; African Commission on Human and Peoples' Rights, Examination of the Initial Report of Namibia, 23rd Ordinary Session (1998), p. 16.

[152] Examination of the Initial Report of Namibia, ibid., p. 19.

[153] Ibid.   [154] Ibid., p. 18.

[155] Resolution on the Right to a Fair Trial and Legal Assistance in Africa, adopting the Dakar Declaration on the Right to a Fair Trial in Africa, DOC/OS(XXVI)INF.19.

[156] Ibid.   [157] Ibid.   [158] Ibid.

[159] Report on the 14th Session of the African Commission on Human and Peoples' Rights, held in Addis Ababa, Ethiopia, 1–10 December 1993, pp. 20–5 (Examination of the Initial Report of Ghana); Examination of the Initial Report of Zimbabwe, note 147 above, pp. 86–8.

rights. In response, for instance, to the Commission's questions at the 14th Ordinary Session regarding the right to work and the consequences of economic structural adjustment, the representative of Ghana answered that:

> The right to work is provided for but is linked to availability of work. The basic principle is that if one satisfies the basic requirements, there are no reasons that one should be denied employment on the basis of sex, religion etc. With regard to retrenchment, we embarked on a structural adjustment programme in April 1983. One major plank of the Economic Recovery Programme was to review the way government services were operating including movement away from central government control, leading to private-oriented economy and also leading to retrenchment. The government realised the effects and a programme for the mitigation of the social cost of adjustment policy (PAMSCAD) was adopted. This led to an initiative by the government, for example the establishment of development projects and the grant of loans to people who had been retrenched, especially in rural communities. There was also assistance for health for those affected by retrenchment. People were not simply sacked without benefits although we admit that the benefits sometimes paid later [*sic*]. But people were not left to their fate in society.[160]

The record of follow-up to the exchanges and disclosures in State reports by the Commission is at best mixed and inadequate. The reports of the States Parties themselves and records of the public consideration of these reports by States Parties' representatives on the floor of the Commission are routinely issued as public documents. However, the written response of the States to outstanding issues revealed in the process of the consideration of the reports have inexplicably not been made public. NGO and other advocates or monitors are, therefore, unable to ascertain whether, and, if so, to what extent, the States Parties respond to the Commission's requests for clarification, follow-up or further information on these rights. Such a step would facilitate independent monitoring of compliance by the States Parties with the Commission's recommendations.[161] There is considerable room for the Commission to further develop the norm-clarification, standard setting, policy-formulation and benchmarking roles of this otherwise invaluable

---

[160] Examination of the Initial Report of Ghana, *ibid.*, pp. 22–3.

[161] For a description of the procedure for State reporting before the African Commission, see A. Danielsen, *The State Reporting Procedure under the African Charter* (Danish Centre for Human Rights, 1994).

procedure of State reporting in relation to the implementation of economic, social and cultural rights.

ECONOMIC, SOCIAL AND CULTURAL RIGHTS IN THE CASEWORK OF THE AFRICAN COMMISSION

The casework of the Commission is regulated by Chapter III of the Charter[162] and by the Commission's Rules of Procedure.[163] Although the Charter allows for both inter-State and non-State communications, the case-based jurisprudence of the African Charter mechanism has been developed through the non-State communications received and considered by the Commission under Article 55 of the African Charter. All but one of the communications so far received by the Commission have been non-State communications.[164] Of over forty-five cases that have proceeded to a decision on the merits, at least fifteen have addressed various aspects of economic, social and cultural rights in the Charter.[165] Economic, social and cultural rights figure prominently in several of the communications currently pending before the Commission.[166] The evidence from the casework of the Commission in these cases affirms the permeability and interdependence of human rights. It also demonstrates that it is unviable to categorise the rights in the Charter.

A case-based approach to economic, social and cultural rights in the African Charter can happen at two levels or stages. At one level, economic, social and cultural rights are a matter of access to the legal process.[167] This

---

[162] African Charter, Articles 46–59.

[163] Rules of Procedure of the African Commission on Human and Peoples' Rights, adopted 6 October 1995, ACHPR/RP/XIX (entered into force 6 October 1995) (hereinafter the 'Rules of Procedure') (*Documents of the African Commission*, p. 21).

[164] The first and only non-State communication so far registered by the Commission is Communication 227/98, *Democratic Republic of the Congo (DRC)* v. *Burundi, Rwanda and Uganda.*

[165] For a recent review of the substantive jurisprudence from the African Commission on various rights in the Charter, see C. A. Odinkalu, 'The Individual Complaints Procedures of the African Commission on Human and Peoples' Rights: A Preliminary Assessment', *Transnational Law and Contemporary Problems* 8 (1998) 360.

[166] Including Communication 155/96, *Social and Economic Rights Action Centre and Centre for Economic and Social Rights* v. *Nigeria* (protection of rights to life, health and the environment); Communication 219/98, *Legal Defence Centre* v. *Gambia* (right to work and employment-related protection); and Communication 226/99, *Union des Syndicats Autonomes du Senegal* v. *Senegal* (trade union rights).

[167] See J. McBride, 'Access to Justice Under International Human Rights Treaties', *Parker School Journal of East European Law* 5 (1998) 3 at 33 *et seq.*

aspect of economic, social and cultural rights arises in the admissibility stage of the proceedings of the Commission.[168] In addition, the Commission also interprets the Charter provisions on these rights in its merits decisions.

ACCESS TO THE AFRICAN COMMISSION AS AN ECONOMIC, SOCIAL AND CULTURAL RIGHT

Article 56 of the African Charter stipulates the conditions that communications must comply with in order to be admissible for consideration on the merits.[169] The most important of these conditions is the requirement in Article 56(5) that communications should be sent only 'after exhausting local remedies, if any, unless it is obvious that this procedure is unduly prolonged'.[170] Availability of and, therefore, access to domestic adjudication procedures, including the means to pursue and exhaust them, is implied in this provision as an exception to the requirement to exhaust domestic remedies. Addressing this point in its *Advisory Opinion on Exceptions to the Exhaustion of Domestic Remedies*, the Inter-American Court of Human Rights concluded that:

> if legal services are required either as a matter of law or as a matter of fact in order for a right guaranteed by the Convention to be recognised and a person is unable to obtain such services because of his indigency, then that person would be exempted from the requirement to exhaust domestic remedies. The same would be true of cases requiring the payment of a filing fee. That is to say, if it is impossible for an indigent to deposit such a fee, he cannot be required to exhaust domestic remedies unless the State provides some alternative mechanism.[171]

Although it has evolved several exceptions to the strict requirement to exhaust domestic remedies, the African Commission has not yet directly confronted the question whether poverty or inability to afford domestic legal procedures is or can be one of such exceptions. Two developments in the case law of the Commission so far are, nevertheless, relevant in this context.

---

[168] For a description and analysis of the processes for the consideration and disposal of communications by the African Commission, see C. A. Odinkalu and C. Christensen, 'The African Commission on Human and Peoples' Rights: The Development of Its Non-State Communications Procedures', *Human Rights Quarterly* 20 (1998) 235.

[169] African Charter, Article 56.   [170] *Ibid.*, Article 56(5).

[171] *Advisory Opinion on Exception to Domestic Remedies*, note 107 above, p. 22, para. 30.

First, the Commission has established that the requirement to exhaust domestic remedies under the Charter is subject to the three principles of availability, adequacy, and effectiveness, so that a complainant is not bound to exhaust remedies that are 'neither adequate nor effective'.[172] Citing non-exhaustion of domestic remedies in Communication 71/92, *Rencontre Africaine pour la Defense de Droits de l'Homme v. Zambia*,[173] the Government of Zambia objected to the admissibility of a case filed on behalf of several hundred West African nationals who had been expelled *en masse* from Zambia. In dismissing the Zambian objection and upholding the admissibility of the communication, the Commission reasoned that Article 56(5) of the Charter 'does not mean . . . that complainants are required to exhaust any local remedy which is found to be, as a practical matter, unavailable or ineffective'.[174] The Commission pointed out that the victims and their families were collectively deported without regard to a possible judicial challenge to such conduct and concluded that the remedies referred to by the respondent State were as a practical matter unavailable.[175] These principles extend to those cases where it is 'impractical or undesirable' for a victim or applicant to approach domestic courts.[176] These cases provide proof that the mere existence of domestic procedures without sufficient assurance of accessibility is not of itself sufficient to meet the standard of availability under Article 56(5). The expense of domestic procedures would surely raise questions of access, and therefore of availability, adequacy and effectiveness. It thus is arguably an exception to the requirement to exhaust domestic remedies under Article 56(5) of the Charter.[177]

Secondly, the Commission has taken the view that the rule regarding exhaustion of domestic remedies is dispensed with in cases of serious and

---

[172] Communication 87/93, *Constitutional Rights Project (in respect of Zamani Lakwot and 6 Others) v. Nigeria*, Eighth Activity Report 1994–1995, Annex VI (*Documents of the African Commission*, p. 391), p. 16 at p. 18, para. 6.

[173] Communication 71/92, *Rencontre Africaine pour la Defense de Droits de l'Homme v. Zambia*, Tenth Activity Report 1996–1997, Annex X (*Documents of the African Commission*, p. 563).

[174] *Ibid.*, para. 12.   [175] *Ibid.*, para. 15.

[176] Communications 25/89, 47/90, 56/91 and 100/93 (joined), *Free Legal Assistance Group, Lawyers' Committee for Human Rights, Union Interafricaine des Droits de l'Homme, Les Témoins de Jehovah v. Zaire*, Ninth Activity Report 1995–1996, Annex VIII (*Documents of the African Commission*, p. 444), p. 2 at p. 6, para. 37. See also Communications 147/95 and 149/96, *Sir Dawda K. Jawara v. The Gambia* (Merits), Thirteenth Annual Activity Report, Annex V, p. 95.

[177] *Advisory Opinion on Exceptions to Exhaustion of Domestic Remedies*, note 107 above.

massive violations of human rights. Thus the Commission holds that it must read Article 56(5) in the light of its duty to:

> ensure the protection of the human and peoples' rights . . . The Commission cannot hold the requirement of exhaustion of local remedies to apply literally in cases where it is impractical or undesirable for the complainant to seize the domestic courts in the case of each individual complaint. This is the case where there are a large number of individual victims. Due to the seriousness of the human rights situation as well as the number of people involved, such remedies as might exist in the domestic courts are as a practical matter unavailable or, in the words of the Charter, 'unduly prolonged'.[178]

This in turn raises potentially two important developments. It provides a justification and basis for the Commission to undertake case-based monitoring of economic, social and cultural rights by investigating, verifying and considering complaints about situations of mass non-compliance with these rights, such as, for instance, mass illiteracy or high maternal mortality. While the outcome of such a hearing may well differ from a communication about an individual violation, such a procedure would nevertheless enable the Commission to undertake a public investigation of the causes of widespread violations where they exist and provide systemic remedies and recommendations. Were such a case to be instituted, there is sufficient basis in the jurisprudence of the Commission examined here to also justify excepting it from the rigours of the requirement to exhaust domestic remedies.

THE SUBSTANTIVE CONTENT OF ECONOMIC, SOCIAL AND CULTURAL RIGHTS IN THE CASE LAW OF THE AFRICAN COMMISSION

Economic, social and cultural rights have usually been presented to the Commission in association with other violations. A majority of the Commission's pronouncements in this regard have arisen in the consideration of deportation and nationality-related cases. In the absence of an express

---

[178] Communications 25/89, 47/90, 56/91 and 100/93 (joined), *Free Legal Assistance Group, Lawyers' Committee for Human Rights, Union Interafricaine des Droits de l'Homme, Les Témoins de Jehovah v. Zaire*, Ninth Activity Report 1995–1996, Annex VIII (*Documents of the African Commission*, p. 444), paras. 56–7; Communications 54/91, 61/91, 98/93, 164/97 and 210/98, *Malawi African Association; Amnesty International; Ms Sarr Diop, Union Interafricaine des Droits de l'Homme and RADDHO; Collectif des Veuves et Ayants-droits; Association Mauritanienne des Droits de l'Homme v. Mauritania*, Thirteenth Activity Report 1999–2000, Addendum, para. 85.

guarantee of a right to housing in the Charter, the Commission has based protection for housing-related rights on the Article 5 guarantee of human dignity, including the prohibition of torture and cruel, inhuman and degrading treatment. In Communication 93/97, *John K. Modise* v. *Botswana*,[179] the complainant was rendered stateless by the respondent State who cancelled his Botswana nationality and deported him to South Africa for political reasons. South Africa in turn deported him to the then homeland of Bophuthatswana who in turn deported him to Botswana. Unable to resolve the question of where to keep the complainant, the authorities of the respondent State made him homeless for a long period on a specially created strip of border territory with South Africa called 'no-man's land'. The Commission found that such enforced homelessness was inhuman and degrading treatment that offended 'the dignity of human beings and thus violated Article 5'.[180] This decision is all the more remarkable given that the Charter contains no *ad hominem* provision for a right to nationality.

In Communication 212/98, *Amnesty International* v. *Zambia*,[181] the Commission similarly found the deportation of two prominent opposition politicians by Zambian authorities to the neighbouring State of Malawi to violate the duty of the respondent State to respect and protect the family. Holding that the acts of the government violated Article 18(1), the Commission declared that 'the government of Zambia has deprived them [the victims] of their family and is depriving their families of the men's support, and this constitutes a violation of the dignity of a human being'.[182] In this case, therefore, the Commission read the guarantee of human dignity in Article 5 of the Charter as reinforcing the protection of the family in Article 18. The Commission has similarly found a combined violation of Articles 5 and 18 of the Charter where detainees were deprived of access to their families.[183]

---

[179] Communication 97/93, *John K. Modise* v. *Botswana*, Tenth Annual Activity Report 1996–1997, Annex X (*Documents of the African Commission*, pp. 349, 567).

[180] *Ibid.*, para. 32.

[181] Communication 212/98, *Amnesty International* v. *Zambia*, Twelfth Annual Activity Report 1998–1999, Annex V (*Documents of the African Commission*, p. 745), p. 52.

[182] *Ibid.*, para. 50.

[183] Communication 151/96, *Civil Liberties Organisation* v. *Nigeria*, Thirteenth Annual Activity Report 1999–2000, Annex V, 71. The Commission held that this was 'a psychological trauma difficult to justify and may constitute inhuman treatment'. *Ibid.*, p. 75, para. 27. See also Communications 143/95 and 150/96, *Constitutional Rights Project and Civil Liberties Organisation* v. *Nigeria*, Thirteenth Annual Activity Report 1999–2000, Annex V, p. 62 at p. 66, para. 29.

In another case against Benin, it was shown that the authorities of the respondent State harassed, detained and tortured the parents of detainees and political opponents of the ruling government. The Commission similarly held these acts to violate human dignity, the prohibition against torture and the protection of the family under the Charter.[184]

In addition to being prohibited under Article 12(5) of the Charter, mass expulsion of non-nationals, defined by the Charter as 'that which is aimed at national, racial, ethnic or religious groups',[185] also violates most of the economic, social and cultural rights in the Charter. Communication 159/96, *Union Interafricaine des Droits de l'Homme et al.,* v. *Angola*, was initiated by five NGOs representing hundreds of West African nationals collectively expelled by Angola in 1996. In finding a violation by Angola of the Charter, the Commission held that:

> Mass expulsions of any category of persons, whether on the basis of nationality, religion, ethnic, racial or other considerations 'constitute a special violation of human rights'. This type of deportations calls into question a whole series of rights recognised and guaranteed in the Charter; such as the right to property,[186] the right to work[187] the right to education,[188] and results in the violation by the State Party of its obligations under Article 18 paragraph 1 which stipulates that 'the family shall be the natural unit and basis of society. It shall be protected by the State, which shall take care of its physical and moral health.' By deporting the victims, thus separating them from their families, the defendant State has violated and violates the letter of this text.[189]

The *Mauritania* cases[190] comprised five consolidated communications arising from developments in Mauritania between 1986 and 1992. Briefly, these

---

[184] Communications 16/88, 17/88 and 18/88, *Comité Culturel pour la Démocratie au Benin, Hilaire Badjogoume and El Hadj Boubacar Diawara* v. *Benin* (Merits), Seventh Annual Activity Report 1993–1994, Annex IX; Eighth Activity Report 1994–1995, Annex VI (*Documents of the African Commission*, pp. 340 and 381).

[185] African Charter, Article 12(5).   [186] *Ibid.*, Article 14.

[187] *Ibid.*, Article 15.   [188] *Ibid.*, Article 17.

[189] Communication 159/96, *Union Interafricaine des Droits de l'Homme, Féderation International des Ligues des Droits de l'Homme, Rencontre Africaine des Droits de l'Homme, Organisation Nationale des Droits de l'Homme au Sénégal and Association Malienne des Droits de l'Homme* v. *Angola*, Eleventh Activity Report 1997–1998, Annex II (*Documents of the African Commission*, p. 615), p. 30 at pp. 31–2, paras. 16–17.

[190] Communications 54/91, 61/91, 98/93, 164/97 and 210/98, *Malawi African Association; Amnesty International; Ms Sarr Diop, Union Interafricaine des Droits de l'Homme and RADDHO; Collectif des Veuves et Ayants-droits; Association Mauritanienne des Droits de l'Homme* v. *Mauritania*, Thirteenth Activity Report 1999–2000, Addendum.

communications alleged the existence in that State of slavery and analogous practices, and of institutionalised racial discrimination perpetrated by the ruling Beydane community against the more populous black community. Among other things, the cases alleged that black Mauritanians were enslaved, routinely evicted or displaced from their lands which were then confiscated by the government. It was also alleged that the members of the black community of Mauritania were excluded from access to employment and were subjected to tedious and unremunerative work. The communication also alleged that some detainees had, among other things, been starved to death, left to die in severe weather without blankets or clothing, and were deprived of medical attention. The Commission decided that the starvation of prisoners and depriving them of blankets, clothing and healthcare violated Article 16 of the Charter.[191] It also found that the forced eviction of black Mauritanians from their homes violated their rights to freedom of movement and property under respectively Articles 12(1) and 14 of the Charter.[192] Regarding some of the allegations of systematic enslavement of the black community of Mauritania, the Commission observed that:

> The Commission considers, in line with the provisions of Article 23(3) of the Universal Declaration of Human Rights, that everyone who works has the right to just and favourable remuneration ensuring for himself and his family an existence worthy of human dignity, and supplemented, if necessary, by other means of social protection. These provisions are complemented by those of Article 7 of the International Covenant on Economic, Social and Cultural Rights. In view of the foregoing, the Commission deems that there was a violation of Article 5 of the Charter due to practices analogous to slavery, and emphasises that unremunerated work is tantamount to a violation of the right to respect the dignity inherent in the human being. It furthermore considers that the conditions to which the descendants of slaves are subjected clearly

---

[191] *Ibid.*, p. 156, para. 122.

[192] *Ibid.*, p. 156, paras. 125–8. The Commission has held that, in addition to being a violation of press freedom, sealing up the premises of newspapers also violates Article 14. See Communications 140/94 and 145/95, *Constitutional Rights Project, Civil Liberties Organisation and Media Rights Agenda* v. *Nigeria*, Thirteenth Annual Activity Report 1999–2000, Annex V, p. 53. The Commission reasoned in this case that 'the right to property necessarily includes a right to have access to one's property and the right not to have one's property invaded or encroached upon', holding that military decrees which permitted this 'cannot be said to be "appropriate" or in the interest of the public or the community in general'. *Ibid.*, p. 60, para. 54.

constitute exploitation and degradation of man, both practices condemned by the African Charter.[193]

In Communication 39/90, *Annette Pagnoulle (on Behalf of Abdoulaye Mazou) v. Cameroon*[194] a Cameroonian magistrate was unlawfully detained and removed from his job. The Commission held that the failure of the State Party to reinstate him after his release from what turned out to be unjustified and illegal detention constituted a violation of his right to work under satisfactory and equitable conditions.[195]

Where a State Party was found by reason of corruption and misman-agement of the resources of the country to have failed to provide basic services necessary for basic health, including safe drinking water, electricity and basic medicine for its health facilities, the Commission adjudged that there was a violation of Article 16 of the Charter.[196] It has also held that the arbitrary closure of universities and secondary schools for two years, accompanied by non-payment of teachers' salaries because of widespread corruption, which prevented students from attending school and teachers from providing education to the students, violated the right to education under the Charter.[197]

Regarding culture as a human rights issue, the Commission takes the view that 'the African Charter should be interpreted in a culturally sensitive way, taking into account the differing legal traditions of Africa'.[198] In the *Mauritania* cases, one of the allegations was that black Mauritanians

---

[193] Communications 54/91, 61/91, 98/93, 164/97 and 210/98, *Malawi African Association; Amnesty International; Ms Sarr Diop, Union Interafricaine des Droits de l'Homme and RADDHO; Collectif des Veuves et Ayants-droits; Association Mauritanienne des Droits de l'Homme* v. *Mauritania*, Thirteenth Activity Report 1999–2000, Addendum, p. 158, para. 135.

[194] Communication 39/90, *Annette Pagnoulle (on behalf of Abdoulaye Mazou)* v. *Cameroon*, Eighth Activity Report 1994–1995, Annex VI; Tenth Activity Report 1996–1997, Annex X (*Documents of the African Commission*, pp. 384 and 555).

[195] *Ibid.*, para. 30.

[196] Communications 25/89, 47/90, 56/91 and 100/93 (joined), *Free Legal Assistance Group, Lawyers' Committee for Human Rights, Union Interafricaine des Droits de l'Homme, Les Témoins de Jehovah* v. *Zaire*, Ninth Activity Report 1995–1996, Annex VIII (*Documents of the African Commission*, p. 444).

[197] *Ibid.*

[198] Communication 140/94, 141/94 and 145/95, *Constitutional Rights Project, Civil Liberties Organisation and Media Rights Agenda* v. *Nigeria*, Thirteenth Activity Report 1999–2000, Annex V, para. 26.

were denied the right to enjoy their culture, including their languages. The Commission considered that these allegations fell within the scope of Article 17(2) and (3) of the Charter. In particular, it emphasised that:

> Language is an integral part of the structure of culture; it in fact constitutes its pillar and means of expression *par excellence*. Its usage enriches the individual and enables him to take part in the community and in its activities. To deprive a man of such participation amounts to depriving him of his identity.[199]

Towards a coherent philosophy and programme of implementation for economic, social and cultural rights under the Charter

The analysis above indicates the outlines of an interesting philosophy for implementing economic, social and cultural rights under the African Charter. Taking its bearing from the integrated normative framework that the Charter embodies, the Commission is inclined to see human rights as an interconnected set of obligations. The notion of and right to respect for human dignity easily emerges as the foundational value and right in the African Charter.[200] It has rightly been said that 'respect for human dignity is a value implicit in almost all the rights enumerated in the Universal Declaration as it must be in any order based on human rights'.[201] The Charter, unlike any of the international Covenants or regional instruments, recognises 'respect of the dignity inherent in the human person' as a distinct right.[202] This simple idea achieves the radical consequence of breaking down the dichotomies and artificial barriers imposed on the implementation of economic, social and cultural rights, for respect for human dignity is a primordial value incapable of being pigeon-holed into any artificial categories of rights. Violations of this precept therefore constitute violations of the Charter attracting legal consequences that must be redressed like any others. This realisation opens

---

[199] Communications 54/91, 61/91, 98/93, 164/97 and 210/98, *Malawi African Association; Amnesty International; Ms Sarr Diop, Union Interafricaine des Droits de l'Homme and RADDHO; Collectif des Veuves et Ayants-droits; Association Mauritanienne des Droits de l'Homme v. Mauritania,* Thirteenth Activity Report 1999–2000, Addendum, 158, para. 137. On the facts of this case, the Commission was, however, unable to find these particular violations established. *Ibid.*, para. 138.

[200] African Charter, Article 5.   [201] Chaskalson, 'Human Dignity', p. 12.

[202] African Charter, Article 5. Article 10(1) of the International Covenant on Civil and Political Rights requires merely that persons deprived of their liberty should be treated with respect for the inherent dignity of the human person. But it does not treat respect for human dignity as a separate right. See the International Covenant on Civil and Political Rights, GA Res. 2200, UN GAOR, 21st Session, Supp. No. 16, p. 52, UN Doc. A/6316 (1966).

up vast and arguably unique possibilities for implementing economic, social and cultural rights under the African regional human rights system.

It is true, therefore, that the fate of economic, social and cultural rights under the African Charter is bound up with the prospects of the African regional human rights mechanism generally. Present records suggest that the system is far from anything close to optimal utilisation. All States Parties remain severely in arrears of their reporting obligations under the Charter, ranging from two years in the case of the most recent signatories to seven years.[203] Similarly, the communications procedures are still severely under-utilised.[204] The imperfections of the Charter do not in any way detract from the challenging normative framework or philosophical premise that it provides for advancing economic, social and cultural rights in Africa and beyond. This requires not just the intellectual awareness and political will on the part of the Commission but, perhaps more importantly, habitual resort to the Charter mechanisms to a level that is currently not the case.

The African Charter mechanisms are uniquely reliant on the States Parties and non-State entities (such as NGOs and individual victims) for their deployment and efficacy. Unless the Commission receives periodic reports, the reporting procedure in Article 62 of the Charter is of little use. Even when they do so, States may well choose to prepare and submit scanty or uninformative reports, thereby calling the credibility and efficacy of the entire procedure into question.[205] To avert this, all that the Commission has at its disposal is the instrument of publicity and its own institutional credibility. The Commission could surely use the former with less reluctance, a development that will help its credibility which remains far from secure. Similarly, unless communications are brought to the Commission and conducted with due diligence and professionalism, the Commission's role in holding States Parties accountable through this process is diminished. To have any meaningful impact the Commission's decisions on communications must in turn influence and shape advocacy agendas at the national level.

---

[203] African Commission on Human and Peoples' Rights, Status on Submission of State Periodic Reports to the African Commission on Human and Peoples' Rights, DOC/OS(SSVI)/INF.16 (1999).

[204] The rate of submission of communications averages at best one communication for every two States Parties per year. See C. A. Odinkalu, 'The Individual Complaints', p. 403.

[205] Welch, 'The African Charter', p. 116, cites the case of Nigeria's first attempt to submit its initial report which owing to 'bureaucratic confusion . . . consisted of nothing more than the table of contents of its suspended constitutions!'.

However, the Commission was not created to be a weak institution entirely at the mercy of forces outside its control and beyond its influence. Quite to the contrary, the Commission enjoys a wide but grossly under-utilised latitude for independent initiative, especially through its promotional and advisory mandates. These could be usefully deployed in stimulating awareness about and interest in the promotion and protection of economic, social and cultural rights in Africa. The Commission currently has three special procedures dealing with Summary, Arbitrary and Extrajudicial Executions, the Human Rights of Women and Prisons in Africa.[206] For a mechanism with responsibility to protect human rights on a continent with pervasive poverty and massive deprivation, the Commission has been remiss in not according adequate priority to economic, social and cultural rights. Problems and themes such as education, healthcare, employment and access to work, child welfare and security, access to basic utilities, and the human rights consequences of structural adjustment would be suitable for close, in-depth and specialised investigation by the Commission. Such an investigation could be undertaken by an independent expert or Special Rapporteur under terms of reference approved by the Commission. The voice and findings of the Commission on such issues would greatly inform policy-making in and about Africa. It could also inform the work of other international mechanisms[207] grappling with aspects of economic, social and cultural rights through programmes of co-operation and mutual support. Similarly, the Commission could hold an Extraordinary Session to consider any or different aspects of economic, social and cultural rights that it considers of priority to the continent.[208]

---

[206] See Ninth Annual Activity Report of the African Commission on Human and Peoples' Rights 1995–6, ACHPR/RPT/9th (*Documents of the African Commission*, p. 428), p. 6.

[207] Excluding cross-cutting mandates, the UN Human Rights Commission currently deploys at least seven special procedures and mechanisms on economic, social and cultural rights, addressing the following: toxic waste, structural adjustment, extreme poverty, education, right to development, foreign debt, and migrants, as well as an open-ended working group on structural adjustment programmes and economic, social and cultural rights. See Report of the Meeting of Special Rapporteurs, Representatives, Experts and Chairpersons of Working Groups of the Special Procedures of the Commission on Human Rights and of the Advisory Services Programme, Geneva, 31 May to 3 June 1999, E/CN.4/2000/5 of 6 August 1999. The Special Rapporteur on Violence Against Women has also recently issued a Report on Economic and Social Policy and its Impact on Violence Against Women. See E/CN.4/2000/68/Add.5 of 24 February 2000.

[208] Rule 3 of the Commission's Rules of Procedure empowers it to hold extraordinary sessions. Since its inception in 1987, the Commission has held only two such sessions.

The Commission should, however, avoid the error of designating a single procedure or special mechanism for these rights. Quite apart from reflecting a conceptual misapprehension, if not repudiation, of the indivisibility and interdependence of human rights so clearly recognised by the Charter, such a measure would also consign economic, social and cultural rights in the Charter to an implementational ghetto, which can only reinforce the popular misconceptions about them. The only realistic option open to the Commission is, as it currently does, to mainstream these rights by adopting a multi-disciplinary and multi-faceted approach to their implementation.

The advisory mandate of the Commission, which is particularly suited to standard-setting on economic, social and cultural rights, has not been activated because the Commission has not yet received a trigger request from 'a State Party, an institution of the OAU or an African organisation recognised by the OAU' as required by the Charter.[209] This provision itself requires to be interpreted to clarify who qualifies as an African organisation recognised by the OAU. In June 1998, the OAU supplemented the Charter with a Protocol creating an African Court on Human and Peoples' Rights.[210] This Protocol, which is yet to come into force, will 'complement the protective mandate of the African Commission on Human and Peoples' rights',[211] and, like the Commission, has an advisory jurisdiction framed in identical terms to that found in Article 45(3) of the Charter itself.[212] Until the Court comes into being, the Commission's advisory mandate is the only source of guidance and authoritative standard setting on the rights in the Charter, especially the economic, social and cultural rights. Thereafter, however, these competing advisory competences will have to be rationalised in some form that is presently difficult to predict.[213]

In 1988, a former Chairman suggested that the Commission had decided to prioritise civil and political rights and postpone the timetabling of economic, social and cultural rights because it would easily be overwhelmed

---

[209] African Charter, Article 45(3).

[210] Protocol to the African Charter on Human and Peoples' Rights on the Establishment of an African Court on Human and Peoples' Rights, OAU/LEG/EXP/AFCHPR/PROT III, adopted by the 36th Ordinary Session of the Assembly of Heads of State and Government of the OAU, Ouagadougou, Burkina Faso, on 9 June 1998 (*Documents of the African Commission*, p. 82) (hereinafter the 'African Court Protocol').

[211] *Ibid.*, Article 2.   [212] *Ibid.*, Article 4.

[213] The Protocol shall come into force thirty days after receipt by the Secretariat of the OAU of the fifteenth instrument of ratification. See African Court Protocol, Article 34(3). As at the end of November 2001 only five states had ratified the Protocol.

with 'too many cases from too many countries'.[214] Since then, the Commission has demonstrated that this was an erroneous statement of its responsibilities under the Charter. In seeking to do something about these rights, the Commission grapples with practical problems affecting the lives of people in Africa and offers the guidance of international human rights law in resolving these problems. It would be easy for the Commission to get lost in defining in the abstract the content of the rights without relating its work to the experiences of peoples in Africa. If it is to resist this temptation, the Commission must grasp the nettle of pioneering a new approach to the protection of economic, social and cultural rights in international human rights law, unencumbered by the cobwebs and qualifications that are found in other human rights standards. In the Charter, it has the normative basis for this undertaking. In Africa, protecting economic, social and cultural rights is not the stuff of academic dissertations; it is a grave matter of human survival. Only when the Commission sees it as such can it begin to fulfil the ambitious human rights protection agenda that the African Charter enunciates.

[214] U. O. Umozurike, 'The Protection of Human Rights Under the Banjul (African) Charter on Human and Peoples' Rights', *African Journal of International Law* 1 (1988) 82.

7

THE CHALLENGE OF CULTURE FOR HUMAN RIGHTS IN AFRICA: THE AFRICAN CHARTER IN A COMPARATIVE CONTEXT

N. BARNEY PITYANA[*]

Culturalism and the universality of human rights

Universality is best stated in the Preamble to the Universal Declaration of Human Rights (UDHR)[1] which proclaims the Declaration to be a:

> common standard of achievement for all peoples and all nations, to the end that every individual and every organ of society shall strive by teaching and education to promote respect for these rights and freedoms and by progressive measures, national and international, to secure their universal and effective recognition and observance.

The basis for this assertion of the universality of human rights is often said to flow from the very fact of being human, this being based on views drawn variously from principles of natural law, morality, philosophy or anthropology.[2] On the basis of such studies, it can be asserted with

---

[*] This chapter is based on a paper which was originally presented at an international symposium on 'Human Rights and the Rule of Law in Africa', held at the University of Illinois in Urbana-Champaign in July 1999, but has been extensively revised for publication in this volume.

[1] UN General Assembly Resolution 217A (III) 1948. It was adopted by forty-eight votes for with none against and eight abstentions. Of those African States then members of the UN (most being under colonial rule at the time), Egypt, Ethiopia and Liberia voted for the adoption of the Declaration, whereas South Africa abstained.

[2] Y. Ghai, 'Universalism and Relativism: Concretising the Debate' (unpublished paper distributed by the International Council on Human Rights Policy, Geneva, June 1999); C. Brown, 'Universal Human Rights: A Critique', *International Journal of Human Rights* 1(2) (1997) 41–65; M. Freeman, 'Universalism, Communitarianism and Human Rights: A Reply to Chris Brown', *International Journal of Human Rights* 2(1) (1998) 79–92; D. O'Sullivan, 'The History of Human Rights Across Regions: Universalism vs Cultural Relativism', *International Journal of Human Rights* 2(3) (1998) 22–48; M. wa Mutua, 'The Banjul Charter

confidence that all cultures everywhere have standard rules or practices which show respect for human beings, that there are rules of natural justice and norms of behaviour. In broad principle, therefore, all cultures should be capable of assenting to the proposition in the Universal Declaration that 'All human beings are born free and equal in dignity and rights' in that they can identify something of their own practices and mores in that statement. Human rights may not have been understood or accepted in all cultures in exactly that terminology or in the absoluteness of its application but a consciousness of those principles has a universal and cross-cultural ring to it.

The universality principle has the enthusiastic support of many prominent human rights figures including Kofi Annan, the Secretary-General of the United Nations, and Mary Robinson, the UN High Commissioner for Human Rights. Writing in the *Human Development Report 2000* which was devoted to the theme of 'Human Development and Human Rights', Mrs Robinson shows impatience with the debate and the challenges to universality, fearing that it takes the focus away from the primary task of monitoring observance and implementation of human rights. She goes on to say:

> Universality is, in fact, the essence of human rights: all people are entitled to them, all governments are bound to observe them, all State and civil actors should defend them. The goal is nothing less than all human rights for all.[3]

Cees Flinterman makes the point that, even if it were to be acknowledged that not many African States were represented at the drafting of the Declaration, they have all subsequently shown adherence to it and to its principles by their participation in the subsequent standard-setting which characterised the period since the adoption of the International Covenants on Civil and Political Rights and Economic, Social and Cultural Rights of 1966.[4] In any event, one can argue that the Vienna Declaration and Programme of

---

and the African Cultural Fingerprint: An Evaluation of the Language of Duties', *Review of the African Commission on Human and Peoples' Rights* 6 (1996–7) 16–48; J. D. van der Vyver, 'Universality and Relativity of Human Rights: American Relativism', *Buffalo Human Rights Law Review* 4 (1998) 43–78, and the authorities cited therein.

[3] UNDP, *Human Development Report 2000: Human Development and Human Rights* (New York: Oxford University Press, 2000), p. 113.

[4] C. Flinterman, 'The Universal Declaration of African Human Rights and the Protection of Human Rights in Africa', *Africa Legal Aid Quarterly* (1998) 19.

Action of 1993 settled the debate about universality when it declared that:

> All human rights are universal, indivisible, interdependent, and interrelated.[5]

The relativist argument challenges the notion that any set of principles or beliefs can be capable of universal application. That view is supported by the argument that different cultures espouse different philosophies and values concerning the human condition and so there cannot, therefore, be a commonly or uniformly applicable theory of human rights. Chris Brown states this position forcefully:

> It is implausible to think that rights can be extracted from liberal polities, decontextualised and applied as a package worldwide. This is not simply because of international value-pluralism; it is decontextualisation that is critical whether international or domestic.[6]

The political argument is that, since there were only a small number of independent African States in 1948, how could colonial powers determine what is universal? In other words, universalism was another function of imperialism, with a few but dominant nations presuming to prescribe principles and philosophies of life for the rest of the world.

A number of variations of relativist arguments can be identified. First, that since civilisations and cultures vary both in time and geographical location so too will their life-worlds vary. On this basis, international human rights standards are simply European or Western norms which are being imposed upon all other contemporary cultures for all time. A second variation of this idea is that, even if it were to be agreed that there are some human rights norms which have universal acceptance, it would be impossible to attach similar value or weight to them irrespective of location and circumstance. Thirdly, although there are some human rights norms that do have universal acceptance, others are negotiable in the light of the prevailing cultural, historical or other values applicable at any given time or place. Fourthly, in any event, the nature of society and of the world is such that there is a multiplicity of cultures and values and these have to be respected since they provide an essential starting point for any understanding of societal norms.

It is therefore unnecessary to assert the existence of a monochromatic global society and it is possible to value difference. Each culture has its own ways of interpreting and understanding universal norms which must be

---

[5] Vienna Declaration and Programme of Action, A/CONF.157/23, para. 5.
[6] Brown, 'Universal Human Rights', p. 49.

viewed only in broad terms. There is value in seeking to understand the dynamics of different cultures and societies and opening up space for dialogue with one another. This fourth version is a moderate form of relativism and it is predicated upon the notion that all human rights must be mediated through local understandings and interpretations.

There have, of course, been some spirited defences of universalism. Kofi Komado argues that, regardless of who actually drafted the UDHR and by whom it was adopted, it cannot be denied that the Declaration reflects human values which are universal to humankind.[7] Justice Abdul Koroma, Judge of the International Court of Justice, provides a more balanced statement on the relevance of the Universal Declaration. He acknowledges the charge that it does not reflect African values and culture and that it propounds an individualistic view of rights.[8] However, he believes human rights have always been part of the African value system and he goes on to say:

> In my view, however, the values and ethos which were proclaimed by the Declaration have neither proved adverse nor injurious to the interests of the African people as a whole. Accordingly, the significance and the impact of the Declaration should not be underestimated, because it was inspired and defined by a certain political philosophy, elements of which are universally shared.

Judge Koroma thus makes the very vital point that all law evolves and is continuously shaped by interpretation in order to enhance justice.[9]

---

[7] International Commission of Jurists, 'Africa and the Universal Declaration of Human Rights', *The Review: Special Issue* 60 (1998) 41. Komado goes on to say (*ibid.*, p. 42): 'For us in Africa, it will be wrong to interpret the Universal Declaration in eurocentric terms or to put an ideological tag on it. The truth is that in the contemporary interdependent and interpenetrating global society of ours, the Universal Declaration and the emerging constitutional law of human rights it has engendered, serve as the web around which our hopes for a better and more just world are woven.'

[8] A. Koroma, 'The Influence of the Universal Declaration of Human Rights in Africa – Fifty Years After Its Adoption – A Legal Perspective', *Africa Legal Aid Quarterly* (1998) 6.

[9] This view is supported by another African judge of the International Court of Justice, Judge Bola Ajibola, who writes that: 'Most of the freedoms guaranteed reflect values which in traditional African society were well respected and cherished. Traditional African society particularly cherished human values such as equality and liberty. Respect and privilege stemmed not from the individual's power and wealth, but from his or her humanity.' B. Ajibola, 'Problems of Human Rights and the Rule of Law', *Africa Legal Aid Quarterly* (July–September 1997) 25. This confidence in African values is also celebrated by Justice Yvonne Mokgoro of the South African Constitutional Court, who says that: 'the values of *ubuntu* [the concept that identity is formed by community], I would like to believe, if consciously harnessed, can be central to a process of harmonising indigenous law with the Constitution and can be integral to a new South African jurisprudence.' Y. Mokgoro, *Buffalo*

It would appear, therefore, that, although worded in universalist terms, international human rights norms are beginning to espouse the moderate version of relativism. This is illustrated by the following examples. First, the Vienna Declaration and Programme of Action of 1993, adopted by 172 Member States of the United Nations, holds both the universalist and the relativist notions in tension. It states that:

> All human rights are universal, indivisible, and interdependent and interrelated. The international community must treat human rights globally in a fair and equal manner, on the same footing and with the same emphasis. While the significance of national and regional peculiarities and various historical, cultural and religious backgrounds must be borne in mind, it is the duty of States, regardless of their political, economic, and cultural systems, to promote and protect all human rights and fundamental freedoms.[10]

Of course, this formulation was seeking to address a number of concerns all at once. At one level, it sought to answer those who claim that there is a hierarchy of rights by attacking the argument that some rights have immediate application and are enforceable and justiciable while others are mere principles of policy direction. At another level, it sought to address the 'universalism v. relativism' debate by having resort to the principle of the margin of appreciation developed within the jurisprudence of the European Convention on Human Rights in order to take account of cultural specificities when applying human rights norms and ever since the *Handyside* case[11] has been used in relation to an expanding number of Convention Articles. In the *Lawless* case, Sir Humphrey Waldock explained that the rationale for the recognition of a margin of appreciation:

> is that the government's discharge of these responsibilities is essentially a delicate problem of appreciating complex factors and balancing conflicting considerations of the public interest.[12]

Human Rights Law Review 4 (1998) 22. Of course, one must not lose sight of the fact that these views may be taking a less critical and even sentimental view of African social structure, customs and history. One can also observe that they seem to take a uniform view of African culture and tradition. Not enough recognition is given to the variances and divergences in such a vast continent.

[10] Vienna Declaration and Programme of Action, para. 5.

[11] *Handyside* v. *United Kingdom*, Judgment, 7 December 1976, Series A, No. 24, (1979–80) 1 EHRR 737.

[12] *Lawless* v. *Ireland*, cited in van der Vyver, 'Universality and Relativity', p. 47.

Macdonald stresses that the margin of appreciation must reflect the appropriate scope and ambit of justifiable variation in the application of the Convention which will vary in each case according to the context and circumstances. In delineating the margin of appreciation, says Macdonald, 'what can be hoped for is the enumeration of the many different factors that are relevant to the question of the proper level of deference, and an indication, perhaps through examples, of the sorts of contexts in which each of those factors has most weight'.[13] Unlike van der Vyver,[14] I believe that the doctrine of the margin of appreciation opens the way to a moderate relativist position by giving due weight to the local context. It seems clear to me that the purpose of the doctrine is essentially just that: an attempt to clarify the scope of the rights in question by interpreting them taking into account the local context and it is not designed to deny rights otherwise recognised by law. The margin of appreciation doctrine does not provide a justification for the violation of a right; it helps define the parameters of the right in question.

A second example, which is also reflected in the Vienna Declaration, concerns the Paris Principles[15] which again demonstrate an awareness of the importance of the context-specific application of human rights norms. The Paris Principles were designed to shape the establishment and development of independent national institutions and mechanisms for the promotion and protection of human rights. In endorsing those Principles, the Vienna Declaration also recognised 'the right of each State to choose the framework which is best suited to its particular needs at national level'.[16]

---

[13] R. St J. Macdonald, F. Matscher and H. Petzold (eds.), *The European System for the Protection of Human Rights* (Dordrecht: Martinus Nijhoff, 1993), p. 85.

[14] Van der Vyver, 'Universality and Relativity', p. 50.

[15] Principles Relating to the Status of National Institutions, UN General Assembly Resolution 48/134, adopted 20 December 1993.

[16] Vienna Declaration, para. 36. It is, however, easier to provide for this in the abstract than in practice, as shown by the following incident. The International Coordinating Committee of National Institutions (ICC) is a voluntary association of national institutions accredited to the United Nations Commission on Human Rights and supported by and working closely with the Office of the UN High Commissioner for Human Rights in Geneva which resolved to establish an accreditation system for national institutions so that there could be uniform founding principles and, broadly, ensure a similar standing for national institutions. It naturally required national institutions, for the purposes of accreditation, to conform to the Paris Principles. The ICC published guidelines and a list of accredited national institutions. The Consultative Human Rights Council of Morocco, however, received only provisional accreditation since five government ministers are ordinary members. Whereas the Paris Principles state that representatives of government departments,

Cultural relativism must, therefore, be viewed as mutually interactive with universalism. Universal principles had their genesis in local situations and traditions. They will be considered an imposition only to the extent that nations are unable to identify something of themselves and their values in the principles.[17] All cultures contribute to the corpus of rights according to their own traditions and understandings. In that case they become simply executives of global governance.[18] International standards are important because they settle some key principles and set norms and standards. And yet national insights and experiences must continue to improve and perfect international standards, revise them or establish new ones as necessity determines. That constant interaction is due to the fact that ordinary human beings who are located in the real world also devise international norms. These norms will only have value to the extent that they meet human needs. This dynamism of rights must be viewed against the universally accepted notion that all culture is dynamic and that intellectual property is subject to change and development.[19] Not all culture is uniformly good or bad and no culture can sit in moral judgment over others. Isaac Nguema, a former Chairman of the African Commission, insists that whatever the origins of specific theories of human rights – whether from within the Western and some Asian codified traditions or from the oral traditions of Africa and indigenous Americans – that is no evidence of moral or intellectual superiority.[20] Moreover, all cultural practices and traditions operate within systems of dynamics which balance each other out and are usually self-correcting.[21]

if included, 'should participate in the deliberations only in an advisory capacity'. African delegates objected to this, claiming that the Committee had failed to appreciate the specific context within which Morocco operated, while Morocco itself argued that the presence of government ministers was essential to ensure better liaison between the government and the Commission. I would suggest that had the ICC applied the principle of the margin of appreciation it might have avoided such objections.

[17] See Lon Fuller's internal morality of the law which requires constancy, consistency, applicability and certainty: L. Fuller, *The Morality of the Law* (New Haven: Yale University Press,1964), pp. 46–91.

[18] O'Sullivan, 'History of Human Rights'.

[19] See B. Pityana, *Beyond Transition: The Evolution of Theological Method in South Africa – A Cultural Approach* (unpublished thesis, University of Cape Town, 1995), pp. 64–80.

[20] I. Nguema: 'Africa, Human Rights and Development', *Review of the African Commission on Human and Peoples' Rights* 7(2) (1998) 91–113 at 93.

[21] For example, the Basotho under Moshoeshoe I had a proverb: *morena ke morena ka sechaba; sechaba ke sechaba ka morena* (a chief is a chief by and through the support of the people, and a people is a people by and through the umbrella of security and good order provided

Mindful of this caution, Yash Ghai argues that the environment around which human rights have been understood and applied has undergone change. First, the world has become more globalised, which suggests that there is a greater degree of cultural fusion and subversion than might have been contemplated before. This has sharpened the sense of neighbourhood, the global village compelling cultures to co-exist. 'The key moral question of our time', writes Professor Yash Ghai,

> is the basis on which diverse peoples can co-exist and interact. More specifically, the question is whether in this multi-cultural world a particular view or belief can be regarded as overriding international consensus on rights and values.[22]

Secondly, there is a greater understanding, even if grudging at times, of the view that all rights must be considered holistically, as was counselled in the Vienna Declaration. This sensitivity to the interrelatedness, indivisibility and interdependence of rights requires that there be greater appreciation of the need to balance competing rights, and cultural relativity plays a part in this process.

Makau wa Mutua places these challenges in the political context of Africa. He pleads that the rhetoric of human rights need not be ensconced in liberal absolutism but 'in the dynamic ability of the human rights movement to accept new dimensions and shifting priorities'. This, he believes by some dialectical argumentation, would preserve the universalism of human rights principles:

> One of the drawbacks of the rights language is its ability to decontextualise concrete struggles through universalisation. But this is a blunder African scholar-activists cannot afford. While the linguistic universalisation of the general struggle against State despotism is a necessary and an essential first step against repressive regimes, it will not undo the concrete localised conditions that allow dictators to flourish.[23]

by the chief). Typically, people changed their allegiances to a brother or relative of the chief or they overthrew the chief whenever he failed to provide security and justice for the people. See S. J. Gill, 'Electoral Systems for Lesotho: Lesotho's Own Political Heritage and Possible Contributions from Other Systems', in C. N. Sello (ed.), *1998 Lesotho National Election: Lessons for the Future* (Lesotho Council of Non-Governmental Organizations, 1998), pp. 22–5. Examples from east and west Africa are set out in Mutua, 'The Banjul Charter', pp. 22–8.

[22] Ghai, 'Universalism and Relativism', p. 5.

[23] M. wa Mutua, 'Human Rights Discourse: African Viewpoint', in R. Savio, R. and D. E. Reoch, E. Dallas, *Human Rights: The New Consensus* (London: Regency Press, 1994), p. 99.

What wa Mutua seeks to achieve is an alignment of the universal language of rights with the appreciation of the concrete African political and cultural environment in which such rights are to be applied. Failure to do so will simply produce a human rights movement in Africa which would be a duplication of Western discourse which, it is argued, would simply lead to a cul de sac. This requires that international norms should not be regarded as an invariable template but as minimum standards or a framework which permit further dynamic development and expressions.

It is evident from the above discussion, therefore, that rights, as part of the fabric of society, must similarly reflect the changing values, perceptions and power relations within and between different worlds. There can be no doubt that within the conceptual framework of rights ideological and hegemonic ideals prevail as they do in other aspects of life. The rights discourse that has been universalised, it must be admitted, reflects a world-view and principles of the State drawn from Western philosophy. Even though all cultures have espoused values of rights, the way these have been expressed and understood is through Westernised language and ideas. What is required is the legitimising of all cultures as sources of rights.[24] More importantly, rights – or understandings of them – change and vary; they are vibrant and dynamic. Having said all that, it must also be conceded that humanity best exists in a rights world. All human beings are bearers of rights. Yash Ghai, in an article celebrating fifty years of the Universal Declaration of Human Rights, expresses this dynamic model of rights as follows:

> Rights – whose moral legitimacy is drawn from several sources, including a critical analysis of social and economic organisation, international negotiations and agreements, and overlapping inter-cultural consensus – are valuable as the basis of interrogating and critiquing culture. Cultural understandings can be informed (and thereby changed) by notions of fairness, and knowledge of rights can awaken awareness of oppression, and its causes. Rights respond to changing perceptions of justice, reflecting the imperatives of particular economic and social systems.[25]

It will be clear from this that one must view rights in a more dynamic and holistic mode. One must not only observe the interaction and interrelatedness of rights but one must also note that rights are best expressed and

---

[24] See M. wa Mutua, 'Savages, Victims and Saviours: The Metaphor of Human Rights', *Harvard International Law Journal* 42(1) (2001) 201–45.

[25] Y. Ghai, 'The Critics of the Universal Declaration', *Interights Bulletin* 12(1) (1989) 45.

applied by balancing various rights claims. Finally, no one can any longer deny that rights best find expression and application in given contexts. One cannot understand and apply rights under a form of universalism that is discrete from the context in which rights are to be applied and experienced. To underscore this, Ghai argues that:

> Such processes provide a basis for inter-cultural dialogues and for adjusting rights to the exigencies of different societies. But they provide for the balance to be struck in a principled way, with a measure of rationality, justification and proportionality, *within a framework of generally accepted values.* In increasingly complex and globalising societies, such a regime of rights provides both a universalising framework and the means of adjusting rights to local circumstances. It facilitates pluralism without compromising essential principles. Without such a binding framework, fair and peaceful co-existence of diverse peoples and cultures would be placed in dire jeopardy.[26]

It is my submission that the African Charter holds the elements of universality and particularity in a dialectic of tension and mutual reinforcement. In many ways the Charter predates the arguments that have surfaced during the process that culminated in the adoption of the 1993 Vienna Declaration and subsequent debates, which were heightened when, on its fiftieth anniversary, the efficacy and relevance of the Universal Declaration was brought under the microscope.

Culture, the African Charter and domestic law: a margin of appreciation to States?

Moving on from these general observations, the second part of this chapter will look at a number of issues which bear upon the nature of the relationship between the Charter and domestic law and practice. The first set of issues arise out of the nature of the concepts found within the Charter itself, the second from its practical application. These will be addressed in turn.

CONCEPTUAL ISSUES

Individual duties

Some have suggested that the inclusion of duties in the African Charter, alongside its references to the family, reinforce a conservative approach to

---

[26] *Ibid.*, p. 46 (emphasis added).

human rights.[27] Scholars such as Makau wa Mutua have argued that the language of duties underplays the force of rights because it emphasises the duty of the individual rather than that of the State, and Evelyn Ankumah also argues that the language of duties 'is vaguely defined and could be used to suppress individual rights such as the freedom of conscience'.[28] There is, accordingly, a preponderance of opinion which suggests that the mere provision of 'duties' creates a reactionary environment for the protection of human rights. There is also an unjustified view that the African Charter is unique in that it provides for the duties of the individual. Not only is there a neat reference to 'duties' in Article 29 of the UDHR but these can also be found in a number of other international instruments such as the Declaration on the Right to Development[29] and, more recently, in the Declaration on Human Rights Defenders.[30] Among regional instruments one can find these in the American Declaration of the Rights and Duties of Man[31] and in the Inter-American Convention on Human Rights.[32] A feature of the African Charter, though, is that these duties are spelt out more elaborately than anywhere else. The Charter does not permit general derogations although 'clawback' limitations of the rights are spelt out. If anything, the chapter on duties, Articles 27–29, represents perhaps the most elaborate limitations of the rights. For example, Article 27(2) provides:

> The rights and freedoms of each individual shall be exercised with due regard to the rights of others, collective security, morality and common interest.

[27] See International Human Rights Policy Council, *Taking Duties Seriously: Individual Duties in International Human Rights Law; A Commentary* (Geneva: International Human Rights Policy Council, 1999).

[28] Ankumah, 'Towards Effective Implementation of the African Charter', *Interights Bulletin* 8(3) (1994) 59–60 at 60. Hatem Ben Salem, a member of the African Commission, has proposed that consideration of the amendment of the African Charter should be seriously considered because 'it is doubtful whether it is necessary to keep in the text of the Charter such heavy duties towards individuals'. H. Ben Salem, 'The African System for the Protection of Human and Peoples' Rights', *Interights Bulletin* 8 (1994) 55–7 at 56.

[29] General Assembly Resolution 41/128, 4 December 1986.

[30] Declaration on the Right and Responsibility of Individuals, Groups and Organs of Society to Promote and Protect Universally Recognised Human Rights and Fundamental Freedoms, General Assembly Resolution 53/144, 8 March 1999.

[31] Adopted by the Ninth International Conference of American States, Bogotá, Colombia, 1948, Chapter 2.

[32] Article 32.

Article 28 provides:

> Every individual shall have the duty to respect and consider his fellow be-
> ings without discrimination, and to maintain relations aimed at promoting,
> safeguarding and reinforcing mutual respect and tolerance.

Article 29(7) provides:

> [The individual shall have the duty] to preserve and strengthen positive
> African cultural values in his relations with other members of the society,
> in the spirit of tolerance, dialogue and consultation ...

Far from duties creating an environment for a gratuitous invasion of rights, duties should be understood as reinforcing rights. Secondly, it becomes necessary to make reference to duties because, in the modern global environment, the key performers are not necessarily the States but non-State actors. To focus solely on States as providers and protectors of rights would be to leave out of consideration a large part of social commerce where rights are exercised. Finally, the African Charter spells out duties in order to save the African system of human rights from over-dependence on individualism. Now that the UN has adopted a declaration on the rights and duties of citizens,[33] I hope that that argument can be laid to rest. The tide is turning against the over-emphasis of rights which was a feature of the traditional human rights regime. It is now affirmed that rights can best be understood alongside or as the flip side of duties and that the two should always be held together. There is, for example, a movement that misguidedly suggests that the human rights agenda elevates the rights of criminals and law-breakers. In any event, no rights are absolute and all rights are subject to limitations. Sensitivity to this attack has led human rights experts to seek to make provision for the rights of victims as well.

Even if one accepts this understanding of individual duties, the concept is not without difficulties. The problem is that duties, being generally in the form of moral rules rather than legal norms, are difficult to enforce. By their nature ethical rules are merely subject to individual conscience. There is, nonetheless, a body of fundamental moral norms which are part of the taken-for-granted world which individuals inhabit. Such norms are 'known' and 'accepted' by people in a particular milieu without question. Such rules are self-evident and warrant no further demonstration. This, of

---

[33] See note 30 above.

course, is quite apart from their observance at all times. They are stated without any need for proof. The point here is that the duties set out in the African Charter are of a different category from the rights expressed elsewhere and must be understood as such. The moral duties referred to must be seen as quite separate from the legal duties. Often legal duties can be exercised as part of the enforcement of the positive duties of individuals. There is evidence, therefore, that rights and duties must always be held together.

Rights of peoples

Comparatively little attention has been given to the meaning and implications of the references in Articles 19–24 of the Charter to 'all peoples'. This reference is particularly confusing if one accepts that from its inception, the OAU insisted upon the territorial integrity of States and respect for the national boundaries of States inherited from the colonial powers at independence.[34] The view has been expressed that the reference to 'peoples' refers simply to the anti-colonial movement or the movement for decolonisation and liberation of then subject peoples. The purpose of the provision, on this view, was simply to express solidarity as well as legal sanction to the liberation movement then struggling for independence in Africa.[35] Others, among them members of the African Commission, argue that the reference to 'peoples' in the Charter is simply another way of referring to the State. In 1963, the predominant philosophy of pan-Africanism was that Africans were a people and that African unity was the ideal championed by the OAU.[36] I consider this to be a flawed argument. Clearly, there is nothing 'African' about the concept of a nation-State. In any event, the

[34] Throughout the history of post-colonial Africa secessionist movements have been suppressed, as was the case in Biafra, Nigeria, Katanga, Congo, Casamance in Senegal, Western Sahara from Morocco, etc. Against this trend, Ethiopia conceded part of its sovereign territory to establish Eritrea, although one must understand that Ethiopia was never colonised. There have also been moves to separate Somalia and create Somaliland, reflecting the Italian and British history of colonialism. For this reason, 'peoples' should not be understood as separate sovereign entities.

[35] See Communication 75/92, *Katangese Peoples' Congress v. Zaire*, Eighth Activity Report 1994–1995, Annex VI (*Documents of the African Commission*, p. 389).

[36] For more details of the denouement of the African Commission's interpretation in mission reports and communications, see R. Murray, *The African Commission on Human and Peoples' Rights and International Law* (Oxford: Hart Publishing, 2000), pp. 104–7.

States at independence were no more than colonial creations. The reality is that the construction of the nation-State cut across a variety of forms of nationhood and political formations which characterised African societies *ab initio.*[37]

Whatever may have been the intention of the drafters and the context in which reference to 'all peoples' was made, it does lend itself to application in cases where indigenous populations in Africa, ethnic communities, seek to establish their rights as a collective within the State. Notwithstanding the *Katanga*[38] decision, the African Commission, for example, appears to have accepted the right of the people of Western Sahara to independence. At its 28th Ordinary Session held in Algiers, the Commission passed a resolution affirming the right of the people of Western Sahara to self-determination.[39] The wording of Articles 20 and 21 of the Charter bears a striking resemblance to the draft UN Declaration on the Rights of Indigenous Populations.[40] The closest the Commission has come to acknowledging minority rights as 'peoples' rights' is in a set of decisions on allegations of systematic oppression targeted at the black minority in Mauritania during the period 1989–91. At this time there was a systematic and brutal removal of black Mauritanians from their lands, victimisation of black Mauritanians in the army and the civil service and a denial of language rights. When finding violations of Articles 19 and 23 of the Charter, the Commission said that 'the unprovoked attacks on the villagers is a denial of the right of the people to live in peace and security' and that:

> Central to the communications in question is the domination of black Mauritanians by a ruling Arab clique, for which the communication presents

[37] For a fuller discussion of this, see my paper, 'On the Situation of Indigenous People in Africa', submitted for discussion at the 26th Ordinary Session of the African Commission held in Kigali, Rwanda, 1–15 November 1999.

[38] Communication 75/92, *Katangese Peoples' Congress* v. *Zaire*, Eighth Activity Report 1994–1995, Annex VI (*Documents of the African Commission*, p. 389). This was the first matter brought before the Commission under Article 20, which provides that: 'All peoples shall have the right to existence. They shall have the unquestionable and inalienable right to self-determination.' The Commission ruled that the sovereignty and territorial integrity of Zaire had to be preserved and that the province of Katanga was 'obliged to exercise a variant of self-determination that is compatible with the sovereignty and territorial integrity of Zaire'.

[39] Resolution on the Western Sahara, Thirteenth Annual Activity Report of the African Commission on Human and Peoples' Rights, 1999–2000, ACHPR/RPT/13th, Annex IV.

[40] Sub-Commission on Prevention of Discrimination and Protection of Minorities, Draft Declaration, 1994/45, 26 August 1994, E/CN.4/1995/2, E/CN.4/Sub.2/1994/56.

abundant evidence. The subsequent discrimination against black Mauritanians goes against a principal objective of the Charter, that of equality. Such oppression constitutes a violation of Article 19.[41]

In the recent decision, *Social and Economic Rights Action Centre/Centre for Economic and Social Rights* v. *Nigeria*, it was alleged that Nigerian military forces constantly raided the villages of the Ogoni people, destroyed their homes, pillaged their crops, subjected them to constant harassment and exposed them to environmental hazards due to the negligence of the oil processing plants in the region. The Commission applied the group rights provisions of the Charter and said that:

> International law and human rights must be responsive to African circumstances. Africa will make its own law where necessary. Clearly, collective rights, environmental rights and economic and social rights are essential elements of human rights in Africa.[42]

With respect, it seems to me that these cases do not provide sufficient evidence of the Commission seriously examining the significance of 'peoples' in the Charter. It is nonetheless interesting that, whereas the Commission could have adjudicated on these by mere reference to the equality provisions in Article 2 of the Charter, it chose to utilise the group rights provisions in Articles 19–23. Strangely enough, it did so without distinguishing the application of the two sets of rights especially as the communication was not necessarily a class action matter and individuals had alleged violations of their rights.[43] Neither does the Commission describe the nature and content of the rights especially as these sets of cases are the only occasions where the Commission has ventured into the application of collective rights or the rights of 'peoples'.

Having said all that, though, it must be accepted that the African Commission is not ready to interpret the provisions of the Charter in a fashion that embraces the secessionist sentiment in parts of the continent. Moreover, its caution in this regard has resulted in the Commission being very

---

[41] Communications 54/91, 61/91, 98/93, 164/97 and 210/98, *Malawi African Association; Amnesty International; Ms Sarr Diop, Union Interafricaine des Droits de l'Homme and RADDHO; Collectif des Veuves et Ayants-droits; Association Mauritanienne des Droits de l'Homme* v. *Mauritania*, Thirteenth Activity Report 1999–2000, Addendum, paras. 65–7.

[42] Communication 155/96, unpublished, paras. 49–50.

[43] On the relationship between individual and peoples' rights, see Murray, *The African Commission*, p. 109.

slow to recognise the rights of indigenous populations in Africa.[44] African States recognise the need for indigenous peoples to receive education and healthcare, as well as the right to speak their language and practise their culture. The problem that is often encountered is the tendency of States to appear to be seeking to assimilate indigenous groups into the dominant culture.[45] The 1989 ILO Convention and the draft Declaration on the Rights of Indigenous Peoples[46] provide guidance as to the States' responsibilities: to consult the peoples concerned in a manner appropriate to their cultures and traditions, to provide for the development of the indigenous communities with their participation and approval, and to teach children to read and write in their own languages. Among the rights recognised are the rights to develop their own histories, cultures and languages.[47]

Given the above interpretation, therefore, the provisions on 'peoples' rights' in the African Charter serve a vital purpose in making room for class actions and in recognising claims to 'self-determination' within a sovereign State although it is my view that this will have to be understood as falling short of secession.

PRACTICAL EXAMPLES

The African Commission has been confronted with situations where the national legislation, including constitutions, of States Parties has been at variance with the express provisions of the African Charter and in many

[44] See my paper on indigenous peoples in Africa (25th Ordinary Session, Bujumbura, 1998); and the resolution adopted by the 28th Ordinary Session in Cotonou, Benin, November 2000. Nevertheless, a working group was appointed by the African Commission at its 28th Ordinary Session in Cotonou, Benin, with the task of aligning the African Charter with developments taking place within the UN and other regional systems but without going as far as recognising self-determination as legitimating separation from the State.

[45] On a recent promotional visit to Botswana, 2–7 April 2001, debate about the appropriate ways in which the State can discharge its responsibilities towards indigenous communities was raised. The State had been grouping and, therefore, relocating indigenous communities so that, as the spokespersons argued, the provision of basic facilities like water, healthcare and schools could be better provided. Others charge that the relocations have been done without regard to indigenous traditions and culture and were essentially assimilationist.

[46] See note 40 above.

[47] For a fuller discussion of the ILO Convention and the draft declaration especially as it affects language rights of minorities and indigenous peoples, see F. de Varennes, *Language, Minorities and Human Rights* (The Hague: Martinus Nijhoff Publishers, 1996), pp. 262 *et seq.*

cases the States concerned had not provided for the domestic application of the Charter. Where there is a strong bias towards domestic law – as in South Africa and Zimbabwe – and in the absence of legislative acts domesticating the international treaty, anomalies may arise and the African Commission could declare a piece of legislation or a governmental act to be contrary to the Charter.[48] This can be avoided, as is the case in South Africa, if national legislation incorporates the principles of international law into domestic law.[49] It has been suggested, and I agree, that this subject tends to be dealt with in a too theoretical manner[50] and therefore I propose to consider the relationship in a concrete fashion by looking at a number of case studies concerning these countries.

Before doing so, however, it is worthwhile recalling the general nature of the relationship between the Commission and the States Parties: the Commission is required to interpret the Charter while States Parties are required to '[r]ecognise the rights, duties and freedoms enshrined in this Charter and . . . undertake to adopt legislative or other measures to give effect to them'.[51] Thus national courts have a critical role in the formation and shaping of international norms and standards of practice. Benedetto Conforti observes that domestic courts can recognise such norms 'if it [the court] recognises that it corresponds to an ideal of justice and of protection of the human person'.[52] Regardless of whether the international human rights treaty concerned has been incorporated into domestic law, the courts should still be able to apply the principles and abide by the spirit of the treaties. It is easy to set up barriers to judicial notice being

---

[48] P. F. Gonidec: 'The Relationship of International Law and National Law in Africa', *African Journal of International and Comparative Law* 10(2) (1998) 244–9 at 247–9.

[49] I do not share the view that, merely by neglecting to domesticate the provisions of an international treaty especially in cases when the treaty is not self-executing, the State Party may blithely ignore its international obligations. Article 1 of the African Charter states clearly that: 'Member States of the OAU parties to the present Charter shall recognise the rights, duties and freedoms enshrined in this Charter and shall undertake to adopt legislative or other measures to give effect to them.' In my opinion, neither can 'clawback' clauses vitiate the commitments solemnly made by the States Parties.

[50] See International Council on Human Rights Policy, *Universality: Local Values, International Standards and Genuine Dilemmas, Mapping Paper for Consultation only* (International Council on Human Rights Policy, August 1998).

[51] African Charter, Article 1.

[52] B. Conforti and F. Francioni (eds.), *Enforcing International Human Rights in Domestic Courts* (The Hague: Martinus Nijhoff, 1997), p. 6.

taken of international norms which fall outside the domestic legal framework. Conforti, however, cautions against resorting too readily to the non-
self-executing nature of particular obligations found in some domestic
settings.[53]

Such dangers are compounded in the context of the African Charter
because of the nature of its 'clawback' clauses which are criticised for undermining its core principles and thus limiting the scope of its applicability.
This, of course, is true of such clauses in any such instrument but is particularly acute in the African Charter because they appear to subordinate
the Charter to domestic law since there is no test that such limitations
be prescribed by a law of general application and be reasonable and justifiable in an open and democratic society based on human dignity, equality
and freedom (as, for example, is required by the South African Constitution). However, the African Commission has made it clear that these
clauses are to be interpreted against the primary objectives of the Charter and with due regard to international human rights law.[54] This needs
to be remembered when assessing the balance struck by the Charter between the international and national legal frameworks but as the following discussion will show, it is apparent that international human rights
norms and standards come into conflict with some African customary
practices and traditions, particularly in relation to matters of family and
religion.

[53] He argues that 'it is necessary to take a cautious approach in accepting the existence of an
exceptional category of international norms that owe their non-self-executing natures to
their substantive content. Such an exception must not lead to political manoeuvring in the
form of non-implementation of rules found to be "undesirable", either because they are
considered contrary to national interest, or because they entrench progressive values, or
finally because they are viewed suspiciously by the internal judge purely by reason of their
origins.' *Ibid.*, p. 8.

[54] See, for example, Communication 212/98, *Amnesty International* v. *Zambia*, Twelfth Activity Report 1998–1999, Annex V (*Documents of the African Commission*, p. 745), para. 42:
'the Commission is of the view that the "clawback" clauses must not be interpreted against
the principles of the Charter. Recourse to these should not be used as a means of giving credence to violations of the express provisions of the Charter. Secondly, the rules
of natural justice must apply . . . It is important for the Commission to caution against
a too easy resort to the limitation clauses in the African Charter. The onus is on the
State to prove that it is justified to resort to the limitation clause.' See also Communications 140/94, 141/94 and 145/95, *Constitutional Rights Project, Civil Liberties Organisation and Media Rights Agenda* v. *Nigeria*, Thirteenth Activity Report 1999–2000, Annex V,
para. 40.

African customary law and discrimination against women

Zimbabwe, a party to the African Charter, the Convention on the Elimination of All Forms of Discrimination Against Women[55] and the ICCPR,[56] has a Constitution which contains a provision that outlaws discrimination on the basis, *inter alia*, of gender or sex. Section 23(3) of the Constitution, however, excludes marriage, divorce and 'the application of African customary law in any case involving Africans' from the scope of that provision. The courts in Zimbabwe display a particular conservativeness in matters relating to customary law, especially family law. Although there have been subsequent amendments by parliament, the courts have been progressive in matters concerning civil and political rights such as the death penalty[57] and the right of Zimbabwean women to bring their foreign husbands to reside in Zimbabwe.[58] Moreover, although international treaties ratified by Zimbabwe under the authority of the President are not self-executing unless passed into law by parliament, Zimbabwe has submitted three reports in accordance with Article 62 of the African Charter.[59] It must be assumed, therefore, that in general Zimbabwe seeks to abide by her international obligations in this regard. However, as matters currently stand, it is evident that the law in Zimbabwe condones discrimination against women in family matters[60] which is demonstrably in violation of the international treaties to which Zimbabwe is party. The Human Rights Committee has noted that, however varied the concept of family may be, 'the rights of women under those systems of law must not be subject to discrimination and must be ensured on the basis of equality with men'.[61]

Nevertheless, Zimbabwean courts have recently handed down some controversial judgments that perpetuate the problems. For example, Vennia

---

[55] Convention on the Elimination of All Forms of Discrimination Against Women (1979), UNGA Res. 34/180.

[56] International Covenant on Civil and Political Rights (1966), UNGA Res. 2200A (XXI), 999 UNTS 171.

[57] *Catholic Justice and Peace Commission* v. *Attorney-General*, 1993 (1) ZLR 242(S).

[58] *Rattigan* v. *Chief Immigration Officer*, 1994 (2) ZLR 54(S).

[59] The second and third report were combined.

[60] See, for example, CEDAW, Concluding Observations: Zimbabwe, 14 May 1998, A/53/38, paras. 120–66 at paras. 141 and 157.

[61] Quoted in A. Armstrong *et al.* (eds.), *Uncovering Reality: Excavating Women's Rights in African Family Law* (Women and Law in Southern Africa Working Paper No. 7), p. 8.

Magaya sought a Supreme Court ruling overturning the decision of the Magistrates' Court that a woman 'cannot be appointed to [her] father's estate when there is a man' in a case of intestate succession under customary law. The Supreme Court ruled unanimously that 'the nature of African society dictated that women were not equal to men. According to cultural norms, women should never be considered adults within the family, but only as a junior male or teenager.' Justice Gibson Muchetere argued that customary law took precedence over statutory law. The Legal Age of Majority Act 1982, which accords majority status to men and women upon reaching the age of 18, did not apply to customary family law and, the judge continued, Zimbabwe's Constitution sanctioned discrimination against African women in family matters:

> Under customary law, women did not have a right to heirship and majority status would not give them that additional right.[62]

In his judgment, Muchetere J made reference to the fact that rural communities still practised customary law and their values would be offended by any reckless disavowal of customs. In justifying his ruling in support of the Magistrates' Court, he said:

> It must be recognised that customary law has long directed the way African people conducted their lives and the majority of Africans in Zimbabwe still live in rural areas and still conduct their lives in terms of customary law.[63]

Chidi Anselm Odinkalu argues that, had the Court applied its mind to the 'repugnancy test', and thereby affirmed the supremacy of non-discrimination, it would have arrived at a different conclusion.[64] Rather than doing

---

[62] Reported in the South African *Mail and Guardian*, 7 May 1999.

[63] *Ibid.* This may suggest that, in urban Zimbabwe, if the case can be made that a particular custom no longer had credence, the court might decide otherwise!

[64] C. A. Odinkalu and C. Christensen, 'The African Commission on Human and Peoples' Rights: The Development of Its Non-State Communications Procedures', HRQ 20 (1998) 235 at 240. This is doubtful because the Court does assert without proving it that society in Zimbabwe does not accept that a woman succeeds to her father's inheritance where there is a surviving male relative. What the Court did not do was to examine the effect of conflict of laws, apply a limitation test and give weight to the provisions and/or intentions of the Constitution of Zimbabwe. Instead, the Court ruled that the Constitution intended to exclude customary law from subjection to the Constitution. That is a problem that needs to be addressed. The Women and Law Working Paper (see note 61 above) argues with reference to Article 18(2) of the African Charter that: 'While traditional values of this sort include those existing in customary law, it seems that they

so, the Court has tended to take a static, conservative view of women and society. If this reactionary interpretation becomes settled law, then the worst of Mutua's fears about the African Charter will become fulfilled.[65]

In another Zimbabwean case, Marita Ncube was jailed for eighteen months for arson after having intentionally set her father-in-law's house on fire because he insisted on having sexual relations with her in accordance, he claimed, with customary law.[66] A coalition of women's groups protesting the trend in the courts stated recently that 'what alarms us is that the Supreme Court reinstates the disadvantages and disabilities women suffered under customary law, which the legislature clearly intended to remove through the Legal Age of Majority Act'. Susan Njani, writing in the *Mail & Guardian*, surmised that 'one section of the current Constitution prohibits discrimination on the grounds of sex, while another states that it is lawful to discriminate in areas of family law, customary law, inheritance, divorce or marriage'.[67]

Some cases brought before the South African Human Rights Commission also suggest the continuation of discriminatory practices. For example, a Mrs Rakoma sought to enforce her rights to her inheritance after her parents died. She discovered that the Bafokeng tribal court had granted the parental estate to her nephew, her late brother's son, to her total exclusion. It was only following the intervention of the South African Human Rights Commission that a higher tribunal of tribal authority reversed the decision of the lower court.[68]

---

are subject to recognition by the community. This is supported by the duty, established in Article 29 of the Charter, to preserve and strengthen *positive* African cultural values in relations with other members of society in the spirit of tolerance, dialogue and consultation and, in general, to contribute to the promotion of the moral well-being of society.' The working paper argues that, in the Zimbabwe cases, the judges have lost sight of the fact that it is *positive* values which are to be preserved, being those relevant to a contemporary, progressive, modern society.

[65] M. wa Mutua, 'The African Human Rights System in Comparative Perspective', *Review of the African Commission on Human and Peoples' Rights* 3 (1993) 5–11 at 8.

[66] He claimed that, according to the customs of the Kalanga people, it was his responsibility to look after his son's possessions while he was away, and that that included his wife.

[67] S. Njani, *Mail and Guardian* (South Africa), 10 June 1999.

[68] In another case before the Commission, Mrs Elizabeth Tumane, who belonged to the Bakgatla tribe and was a Jehovah's Witness, was restricted to her compound because she refused to comply with traditional mourning practices which, she argued, were contrary to her religious beliefs. But cf. Thandabantu Nhlapo, who takes a more positive view of the effect of South Africa's new constitutionalism on the practice of African traditions and

On the other hand, following *Makwanyane*,[69] the courts have been taking a more purposive approach to constitutional interpretation in order to achieve substantial equality. Drawing extensively from an article by Albertyn and Kentridge on the right to equality in the interim Constitution, Kathree has argued that:

> A purposive, contextual approach to interpretation will not only 'seek to maximise its coherence' and to promote the values of an 'open and democratic society based on freedom and equality' but it will place equality 'at the centre' of constitutionalism in South Africa. It is this 'appreciation of the centrality of equality to the task of democratic reconstruction' that guides us towards a substantive understanding of the right to equality in Section 8 of the Bill of Rights. They [Albertyn and Kentridge] argue that the purposive approach 'reveals that within the constitutional vision of democracy lies an expansive and substantive conception of equality which encompasses the need to remedy inequality as well as remove discrimination'.[70]

It is evident, therefore, that South African jurisprudence is moving towards the practice of 'purposive' interpretation that aims to ensure a contextualised understanding of the intention of the law. This is now reinforced by the Promotion of Equality and Prevention of Unfair Discrimination Act 2000, which entered into force on 21 March 2001, which seeks to give effect to the equality provision of the Constitution and to provide for the domestic application of relevant international treaties such as the Convention on the Elimination of Racial Discrimination and the Convention on the Elimination of All Forms of Discrimination Against Women to which South Africa is a party. The purpose of the new law is stated as 'to promote substantive equality' and it is to be hoped that this will be recognised domestically with regard to customary law and internationally in the elaboration of the proposed Draft Protocol to the African Charter on Human and Peoples' Rights on the Rights of Women in Africa.[71]

---

customs. He holds that the new constitutional dispensation could be guaranteed to give fair scrutiny to African tradition and custom in the light of the tenets of the constitution. He refers to two cases decided by the lower courts: the Transvaal Provincial Division, *Mthembu* v. *Letsela*, 1997 (2) SA 936 (T) confirmed by the Supreme Court of Appeal (*per* Mpati AJA, Case No. 71/98, delivered on 30 May 2000) and *Mabena* v. *Letsoalo*, 1998 (2) SA 1068 (T).

[69] 1995 (6) BCLR 665; 1995 (3) SA 391; 1995 (2) SACR 1 (CC); 1999 (1) 18 (SCA).

[70] F. Kathree, 'The Convention on the Elimination of All Forms of Discrimination Against Women', *South African Journal of Human Rights* 11 (1995) 421–37 at 435.

[71] Final Version, 13 September 2000, CAB/LEG/66.6. This must be submitted to an expert group of the OAU before being submitted for adoption by the Council of Ministers and

Religion

Human rights and gender activists have been outraged by the recent adoption and application of *Shari'a* law among the northern states of Nigeria which raises serious questions concerning the application of the African Charter, both as regards conflicts with religious law and with the application of the Charter in federal States.[72] In South Africa such matters are easier to deal with and a balance has been struck between the respective sets of concerns in a fashion which seems to mirror that adopted by the African Commission itself. In recent cases against Sudan concerning the application of *Shari'a* against non-Muslims, the African Commission held:

> There is no controversy as to *Shari'a* being based upon the interpretation of the Muslim religion. When Sudanese tribunals apply *Shari'a*, they must do so in accordance with the other obligations undertaken by the State of Sudan. Trials must always accord with international fair-trial standards. Also, it is fundamentally unjust that religious laws should be applied against non-adherents of the religion. Tribunals that apply only *Shari'a* are thus not competent to judge non-Muslims, and everyone should have the right to be tried by a secular court if they wish.[73]

As regards the alleged persecution of non-Muslims to force their conversion to Islam, the African Commission similarly held:

ultimately the Assembly of Heads of State and Government. The Protocol seeks to address the continuing discrimination against women prevalent in Africa and to eliminate the harmful practices associated with gender discrimination. The draft requires States to pass legislation and develop policies which will ensure equality and equal participation of women, eliminate harmful social and cultural practices and conduct, eliminate violence against women and regulate matrimonial relations so as to protect women against exploitation. The passage of this protocol would mark a radical development by African States in progressively ensuring the rights of women in Africa.

[72] In Zamfara State, a teenage woman, Bariya Ibrahim Magazu, was sentenced to a total of 180 lashes with a whip by an Islamic court because she became pregnant out of wedlock. She was found guilty by a court in Tsafe for the offences of *zina* (pre-marital sex or fornication) and *qadhf'* (making false accusations against the men she accused of fathering her child). The men identified by the woman were all found not to be responsible. Ms Magazu gave birth and the punishment was due to be handed out forty days after the birth of the baby. In Katsina State, 18-year-old Attine Tanko was sentenced to a public flogging after having been found guilty by an Islamic court of engaging in pre-marital sex.

[73] Communications 48/90, 50/91, 52/91 and 89/93, *Amnesty International; Comité Loosli Bachelard; Lawyers' Committee for Human Rights; Association of Members of the Episcopal Conference of East Africa* v. *Sudan*, Thirteenth Activity Report 1999–2000, Addendum, para. 73.

Other allegations refer to the oppression of Christian civilians and religious leaders and the expulsion of missionaries. It is alleged that non-Muslims suffer persecution in the form of denial of work, food aid and education. A serious allegation is that of unequal food distribution in prisons, subjecting Christian prisoners to blackmail in order to obtain food. These attacks on individuals on account of their religious persuasion considerably restrict their ability to practise freely the religion to which they subscribe. The government provides no evidence or justifications that would mitigate this conclusion. Accordingly, the Commission holds a violation of Article 8.[74]

Turning now to the South African practice, in a groundbreaking case on freedom of religion,[75] the court took judicial notice of Article 2 (on equality) and Article 8 (on the right to free practice of religion) and found that attendance at religious observances in State schools was 'free and voluntary' and that any form of coercion would be unconstitutional. The court found that, by subjecting herself to the constitution of the school association, the plaintiff waived her right to exclude herself from participating in obligations which flowed from a freely chosen affiliation: she had the option of renouncing her membership but chose not to do so.

Two other cases have recently come before the South African Constitutional Court which touch upon the right to religious belief and its practice. In *Christian Education South Africa* v. *Minister of Education*,[76] the constitutionality of the Schools Act which declared corporal punishment in schools to be an offence was challenged. Sachs J, giving the unanimous verdict of the court, recalled that:

> courts throughout the world have shown special solicitude for protecting children from what they have regarded as the potentially injurious consequences of their parents' religious practices. It is now widely accepted that in every matter concerning a child, the child's best interests must be of paramount importance.

Confronted with the consequences of the parties operating from different starting points, one on the basis of human rights and the other from a religious viewpoint,[77] Sachs J decided that the appellants had to be bound

---

[74] *Ibid.*, para. 76.
[75] *Wittman* v. *Deutscher Schulverein Pretoria and Others*, 1999 (1) BCLR 92 (T).
[76] CCT 13/98.
[77] Albeit a particularly narrow religious interpretation which was expressed thus: 'For believers, including the children involved, the indignity and degradation lay not in the punishment, but in the defiance of the scriptures represented by leaving misdeeds unpunished;

by the limits of the common law and found that it was not unreasonable to expect the schools to make adaptations to uphold the principle of non-discrimination.[78]

The second is an inconclusive case, *Prince v. President of the Law Society of the Cape of Good Hope.*[79] The appellant, a devotee of Rastafarianism, sought to overturn the decision of the Law Society that he was not a 'fit and proper person' to be admitted as an attorney because of his previous convictions for use of cannabis and his declaration that he intended to continue using the substance. He argued that criminalising its use was an unconstitutional restriction upon his right to religious belief and practice. Although the court felt that additional evidence was required before it could determine the constitutional issue,[80] the judge noted that Rastafarians were a vulnerable minority deserving of protection and, in a statement which seems to reflect the current approach to the question, it was said that:

> Our Constitution recognises that minority groups may hold their own religious views and enjoins us to tolerate and protect such views. However, the right to freedom of religion is not absolute. While members of a religious community may not determine for themselves which laws they will obey and which they will not, the State should, where it is reasonably possible, seek to avoid putting the believers to a choice between their faith and respect for the law.

Conclusions

Calling for a more liberal and progressive interpretation of the African Charter, Ankumah observes that:

> A major threat to the enjoyment of fundamental rights regards the conservative interpretation of those rights. Too often, arguments are made that a particular human rights notion is a Western invention with no relevance to

---

subjectively for those who shared the religious outlook of the community, no indignity at all was involved.' *Ibid.*

[78] He was also of the view that '[t]he parents are not being obliged to make an absolute and strenuous choice between obeying the law of the land or following their conscience. They can do both simultaneously.' *Ibid.*

[79] CCT 36/00.

[80] 'To answer the constitutional question presented in this appeal', said Ngcobo J, 'it is necessary to have information on how, where, when and by whom cannabis is used within the Rastafarian religion in South Africa, how cannabis is obtained and whether the religion regulates the use and possession of cannabis by its members'.

Africa. Those notions are often said to be inconsistent with African tradition and values.[81]

She gives the example of how the African Commission dealt with a communication from Zimbabwe on the rights of gay and lesbian people. On the basis of an untested allegation that 'homosexuality offends the African sense of dignity and morality and is inconsistent with positive African values', the communication was declared inadmissible.[82] Another similar example concerns a group of consolidated cases against Mauritania in which the Commission declined to pronounce on the social practice of slavery in part because the State delegates denied that there was slavery although they acknowledged that historical relations of inequality still persisted.[83] An outline for a more progressive interpretation of the Charter is evidenced in the recent cases against Zambia and Nigeria where the Commission ruled that limitations on rights must be compatible with international law.[84] Clearly, this reflects the form of progressive development in the jurisprudence of the Commission for which many are clamouring. It is also consistent with Article 60 of the Charter which enjoins the Commission to interpret the Charter in the light of other international human rights conventions.

It is my sincere belief that, more than ever before, the African Commission now has tools to interpret the Charter more effectively. Not only did the OAU First Ministerial Conference on Human Rights, in the Grand Bay (Mauritius) Declaration and Programme of Action (1999),[85] pronounce on the fact that many of the problems experienced in Africa have their roots in human rights violations, it also affirmed a number of human rights norms and undertook to support the work of the African Commission. It is also noticeable that, in

---

[81] E. Ankumah, *The African Commission on Human and Peoples' Rights. Practice and Procedures* (The Hague: Martinus Nijhoff, 1997), p. 17.

[82] *Ibid.*; Communication 136/94, *William Courson* v. *Zimbabwe*, Eighth Activity Report 1994–1995, Annex VI (*Documents of the African Commission*, p. 397).

[83] Communications 54/91, 61/91, 98/93, 164/97 and 210/98, *Malawi African Association; Amnesty International; Ms Sarr Diop, Union Interafricaine des Droits de l'Homme and RADDHO; Collectif des Veuves et Ayants-droits; Association Mauritanienne des Droits de l'Homme* v. *Mauritania*, Thirteenth Activity Report 1999–2000, Addendum.

[84] See, for example, Communication 212/98, *Amnesty International* v. *Zambia*, Twelfth Activity Report 1998–1999, Annex V (*Documents of the African Commission*, p. 745); Communications 140/94, 141/94 and 145/95, *Constitutional Rights Project, Civil Liberties Organisation and Media Rights Agenda* v. *Nigeria*, Thirteenth Activity Report 1999–2000, Annex V.

[85] CONF/HRA/DECL (I).

the context of the OAU reform process currently in process, the Assembly of Heads of State and Government meeting at Lomé, Togo, in July 2000 adopted the 'Constitutive Act of the African Union' which affirms the principles already enshrined in the Charter, namely, the promotion of gender equality; respect for democratic principles, human rights and the rule of law, good governance; and the promotion of social justice to ensure balanced economic development.

What then does this say about cultural relativity? I wish to reiterate the central message contained in the first section of this chapter, that the polarisation of the debate simply misses the point. In reality international human rights standards make us all both universalists and relativists. Concerns about Western hegemony simply turn those of us who are from Africa and elsewhere into reactionaries and we concede too much of the moral high ground to those who, in any event, have perfected into an art form the application of international human rights norms selectively. Secondly, what demands attention, rather, are the ground rules or guidelines for the application of contextualisation or 'margin of appreciation' principles. The second part of this chapter has attempted to illustrate how this finds reflection in the concepts in and practice under the Charter.

I would argue that this demonstrates that a theory of applied cultural relativism is unavoidable if we are to have a truly fair and just application and understanding of international human rights law. Makau wa Mutua captures perfectly the conclusions arrived at in this chapter:

> Ultimately, a new theory of internationalism and human rights, one that responds to diverse cultures, must confront the inequities of the international order. In this respect, human rights must break from the historical continuum – expressed in the metaphor and the grand narrative of human rights – that keeps intact the hierarchical relationships between European and non-European populations.[86]

[86] Mutua, 'Savages, Victims and Saviours', p. 243.

8

NON-GOVERNMENTAL ORGANISATIONS
IN THE AFRICAN SYSTEM

AHMED MOTALA

The African Commission

Throughout its existence over little more than a decade, non-governmental organisations (NGOs) have provided crucial support in strengthening the mandate of the African Commission on Human and Peoples' Rights (the Commission) and in improving its efficiency. Even prior to the establishment of the Commission, NGOs played a role in the drafting of the African Charter on Human and Peoples' Rights (the African Charter),[1] its adoption by the Organization of African Unity (OAU) and its ratification by African States. Since its establishment, a close and beneficial relationship has developed between the Commission and NGOs. This unique alliance enables NGOs to provide the Commission with much-needed support and assistance. However, more needs to be done by NGOs to improve their relationship with the Commission and to contribute effectively to the various aspects of its mandate of promotion and protection of human rights in Africa.

The African Charter recognises the role of NGOs in the work of the Commission, albeit without specifically referring to NGOs. Article 45(1)(a) of the African Charter requires the Commission to promote human and peoples' rights by encouraging 'national and local institutions concerned with human rights', and Article 45(1)(c) requires the Commission to 'co-operate with other African and international institutions concerned with the promotion and protection of human rights'. The important role of NGOs in bringing complaints of human rights violations before the Commission

---

[1] African Charter on Human and Peoples' Rights, adopted 27 June 1981, OAU Doc. CAB/LEG/67/3, rev.5, entered into force on 21 October 1986 and has universal ratification of Member States of the Organization of African Unity.

is given recognition in Article 55 of the African Charter, although the drafters of the treaty refer to 'communications other than those from States Parties to the present Charter'.[2] The Rules of Procedure of the Commission[3] are explicit about the role to be played by NGOs in its work from proposing items for the agenda of its sessions,[4] to the granting of observer status,[5] and consultations with NGOs.[6] Although the previous Rules of Procedure of the Commission specifically referred to the submission of complaints by NGOs,[7] the current Rules of Procedure make no reference to NGOs in its provisions relating to 'other communications'.[8]

The African Commission clearly recognises the excellent relationship it has with NGOs and the important contribution that they provide to its work. Its plan of action for 1996–2001 includes the establishment of an exchange and communications network and the strengthening of links with NGOs.[9] In its most recent report the Commission acknowledges the contribution of NGOs to its work including through the provision of funding for additional staff and promotional visits of Commissioners and the organisation of meetings and seminars.[10]

In its early years the Commission faced considerable criticism, including about the lack of resources, its efficiency and its ability to have any impact on the serious human rights situation in Africa. One commentator stated:

> The Commission's operation and effectiveness to date is, to be honest, appalling. It is inconceivable that an institution charged with the responsibilities that the Commission has could function at all, even assuming that the

---

[2] Article 55 of the African Charter.

[3] Amended Rules of Procedure of the African Commission on Human and Peoples' Rights, adopted by the Commission at its 18th Session held in October 1995 in Praia, Cape Verde, ACHPR/RP/XIX; R. Murray and M. Evans (eds.), *Documents of the African Commission on Human and Peoples' Rights* (Oxford: Hart Publishing, 2001), p. 21 (hereinafter *Documents of the African Commission*).

[4] Rule 6(f).   [5] Rule 75.   [6] Rule 76.

[7] Rule 114(1) and (2) of the Rules of Procedure of the African Commission on Human and Peoples' Rights, adopted on 13 February 1988, Dakar, Senegal, First Activity Report of the African Commission on Human and Peoples' Rights, Documentation No. 1, Annex V (*Documents of the African Commission*, p. 136).

[8] Chapter XVII of the Rules of Procedure.

[9] Mauritius Plan of Action, Section IV, 6 *Review of the African Commission on Human and Peoples' Rights* (1996–7) 224 (*Documents of the African Commission*, p. 579).

[10] Thirteenth Annual Report of the African Commission on Human and Peoples' Rights 1999–2000, AHG/222 (XXXVI), p. 12.

Commissioners were of the highest professionalism and courage, without at least a properly stocked library, a permanent hall or halls for public and private sessions, and a competent and able research and investigation team. Yet, the Commission as of October 1991 did not have any of the above, except their good intentions, potential professionalism of a few of the members of the Commission, and the willingness to look for solutions to the material and professional deprivations that could provide the basis for more effective concentration on the more substantive responsibilities of protection and promotion of human and peoples' rights on the continent.[11]

The ability of the Commission to function efficiently and fulfil its mandate competently was undermined not only by the failure of the successive Gambian Governments to fulfil their promises of facilities and resources,[12] but also by the failure of its parent body, the OAU, to provide adequate financial resources and professional staff.[13] Apart from the Secretary to the Commission and a few administrative and support staff, the Commission continues to rely on *ad hoc* arrangements for professional staff, most of who are on temporary contracts and funded mainly by European donor governments.

The role and functioning of the Commission was not well known within Africa and the first NGOs to attend its sessions and apply for observer status were international NGOs and not African.[14] Failure by the Commission to publicise its work, especially during its sessions, and the rules of confidentiality regarding complaints considered by it, contributed to the ignorance of African NGOs about the African Charter and the Commission.

[11] S. B. O. Gutto, 'Non-Governmental Organizations, Peoples' Participation and the African Commission on Human and Peoples' Rights: Emerging Challenges to Regional Protection of Human Rights', in *Human Rights in Developing Countries Yearbook* (Scandinavian University Press, 1999), p. 49.

[12] The Secretariat of the Commission is accommodated in temporary headquarters provided by The Gambian Government, which it shared until recently with an NGO, the African Centre for Democracy and Human Rights Studies, created by The Gambian Government but which became autonomous in 1994.

[13] The Commission received an amount of US$576,000 for the financial year 1996/7, which constituted about 1.95 per cent of the total programme budget of the OAU. Amnesty International, *Organization of African Unity: Making Human Rights a Reality for Africans*, AI Index: IOR 63/01/98, p. 36. This amount was increased to approximately US$750,000 in the 1998/9 budget of the OAU.

[14] Amnesty International and the International Commission of Jurists obtained observer status at the 3rd Session of the African Commission in April 1988. At the 9th Session of the African Commission in April 1991 in Lagos, Nigeria, only two African NGOs, apart from Nigerian NGOs, were present.

Few governments were submitting reports to the Commission, not allowing it to fulfil its role of monitoring compliance with the African Charter, and apart from the host government, few representatives of other African governments attended the sessions. Therefore at the beginning of the 1990s the Commission needed to be invigorated. Consequently, the International Commission of Jurists (ICJ), the Geneva-based NGO, decided to organise workshops prior to each session of the Commission at which primarily African NGOs would be invited to participate. The objectives of these workshops were to develop NGO strategies for promoting the African Charter in their own countries, to develop dialogue between NGOs and the Commission and to allow NGOs to attend the Commission's sessions.[15] The first workshop, which was held in October 1991 prior to the 10th Session of the Commission, made several recommendations including on the independence of the Commission, dissemination of information and the role of NGOs.[16] That workshop and the many that followed provided the impetus for NGOs to become more involved in the work of the Commission and in providing assistance in the fulfilment of its mandate.

Observer status

By the end of its 28th Session in November 2000, 247 NGOs had been granted observer status by the Commission, the majority of which are African NGOs. While the large number of NGOs obtaining observer status has to be welcomed, it is regrettable that many do not fulfil their responsibilities of co-operation with the Commission.

The granting of observer status by the Commission began as a cursory procedure without a careful examination of the information being provided by organisations seeking observer status. An NGO seeking observer status applies in writing to the Commission providing information about its constitution, by-laws, a list of officers, sources of funding, publications and other relevant information. While well-known African and international

---

[15] International Commission of Jurists, *ICJ Workshops on NGO Participation in the African Commission on Human and Peoples' Rights 1991 to 1996: A Critical Evaluation* (ICJ, 1996), p. 33.
[16] International Commission of Jurists, *The Participation of Non-Governmental Organizations in the Work of the African Commission on Human and Peoples' Rights: A Compilation of Basic Documents* (ICJ, 1996) provides the conclusions and recommendations of the ten workshops held between October 1991 and March 1996.

organisations may not require scrutiny, with the proliferation of NGOs it became necessary for the Commission to scrutinise the applications being presented. The Commission often considered applications for observer status without a representative being present to answer questions or present additional information that may be required. In some instances, representatives of NGOs simply handed to a member of the Commission all the relevant documents during a session and had their applications granted during the session without the information being processed by the Secretariat, whereas in other instances applications have been inexplicably lost or the granting of observer status delayed without reasons.

During the 20th Session of the Commission in October 1996 in Mauritius, and again at the 21st Session of the Commission in April 1997 in Mauritania, a question was raised regarding the granting of observer status to NGOs that were not recognised by the government of the country in which they were based or not registered in accordance with national laws. At the meeting in Nouakchott, the Mauritanian Government raised the issue after it had tried to prevent local NGOs from attending the public session of the Commission. The government argued that NGOs not registered in accordance with national legislation should not be granted observer status. On both occasions on which this issue was raised, the majority view of the Commission was that, as there were many reasons for governments failing or refusing to recognise NGOs in their countries, it would be difficult for the Commission to examine all these reasons. More importantly, the Commission pointed out that as a body of independent experts it had to consider applications for observer status in accordance with the African Charter, its own Rules of Procedure and the criteria it has established. A Commissioner drew the attention of the Commission to the fact that observer status had at that stage already been accorded to a number of NGOs that were not recognised by the governments of the countries in which they were based and that such recognition or registration in accordance with national laws was not a prerequisite for the granting of observer status.[17]

In its report to the 27th Session on the status of the submission of NGO activity reports, the Secretariat of the Commission presented a long list of NGOs that had failed to submit reports of their activities once every two

---

[17] As the Commission does not make public the final summary minutes of its sessions, as it is required to do under Rule 40 of its Rules of Procedure, the author had to rely on personal notes and unofficial transcripts of the proceedings of the sessions.

years as required by the Commission.[18] While about half of these NGOs have submitted at least one report to the Commission, most have not submitted either their initial or subsequent reports.[19] A large number of NGOs have ceased to communicate with the Commission and have not sent representatives to any of the Commission's meetings. These failings on the part of NGOs seem to have prompted the 34th Assembly of Heads of State and Government of the OAU to adopt a decision in which it requested 'the Commission, for reasons of efficiency, to review its criteria for granting observer status and to suspend further granting of observer status until the adoption of new criteria'.[20] In accordance with this request the Commission adopted a resolution at its 24th Session in Banjul, The Gambia, in October 1998, in which it decided that representatives of NGOs applying for observer status be present at the consideration of their applications, to review the criteria for the granting of observer status and to revoke the observer status of NGOs that do not submit any activity reports at the 27th ordinary session in October 1999.[21]

Subsequently, at its 25th Session in Burundi, in May 1999, the Commission adopted revised criteria for the granting of and maintaining observer status.[22] The revised criteria were adopted in a closed session of the Commission without prior consultations with NGOs, despite requests from NGOs, including the Arab Organization for Human Rights, that they be allowed to comment on the draft criteria. The criteria are divided into four sections: requirements for the obtaining of observer status; participation of observers in the proceedings of the Commission; relations between the Commission and observers; and final provisions that list the sanctions that

[18] Decision taken at the 11th Session of the Commission, Fifth Annual Activity Report of the African Commission on Human and Peoples' Rights 1991–1992, ACHPR/XI/AN. Rpt/5 Rev.2, p. 7 (*Documents of the African Commission*, p. 217).

[19] Status of Submission of NGO Activity Reports, March 2000, DOC/OS (XXVII)/153a.

[20] Declaration and Decisions adopted by the Thirty-Fourth Ordinary Session of the Assembly of Heads of State and Government, Ouagadougou, Burkina Faso, June 1998, AHG/Dec. 126 (XXXIV).

[21] Resolution on the Co-operation Between the African Commission on Human and Peoples' Rights and NGOs Having Observer Status with the Commission, Twelfth Annual Activity Report of the African Commission on Human and Peoples' Rights (1998–9), AHG/215 (XXXV), Annex IV (*Documents of the African Commission*, p. 699).

[22] Resolution on the Criteria for Granting and Enjoying Observer Status to Non-Governmental Organizations Working in the Field of Human Rights with the African Commission on Human and Peoples' Rights, Twelfth Annual Activity Report 1998–1999 (*Documents of the African Commission*, p. 705).

could be applied to NGOs. The criteria for the obtaining of observer status have been improved in that they set out clearly what documentation and information is required and necessitate all applications to be processed by the Secretariat. One of the requirements is that an NGO is obliged to provide 'proof of its legal existence'. Although the Commission is yet to determine the nature and extent of this requirement, it would be of concern if the Commission intends by this that NGOs have to produce proof of registration in the country in which the NGO is based. The second chapter of the criteria defines the role of NGOs during the sessions of the Commission, recognising their entitlement to documents of the Commission and expanding on the role played by NGOs until then.[23] The privilege enjoyed by NGOs to make statements at the sessions is recognised but the requirement of prior notification has been added. The third chapter of the criteria reiterates the need for close co-operation between NGOs and the Commission and the requirement that NGOs present their activity reports every two years. The final chapter provides for sanctions against NGOs that do not fulfil their obligations including non-participation in sessions, denial of documents and information and denial of the opportunity to propose items for the Commission's agenda. Observer status of an organisation that does not fulfil the criteria may also be suspended or withdrawn.

Participation in sessions

The most visible role of NGOs has been during the sessions of the Commission. They have availed themselves of the provision of the Rules of Procedure of the Commission that permits NGOs to suggest items for the agenda of the Commission and have suggested topics pertaining to human rights situations in African countries, for example Sierra Leone, and thematic issues such as economic, social and cultural rights. Besides presenting information on the agenda item they have suggested, NGOs often make concrete proposals to the Commission on measures it could adopt to investigate the specific country situation or violations or mechanisms it could establish to deal with thematic issues. Examples of such initiatives include urging the Commission to undertake investigative missions to countries where serious human rights violations have been occurring, and the establishment of the

---

[23] Observers may be invited to be present at closed sessions dealing with particular issues of interest to them.

mechanism of Special Rapporteur to investigate specific recurring human rights violations NGOs have identified.

Since 1991, with a few exceptions, workshops have been arranged by NGOs in collaboration with the Commission prior to each of its sessions. While the workshops have been primarily the work of the ICJ, it has often worked in conjunction with African NGOs in countries where the sessions of the Commission have been held, and more recently African NGOs have been arranging these workshops independently of international NGOs.[24] The workshops, which have tried to influence the work and efficiency of the Commission, have had some impact. Resolutions proposed to the Commission by workshop participants on country situations or thematic issues have often been adopted by it with little or no amendment.[25] The participation of Commissioners at the workshops has allowed for a free exchange of views, sometimes critical, to the enhancement of the relationship between the Commission and NGOs. However, the participation of the representatives of some governments in these workshops has prevented NGO representatives from those countries from expressing their views openly and, at least on one occasion, an attempt was made to prevent a resolution being adopted.[26]

Public statements by NGOs during the Commission's sessions have both criticised it and cajoled it to improve its efficiency and effectiveness. The opportunity for such statements was created by the Commission and is now a permanent item on its agenda on 'Relationship with Observers'. However, NGOs are not restricted to this agenda item and are permitted with few restrictions to contribute to each item on the agenda, including through the raising of questions or concerns about reports presented by Commissioners, Special Rapporteurs or the Secretariat.

---

[24] For example, the African Centre for Human Rights and Democratic Studies arranged the workshop prior to the 27th Session in April 2000.

[25] For example, at its 19th Session, the Commission adopted resolutions on the respect for and strengthening of the independence of the judiciary and on the role of lawyers and judges in the integration of the African Charter in national systems. These resolutions were proposed by NGO participants at a workshop on the independence of the judiciary that preceded that session. Final Communiqué of the 19th Session of the African Commission on Human and Peoples' Rights, 24 March – 4 April 1996, Ouagadougou, Burkina Faso, ACHPR/FIN/COM/XIX (*Documents of the African Commission*, p. 487), paras. 9 and 17.

[26] At the workshop that preceded the 20th Session in Mauritius in October 1996, the representatives of Tunisia tried to prevent a resolution being adopted on the human rights situation in that country. Resolution on the Human Rights Situation in Tunisia, Statement and Summary Report of the Eleventh ICJ Workshop on Participation in the African Commission on Human and Peoples' Rights (no reference).

International organisations such as Amnesty International present an oral statement at each session in which they highlight the human rights situation in a few African countries and address a thematic issue. African NGOs often deal with the human rights situation in their own countries and make recommendations to the Commission to adopt resolutions or undertake investigative missions. The close co-operation among NGOs ensures that they present different perspectives of the same message, which results in greater impact on the Commission. For example, at the 26th Session in November 1999 in Rwanda, Amnesty International, Human Rights Watch, Interights and representatives of the Sierra Leone Bar Association teamed up to present information to the Commission on the serious human rights situation in Sierra Leone. The Commission acted upon that information by undertaking a mission to Sierra Leone in February 2000. Although the representatives of several Nigerian NGOs attend each session of the Commission, there is always a collaborative effort among them and they often present a single joint statement.[27] While the relationship between most NGOs that attend the Commission's sessions is cordial and co-operative, sometimes competitiveness and confrontation between NGOs from the same country is also evident. Such confrontations emanate from some NGOs seeking legitimacy, competition for funding and the stance of the NGO, especially those that may be perceived to be pro- or anti-government.

Many resolutions adopted by the Commission have been the result of the close collaboration between NGOs and the Commission. Even in instances where draft resolutions have not been proposed by NGOs, representatives of NGOs have assisted in the drafting of resolutions. For example, at the 26th Session representatives of Amnesty International, the African Society for International and Comparative Law and Prisoners Rehabilitation and Welfare Action assisted the Special Rapporteur on extrajudicial, summary or arbitrary executions in drafting a resolution on the death penalty which was adopted by the Commission.[28] Since its 17th Session, the Commission has tried to act independently of NGOs in the drafting of resolutions after the Government of Algeria protested against a resolution on that country and as more governments began sending representatives to the Commission's

---

[27] See, for example, Submission by Nigerian Human Rights NGOs to the 23rd Session of the African Commission on Human and Peoples' Rights, 20–29 April 1998, Banjul, The Gambia.

[28] Resolution Urging the States to Envisage a Moratorium on the Death Penalty, Thirteenth Annual Activity Report 1999–2000, Annex IV.

sessions. While it is important that the Commission acts independently from NGOs as much as it does from governments, the expertise and often first-hand experience of NGOs proves invaluable in encapsulating in a resolution the concerns regarding human rights in a particular African country or a human rights theme.

The Commission's sessions provide the ideal opportunity for NGOs to share their information with members of the Commission, other NGOs and government representatives. The information, in the form of documents, reports and press releases, is presented mainly in English and French and sometimes in Arabic and languages indigenous to Africa. The array of publications distributed at each session of the Commission attests to the efforts being made by NGOs to promote and protect human rights in Africa. Many publications promote the African Charter and the work of the Commission,[29] while others report on the human rights situation in different African countries.

The Commission has on several occasions called on NGOs to create a body to ensure better co-ordination of their activities at each session. While there has been informal co-ordination among NGOs at each session, many NGOs, especially African ones, have been reluctant to form a body for co-ordination of their activities. This reluctance is based on several uncertainties: whether the Commission would communicate with NGOs only through the co-ordinating body; whether NGOs would be required to present a composite oral statement to each session; whether northern NGOs would play a dominant role in the co-ordinating body; and whether the co-ordinating body would assist the Commission in the consideration of applications for observer status. Some NGOs such as the ICJ have suggested that in order to improve the relationship between the Commission and NGOs a specific post for liaison with NGOs should be established within the Secretariat, similar to that in the UN and the Council of Europe. The Commission has yet to act on this suggestion.

Media and publicity

The media is an important tool for human rights work as it provides the means for the transmission of information about human rights issues. The

---

[29] For example, Lawyers for Human Rights, *An Introduction to the African System for the Protection of Human and Peoples' Rights* (September 1995).

media also provides a forum for the education of the general public about human rights. It is therefore unfortunate that the Commission has not made full use of this tool despite identifying a media programme as a priority.[30] The Commission has preferred to maintain a low-key attitude towards the media even in instances where media attention could have enhanced its work and image, for example during missions to investigate human rights violations.

It has been left largely to NGOs to publicise the African Charter and the work of the Commission through the media. Often the publicity coincides with the biannual sessions of the African Commission. For example, when the Commission was celebrating its tenth anniversary during the 20th Session in Mauritius in November 1996, the efforts of Amnesty International Mauritius ensured that journalists reported on every public session. The NGO arranged a briefing meeting between the Secretary of the Commission and journalists during a preparatory visit, provided journalists with information regarding the agenda and arranged interviews with Commissioners and other participants at the session. NGOs have also used the occasion of the African Human Rights Day, which falls on 27 October each year, and the Day of the African Child, which occurs on 16 June every year, to promote human rights generally but also African human rights treaties and the work of the Commission. NGOs have produced teaching materials, reports and publications on the African Charter and the work of the Commission, which they have distributed widely to schools, universities, government departments and judicial officials.[31] The African Charter has also been translated into numerous indigenous African languages by NGOs for distribution to communities. NGOs have also ensured that decisions by the Commission regarding complaints of human rights violations in their own countries receive wide media attention.[32]

While the efforts of NGOs are laudable, this has to be co-ordinated with the Commission to ensure that its message reaches its target audience in

---

[30] Mauritius Plan of Action, Section II, para. 11, p. 217.

[31] Some examples include publication of the African Charter and Rules of Procedure of the Commission by the African Centre for Democracy and Human Rights Studies, January 1995; Amnesty International, *A Guide to the African Charter on Human and Peoples' Rights* (September 1991), AI Index: IOR 63/05/91, which has been translated into indigenous African languages such as Bambara and Zulu.

[32] For example, the Southern African Human Rights NGO Network (SAHRINGON) publicised the African Commission's decision in *Amnesty International* v. *Zambia* which was reported in the Zambian newspaper *The Post* on 8 October 1999.

African countries and can be followed up accordingly through the dissemination of relevant materials, such as the African Charter.

Complaints mechanism

Although the African Charter in Article 55, by referring to 'communications other than those of States Parties', does not specifically identify or recognise the role of NGOs in the filing of complaints regarding human rights violations, in practice the complaints procedure before the Commission has been used mainly by NGOs who have filed complaints on behalf of individuals or groups alleging violations of the rights enshrined in the African Charter.[33] In some cases, the Commission has received communications from NGOs that 'relate to special cases which reveal the existence of a series of serious or massive violations of human and peoples' rights' and has dealt with such cases under the procedure prescribed by Article 58 of the African Charter.[34]

At the beginning of the last decade the joint responsibility of the Commission and the NGOs 'of developing a strong and progressive African jurisprudence' was recognised.[35] This responsibility has been taken seriously by NGOs, and, during the first decade of the Commission's existence up to June 1997, it had received more than 200 communications from individuals and NGOs, and a final decision had been reached in 119.[36] At its 26th and 27th Sessions alone, the Commission had 151 complaints before it including six new ones. It considered 130 communications at these sessions, of which it reached a final decision in fifty-three, all except four of which were filed by NGOs.[37]

NGOs have made a considerable contribution to the jurisprudence of the Commission in relation to almost every substantive provision of the Charter. However, complaints filed by NGOs were often influenced by events in their

---

[33] See C. A. Odinkalu and C. Christensen, 'The African Commission on Human and Peoples' Rights, Human Rights: The Development of its Non-State Communications Procedure', *Human Rights Quarterly* 20 (1998) 235–80, for a critical analysis of the procedure for consideration of complaints filed by NGOs and individuals.

[34] For example, Communications 25/89, 47/90, 56/91 and 100/93 (joined), *Free Legal Assistance Group, Lawyers' Committee for Human Rights, Union Interafricaine des Droits de l'Homme, Les Témoins de Jehovah v. Zaire*, Ninth Activity Report 1995–1996, Annex VIII (*Documents of the African Commission*, p. 444).

[35] Gutto, 'Non-Governmental Organizations', p. 42.

[36] Odinkalu and Christensen, 'The African Commission', p. 238.

[37] Thirteenth Annual Activity Report 1999–2000, Annex V.

own countries and related to violations occurring at a specific time. Most of the cases filed by Nigerian NGOs therefore relate to the right to a fair trial and access to courts enshrined in Article 7 of the African Charter. The opportunity to present allegations of human rights violations to a supranational body that considered these in regard to the treaty obligations of a State allowed some NGOs to obtain decisions that had been denied to them by their own national courts. This was particularly true of Nigerian NGOs that filed complaints relating to violations committed under the military regime of General Abacha who were often denied even access to a court to seek remedies for such violations.[38]

The practice of the Commission to allow complainants to present their case orally during its private sessions has been welcomed by NGOs as it has enabled them to present succinct and precise arguments to the Commission which can assist the Commission to reach a reasoned decision. This practice has permitted NGOs to present witness testimony to the Commission and for Commissioners to raise questions directly with the victim of the human rights violation. Where it has considered it necessary, the Secretariat of the Commission has sometimes requested an NGO to represent an individual complainant during proceedings before the Commission. An important effect of the oral presentation of a case has been an increase in the number of governments willing to participate in the proceedings. The participation of representatives of States has contributed to an improvement in the deliberations of the Commission and its decisions. What is to be hoped for is the implementation by States of the decision of the Commission. The Commission stated that the non-compliance of States Parties with recommendations adopted on communications was one of the major factors in the erosion of the Commission's credibility.[39]

The reluctance of many NGOs to utilise the complaint procedure before the Commission has to do with a lack of confidence in the mechanism. The lack of an enforcement mechanism and the failure of the OAU Assembly of Heads of States and Government, to which the Commission reports, to do anything beyond the adoption of the Commission's report

---

[38] See, for example, Communications 140/94, 141/94 and 145/95, *Constitutional Rights Project, Civil Liberties Organisation and Media Rights Agenda* v. *Nigeria,* Thirteenth Activity Report 1999–2000, Annex V.

[39] Non-Compliance of States Parties to adopted recommendations of the African Commission: A Legal Approach, DOC/OS/50b (XXIV) (*Documents of the African Commission,* p. 758).

has contributed to this reluctance. Furthermore, in the past there have been considerable delays in the consideration of complaints by the Commission, although the length of time taken to reach a decision has progressively grown shorter.[40]

It is unfortunate that a large number of complaints filed by NGOs have been considered inadmissible by the Commission on the basis that they failed to fulfil the requirements of Article 56 of the Charter. In most instances, the inadmissibility is based on the failure of the author of the complaint to exhaust domestic remedies or to articulate why local remedies could not be exhausted or because they would be unduly prolonged.[41] Although the Commission has granted considerable latitude when there has been no exhaustion of local remedies, it has been criticised for taking a too formalistic approach in some instances or for not considering the effectiveness of the remedy that would have been obtained at the domestic level.[42]

State reporting procedure

The State reporting procedure under Article 62 of the African Charter provides the Commission with an important opportunity to scrutinise the compliance of a State Party with its obligations under the treaty through dialogue.[43] While many States have failed to comply fully with their obligations under Article 62 to file reports with the Commission every two

---

[40] For example, it took the Commission about fourteen months to render a decision in Communication 212/98, *Amnesty International* v. *Zambia*, from the date on which it was filed, Twelfth Activity Report 1998–1999, Annex V (*Documents of the African Commission*, p. 745). On the other hand, it has taken the Commission almost ten years to render a final decision in Communications 48/90, 50/91, 52/91 and 89/93, *Amnesty International; Comité Loosli Bachelard; Lawyers' Committee for Human Rights; Association of Members of the Episcopal Conference of East Africa* v. *Sudan*, Thirteenth Activity Report 1999–2000, Addendum; and Communications 54/91, 61/91, 98/93, 164/97 and 210/98, *Malawi African Association; Amnesty International; Ms Sarr Diop, Union Interafricaine des Droits de l'Homme and RADDHO; Collectif des Veuves et Ayants-droits; Association Mauritanienne des Droits de l'Homme* v. *Mauritania*, Thirteenth Activity Report 1999–2000, Addendum.

[41] See, for example, Communication 201/97, *Egyptian Organisation for Human Rights* v. *Egypt*, Thirteenth Activity Report 1999–2000, Annex V; Communication 209/97, *Africa Legal Aid* v. *The Gambia*, Thirteenth Activity Report 1999–2000, Annex V.

[42] Odinkalu and Christensen, 'The African Commission', pp. 258 and 259.

[43] See Chapter 2 above for a detailed discussion of the State reporting procedure; and A. Danielsen, *The State Reporting Procedure Under the African Charter* (Danish Centre for Human Rights, 1994).

years,[44] recently more States have presented their reports.[45] The role of NGOs is vital to the dialogue between the Commission and States especially as the Commission does not have the resources or the capacity to monitor the human rights situation and to keep abreast of developments throughout the continent. The Commission has acknowledged that 'the public discussion of periodic reports also provides an opportunity for NGOs to make their contribution to the process of dialogue'.[46]

NGOs provide the Commission with vital background and factual information on the country under consideration to enable Commissioners to raise questions with and seek clarification from government representatives. Without such information the Commissioners are rarely able to enter into meaningful dialogue. In recognition of this role, the Commission has often invited NGOs to provide information in advance of a State Party report being considered. Such information could complement information obtained by the Commission from other sources including United Nations bodies to enable better scrutiny of legislative, policy and practical weaknesses that impede implementation of the African Charter by a State Party. NGOs are not allowed to intervene in the discussions between the Commission and government representatives in the public sessions.

However, in order for NGOs to play a meaningful role in this process, they should know in advance which reports are to be considered by the Commission at its forthcoming session. It has to be acknowledged though that often the Commission is unable to consider a particular State's report because of the failure of government representatives to attend the session at which the report is to be considered. It is often very difficult for NGOs to obtain State reports filed with the Commission, despite NGOs requesting it from the State that is reporting. Requests to the Secretariat of the Commission for copies of State reports have also often gone unheeded. The Commission

---

[44] See Chapter 2 above; and Status of Submission of State Periodic Reports to the African Commission on Human and Peoples' Rights, 27th Ordinary Session, 27 April to 11 May 2000, DOC/OS (XXVII)/INF. 22.

[45] At the 27th Session of the Commission in May 2000, Burundi, Libya, Rwanda, Swaziland and Uganda presented their reports to the Commission, and the reports of Benin, Egypt, Ghana and Namibia were to be considered at its 28th Session in November 2000, Thirteenth Annual Activity Report 1999–2000, p. 3. The reports of Benin and Egypt were considered at the 28th Session but consideration of the reports of Ghana and Namibia was postponed due to the representatives of these States not attending the session.

[46] Mauritius Plan of Action, p. 220.

should make a State report publicly available to all participants at its session prior to the session at which the report is to be considered. Furthermore, the report should be sent to NGOs with observer status in the country whose report is to be considered with a specific request for information. NGOs should be given sufficient time to prepare observations on the report or a 'shadow' report that would enable Commissioners to raise pertinent questions with government representatives. Such advance notice would not be possible if the Commission repeats what it did in regard to the consideration of the report of Uganda at its 27th Session. Representatives of the Ugandan Government arrived at the session and informed the Secretariat that they had come prepared to present their report to the Commission. Without further consideration and without even providing the Secretariat an opportunity to prepare any background information or questions, the Commission acceded to the request of the Ugandan representatives. The result was that the examination of the report was cursory with questions being raised mainly by the Chairperson of the Commission based upon a recent visit to Uganda to investigate prison conditions. Some Commissioners also raised questions about Uganda's participation in the war in the Democratic Republic of Congo that seemed to be based on general knowledge rather than detailed information about the human rights situation or violations of international humanitarian law.

It is such cursory examination of State reports that discourages NGOs from contributing to the process of the scrutiny of State reports. Although some Commissioners ask incisive questions on a range of violations, such questions are often ignored by government representatives and then not followed up during the dialogue. In most instances the questions asked by Commissioners are of a general nature and are not detailed, probing and specific and fail to elicit substantive responses. The failure of the Commission to issue recommendations that would provide guidance to governments on legislative and practical shortcomings and to establish a yardstick by which to measure improvements also make the entire process look weak to NGOs, discouraging them from co-operating with the Commission.

However, NGOs should realise that the process of examination of State reports would only improve if the NGOs fulfilled their role to supply information to the Commission on a regular basis and took the initiative to prepare detailed shadow reports. The Commission has requested NGOs to submit regular written reports on the human rights situation in Africa to assist it in the execution of its mandate.[47] Attendance at the session of the Commission would also enable them to provide updated information to Commissioners and inform them of the priority issues that should be raised with government representatives. It is regrettable that so few NGOs with observer status take this procedure seriously.

Assistance in regard to missions

The African Charter, under Article 46, permits the Commission to 'resort to any appropriate method of investigation' in the fulfilment of its mandate. Such broad authority has enabled the Commission to undertake missions after receiving several complaints from NGOs concerning a particular country. Although NGOs considered these as investigative missions in fulfilment of the Commission's protective mandate, the Commission often perceived them as promotional missions. This lack of clarity has affected the way in which the Commission has conducted the missions and the final outcome of the missions. In most instances, the Commission has relied exclusively on the government for resources and logistical support while in the country, the same government that was the subject of the complaints of violations of the African Charter. The earliest missions of the Commission were to Sudan, Nigeria and Mauritania.

In addition to missions that had a clearly investigative purpose, Commissioners have also undertaken visits to countries to promote the work of the Commission and to encourage governments to participate in the Commission's sessions and to abide by their obligations under the African Charter. During 2000 Commissioners undertook promotional visits to several countries including Chad, Djibouti, Mozambique and Tanzania.[48]

NGOs played an important role in assisting the Commission with its preparations for its missions, whether investigative or promotional. They have suggested guidelines that would form the framework for missions of the Commission and have recommended methodologies for the investigations. NGOs were forthcoming with current information on the country that would have enabled Commissioners participating in the mission to understand the context in which they were working. NGOs such as Amnesty

---

[47] Resolution on the Human Rights Situation in Africa, Thirteenth Annual Activity Report 1999–2000, Annex IV.

[48] See Thirteenth Annual Activity Report 1999–2000, p. 8, for a list of missions undertaken between May 1999 and May 2000.

International were even requested by the Secretariat to provide details of relevant government officials that Commissioners intended to meet during the mission. International and regional NGOs always consider it necessary for the Commissioners to meet with credible local NGOs during the mission and therefore make an effort not only to provide the Secretariat with details of such NGOs but also to inform local NGOs of the mission.

The manner in which the Commission has conducted investigative missions and their outcome has in general been very disappointing for NGOs. The failure of the Commission to adopt clear guidelines for the conduct of missions that would ensure its independence and impartiality and a thorough investigation of the allegations is of concern to NGOs. This is despite NGOs having made available to the Commission guidelines adopted by intergovernmental bodies such as the United Nations and human rights NGOs. The lack of serious preparation for such missions and inexplicable delays in publishing reports of missions has undermined the effectiveness of this important investigative procedure. For example, the report on the mission to Mauritania which took place in June 1996 was published a year later.[49] The report of the mission to Nigeria in March 1997 has still to be published.

A recent investigative mission of the Commission was to Sierra Leone in February 2000. Interights, as it was entitled to do under the Commission's Rules of Procedure, requested the Commission to include on its agenda for the 26th Session a specific item on the situation in Sierra Leone.[50] At that session in November 1999, Amnesty International, Human Rights Watch and Interights combined their efforts with the Sierra Leone Bar Council. The NGOs expressed concern about the impunity granted to perpetrators of serious human rights violations in the peace agreement signed in July 1999 by the warring parties in Sierra Leone, and the failure of the African Commission to condemn the atrocities or to undertake a mission to that country. The NGOs convinced the Commission of the need to investigate the serious human rights situation in Sierra Leone and it adopted a resolution in which it decided to send a mission to Sierra Leone to seek

[49] Report of the Mission to Mauritania, Tenth Annual Activity Report of the African Commission on Human and Peoples' Rights 1996–7, DOC/OS/(XXII), Annex IX (*Documents of the African Commission*, p. 538).

[50] Human Rights Situation in Africa: Memorandum on the Peace Agreement and the Issue of Human Rights Violations During the Civil War in Sierra Leone, DOC/OS(XXXVI)/129.

information and engage in dialogue with the authorities.[51] While the Secretariat awaited a response from the Sierra Leonean Government to its request to visit the country, NGOs provided the Commissioners who were delegated to undertake the mission with information about the human rights situation and suggestions regarding the conduct of the investigations. In January 2000, NGOs established that the government had granted its consent but that the mission was to take place within two weeks, leaving little or no time for preparations. Suggestions by NGOs to postpone the mission to allow for adequate preparations were ignored and the mission went ahead. At the 27th Session of the Commission in April 2000, NGOs, including Interights, expressed concerns that the report of the mission had not been published, given the serious human rights situation in Sierra Leone. Again, during the 28th Session in October 2000, NGOs expressed concern that the report of the mission had not been published. Although the Commission indicated then that the draft report would be finalised and made available to NGOs, by the end of December 2000 this had not been done.

Workshops and seminars

The Commission and NGOs regularly identify issues that are of concern in Africa and which require further discussion in seminars or workshops. The Commission has few financial or other resources to arrange such meetings and therefore encourages the involvement of NGOs. While some of the seminars and workshops have ended in declarations with little or no progress in addressing the issue, others have resulted in the formulation of principles or the adoption of a plan of action to tackle the specific human rights violation. An example illustrates the initiatives taken by NGOs to support efforts by the Commission to bring together NGO representatives and experts to discuss issues of importance to it.

At the 14th Session of the Commission in December 1993, a number of NGOs raised the issue of human rights education, explaining their efforts and the difficulties they were facing in many countries. In its resolution on the issue, the Commission decided 'to intensify the cooperation between the African Commission and African Non-Governmental Organizations on

---

[51] Resolution on the Human Rights Situation in Africa, Thirteenth Annual Activity Report 1999–2000, Annex IV.

human and peoples' rights education'.[52] The Commission also welcomed the initiative taken by NGOs to organise a workshop on human rights education and agreed that it would be organised in collaboration with Lawyers for Human Rights of South Africa.[53] A coalition of African NGOs, led by Lawyers for Human Rights, organised the workshop on human rights education that brought together NGO representatives from almost every country in Africa. Two members of the African Commission also attended the workshop, which was held in South Africa. One of the objectives of the workshop was to establish a network of NGOs for the sharing of information and techniques in human rights education. In 1995, and 1997, follow-up workshops on human rights education were also organised in Egypt by the Legal Resources and Research Centre for Human Rights and in Ethiopia by the Action Professionals' Association for the People. The report and conclusion of each workshop was presented to the Commission. Furthermore, the NGOs involved in the workshops demonstrated their efforts in promoting awareness of the African Charter and the work of the Commission.

NGOs have collaborated with the Commission to arrange seminars and workshops on a range of human rights issues, including fair trial, prison conditions and economic, social and cultural rights and a recent seminar, on freedom of expression, was arranged by Article 19 in November 2000.

Elaboration of principles and standards

The African Commission has relied considerably on NGOs to assist it in the elaboration of principles and standards that give content to the provisions of the African Charter or strengthen the regime of human rights protection. Highlighted below are two key initiatives in which NGOs have been involved.

PRINCIPLES ON THE RIGHT TO A FAIR TRIAL

At its 11th Session in March 1992 the Commission considered a proposal by Amnesty International to define the right to a fair trial in Article 7 of the African Charter in accordance with other international standards such

---

[52] Resolution on Human and Peoples' Rights to Education, Seventh Annual Activity Report of the African Commission on Human and Peoples' Rights 1993–4, AHG/198/(XXX), Annex X (*Documents of the African Commission*, p. 350).

[53] *Ibid.*, para. 19.

as the International Covenant on Civil and Political Rights. The Commission adopted the Resolution on the Right to Recourse and Fair Trial that gave content to the right to fair trial including by recognising the right to be presumed innocent, the right to defence and the right to appeal to a higher tribunal.[54] However, NGOs recognised that this resolution was not adequate for the protection of the rights of accused persons and did not fully encompass international standards. Furthermore, the Commission had indicated its intention to hold a seminar on the right to a fair trial to assist it in elaborating principles.[55] The Commission collaborated with Interights and the African Society for International and Comparative Law in arranging a seminar on the right to a fair trial. The seminar, which brought together African jurists and some experts from other parts of the world, was held in September 1999 and adopted a declaration on the right to a fair trial. Subsequently, in November 1999, the Commission adopted the declaration, which recognised the need for the Commission to adopt detailed principles on the right to a fair trial including those applicable to matters before traditional and customary courts. The Commission also adopted a resolution in which it decided to establish a working group that included NGO representatives to draft principles and guidelines on the right to a fair trial.[56] The draft principles were presented to the Commission at its 30th Session in October 2001.

PROTOCOL ON WOMEN'S RIGHTS

The 17th Session of the African Commission in March 1995 was preceded by a seminar on the African Charter on Human and Peoples' Rights and the rights of women in Africa organised by the Commission in collaboration with Women in Law and Development in Africa (WILDAF). The Commission acceded to one of the recommendations of the seminar by appointing Commissioners Victor Dankwa and Julienne Ondziel-Gnelenga to a working group to draft a protocol on women's rights.[57] The OAU Summit

---

[54] Resolution on the Right to Recourse Procedure and a Fair Trial, Fifth Annual Activity Report 1991–1992, Annex VI (*Documents of the African Commission*, p. 224).

[55] See, for example, Final Communiqué of the 19th Ordinary Session, para. 18.

[56] Resolution on the Right to Fair Trial and Legal Aid in Africa, Thirteenth Annual Activity Report 1999–2000, Annex IV.

[57] Final Communiqué of the 17th Ordinary Session of the African Commission on Human and Peoples' Rights, Lomé, Togo, 12–22 March 1995, ACHPR/COM/FIN/XVIII/Rev.3 (*Documents of the African Commission*, p. 418), para. 31.

endorsed the proposal of the Commission that a protocol on women's rights be elaborated and entrusted the Commission with the task.[58] Prior to the 21st Session of the Commission, in April 1997, the ICJ brought together representatives of African NGOs and other independent experts to begin the process of drafting a protocol. Several Commissioners participated in the deliberations. Subsequently, the draft was presented to the first meeting of the working group on the additional protocol to the African Charter on women's rights. Again at that meeting representatives of ICJ, WILDAF and the African Centre for Democracy and Human Rights Studies assisted the Commissioners in the refining of the draft. The meeting also considered draft terms of reference for the proposed Special Rapporteur on the rights of women in Africa.[59] Subsequent meetings of the working group were held in June and November 1998 which considered previous drafts and proposals by NGOs for the purpose of developing a final draft protocol for submission to the OAU.[60] Representatives of ICJ, WILDAF and the African Centre participated at each meeting.

After the draft protocol was submitted to the OAU Secretariat, the Commission was informed that an NGO, the Inter-African Committee on Traditional Practices with a Harmful Effect on the Health of Women and the Girl Child, had also submitted a draft Convention on the Elimination of All Forms of Harmful Practices Affecting the Fundamental Rights of Women and Girls. The OAU Secretariat requested the Commission to incorporate the draft convention into the draft protocol, to create a single document. The Commission was of the view that it would not be possible to restart the work it had already done and suggested that the OAU Secretariat submit the draft protocol to a meeting of government experts together with all other contributions.[61] The OAU Secretariat produced a draft protocol that incorporates some provisions of the draft prepared by the Commission's working group, which will be presented to an OAU meeting of government experts some time in 2001.

---

[58] Decision AHG/Dec.126 (XXXIV), 34th Ordinary Session of the Assembly of Heads of State and Government.

[59] Report of the First Meeting of the Working Group on the Additional Protocol to the African Charter on Women's Rights, DOC/OS/34c(XXXIII).

[60] See Draft Protocol to the African Charter on the Rights of Women in Africa, DOC/OS(XXVI)/125, for the report of the third meeting of the Working Group held in October 1999 in Kigali.

[61] Thirteenth Annual Activity Report 1999–2000, 7.

Supporting the work of Special Rapporteurs

It is clear that NGOs provide crucial support to the work of the Special Rapporteurs intended to enable them to fulfil their mandate. However, the question that needs to be asked is whether the almost complete reliance of the Special Rapporteurs on NGOs for financial and other resources may create a dependency which governments may perceive as affecting their independence. NGOs are also concerned at the practice developed at the Commission for the appointment of its members as Special Rapporteurs rather than independent experts, as is the practice at the UN Commission on Human Rights. Some NGOs are of the view that there would be fewer constraints on independent experts in the fulfilment of their mandates.

Special Rapporteur on extrajudicial, summary or arbitrary executions

During its 15th Session in April 1994, Amnesty International alerted the Commission to the killings that were then taking place in Rwanda which were the precursor to the genocide in that country in which almost one million people were killed. The NGO urged the Commission to investigate the killings in Rwanda and in other countries through the establishment of the mechanism of Special Rapporteur. The Commission considered this recommendation favourably and appointed Commissioner Hatem Ben Salem as its first Special Rapporteur on extrajudicial, summary or arbitrary executions.[62] In its resolution on Rwanda the Commission requested the Special Rapporteur to 'pay special attention to the situation in Rwanda and to report back to the 16th Session'.[63]

NGOs had hoped that the establishment of this mechanism would enable the Commission to undertake effective investigations into extrajudicial killings and to draw attention to these serious violations through the publication of the Special Rapporteur's report. However, over the past six years, the lack of political will on the part of the Special Rapporteur and the lack of

---

[62] Final Communiqué of the 15th Ordinary Session of the African Commission on Human and Peoples' Rights, Banjul, The Gambia, 18–27 April 1994, ACHPR/FIN/COM/XIV (*Documents of the African Commission*, p. 362). Commissioner Ben Salem resigned from this post in December 2000. For further discussion of the Special Rapporteurs, see Chapter 9 below.

[63] Resolution on Rwanda, Eighth Annual Report of the African Commission on Human and Peoples' Rights 1994–5, ACHPR/RPT/8th/Rev.1, Annex VII (*Documents of the African Commission*, p. 401).

adequate resources has made this mechanism ineffective. Through cajoling and criticism NGOs have tried without success to encourage the Special Rapporteur to fulfil his mandate.[64] In 1999, realising that the Special Rapporteur could not rely on administrative support from the Secretariat due to the lack of resources, the Institute for Human Rights and Development, an NGO based in The Gambia, agreed to provide the necessary assistance to enable him to fulfil his mandate. Although with this assistance the Special Rapporteur began sending communications to States containing allegations of killings, he did little more. Therefore in October 2000 at the 28th Session of the Commission, once again NGOs expressed concerns at the failure of the Special Rapporteur to fulfil his mandate adequately. Despite extrajudicial killings continuing in many countries throughout Africa and requests by NGOs for the Special Rapporteur to undertake missions to specific countries to investigate killings, he has yet to undertake an investigative mission to an African country.

NGOs have often referred to a lack of confidence in the Special Rapporteurs for their failure to send allegations of extrajudicial executions. However, NGOs such as Amnesty International faltered from the outset in not establishing a system for sending information regularly to the Special Rapporteur, as they have with the UN Special Rapporteur on extrajudicial executions. On the other hand, the Special Rapporteur not only expects NGOs to send information, but also expects NGOs such as the Institute for Human Rights and Development to raise funds for his work. While it could be expected of NGOs to provide some financial support, the primary source of funding should be either the regular budget of the Commission or derived from funds raised by the Commission.

Special Rapporteur on prisons and conditions of detention in Africa

Penal Reform International (PRI) commenced efforts for the establishment of a mechanism to investigate prisons and conditions of detention in Africa in 1995. In March 1995, at its 17th Session the Commission, at the urging of PRI, considered the question of penal reform and prison conditions in Africa and decided in principle to appoint a Special Rapporteur.[65] The Commission

---

[64] See, for example, Amnesty International, *African Commission on Human and Peoples' Rights: The Role of the Special Rapporteur on Extrajudicial, Summary or Arbitrary Executions* (November 1997), AI Index: IOR 63/05/97.

[65] Final Communiqué of the 17th Session, para. 29.

also decided to organise a seminar on prison conditions and penal reform in collaboration with PRI.

At the 18th Session of the Commission in October 1995, the representative of PRI presented a draft resolution on the appointment of a Special Rapporteur on prisons and conditions of detention in Africa. At the request of the Commission, PRI provided information and details regarding African experts who would have been suitable for appointment to the position of Special Rapporteur. That provided a glimmer of hope to NGOs that the Commission would appoint an independent expert to the position.

PRI arranged a seminar on behalf of the Commission on prison conditions in Africa in Kampala, Uganda, in September 1996. The seminar, which brought together human rights defenders, prison officials and experts in penal reform from throughout the continent, provided members of the Commission with an overview of the issues regarding prisons in Africa.

A year after the decision to appoint a Special Rapporteur, Commissioner Victor Dankwa was appointed to the position at the 20th Session of the Commission in October 1996.[66] From the outset, PRI provided financial and administrative support to the Special Rapporteur. It raised funds, arranged visits once the consent of governments had been received, provided assistants to accompany the Special Rapporteur during country missions and published the reports. The considerable support provided by PRI is reflected in the adequate manner in which the Special Rapporteur has fulfilled his mandate since his appointment to the position. The Special Rapporteur has undertaken visits to several countries including Benin, The Gambia, Mali, Mozambique, Madagascar, Zimbabwe and Uganda. At the 28th Session in November 2000, the Special Rapporteur presented a brief oral report on his visit to prisons in the Central African Republic which he had undertaken in June that year. In some instances, the visit by the Special Rapporteur has resulted in changes in prison conditions, for example in Mali which invited the Special Rapporteur to return to the country to witness the changes.[67]

---

[66] Final Communiqué of the 20th Ordinary Session of the African Commission on Human and Peoples' Rights, Grand Bay, Mauritius, 21–31 October 1996, para. 18, ACHPR/FIN/COMM/XX (*Documents of the African Commission*, p. 576). In November 2000, Commissioner Dankwa resigned as Special Rapporteur and has been replaced by Commissioner Vera Chirwa.

[67] Prisons in Mali. Report of the Special Rapporteur on Prisons and Conditions of Detention in Africa to the 22nd Session of the African Commission on Human and Peoples' Rights,

Special Rapporteur on women

The two recommendations of the seminar on women's rights in Africa held in March 1995 were that an additional protocol to the African Charter on the rights of women should be drafted and that the Commission should appoint a Special Rapporteur on women. While the Commission entrusted two of its members to begin drafting an optional protocol, it did not accept the recommendation to appoint a Special Rapporteur.[68]

At the 18th Session of the Commission, held in October 1995, the ICJ pursued the matter by presenting a draft resolution on the appointment of a Special Rapporteur on women's rights.[69] The Commission, due to a heavy workload, postponed the consideration of the resolution to the next session, but at the 19th Session it did not make any decision regarding the appointment of a Special Rapporteur on women's rights.

At the 20th Session in October 1996, the Commission again reiterated its commitment to appoint a Special Rapporteur and decided to consider the proposals of its working group at the next session.[70] It was only at the 23rd Session in April 1998 that the Commission appointed Commissioner Julienne Ondziel-Gnelenga to the position of Special Rapporteur on women's rights on the basis of a proposal by the Commission's working group on the draft protocol on women's rights.[71] One of the main tasks of the Special Rapporteur was to oversee the drafting of the protocol on women's rights.

As NGOs had advocated for the appointment of a Special Rapporteur to investigate and report on the rights of women in Africa, it placed an obligation on them to provide support and assistance to Commissioner Ondziel-Gnelenga. In her report to the 26th Session in November 1999 the Special Rapporteur recognised the important role of NGOs in her work, but lamented that, while some NGOs provided information and support,

---

Series IV, No. 2; Mali Prisons Revisited. Report of the Special Rapporteur on Prisons and Conditions of Detention in Africa, Series IV, No. 4.

[68] Final Communiqué of the 17th Session, paras. 30 and 31.

[69] Final Communiqué of the 18th Ordinary Session of the African Commission on Human and Peoples' Rights, Praia, Cape Verde, 2–11 October 1995, ACHPR/FIN/COM/XVIII (*Documents of the African Commission*, p. 457), para. 23.

[70] Final Communiqué of the 20th Ordinary Session, para. 19.

[71] Final Communiqué of the 23rd Ordinary Session of the African Commission on Human and Peoples' Rights, April 1998, DOC/OS/45(XXXIII) (*Documents of the African Commission*, p. 674), para. 11.

many were slow to respond to requests for information.[72] WILDAF provided funding and assistance for the Special Rapporteur's first mission, to Liberia, to gather information and raise awareness. In a bold move, the Special Rapporteur tackled the issue of the death penalty by taking on a case, referred to her by WILDAF, of a Zimbabwean woman, Sokoluhle Kachipare, who was facing execution. In her report, the Special Rapporteur declared capital punishment to be a 'grave violation to the right to life and to the right of every individual not to be subjected to cruel, inhuman and degrading treatment'.[73] This statement encouraged NGOs campaigning against capital punishment who had hoped that the Commission's Special Rapporteur on extrajudicial executions would have taken up the issue during the early years of his appointment.

In her recommendations to the Commission in November 1999, the Special Rapporteur requested that she be provided with a budget and an assistant. Since then the Special Rapporteur has been provided with an assistant funded by the International Centre for Human Rights and Democratic Development, a Canadian NGO.

Supporting the Secretariat

In the interests of improving the efficiency and effectiveness of the Commission, NGOs have provided support to the Commission's Secretariat, especially as the resources provided by the OAU were insufficient for the proper functioning of the Secretariat. This support took many forms, including the distribution of invitations and reports of the Commission to NGOs in Africa, the provision of additional staff and the setting up of the documentation centre. Several NGOs were involved in these initiatives, including the African Centre for Human Rights and Democratic Studies, the African Society for International and Comparative Law, the Danish Centre for Human Rights, Human Rights Internet and the International Commission of Jurists.

A recent report of the Commission recognises the role of NGOs in providing support to its Secretariat.[74] It mentions the assistance provided by the Danish Centre for Human Rights that has enabled the hiring of

---

[72] Report of Activities of the Special Rapporteur on the Rights of Women in Africa, November 1999, DOC/OS(XXXVI)124, p. 11.

[73] *Ibid.* p. 5.   [74] Thirteenth Annual Activity Report 1999–2000, p. 12.

seven additional staff at the Secretariat. It also recognises the contribution of the African Society of International and Comparative Law, who have regularly provided young lawyers on internships extending over a year, and the Raoul Wallenberg Institute, which provided funding for the publication of the Commission's review and for promotional visits by Commissioners. The African Centre for Democracy and Human Rights Studies and the ICJ are also recognised for their contributions to the work of the Commission.

While NGOs continue to rally support for the Commission's Secretariat, some have been concerned about the poor management of the Secretariat staff and a lack of proper procedures for financial management. This has led to a deficiency in the ability of the Secretariat to provide effective and efficient support to the Commissioners and their work. At the first workshop in October 1991, which coincided with the Commission's tenth session, NGOs made recommendations for improvements in the functioning of the Secretariat.[75] Many years later, similar recommendations are still being made by NGOs.[76]

Extraordinary session on Nigeria

When the Nigerian authorities executed nine members of the Movement for the Survival of the Ogoni People in 1995 after a grossly unfair trial, NGOs urged the African Commission to convene a special session to consider the serious human rights situation in Nigeria. NGOs were eager to ensure that the African institution responsible for human rights added its voice to the condemnations from the United Nations, the Commonwealth and the European Union, especially as the Nigerian authorities had ignored the provisional measures adopted by the Commission urging them not to execute the nine, pursuant to a complaint filed by a Nigerian NGO and its resolutions.[77] Interights approached donors on an urgent basis to raise funds to cover the costs of convening an extraordinary session and together with

---

[75] International Commission of Jurists, *The Participation of Non-Governmental Organizations*, p. 17.

[76] See, for example, Amnesty International, *Credibility in Question: Proposals for Improved Efficiency and Effectiveness of the African Commission on Human and Peoples' Rights*, AI Index: IOR 63/02/98.

[77] See, for example, Resolution on Nigeria, Eighth Annual Activity Report 1994–1995, Annex VIII (*Documents of the African Commission*, p. 404).

the ICJ ensured that NGOs participated in the meeting. The Pan African Movement successfully requested the Ugandan Government to invite the Commission to hold the session in Kampala.

The second extraordinary session[78] of the Commission was held in December 1995, when NGOs presented information on the serious human rights situation in Nigeria.[79] The presence of representatives of the Nigerian Government enabled members of the Commissions to convey their serious concerns about the situation directly to them. Some NGOs also raised concerns about the rapidly deteriorating situation in Burundi and the Commission decided to consider it at its 19th Session.

African Court on Human and Peoples' Rights

At the time of the drafting of the African Charter, Member States of the OAU chose not to establish an African Court but to establish only the Commission. After the adoption of the African Charter States were unlikely to put forward a proposal to establish a court to receive complaints of human rights violations given that they have done little to strengthen the Commission over the past fourteen years.[80] An NGO therefore had to begin the initiative. At the workshop that preceded the 14th Session of the Commission in December 1993, the ICJ brought together NGOs and a few experts to begin the process of drafting a protocol to the African Charter for the establishment of an African Court on Human and Peoples' Rights.[81] Subsequently, the ICJ established a working group that included representatives of Lawyers for Human Rights (a South African NGO) and the African Centre for Human Rights and Democratic Studies to produce a draft protocol.

---

[78] The first extraordinary session of the Commission was held in February 1988 to draft its Rules of Procedure.

[79] Final Communiqué of the Second Extraordinary Session of the African Commission on Human and Peoples' Rights, Kampala, Uganda, 18–19 December 1995, ACHPR/ FINCOMM/2nd Extra Ordinary/XX (*Documents of the African Commission*, p. 463).

[80] A list of measures to strengthen the African Commission were proposed during the first meeting of government experts to consider the draft Protocol to the African Charter to establish an African Court, but most of these have yet to be implemented. Report of the Government Experts Meeting on the Establishment of an African Court of Human and Peoples' Rights, 6–12 September 1995, Cape Town, South Africa, OAU/LEG/EXP/AFC/HPR(I), Section VI. For further discussion of the Court, see Chapter 10 below.

[81] Conclusion and Recommendations of the Fifth Workshop, November 1993, in International Commission of Jurists, *The Participation of Non-Governmental Organizations*, p. 39 at p. 41.

The OAU Assembly of Heads of State and Government adopted a resolution in June 1994 in which it requested the Secretary-General to 'convene a Government experts' meeting to ponder, in conjunction with the African Commission, over the means to enhance the efficiency of the African Commission and to consider in particular the establishment of an African Court on Human and Peoples' Rights'.[82] The task of producing the first draft was left almost entirely to NGOs, led by the ICJ. The OAU Secretariat arranged three meetings of government legal experts to finalise the draft protocol, held respectively in Cape Town (September 1995), Nouakchott (April 1997) and Addis Ababa (December 1997). Prior to each of these meetings the ICJ arranged a meeting of NGO representatives, judges and other experts to consider the draft protocol and comments from governments in order to suggest formulations for the various Articles. Thereafter NGO representatives participated alongside government experts at the OAU meeting as invited experts.[83]

NGOs tried to ensure that the Protocol provided a strong framework for the establishment of a human rights court in Africa by providing, for example, for adequate representation of women among the eleven judges; making the decisions of the African Court binding and implementable through national courts; and entitling NGOs and individuals to have access to the African Court. However, NGOs remain concerned about some provisions in the Protocol; for example, the final decision for suspension or removal of a judge would not rest with the African Court, but with the OAU Assembly of Heads of State and Government.[84]

There is also disappointment that NGOs and individuals are not authorised to access the African Court except through the declaration of States ratifying the Protocol. The delays that could occur before a referral of a case by the Commission to the Court were of particular concern to NGOs

---

[82] AHG/Res. 230 (XXX), Assembly of Heads of State and Government, June 1994.

[83] At the first meeting of government experts held in Cape Town in September 1995, several NGO representatives were part of the South African delegation and NGO representatives were nominated to be the leader and deputy leader of the delegation.

[84] Article 19(2) states: 'Such a decision of the Court [suspending or removing a judge] shall become final unless it is set aside by the Assembly at its next session.' The OAU Legal Department also raised concerns about some aspects of the draft Protocol. See The African Court of Human and Peoples' Rights – Factors Which May Limit the Court's Competence and Hamper its Functioning, Annexure III to the Report of the Secretary-General on the Draft Protocol on the Establishment of an African Court of Human and Peoples' Rights, Council of Ministers, 26th Ordinary Session, 26–30 May 1997, CM/2020(LXVI).

that were involved in the drafting of the Protocol. Therefore the first draft included a provision that allowed NGOs or individuals to approach the Court directly on 'exceptional grounds', without first approaching the Commission, in urgent cases or cases involving serious, systematic or massive violations of human rights. This unique provision was intended to allow victims of human rights violations and NGOs to file complaints directly with the African Court without first approaching the Commission, especially where irreparable harm may be caused by the delay in consideration of the matter.[85] However, this provision turned out to be very controversial and led to lengthy discussions among the government experts. While State representatives accepted that individuals and NGOs should have access to the Court and conceded that it was mostly NGOs that filed complaints, they were of the view that States should make an additional declaration accepting the authority of the court to receive petitions from NGOs and individuals.[86] This view prevailed and Article 34(6) of the Protocol requires a State to make a declaration if it accepts the authority of the Court to receive petitions from NGOs and individuals. The Protocol emphasises that '[t]he Court shall not receive any petition under Article 5(3) involving a State Party which has not made such a declaration'. Where a State Party has made a declaration, it is not certain whether an NGO would be entitled to file a case in the African Court which has already been considered by the African Commission.

The Protocol to the African Charter on Human and Peoples' Rights on the Establishment of an African Court on Human and Peoples' Rights was adopted by the OAU Summit in June 1998 and was opened for ratification.[87] Article 5(3) of the Protocol provides: 'The Court may entitle relevant NGOs with observer status before the Commission, and individuals to institute cases directly before it, in accordance with Article 34(6) of this Protocol.' Of the five States that have thus far ratified the Protocol, only Burkina Faso

---

[85] Explanatory Notes to the Protocol to the African Charter on the Establishment of an African Court on Human and Peoples' Rights, p. 3, annexed to Report of the Government Experts Meeting on the Establishment of an African Court on Human and Peoples' Rights.

[86] Report of the Secretary-General on the Draft Protocol on the Establishment of an African Court of Human and Peoples' Rights, Annexure II, p. 6. See also Report of the Government Experts Meeting on the Establishment of an African Court of Human and Peoples' Rights, para. 23.

[87] OAU/LEG/MIN/AFCHPR/PROT(I) Rev.2. The Protocol, which has thus far been ratified by five states, requires ratification by fifteen States for it to come into effect (Article 34(3)).

has made a declaration under Article 34(6) of the Protocol accepting this jurisdiction of the African Court. In regard to cases filed directly before it under Article 5(3) of the Protocol, the African Court is required by Article 6 of the Protocol to consider the admissibility of the case, taking into consideration the provisions of Article 56 of the African Charter. It may seek the opinion of the Commission in this regard. The African Court may either consider the case or refer it to the Commission. Where the case is referred to the Commission, it may be brought again before the African Court after the Commission has decided the matter.

Even if States do not make the declaration, as is most likely, NGOs could still play an important role in shaping the jurisprudence of the African Court, as they have done at the Commission. It would be important for NGOs to ensure that complaints filed with the Commission include strong legal arguments that would be upheld if the Commission or a State refers the matter to the African Court. Furthermore, NGOs would be required to provide support in the presentation of the case before the African Court, especially if the Rules of Procedure of the African Court would permit the legal representative of the victim or claimant to be part of the Commission's legal team.[88] The knowledge and legal expertise of NGO representatives could contribute to the development of the Court's jurisprudence. NGOs would also have an important role to play in monitoring the implementation of the binding decisions of the African Court, in publicising the decisions within their own countries and ensuring that lawyers bringing cases in the national courts refer to the decisions in order to strengthen domestic jurisprudence.

The Protocol authorises the African Court to provide advisory opinions 'at the request of a Member State of the OAU, the OAU, any of its organs, or any African organisation recognised by the OAU'.[89] There are several African NGOs that are recognised by the OAU, which has granted them observer status. Under this provision these NGOs may be able to request an advisory opinion from the African Court on a legal matter relating to the African Charter or 'any other relevant human rights instrument ratified by the States'. A well-formulated request for an advisory opinion brought by an NGO could contribute to the jurisprudence on the interpretation of the Charter or other human rights instruments.

---

[88] Such a provision is contained in the Rules of Procedure of the Inter-American Court on Human Rights, 1 January 1997, Article 22(2).
[89] Article 4(1).

African Charter on the Rights and Welfare of the Child

The African Charter on the Rights and Welfare of the Child[90] came into effect in November 1999, and as at December 2000 had been ratified by twenty-one Member States of the OAU. It is the first regional treaty on the rights of the child. The African Children's Charter has similar provisions to the African Charter regarding the role of NGOs, and provides for the establishment of an African Committee of Experts on the Rights and Welfare of the Child comprising eleven members. The Committee of Experts is required to 'encourage national and local institutions concerned with the rights and welfare of the child'[91] and to 'cooperate with other African, international and regional institutions and organisations concerned with the promotion and protection of the rights and welfare of the child'.[92] However, unlike the African Charter, the complaint procedure specifically recognises the role of NGOs in the filing of complaints before the Committee of Experts. Article 44(1) states: 'The Committee may receive communication, from any person, group or non-governmental organisation recognised by the Organization of African Unity, by a Member State, or the United Nations relating to any matter covered by this Charter.'

Since the adoption of the treaty by the OAU, NGOs have been encouraging States to ratify the African Children's Charter,[93] especially as the Convention on the Rights of the Child has almost universal ratification in Africa.[94] However, States have been reluctant to commit themselves to this regional treaty which has taken more than nine years to come into effect. The failure initially of States Parties to nominate a sufficient number of candidates to be elected to create the Committee of Experts also shows a lack of interest in establishing the mechanism that would scrutinise their compliance with their obligations under the treaty.[95] NGOs encouraged States to nominate

---

[90] OAU Doc. CAB/LEG/24.9/49 (1990), adopted in June 1990.

[91] Article 42(1)(a)(i).   [92] Article 42(1)(a)(iii).

[93] See, for example, Amnesty International, *Organization of African Unity: The African Charter on the Rights and Welfare of the Child*, IOR 63/06/98.

[94] Somalia is the only country in Africa not to have ratified the treaty. The US is the only other State not to have ratified the Convention on the Rights of the Child.

[95] The Committee of Experts was to have been elected by the OAU Assembly of Heads of States and Governments in June 2000 in Lomé, Togo, but the elections had to be postponed to the OAU Summit in July 2001 due to too few nominations having been received from States Parties. By the end of December 2000 the OAU had still not received sufficient nominations, with only nine candidates being nominated. Members were eventually elected at the OAU Summit in July 2001.

competent individuals with particular experience in the rights and welfare of the child. It is important for NGOs that the Committee of Experts consists of members who are more than nominally independent, as has been the experience with some members of the African Commission.

NGOs have also made representations to the OAU regarding the drafting of the Rules of Procedure of the Committee of Experts with a view to ensuring the participation of NGOs in its meetings and deliberations. An international NGO that specialises in children's rights has also offered to provide support in the establishment of the secretariat of the Committee of Experts. As with the Commission, the role of NGOs would be important in strengthening and supporting the work of the Committee of Experts. NGOs would play a beneficial role in regard to the examination of State reports, the filing of complaints and in the conducting of investigations. NGOs would also have an opportunity to help the Committee of Experts develop principles and standards relating to the rights of the child, just as they have done with the African Commission.

Conclusion

The Commission, the primary regional mechanism for the protection and promotion of human rights in Africa, still has a long way to go before it could be considered to be effective in tackling the serious human rights issues that prevail throughout the continent. While NGOs have contributed to the improvement of its effectiveness and efficiency, they cannot afford to become complacent. NGOs, especially those within Africa, have to take seriously their responsibility of supporting and critiquing the Commission. They should focus more on the obstacles that hamper the Commission. These include: the deficiencies within its Secretariat; the lack of political will and initiative on the part of some Commissioners; the failure of States to honour their obligations under the African Charter or to comply with the decisions of the Commission; and the unwillingness of the OAU to hold accountable Member States for serious violations of human rights brought to its attention by the Commission or to provide adequate resources for the proper functioning of the Commission.

9

THE SPECIAL RAPPORTEURS IN THE AFRICAN SYSTEM

MALCOLM EVANS AND RACHEL MURRAY

Introduction

The practice of appointing Special Rapporteurs to explore the human rights situation either in a particular State or pertaining to a particular theme has become a well-established feature of the United Nations human rights machinery and ranks among its most innovative achievements.[1] It is, then, no surprise to find that it has been adopted within other systems of human rights protection, including the African regional mechanism. In its relatively short existence the African Commission has appointed three Special Rapporteurs on thematic issues: one on extrajudicial executions, one on prisons and other conditions of detention and one on women's rights. It has not created any country-specific Special Rapporteurs but this is hardly surprising. Unlike the UN Commission on Human Rights, the African Commission has an explicit treaty-based competence to examine the situation on a country-by-country basis through the Charter's reporting

[1] See, for example, under the UN, where there are Special Rapporteurs on the sale of children, child prostitution and child pornography; the right to education; extrajudicial, summary or arbitrary executions; promotion and protection of the right to freedom of opinion and expression; the independence of judges and lawyers; human rights of migrants, religious intolerance; and torture, among others. The Inter-American Commission has a Special Rapporteur on the rights of women and has established an Office of the Special Rapporteur on the Right to Freedom of Expression. See D. Weissbrodt, 'The Three "Theme" Rapporteurs of the UN Commission on Human Rights', *American Journal of International Law* 80 (1986) 693–5; Association for the Prevention of Torture, Standard Operating Procedures of International Mechanisms Carrying out Visits to Places of Detention, Workshop, 24 May 1997 (Association for the Prevention of Torture, Geneva, 1997).

procedures.[2] Further, a number of ancillary country-specific activities are implicitly addressed through the promotional mandate of the Commission, which is exercised by allocating responsibility for particular countries to individual Commissioners[3] and by its visits to States where there have been allegations of serious or massive violations through the communication procedure.[4]

On first glance, then, the record of the Commission is impressive. A closer examination reveals, however, that the decisions to appoint these three Special Rapporteurs appear to have come about more as the result of a combination of NGO lobbying, the impact of particular sets of circumstances and the Commission's desire to be seen to be doing something, rather than as the product of any well-thought-out programme or as a reflection of a belief that these areas represented the most pressing concerns that it faced. In the light of this, it is perhaps not surprising that the record of achievement under these mandates has been modest – indeed, in two cases the achievements could fairly be described as minimal. The following sections will consider the dynamics of the process that led to the Commission appointing these Special Rapporteurs in the first place and give an overview of their work so far. The chapter will conclude with some observations upon the possible reasons for their successes and failures.[5] For the sake of clarity, one particular feature of the African practice needs to be highlighted at the outset: all mandate holders are serving members of the Commission itself. In what follows, they will be referred to as Special Rapporteurs of the Commission but it must not be forgotten that they also form a part of the Commission.

---

[2] For a consideration of the reporting procedure under the African Charter, see Chapter 2 above.

[3] For a detailed consideration of the promotional activities of the Commission, see Chapter 11 below.

[4] For further information on missions undertaken by the African Commission, see R. Murray, 'On-Site Visits by the African Commission on Human and Peoples' Rights: A Case Study and Comparison with the Inter-American Commission on Human Rights', *African Journal of International and Comparative Law* 11 (1999) 460.

[5] The system of Special Rapporteurs is relatively under-explored. Given the lack of up-to-date, reliable and accessible sources relating to the UN system, it is impossible in a chapter of this length both to present that material and to draw in the construction of a comparative analysis. Consequently, this chapter limits itself to an essentially factual presentation of the work of the three African Special Rapporteurs and to making a number of points concerning them, as is consonant with the aims of this particular collection of essays. It is to be hoped that this may assist others who wish to attempt the broader task.

The Special Rapporteur on Extrajudicial, Summary and Arbitrary Executions

The willingness of the Commission to appoint a Special Rapporteur on Extrajudicial, Summary and Arbitrary Executions at its 15th Session in 1994 has been attributed to the timing of that particular session,[6] coming as it did during the genocide in Rwanda to which the Commission had at that time made no response.[7] This was reflected in the decision to establish the terms of the mandate, the – admittedly scanty – record of which expressly provided that the Special Rapporteur, Commissioner Dr Hatem Ben Salem, was 'mainly to focus on the situation in Rwanda'.[8] This linkage is apparent in the 'Resolution on the Situation in Rwanda', adopted at the same session, paragraph 4 of which '[i]nvites the Special Rapporteur . . . to pay special attention to Rwanda and report back to the 16th Session'.[9] At this stage this was the only explicit guidance given regarding the scope of the mandate, which seemed therefore to focus on but not be limited to Rwanda. Moreover, no guidance was given concerning precisely what the Special Rapporteur was actually expected to do or how he was to go about his work.

[6] J. Harrington, 'Special Rapporteurs of the African Commission on Human and Peoples' Rights' (paper submitted to the Conference on Reform of the African Human Rights System, Centre for Human Rights, University of Pretoria, 26–28 March 2001). There is nothing particularly unique in this and it has been suggested that the appointment of some of the UN Special Rapporteurs has been motivated by similar impulses. See, for example, P. Alston, 'The Commission on Human Rights', in P. Alston, *The United Nations and Human Rights. A Critical Appraisal* (Oxford: Clarendon, 1992), pp. 126–210 and 174–5.

[7] The 15th Session of the Commission took place on 18–27 April 1994 in Banjul, The Gambia. The only action taken by the Commission at this time, in addition to appointing the Special Rapporteur, was the adoption of a resolution in which it noted that it was 'deeply concerned about the alarming human rights situation in Rwanda characterised by serious and massive human rights violations', condemning the violence and the massacre, and calling on all parties to resolve the conflict and to respect humanitarian law: Resolution on the Situation in Rwanda, Seventh Activity Report 1993–1994, Annex XII; R. Murray and M. Evans (eds.), *Documents of the African Commission on Human and Peoples' Rights* (Oxford: Hart Publishing, 2001), p. 353 (hereinafter *Documents of the African Commission*). The Commission also produced a press release: see Press Release, Seventh Activity Report 1993–1994, Annex XIII (*Documents of the African Commission*, p. 354). Later action included another resolution on Rwanda, adopted at its 16th Session in October/November 1994: see Resolution on Rwanda, Eighth Activity Report 1994–1995, Annex VI (*Documents of the African Commission*, p. 401).

[8] Seventh Activity Report of the African Commission on Human and Peoples' Rights 1993–4, ACHPR/RPT/7th (*Documents of the African Commission*, p. 317), para. 26.

[9] Resolution on the Situation in Rwanda.

Although, as requested, the Special Rapporteur did set out some of his ideas concerning his vision for his mandate at the following session, the terms of reference were still not formalised or adopted by the Commission at this stage.[10] It was not until the 17th Session in March 1995, nearly a year after his initial appointment, that the Commission approved draft terms of reference which had been presented to the Commission by the Special Rapporteur himself and which dealt with the scope, duration and methods of his work and the proposed budget,[11] and not until the 18th Session in October 1995 that the terms of reference of the mandate were finally approved.[12]

Although the significance of the Special Rapporteur's contribution to the formulation and solidification of the mandate should receive due recognition, it must be noted that in the six years from 1995 until 2001 he succeeded in producing only one written report, submitted to the 20th Session in October 1996, supplemented by general comments made at subsequent sessions of the Commission – a record suggestive of ossification. It appears from the record that a further report from the Special Rapporteur was considered at the following 21st Session in April 1997 and that the Commission was prepared to 'commend the Special Rapporteur for the work he has done so far', but this was the first and last overt signal of approval.[13]

The Special Rapporteur's 1996 report sets out the terms of reference, and this provides a template against which to judge his activities, although for reasons which will become apparent it is hardly necessary to adopt so refined

---

[10] Report of the Special Rapporteur on Extrajudicial Executions in Africa, Eighth Annual Activity Report 1994–1995 (*Documents of the African Commission*, p. 370), paras. 17–19. The Commission noted the need to avoid duplication with the work already undertaken by the UN, and agreed that it would be appropriate to focus on two particular aspects: (a) compensation to the families of victims of such executions; and (b) the responsibility of instigators and authors of such executions.

[11] *Ibid.*, paras. 19–21. See also Final Communiqué of the Seventeenth Ordinary Session, Lomé, Togo, 12–22 March 1995, ACHPR/COM.FIN/XVII/Rev.3 (*Documents of the African Commission*, p. 418), para. 25. The precise content of the terms of reference is not recorded.

[12] See Report on Extrajudicial, Summary or Arbitrary Executions, Tenth Activity Report 1996–1997, Annex VI, Section III (*Documents of the African Commission*, p. 508). Somewhat ironically in the light of subsequent developments, the delay in the implementation of the mandate was said to be due to 'the wish expressed by members of the Commission to begin this first experience on a solid foundation'.

[13] See *ibid.*, para. 18. However, this latter report is not found in the documentation produced by the Commission and is not, apparently, otherwise available.

an approach to be able to proceed to an evaluation. The report includes a number of general statements, such as the importance of the right to life and the principle that no one should be deprived of their right arbitrarily.[14] It also provides an insight into a number of substantive matters which are considered to fall within the scope of the mandate. Thus the report identifies the following as issues to be addressed as comprising the core 'mission' of the mandate:[15]

1. To propose the implementation of a reporting system on cases of extrajudicial, summary and arbitrary executions in African States, especially by keeping a register of the identity of the victims.
2. To follow up, in collaboration with government officials, or failing that, with international, national or African NGOs, all enquiries which could lead to discovering the identity and extent of responsibility of authors and initiators of extrajudicial, summary or arbitrary executions.
3. To suggest ways and means of informing the African Commission in good time of the possibility of extrajudicial, summary or arbitrary executions, with the goal of intervening before the OAU Summit.
4. To intervene with States for trial and punishment of perpetrators of extrajudicial summary or arbitrary executions, and rehabilitation of the victims of these executions.
5. To examine the modalities of creation of a mechanism of compensation for the families of victims of extrajudicial, summary or arbitrary executions, which might be doing [sic] through national legal procedures, or through an African compensation fund.

The 1996 report also considered the nature of the information that was to be collected in the course of the fulfilment of the mandate, and in particular the credibility of sources of information. The task of the Special Rapporteur is to be to verify the facts underpinning allegations, and it is made clear that, although he cannot 'in any way, substitute for the police and judicial organs of the concerned country, nor play the role of detective, it nevertheless remains that he must evaluate the adequacy of the means of inquiry made by national organs and the credibility of the conclusions adopted by national investigative organs'.[16] In order to carry out these functions, the Special Rapporteur is to have 'recourse to all methods of investigation, specifically by requesting the assistance of States and national, international and African

---

[14] Report on Extrajudicial, Summary or Arbitrary Executions.
[15] Ibid., Section II, A.   [16] Ibid., Section III, B.

NGOs'.[17] Moreover, 'he can be assisted in his mission by any person whom he judges competent to perform this task well'.[18]

These, then, are a number of the substantive and procedural elements that were to be part of the work of the Special Rapporteur. The 1996 report goes further, however, and identifies a number of priority 'fields of investigation' that are to be addressed in the fulfilment of the 'mission' set out above. Unsurprisingly, it states that the Special Rapporteur 'can decide to choose a country where he believes the incidence of execution is the most frequent or massive',[19] but it enjoins him to produce a report on the extrajudicial executions of women, children, demonstrators and human rights opponents and activists 'as a priority'.[20] Quite why these particular categories were singled out is not at all clear. Nevertheless, the expectation set out in the 1996 report is that the 'mission' of the Special Rapporteur – presumably the execution of the tasks outlined above, taking into account the particular fields of investigation highlighted – is to be achieved within a two-year period, although this could be extended.[21] This rather suggests that the mandate was seen as a finite project.

As regards the flow of information concerning the work of the mandate holder, the 1996 report envisaged the publication of a bulletin containing information collected on the eve of each session of the Commission. More generally, the Special Rapporteur was to report to the Commission at each session and to the Assembly of Heads of State and Government of the OAU annually, in a report annexed to that of the Commission.[22]

In order to service these activities, the report also records that Commission had approved a budget totalling some US$57,000 to fund the mandate, of which US$16,000 was furnished by the North–South Centre of the Council of Europe and the Swiss Directorate of Co-operation in Development and Humanitarian Aid.[23] The remainder of the 1996 report chronicles a number of activities that the Special Rapporteur had already undertaken in fulfilment

---

[17] *Ibid.*, Section II, D. [18] *Ibid.* [19] *Ibid.*, Section II, B.

[20] *Ibid.* Other ancillary tasks that are programmed include, for example, in relation to creating a trust fund for compensation, 'a joint reflection with interested NGOs and a report will be submitted for the advice of the Commission, which will pronounce on this question'. *Ibid.*, Section III, B.

[21] *Ibid.*, Section II, C. [22] *Ibid.*, Section II, E.

[23] *Ibid.*, Sections III and IV. Costs included computer, phone and secretariat expenses. Additional expenses of US$41,000 were required for the second phase which included visits to particular countries and administrative expenses.

of his mandate. This amounted to little more than planning to contact or making initial inquiries with relevant organisations to consider setting up a register of victims.[24]

Although the setting out of tentative plans does not reflect a particularly pro-active stance, as this report covered only a relatively short period since the formalisation of terms of reference this might be understandable. However, in most regards the subsequent performance falls significantly short of the aims set out in the 1996 report. Indeed, with the exception of the submission of two reports pertaining to country situations, it appears that hardly any of the aspirations set out in the 1996 report became a reality. In the light of this, there is little to be gained in probing the *modus operandi* of the Special Rapporteur and the remainder of this section will set out what evidences of activity exist, and the denouement to which it led.

One of the overriding problems appears to be a lack of clarity concerning the principal focus of the Special Rapporteur's work. Recalling the initial motivation for establishing the mandate, there is appended to the 1996 report a 'Progress Report on Extrajudicial, Summary or Arbitrary Executions' which focuses exclusively on Rwanda and Burundi,[25] but the body of the 1996 report notes that:

> If in the first place the case of Rwanda and of Burundi will be a priority for the collection of information and creation of the computer database, as a matter of course all available information on extrajudicial executions in other African countries will be registered, especially for Liberia. To do so, and collect more testimony, the reports submitted by the organs of the UN as well as the OAU will be taken into consideration.[26]

This diffusing approach is reflected elsewhere in the report, with reference made to other country situations and themes, although with no great

---

[24] It is worth noting in passing that it appears that the Special Rapporteur had little prior experience or knowledge of how to create a database and collect such information, as he had to be alerted to the existence of well-known organisations by others. *Ibid.*, Section III, A (2).

[25] Progress Report on Extrajudicial, Summary or Arbitrary Executions, Tenth Activity Report 1996–1997, Annex VI (*Documents of the African Commission*, p. 516). This notes meetings held with NGOs and Rwandan refugees but it does not record that the Special Rapporteur himself visited either country, although it does say that such visits might be organised in the future. Names of alleged victims were also presented to him at these meetings but the report records that the Special Rapporteur advised the Secretariat to pass these on to the International Criminal Tribunal for Rwanda.

[26] Report on Extrajudicial, Summary or Arbitrary Executions, Section III, A (2).

consistency.[27] This practice spilled over and is reflected in what evidences of further output exist.

Records of the 23rd Session of the Commission in April 1998 note that the Special Rapporteur had 'presented the final report on the summary, arbitrary and extrajudicial executions in Rwanda, Burundi, Chad, Comoros and the [Democratic Republic of the Congo]' and that '[t]his report contains the names of people about whom the Special Rapporteur is expecting information from the States concerned'.[28] It is not possible to analyse this development in any detail since the final report that is referred to has not been disseminated in written form. But it is clear that the States which are listed as the subject of the Special Rapporteur's attention are different from those previously identified.[29] Further confusion as to the focus of the mandate is produced by the Special Rapporteur's statement at the 24th Session of the Commission in October 1998 in which he 'drew the Commission's attention to the new cases of extrajudicial executions in Chad, the Democratic Republic of the Congo, Angola, the Comoros and Sierra Leone',[30] and at the subsequent 25th Session in April/May 1999 when he presented an oral report on executions in Rwanda, Burundi and Chad.[31]

There is in principle nothing objectionable in the Special Rapporteur shifting his focus in order to address the situations that may emerge from unexpected quarters and which require his attention. Indeed, it is highly desirable and foreshadowed in the 1996 report. The problem is that there seems to be a trail of unfinished business which the constant shifts in focus and emphasis do little to disguise. If there is any substantial and substantive output from these efforts, they are not apparent to the most well informed of external observers, although the prospect of this work having borne fruit which has not been properly recorded or reported cannot be

---

[27] Although initially it would appear that he was to focus on certain groups such as women and children, the lists are not consistent throughout the report. In relation to the countries which merit particular attention, again the report later extends this beyond Rwanda and Burundi to Zaire, and also calls for information from NGOs on Sudan, Nigeria and Liberia.

[28] Eleventh Activity Report of the African Commission on Human and Peoples' Rights 1997–8, ACHPR/RPT/11th (*Documents of the African Commission*, p. 599), para. 29.

[29] It might be presumed that this refers to the report on the fulfilment of the Special Rapporteur's 'mission' called for in the 1996 report, and it may be that it is a development of the interim report on Rwanda and Burundi that was annexed to that report. This is, of course, supposition.

[30] Twelfth Activity Report of the African Commission on Human and Peoples' Rights 1998–9, ACHPR/RPT/12th (*Documents of the African Commission*, p. 685), para. 24.

[31] *Ibid.*, para. 25.

wholly discounted, unlikely though this may seem in the light of subsequent events.

Moreover, the picture of general ineffectiveness finds some reflection in both the working methods of the Special Rapporteur and in the work of the Commission mission itself in other spheres. Thus in the period of his appointment, the Special Rapporteur has not been able to conduct any visits to States. There was recently some discussion of his visiting Chad to verify allegations but this did not materialise.[32] Nor does the Commission appear to see the Special Rapporteur as central to its more general discussions and activities pertaining to the countries that he himself has chosen to focus on from time to time.[33] There are, however, some evidences of concrete, albeit limited, action in which the Special Rapporteur has been known to be involved.[34]

From 1998 the Special Rapporteur has had the assistance of a Gambian-based NGO, the Institute for Human Rights and Development, yet despite some initial encouraging signs this does not seem to have changed the situation in any significant fashion. NGOs and subsequently other Commissioners have called on the Special Rapporteur to take some action, and have

[32] Thirteenth Activity Report of the African Commission on Human and Peoples' Rights 1999–2000, AHG/222 (XXXVI), para. 24. There was some indication that the government was not responding to his letters or contacts.

[33] For example, on those occasions where the Commission has contemplated sending missions to Rwanda, it has not included the Special Rapporteur as a member of the proposed delegation: see Ninth Activity Report of the African Commission on Human and Peoples' Rights 1995–6, ACHPR/RPT/9th (*Documents of the African Commission*, p. 428), para. 20. Similarly, in a resolution on Burundi, the Commission has called on the authorities to permit the Special Rapporteurs from the UN and the African Commission to visit the country, but makes no other mention of the Special Rapporteur: Resolution on Burundi, Ninth Activity Report 1995–1996, Annex VII (*Documents of the African Commission*, p. 443).

[34] For example, at the 23rd Session of the Commission in April 1998, Amnesty International alerted the Commission to the possible execution of a number of individuals in Rwanda the following day, and it urged the Commission to contact the authorities in order to call upon them to halt the execution. During the ensuing discussion at the session, Amnesty liaised with the Special Rapporteur over the drafting of a fax to this effect. This was subsequently dispatched, albeit in vain. The Final Communiqué notes that, having heard that the executions were indeed carried out in public, 'the Commission authorised the Chairman to write to the government of Rwanda and express the outrage of the Commission at this blatant disregard of the provisions of the Charter', and a press release to this effect was also issued: Final Communiqué of the 23rd Ordinary Session of the African Commission on Human and Peoples' Rights, DOC/OS/45(XXIII), para. 9 (*Documents of the African Commission*, p. 674).

shown signs of becoming increasingly impatient with his failure to produce any clear evidence of significant activity and outcomes from one session to another. At the 26th Session in November 1999, the Government of Rwanda criticised him for failing to verify allegations that had been made and for the poor quality of his work, although it was forced to withdraw its statement after the Chair noted that the criticism was directed against the Commission rather than one of its members.[35] After some quite vociferous criticism from a number of NGOs at the 28th Session in Benin and from other members of the Commission, Commissioner Ben Salem resigned from his position as Special Rapporteur. It is unclear whether other Commissioners will step in or whether the mandate will now fall into disuse. Taking up this mandate, which has received so little attention and which has been so poorly implemented, is clearly not likely to be an attractive option even for the most dynamically minded Commissioner.

It is difficult to resist the conclusion that this has been a largely wasted opportunity and a matter of some considerable embarrassment for the reputation of the African human rights system in general and the African Commission in particular. This experience may also have contributed to the reticence which clearly exists on the part of the Commission to utilise the Special Rapporteur system and on the part of NGOs to advocate it. However, as will be seen in the following section, its next experiment has shown that it is possible for such a position to function in a much more effective fashion within the African context.

The Special Rapporteur on Prisons and Conditions of Detention

At its 19th Session in 1996 the Commission agreed in principle to appoint a Special Rapporteur on Prison Conditions in Africa.[36] This appears to have been largely in response to requests made by Penal Reform International, an international NGO headquartered in Paris, although this proposal was also supported by other NGOs[37] and the Commission clearly

---

[35] R. Murray, 'Report of the 1999 Sessions of the African Commission on Human and Peoples' Rights', *Human Rights Law Journal*, forthcoming.

[36] Ninth Activity Report, para. 18.

[37] For example, at the 18th Session of the Commission, a draft resolution that had been adopted at the ICJ 9th Workshop for NGOs held prior to the session concerning the appointment of Special Rapporteurs on both Prisons and Women's Rights was presented: see Final Communiqué of the 18th Ordinary Session, Praia, Cape Verde, 2–11 October 1995, ACHPR/FIN/COMM/XVIII (*Documents of the African Commission*, p. 457),

perceived from the outset that NGOs would have an important role in the development and implementation of the mandate.[38] Prior to the session, the first all-African Conference on Prison Conditions had been held in Kampala and this formed a part of the background and general climate in favour of the appointment at the following session.[39] It also appears that the Commission initially considered appointing as Special Rapporteur a person who was not already a member of the Commission but who would 'work under a designated Commissioner', and calls were made for CVs to be submitted from interested candidates.[40] However, this was not followed through, and at the 20th Session in October 1996.[41] Commissioner Dankwa was appointed to this position. The mandate was initially established for a fixed period of two years and allocated a budget of some US$40,000,[42] but at its 25th Session in May 1999 the Commission extended the mandate for a one-year period, until 31 October 2000.[43] At its 28th Session in 2000 the Commission appointed Commissioner Chirwa to the position.[44]

paras. 22–3. Indeed, the report of the Special Rapporteur on Prisons and Conditions of Detention at the 21st Session of the Commission noted that PRI was to support his work and would 'endeavour to mobilise resources at local and international levels for the work of the Special Rapporteur' as well as offer assistance in 'alternatives to imprisonment; prison conditions and rehabilitation; and strengthening of regional, sub-regional and local NGOs working on prisons', as well as making available other information and data: see Report of the Special Rapporteur on Prisons and Conditions of Detention to the 21st Session of the African Commission on Human and Peoples' Rights, Tenth Activity Report 1996–1997, Annex VII (*Documents of the African Commission*, p. 518).

[38] *Ibid.*

[39] See the comments of the Special Rapporteur in his Report on Visit to Prisons in Zimbabwe, reproduced as an appendix to the Report of the Special Rapporteur of Prisons, *ibid* (*Documents of the African Commission*, p. 522).

[40] Ninth Activity Report, para. 18. Indeed, CVs were submitted to the Secretariat of the Commission.

[41] Tenth Activity Report of the African Commission on Human and Peoples' Rights 1996–7, ACHPR/RPT/10th (*Documents of the African Commission*, p. 492), para. 19.

[42] Report of the Special Rapporteur on Prisons. This included US$5,000 for equipment such as a computer; US$8,600 for secretarial support; US$25,000 for travel and the remainder for miscellaneous expenses.

[43] Resolution on the Extension of the Mandate of the Special Rapporteur on Prisons and Conditions of Detention in Africa, Twelfth Activity Report 1998–1999, Annex IV (*Documents of the African Commission*, p. 710).

[44] Final Communiqué of the 28th Ordinary Session of the African Commission on Human and Peoples' Rights, Cotonou, Benin, 23 October to 6 November 2000, ACHPR/FIN.COMM/XXVIII, Rev.2.

The terms of reference finally adopted[45] summarise the mandate as empowering the Special Rapporteur to 'examine the situation of persons deprived of their liberty within the territories of States Parties to the African Charter on Human and Peoples' Rights'.[46] It then spells out a number of tasks which are intended to breathe life into this process, the key elements of which are:[47]

1. conducting an examination of the state of prisons and conditions of detention and making recommendations for their improvement;
2. advocating adherence to the African Charter and other relevant international human rights norms;
3. examining the national laws and making recommendations concerning their compliance with international norms;
4. at the request of the Commission, making recommendations on any communications filed with the Commission related to the subject-matter of the mandate;
5. proposing to States any urgent action which needs to be undertaken;
6. conducting studies into conditions which contribute to detentions and proposing preventative measures;
7. co-ordinating his activities with those of other Special Rapporteurs and working groups.

In order to carry out these tasks the Special Rapporteur is empowered to 'seek and receive' information from States Parties to the African Charter and from individuals and other bodies on cases or situations falling within the scope of the mandate,[48] and the Special Rapporteur 'should be given all the necessary assistance and co-operation to carry out on-site visits and receive information from detained persons, their families or representatives, from governmental or non-governmental organisations and others'.[49]

The terms of reference frame the task of the Special Rapporteur in a generalised fashion, calling on him to conduct an 'evaluation of the conditions

---

[45] These are set out as an appendix to the Report of the Special Rapporteur on Prisons. The text of the Special Rapporteur's report says that these were based on an earlier draft, and were revised at the request of the Commission at its 20th Session in October 1996. This would appear to refer to the outcome of a consultation that was held in The Gambia in January 1996 and which was probably circulating at the 20th Session later that year.

[46] *Ibid.*, para. 2.   [47] *Ibid.*, paras. 3–5.   [48] *Ibid.*, para. 7.   [49] *Ibid.*, para. 8.

of detention in Africa' but also setting out a number of priority areas to be focused upon within that context.[50] Some of these priority areas relate to particular and pervasive problem areas, such as arbitrary detention, treatment in detention and healthcare. Others relate to particular categories of detainees, including women (the entire operation of the mandate is to be conducted against the background of 'paying special attention to problems related to gender'[51]), children, and vulnerable groups including refugees and those suffering from forms of disability. The terms of reference also make it clear that the Special Rapporteur is expected to submit an annual report to the Commission which should be 'published and widely disseminated in accordance with the relevant provisions of the Charter'.[52]

In contrast to the Special Rapporteur on Extrajudicial, Summary and Arbitrary Executions, the Special Rapporteur on Prisons and Conditions of Detention took concrete action almost immediately after his appointment by conducting a mission to Zimbabwe and, as noted above, duly submitted his first report to the 21st Session of the Commission. This presented a summary of his planned activities for the first two years of the mandate as well as a report on his visit to Zimbabwe.[53]

The report sets out the general criteria employed by the Special Rapporteur when deciding which countries to visit first, noting 'the importance of covering the main geographical areas of Africa, the main languages of the OAU, big and small countries as well as island and mainland countries'.[54] Zimbabwe was chosen as the first country to be visited and the factors which were taken into account were principally practical in nature, including 'language, [the] likelihood of co-operation from both government and non-governmental organisations, good road network which will not make internal travel difficult'.[55] Taking account of these criteria, the Special Rapporteur's report set out a Programme of Activities which included the following missions: to Senegal or Mali between May and October 1997; to Uganda or Mauritius between November 1997 and March 1998; to Mozambique or Sao Tomé between May and October 1998; and to Tunisia and South

---

[50] *Ibid.*, para. 11.   [51] *Ibid.*   [52] *Ibid.*, para. 5.
[53] Report of the Special Rapporteur on Prisons and Conditions of Detention to the 21st Session of the African Commission on Human and Peoples' Rights, Tenth Activity Report 1996–1997, Annex VII (*Documents of the African Commission*, p. 518).
[54] *Ibid.*, Part I.   [55] Report on Visit to Prisons in Zimbabwe.

Africa between November 1998 and January 1999, a total of five visits in twenty months.[56]

The Special Rapporteur certainly conducted the number of visits he had planned to undertake, but the countries visited varied somewhat from those set out in the original plans, the missions having been conducted to: Zimbabwe (February/March 1997), Mozambique (December 1997),[57] Madagascar (1998),[58] Mali (twice, August 1997 and November/December 1998),[59] The Gambia (June 1999),[60] Benin (August 1999)[61] and the Central African Republic (June 2000).[62]

The published reports on these visits reveal the basic methodological approach to the conduct of a visit, which usually lasts for between a week and ten days. During this time the Special Rapporteur meets with relevant government officials – including the Attorney-General, Secretaries and Ministers for Justice, Commissioners or Directors for Prisons, magistrates and police officials – as well as local NGOs working in prison reform. He is usually accompanied on his visits by a representative from Penal Reform International (PRI). The number of places of detention visited varies but there has been an attempt to cover prisons outside as well as within the capital city. At these institutions the Special Rapporteur spends some time talking with prisoners in private.

At the end of each visit, the Special Rapporteur draws up a report which may begin with a description of the background concerning the country concerned before going on to note the number of prisons and the prison

---

[56] Reports of the Special Rapporteur to the 21st Session of the Commission, 1997, Part I (*Documents of the African Commission*, p. 518).

[57] Prisons in Mozambique: Report of the Special Rapporteur on Prisons and Conditions of Detention, Report on a Visit 14–24 December 1997, by Professor E. V. O. Dankwa, Series IV, No. 3 (*Documents of the African Commission*, p. 645).

[58] No report arising from this visit has been produced.

[59] Prisons in Mali: Report of the Special Rapporteur on Prisons and Conditions of Detention, Report on a Visit 20–30 August 1997, by Professor E. V. O. Dankwa, Series IV, No. 2 (*Documents of the African Commission*, p. 625); Mali Prisons Revisited: Report of the Special Rapporteur on Prisons and Conditions of Detention in Africa, Report of a Visit 27 November to 8 December 1998, Series IV, No. 4.

[60] Prisons in The Gambia: Report of the Special Rapporteur on Prisons and Conditions of Detention in Africa, Report on a Visit 21–26 June 1999, Series IV, No. 5.

[61] Prisons in Benin: Report of the Special Rapporteur on Prisons and Conditions of Detention in Africa, Report on a Visit 23–31 August 1999, Series IV, No. 6.

[62] Prisons in the Central African Republic, 19–29 June 2000, Report of the Special Rapporteur on Prisons and Conditions of Detention in Africa, Series IV, No. 7.

population. The reports do not follow a stereotypical pattern but almost all demonstrate a particular interest in and awareness of issues concerning overcrowding, whether females are housed with males and children with adults, the number of remand prisoners, discipline and disappearances as well as the judicial process. Other more particularised concerns are also raised.[63]

Reports themselves are detailed and give clear recommendations directed both to the State and to particular institutions. Examples include: the attire of the prisoners, the need to reduce the period of remand, training in human rights for officers, the need to 'orient public attitude to accepting that rehabilitation does occur by employing ex-convicts whenever there is the opportunity to do so', and to consider 'the appropriateness of extending community service to juveniles'.[64] They have also covered the need for speedy investigation of cases and trials, to reconsider criminalisation of street vending, requirements that the diet of prisoners be supplemented by crops and fruit that they grow on the prison land themselves, and enabling prisoners to use the soap that they make.[65] The Special Rapporteur has issued press releases at the end of his visits[66] and has developed the practice of publishing the comments of the governments on his recommendations alongside the report.[67]

It is always difficult to assess the impact and effectiveness of any human rights mechanism but some degree of success of the Special Rapporteur on Prisons and Conditions of Detention is perhaps evidenced by his follow-up visit to Mali conducted in November/December 1998.[68] As a result,

---

[63] For example, the 1997 Report on Prisons in Mali raised the following issues: the state of the buildings, staffing and training, workshops for prisoners, how young offenders are dealt with, possibilities for community service, provision of healthcare, the standard and quantity of food, mail, clothing, visits, games and exercise, complaints procedures, and personal hygiene.

[64] Report on Visit to Zimbabwe, Recommendations 1, 3, 4, 7 and 8.

[65] Prisons in Mozambique, Recommendations 1, 7, 9 and 10.

[66] Prisons in Mali, Press Release.

[67] See, for example, Comments by Government of Mali, *ibid.*, p. 636 and by the Government of Mozambique, *ibid.*, pp. 662–4. Neither, it should be said, were fulsome or comprehensive. The comments of Mali amounted to two short and terse paragraphs, while those of Mozambique, though longer, were principally confined to factual clarifications of the periods of pre-trial custody sanctioned by law.

[68] Following his first visit in 1997 a long list of recommendations was made, including: (1) the need for light and air and improvement of conditions in cells in Mopti prisons; (2) that there should be no more chaining of prisoners; (3) that there should be no more assaults on prisoners and an inquiry should be held into certain such instances; (4) that guards should be trained not to assault prisoners; (5) that those on remand should be given early

his appointment has been hailed as a success and there appears to be a certain amount of relief from the Commission which felt blighted by the inactivity of its previous appointment. Clearly, there are concrete positive results and these are enhanced considerably by the dynamism and commitment of the Special Rapporteur himself. However, there is also a recognition that these successes have also been heavily dependent upon the support given by NGOs.[69] Commissioner Dankwa resigned his position when the mandate expired in October 2000 and it is clear that such levels of support have been offered to his successor as Special Rapporteur on Prisons and Conditions of Detention, Commissioner Chirwa.

The Special Rapporteur on the Rights of Women in Africa

The initial impetus for the appointment of a Special Rapporteur on the Rights of Women in Africa appears to have come from a seminar on the Rights of Women in Africa organised in 1995, the recommendations of which suggested that such a person would be responsible for 'the protection of women's rights'.[70] At this stage the Commission itself did not adopt a position regarding this proposal, but at the 19th Session in March/April 1996 it approved the creation of the mandate.[71] As with the Special Rapporteur on Prisons and Conditions of Detention, and unlike the Special Rapporteur on Extrajudicial, Summary and Arbitrary Executions, however, the Commission refrained from appointing an individual to the position

release or tried; (6) that certain prisons should receive urgent attention; (7) that keeping female prisoners in private houses is not satisfactory; (8) that new prisons should be built with separate sections for women and children; (9) that remand prisoners should be kept separate from convicted prisoners; (10) that the tense atmosphere within the institution should be reduced; (11) that guards should not be made to work 24 hours a day or seven days a week; (12) that preferential treatment should not be given to civil servants; (13) that prisoners should have blankets, mats, soap and clothing; (14) that the granting of an amnesty should be considered; (15) that female guards be trained for some duties; and (16) that NGOs should be encouraged to visit prisons. Despite concerns noted during his second visit a year later, he concluded that the 'government is serious about prison reform. It is willing to learn from and share ideas on the subject with others. It recognises that much work has to be done in this area.' The Special Rapporteur noted that the government had been willing to open its prisons, that there were 'dedicated and conscientious prison staff', and that it had 'implemented some of the recommendations' in his first report. See Mali Prisons Revisited, p. 44.

[69] This will be discussed below.   [70] Final Communiqué of the 17th Session, para. 28.
[71] Ninth Activity Report, para. 19.

until draft terms of reference had been determined, the clear intention being that the appointment be made at the following session.[72] This did not in fact happen, although the Commission's activity report for the period records in a section headed 'Special Rapporteur on the Rights of Women' that three Commissioners were appointed to work on a draft protocol on the rights of women, these being Commissioners Dankwa, Duarte Martins and Ondziel-Gnelenga.[73] Nevertheless, the Final Communiqué of the session reiterated the Commission's commitment to the appointment of the Special Rapporteur.[74]

As with the appointment of the Special Rapporteur on Prisons and Conditions of Detention, it appears that the Commission was prepared to consider applications from experts in the field rather than limit the field of choice to serving Commissioners.[75] The draft terms of reference[76] also support this view: they set out a number of criteria concerning the appointment of the Special Rapporteur[77] and established a procedure by which the working group – presumably that created at the 20th Session to draft the protocol on women's rights – was to propose a candidate.[78] There is, however, a sense of inevitability about the outcome and the working group ultimately proposed that one of its own members, Commissioner Ondziel-Gnelenga,

---

[72] *Ibid.*

[73] Tenth Activity Report, para. 20. Such a Protocol had also been called for at the 1995 Seminar and was agreed upon by the Commission at the 19th Session. See Final Communiqué of the 17th Session, para. 28(i).

[74] Final Communiqué of the 20th Session, para. 19.

[75] Ninth Activity Report, para. 19, certainly implies that it was envisaged that the appointment might be made from outside the ranks of the Commission itself.

[76] Draft Terms of Reference for the Special Rapporteur on the Rights of Women in Africa, DOC/OS/34c (XMII), Annex II (*Documents of the African Commission*, p. 490), para. I.

[77] They provide that the appointed person should be a citizen of a State Party to the Charter, 'have a high consideration and competence in matters of women's rights' and 'must accept and be committed to execute, within the time allowed, the duty as defined in the terms of reference and [be] wholly responsible to the Commission', Draft Terms of Reference, Section II.

[78] See Draft Terms of Reference, Section III. The record concerning the drawing up of the terms of reference for the mandate appears confusing. It appears that they were drawn up by the working group in January 1998. However, the opening sections of the draft imply that it was being drawn up prior to the 20th Session at which the appointment was to have been made, and the sections concerning the criteria for appointment would support that. They certainly seem odd – even embarrassing – in the light of the recommendation made at that very meeting to appoint a member of the working group to the position (for which see below). It may well be a composite document.

should occupy the position,[79] although this was not formally endorsed by the Commission until the 25th Session of the Commission in April/May 1999, this being retrospective with the appointment taking effect from 31 October 1998.[80]

The terms of reference themselves are couched in expansive terms, and provide that the Special Rapporteur is:[81]

(a) To carry out a study on the situation of the human rights of women in Africa.

(b) To draw up guidelines on the drafting and examination of States Parties' reports on the rights of women in Africa.

(c) Ensure or make a follow up on the implementation of the Charter by States Parties. In this vein, the Special Rapporteur will prepare a report on the situation of violations of women's rights and propose recommendations to the Commission.

(d) The Special Rapporteur will assist African Governments in the development and implementation of their policies of promoting and protecting women's rights in Africa.

(e) He or she will encourage and work with NGOs in the field of promotion and protection of women's rights.

(f) He or she will serve as a link between the Commission and intergovernmental and non-governmental organisations at regional and international levels in order to harmonise the initiatives on the rights of women.

(g) In this regard, the Special Rapporteur will collaborate with Special Rapporteurs from the UN and other regional systems.

The mandate was initially set to expire in 2002, a relatively long four-year timescale, and an interim report addressing the substance of the subject-matter of the mandate was to be submitted within two years, along with proposals for the future.[82] In addition, the Special Rapporteur was required

---

[79] Draft Terms of Reference, Section III, 'Nota Bena'. It should also be noted that, when taking the original decision to appoint a Special Rapporteur, the Commission had called for CVs from interested individuals who would work under the guidance of two named Commissioners, Professor Dankwa and Dr Duarte Martins, 'who have experience in this field' (see Ninth Activity Report, para. 19). The particular experience in the field of women's rights of the Special Rapporteur has not been made manifest, other than her having been the third member of the working group appointed to draft the Protocol, which is presumably relevant expertise.

[80] Resolution on the Designation of a Special Rapporteur on the Rights of Women in Africa, Twelfth Activity Report 1998–1999, Annex IV (*Documents of the African Commission*, p. 711). Her appointment to this position by the working group had been noted at the 23rd Session of the Commission in April 1998. See Eleventh Activity Report, para. 33.

[81] Draft Terms of Reference, Section I, 1.   [82] *Ibid.*, Section I, 2.

to submit a progress report to the Commission at each session and present an annual report to the Assembly of Heads of State and Government, annexed to that of the Commission.[83] At this stage, however, the question of financial provision remained to be settled.[84]

In its 11th Report the Commission noted that the Special Rapporteur was expected to submit an interim report to the 24th Session of the Commission,[85] and at that session it was noted that she had indeed presented a preliminary report pertaining to her mandate, as well as reporting on activities so far undertaken.[86] At the 30th session of the Commission in October 2001, one of the new Commissioners, Dr. Angelo Melo, took over the position, with a mandate of two years. With the exception of items of information gleaned from *ad hoc* comments made at the session of the Commission, this information appears to be the sum total of public knowledge on the fulfilment of the mandate. The Commission's official documentation gives the impression that, although the Special Rapporteur has more recently spent time visiting African countries and collecting information in respect of her wider mandate, up until then she focused less on her programme of work, and concentrated instead on the development of the draft protocol on the rights of women. Given that this appears to have been the context out of which the appointment was made, this is not, perhaps, surprising. Much of the detail on any recent research carried out, however, has once again been provided orally at sessions. The very visibility of the work of the Special Rapporteur on Prisons and Conditions of Detention also seems to militate against the more benign interpretations of the available written record. These are considered in turn below.

Assessment and difficulties

There would appear to be a number of issues relevant to the appointment of all the Special Rapporteurs which are central to an evaluation of their successes and failures.

ALL SPECIAL RAPPORTEURS HAVE BEEN COMMISSIONERS

As the result of what would appear to be a reticence on the part of the Commission to delegate some responsibility to those outside of its membership,

---

[83] *Ibid.*, Section I, 4.   [84] *Ibid.*   [85] Eleventh Activity Report, para. 33.
[86] Twelfth Activity Report, paras. 28–9.

all three Special Rapporteurs have been serving members of the Commission. This is despite the fact that in the latter two cases the Commission appears at some stage to have contemplated and started the process of advertising for non-members to be appointed.

There are a number of difficulties with appointing members of the Commission as Special Rapporteurs. Despite the belief that having these roles occupied by its own members will ensure that the Commission would have a degree of control over their functioning, the Commission has, ironically though unsurprisingly, found it difficult and uncomfortable to have to reprimand its own members for any shortcomings. It might be less reticent in doing so if the individual in question were answerable to the Commission but were not a part of it.

In addition, adding further burdens to Commissioners who already only act in that capacity on a part-time basis is wholly unrealistic, and compounded by their being required to function in areas which may be far removed from their full-time professional expertise.[87] Indeed, the very independence of some Commissioners has been a constant source of debate and, while political connections of members need not necessarily conflict with their work as members of the Commission, the sensitivity of some tasks – particularly in relation to extrajudicial executions – is such that it is certainly arguable that it is inappropriate for those holding ambassadorial, government or similar office to undertake such roles.

This raises the question of whether it might be more appropriate to establish working groups acting under the leadership and guidance of a Commissioner but involving outside assistance, rather than appoint Special Rapporteurs. Certainly, previous experience suggests that this might be a useful way forward. For example, a working group was established for drafting the protocol on women's rights which comprised a combination of Commissioners and representatives of relevant NGOs. This met relatively frequently and was successful in producing a draft protocol in September 2000. Similarly, the working group established at its 26th Session in November

---

[87] For example, Commissioner Ben Salem is an Ambassador for Tunisia; Commissioner Dankwa is a Professor in Law; and Commissioner Ondziel-Gnelenga was a barrister. While these Commissioners themselves may have a more general understanding of international human rights law, none has been acknowledged expert in the field for which they were chosen as Special Rapporteurs. Equally, where there is relevant expertise within the Commission, it is not clear whether attempts have been made to utilise it in this fashion.

1999 to prepare a draft of general principles on the right to fair trial which was established after a seminar had been held on the topic.[88] It is composed entirely of Commissioners but collaborated closely with NGOs.[89] It could be argued therefore that thematic groups which embrace external assistance and expertise have a better track record of delivering results. Similarly, the establishment of a working group in late 2000 on indigenous peoples' rights.[90] This group, composed of two Commissioners and three experts on indigenous peoples, met and held a workshop at the 29th Session of the Commission in Libya in May 2001.

RELIANCE ON NGOs

All of the Special Rapporteur mandates have come about as the result of lobbying by NGOs. Certainly, the success of the Special Rapporteur on Prisons appears to have been greatly assisted by the support provided both before and after his appointment by PRI. PRI obtained funding prior to his appointment, suggested names of individuals who might be appointed to the position, and drafted a resolution and terms of reference for the Commission. After the appointment of Commissioner Dankwa as Special Rapporteur, PRI facilitated visits to various States, provided considerable administrative and secretarial support, accompanied him to prisons and other detention centres and produced and helped publish his reports. This contrasts with the assistance offered by the Commission's Secretariat, which has played a minimal role.

While the success of these endeavours can be applauded, it is a matter of concern that the Commission appears to have largely abdicated responsibility for the operation of the mandate to the NGO, although it is quite prepared to accept the praise for its success. The manner in which this

---

[88] Seminar on the Right to Fair Trial in Africa, in collaboration with the African Society of International and Comparative Law and Interights, Dakar, Senegal, 9–11 September 1999.

[89] For the establishment of this body, see Resolution on the Right to Fair Trial and Legal Assistance in Africa, Thirteenth Activity Report 1999–2000, Annex IV.

[90] This is composed of Commissioners Pityana, Rezzag-Bara and Ben Salem: Resolution on the Rights of Indigenous Peoples/Communities in Africa, 28th Ordinary Session, Cotonou, Benin, October/November 2000.

particular Special Rapporteur mandate has operated appears to have resulted in the Commission itself accepting that responsibility for the support and functioning of Special Rapporteurs lies with NGOs rather than with the Commission. Indeed, during discussion at sessions, many Commissioners and the Secretary himself have called on NGOs to assist the Special Rapporteurs with their work in terms which suggest such a shift.

It does not appear that an appropriate balance has been struck between the roles and responsibilities of NGOs and the Commission. Clearly, NGO support is as immensely valuable to the operation of this as to any other human rights mechanism, but the Commission must take responsibility for the actions of its own members and actions taken in its name. Its failure to do so will only encourage those who have criticised the NGOs for pursuing their own agenda in the name of the Commission. While it would be unwarranted to tarnish all NGOs in this way – and there is certainly no justification for doubting that organisations such as PRI have been doing anything other than showing their wholehearted commitment to the cause of improving prison and detention conditions – it cannot be assumed that all such organisations will be as scrupulous and the Commission must proceed with due circumspection if it is to retain the confidence of States Parties and NGOs alike. Above all, it must be clear that it is the Commission which takes ultimate responsibility for work conducted under the auspices of the mandates which it has created.

FUNDING

A constant source of complaint by both the Special Rapporteur on Extrajudicial, Summary and Arbitrary Executions and the Special Rapporteur on Women's Rights, given as a reason for their relative inactivity, has been lack of funding.[91] Although some budgetary allocations have been made at the commencement of two of the mandates, the Commission has not created a particular budget stream for the Special Rapporteurs to tap into, and it has been suggested that a certain amount of core funding should be allocated for administrative purposes to support the Special Rapporteurs in their mandate.[92] The Commission should seriously consider such an approach

---

[91] Thirteenth Activity Report, paras. 28 and 29.
[92] Suggestions made by the Institute of Human Rights and Development (an NGO) at the 28th Session of the Commission.

but given its failure to address this problem itself, the Special Rapporteurs have found themselves in the position of frequently calling on NGOs to find financial support for their activities. It is a matter of concern, although it is probably because it would be perceived as a purposeless activity, that neither the Commission nor its Secretariat have been the focus of their requests, since they surely ought to bear the primary responsibility in this regard.

Clearly, financial and logistical support is required by the Special Rapporteurs if they are to liaise with governments and organisations, undertake research and conduct visits. The lack of financial assistance may be used as a smokescreen to mask other causes of inaction. Several offers of support have been made by NGOs and others for the work of the Special Rapporteurs,[93] and in cases where funds have been secured it is not clear from the record that this has had an impact as regards output. This can hardly be a source of encouragement to potential donors.

Before appointing individuals to such roles, the Commission must determine whether it can provide the financial and logistical support to enable them to function effectively. The success of the Special Rapporteur on Prisons was due at least in part to funding being provided by NGOs in advance of its establishment, thus enabling the Special Rapporteur to start his work immediately upon his appointment. Concrete results were produced and further funding was therefore forthcoming. It is this virtuous circle that needs to be established although, as has been argued above, the Commission itself should play a major role in establishing and securing the basic funding.

THE LACK OF A CLEAR MANDATE

As has already been mentioned, an important issue in respect of the Special Rapporteur on Extrajudicial, Summary and Arbitrary Executions was the lack of a clear mandate in the first years, which arguably could have had a debilitating impact on the mandate holder as he sought to establish his role and function in a difficult and shifting political climate. This problem was clearly recognised and the subsequent Special Rapporteurs' mandates were

---

[93] Commission documents have indicated that the ICJ provided some assistance, but it does not detail what this was. See, for example, Twelfth Activity Report, para. 52; Thirteenth Activity Report, para. 60.

more clearly defined at the outset. The mandate of the Special Rapporteur on Prisons and Conditions of Detention appears to have been realistic and to have worked well, whereas it is possible that the mandate of the Special Rapporteur on Women's Rights is too wide to be achievable, but, given the dearth of material upon which it can be judged, it is impossible to say. Clearly, it embraces a number of fairly precise and achievable functions, such as drafting guidelines for State reporting, but other tasks, such as an evaluation of women's rights in Africa, are of immense scope and complexity and arguably require many years' work if they are to be undertaken properly. Certainly, the timescale set out in the draft terms of reference for the completion of this project appears hopelessly inadequate and this can hardly encourage the Special Rapporteur to embrace the project with enthusiasm.

Conclusion

The experience of Special Rapporteurs within the African human rights system has been mixed: on the whole it has been disappointing and in some regards downright embarrassing. The potential that such mandates have to enhance the protection of human and peoples' rights and to develop the law and practice in the relevant areas is considerable, but clearly mandates have not been used as well as they might.

If there is one single reform of current practice that needs to be implemented it is the practice of appointing serving Commissioners as Special Rapporteurs which merely assists in compounding the problems which flow from the lack of clarity in the mandates. Indeed, at the 27th Session of the Commission, the Special Rapporteur on Women's Rights observed that 'when I'm approached in my capacity as Special Rapporteur, I have reservations because I don't know if the Commission is not going to receive a communication concerning that situation and then what would my role be? The Special Rapporteurs of the Commission are not like those of the UN who are independent from the Commission'.[94] This prompts her to suggest that those outside of the Commission should be appointed to this position. Coming from a postholder, this is a powerful call.

At the 27th and 28th Sessions, representatives of both Amnesty International and Interights asked the Commission to review the whole process of its Special Rapporteur mechanisms. The Institute for Human Rights and

[94] R. Murray, 'Transcripts of 27th Session', p. 48, on file with the author.

Development, citing its experience with the Special Rapporteur on Extrajudicial, Summary and Arbitrary Executions, asked the Commission to consider in the future appointing non-members of the Commission as Special Rapporteurs, to ensure that the terms of reference, the duration of mandates and the aims of each Special Rapporteur are made clear, to appoint special working groups to advise the Special Rapporteur, and to allocate a portion of the Commission's own budget to the Special Rapporteur to fund the core activities of the Special Rapporteurs, accepting that additional funding could be sought from elsewhere. The only response from the Commission to these eminently sensible suggestions was a request by the Chair that this statement be made available in writing to the Secretariat.

The Special Rapporteur on Extrajudicial, Summary and Arbitrary Executions has recently resigned and the mandate holders of the Special Rapporteurs on Prisons and Conditions of Detention and on Women's Rights have recently changed. It would seem to be an apposite moment for the Commission to embark upon a detailed and serious evaluation of the role and functioning of all its Special Rapporteurs. Recent calls have been made by various NGOs for the Commission to appoint Special Rapporteurs on Human Rights Defenders[95] and on Freedom of Expression. Both NGOs and the Commission must bear in mind the failures of the Special Rapporteur on Extrajudicial Executions, the dependency of the success of the Special Rapporteur on Prisons on NGOs and the yet unexploited potential of the Special Rapporteur on the Rights of Women, before being quick to create yet another thematic position. It would seem unwise to go further down this road until the reappraisals that have been called for have taken place.

[95] The 14th International Commission of Jurists Workshop for NGOs reiterated this suggestion: see Recommendation on the Human Rights Situation in Africa, 14th ICJ Workshop.

10

THE AFRICAN COURT ON HUMAN AND PEOPLES' RIGHTS

JULIA HARRINGTON

Introduction

The African Court on Human and Peoples' Rights[1] should become a reality sometime in the next decade and will form part of the African regional human rights system,[2] joining the African Commission on Human and Peoples' Rights as one of three mechanisms established by the Organization of African Unity to enforce the African Charter on Human and Peoples' Rights.[3] The African Commission was created in 1987 following the entry into force of the African Charter in 1986 and was the subject of considerable commentary from human rights activists and international law scholars, both as regards its mandate as set out in the Charter[4] and its practices

---

[1] Protocol to the African Charter on Human and Peoples' Rights on the Establishment of an African Court on Human and Peoples' Rights, OAU/LEG/AFCHPR/PROT (III), adopted by the Assembly of Heads of State and Government, 34th Session, Burkina Faso, 8–10 June 1998.

[2] If, by 'the African system', we mean the constellation of human rights treaties and supporting mechanisms promulgated by the OAU, it first came into existence in 1973, with the entry into force of the Convention on Specific Aspects of the Refugee Problem in Africa. However, the OAU Refugee Convention, as it is commonly called, has no implementation mechanism. Thus, the African system changed dramatically in character in 1986 when the African Charter came into force, necessitating the creation of the African Commission in 1987. All OAU treaties adopted since the Refugee Convention have provided for implementation mechanisms.

[3] African Charter on Human and Peoples' Rights, ILM 21 (1987) 59.

[4] R. Gittleman, 'The African Charter on Human and Peoples' Rights: A Legal Analysis', *Virginia Journal of International Law* 22 (1981–2) 667–714; M. wa Mutua, 'The African Human Rights System in Comparative Perspective', *Review of the African Commission on Human and Peoples' Rights* 3 (1993) 5–11; W. Benedek, 'The African Charter on Human and Peoples' Rights: How to Make it More Effective', NQHR 11 (1993) 26–7.

and procedures.[5] When it comes into being, the African Court will have a powerful effect on the Commission's role and procedures and it is not too early to begin considering the nature of its impact.

The notable absence of a Court at the inception of the African regional system provoked much comment. It was argued by some that the omission of a court was not only understandable but natural, and that a commission standing alone reflected African traditions of conciliation rather than confrontation.[6] Others, perhaps more pragmatically minded, saw the absence of a court as representing a concession to the prevailing political climate at the time that the African Charter was drafted, and maintained that a court would have to be created in the future. It was the latter view that ultimately won out, and the process of drafting the Protocol to the African Charter on the Establishment of an African Court on Human and Peoples' Rights was itself an acknowledgment that the African system was incomplete, a work in progress.

The devisers of the African system – African States themselves acting collectively – did not have an opportunity to pass judgment on their most concrete human rights handiwork, the African Commission, until the consultations for the African Court began. While individual States, through their representatives, have made public statements on the African Commission's

---

[5] Due to its relatively short history, there is not as much scholarship on the African Commission as on the other regional (European and Inter-American) systems, but by now most facets of the Commission's work have come under analysis and, frequently, criticism. See, for example, Amnesty International, *The African Commission on Human and Peoples' Rights: The Role of the Special Rapporteur on Extrajudicial, Summary or Arbitrary Executions*, AI Index, IOR 63/05/97 (London: Amnesty International Secretariat, November 1997); E. Ankumah, *The African Commission on Human and Peoples' Rights: Practices and Procedures* (The Hague: Martinus Nijhoff, 1996); R. Murray, *The African Commission on Human and Peoples' Rights and International Law* (Oxford: Hart Publishing, 2000); C. A. Odinkalu, *The Communications Procedure of the African Commission on Human and Peoples' Rights* (University of Iowa, 1999); R. Murray, 'Decisions of the African Commission on Individual Communications under the African Charter on Human and Peoples' Rights', *International and Comparative Law Quarterly* 46 (1997) 412–34; and Interights, Civil Liberties Organisation and RADDHO, 'Missions for Protective Activities' (submitted to the 21st Session of the African Commission, 1997).

[6] K. M'Baye, 'Introduction to the African Charter on Human and People's Rights', in K. M'Baye, *The African Charter on Human and Peoples' Rights: A Legal Analysis* (1985), p. 27; U. O. Umozurike, 'The African Charter on Human and Peoples' Rights', *American Journal of International Law* 77 (1983) 908.

practices,[7] the meetings called to develop the Court Protocol formed a distinct, high-profile collective process which endeavoured to envision the future of the African regional human rights system, inevitably building upon the foundations provided by the Commission's practice in its first decade.[8] The results of this process were ultimately embraced by the Assembly of Heads of State and Government of the OAU itself, in the form of the Protocol.

Thus, it is fair to say that, where the provisions for the Court's organisation and mandate differ from those of the Commission, this reflects a decision to reorientate the future direction of the system. Although the substantive provisions of the African Charter could not be changed by a Protocol, by their shaping the procedures of the Court, and in some cases by making them very different from those of the Commission, African Heads of State and Government indicated precisely how much scrutiny and potential censure they were willing to accept from their regional human rights system.

This chapter will consider how African States have undertaken to change the OAU human rights system through the establishment of an African Court on Human and Peoples' Rights. The first part of the chapter analyses the process of drafting the Protocol. The second part of the chapter analyses the text of the Protocol itself. The third part of the chapter speculates on what may occur once the Protocol enters into force, the principal obstacles that will need to be overcome and the legal issues that will need to be resolved. This will be done within the context provided by the current African system: how the experience of the African Commission over the past fifteen years has influenced States' preferences for how the Court will operate, and how

---

[7] See, for example, R. Murray, 'Report on the 1996 Sessions of the African Commission on Human and Peoples' Rights', HRLJ 18 (1997) 16–27; R. Murray, 'Report on the 1997 Sessions of the African Commission on Human and Peoples' Rights', HRLJ 19 (1998) 169–87.

[8] While consultations had taken place within the OAU to draft the African Charter on the Rights and Welfare of the Child (ACRWC) in the years preceding 1990, the early date of these discussions (before the African Commission had developed much in the way of practice), the lack of a direct relationship between the African Commission and the Committee established under the ACRWC and, probably, the fact that children's rights were less controversial than the proposed Court, make the ACRWC less symbolically significant as a commentary on the African Charter. In fact, the provisions of the ACRWC are nearly identical to those of the African Charter, especially in the sensitive area of adjudication of alleged violations, aside from a small restriction on *locus standi*. See African Charter on the Rights and Welfare of the Child, OAU Doc. CAB/LEG/24.9/49 (1990), Article 44(1).

the factors influencing the work of the Commission will similarly affect the prospects for the success of the Court.

The drafting process

Reading the Preamble to the Protocol on the creation of an African Court, it might be thought that the first formal consideration of the idea was undertaken by a 'government legal experts' meeting' held in Cape Town, South Africa, on 6–12 September 1995.[9] In reality, a draft protocol for an African court had first been made by Karl Vasak, a Czech jurist, in 1993, at the request of the International Commission of Jurists (ICJ), an NGO based in Geneva.[10] An experts' meeting prior to the African Commission's 14th Session in Addis Ababa in December 1993 produced another draft, and in 1994 this was reworked by a group in Geneva co-ordinated by the ICJ.[11]

There was also a meeting of apparently *non-government* legal experts convened in Cape Town immediately before the meeting of 'government legal experts' mentioned in the Protocol.[12] This prior meeting was convened by the ICJ in collaboration with the OAU General Secretariat and the African Commission on Human and Peoples' Rights.[13] The draft Protocol submitted to the subsequent government experts workshop was the product of this meeting, although only the government experts' meeting is mentioned in the Preamble.

One reason why the recitation of the history of the Protocol given in the Preamble fails to mention the several preliminary drafts, and indeed an entire conference, may be that it reflects the discomfort of African States with the important role played by non-State actors in the drafting process. Officially – that is, according to the Protocol[14] – NGOs played no part in

---

[9] Preamble to the Protocol, para. 7.

[10] A. George, 'The African Court Demystified' (paper prepared for the African Centre for Democracy and Human Rights Studies, March 1998), p. 1.

[11] *Ibid.*, p. 1.

[12] Government Legal Experts Meeting on the Question of the Establishment of an African Court on Human and Peoples' Rights, 6–12 September 1995, Cape Town, South Africa, Report, OAU/LEG/EXP/AFC/HPR(I), reproduced in *African Journal of International and Comparative Law* 8(2) (1996) 493–500.

[13] *Ibid.*, para. 15.

[14] Other documents of the OAU Secretariat keep to the same practice of omitting mention of NGO calls for and work towards the Court. For example, para. 4 of the Report of the Secretary-General on the Draft Protocol on the Establishment of an African Court on

the process and only the meetings composed of 'experts' in the employ of governments are acknowledged. But the fact that a (non-governmental) legal experts' meeting was held in collaboration with the OAU Secretary-General and the African Commission immediately before the Cape Town *government* legal experts' meeting suggests a willingness within some quarters of the OAU to involve NGOs in the process. Even at the 'government legal experts' meeting mentioned in the Preamble to the Protocol there was a significant number of non-government participants,[15] and, without their prodding, lobbying and legal and financial support, it is unlikely that the process of drafting a protocol would have occurred at all and certainly not as soon as it did.[16] It should also be remembered that such involvement at the earliest stage of the development of the Protocol was particularly significant: the act of tabling a draft is a powerful one, directly affecting the range of issues to be considered and how they are framed.

The 1995 Cape Town meeting produced a draft Protocol which provided for a Court of eleven judges, including a full-time President, who were to be nominated by their States and elected by the OAU Assembly of Heads of State and Government to serve in their private capacities, in the same fashion as members of the African Commission.

The Cape Town draft Protocol was circulated[17] to all Member States

---

Human and Peoples' Rights, Council of Ministers/1996 (LXV), states: 'The initiative for the establishment of the Court started when the Assembly of Heads of State and Government, meeting in 1994 adopted resolution Assembly of Heads of State and Government/Res. 230 (XXX).'

[15] According to the report of the meeting, it was attended by fifty-six people, but only 23 Member States sent representation, 43 per cent of the total OAU membership. Even assuming a few States sent multi-person delegations, nearly half of the participants must have been 'members of the African Commission [which could not surpass eleven individuals], national and international observers, legal experts and representatives of international organisations'. See OAU/LEG/EXP/AFC/HPR(I), para. 3.

[16] There is substantial precedent for the involvement of NGOs in the creation of OAU treaties, including the drafting of the African Charter and the African Committee on the Rights and Welfare of the Child where NGOs played a vital part. The first formal call for an African regional human rights instrument was the 'Law of Lagos', the culminating resolution of a conference convened by the ICJ in Lagos in 1961, followed by similar conferences at least once a decade until the African Charter was adopted. The ICJ has been instrumental in drafting and lobbying for the African Charter on the Rights and Welfare of the Child, and a Protocol to the African Charter on the Rights of Women which is still in the drafting stage.

[17] The procedure for adoption of new OAU treaties is: the circulation of a draft, the product of an experts' meeting, for comments by Member States; approval by the OAU Council of (Foreign) Ministers; and finally adoption by the OAU Assembly of Heads of State and

of the OAU[18] for their comments. However, only three States[19] submitted comments in the seven months between the Cape Town meeting and the 64th Session of the OAU Council of Ministers held in July 1996. The 64th Session of the OAU Council of Ministers, without giving reasons, deferred consideration of the Protocol and asked that the draft be recirculated and reconsidered at its 65th Session, six months later. By the time of that session, in February 1997, ten States had submitted comments on the Protocol.[20]

These comments raised a number of detailed concerns relating to the general principles of establishing the Court and the actual provisions of the draft Protocol.[21] However, it was accepted from the outset that the centrepiece of any such Court's work was to be the hearing of cases of alleged violations of the African Charter brought against States Parties. What was less clear from the outset was who should be permitted to bring such cases. The most controversial point in the Cape Town draft appears to have been draft Article 6, which permitted the Court to exercise 'exceptional jurisdiction' to hear cases that had not yet been heard and decided by the African Commission. Since *locus standi* before the African Commission is very broad – anyone, even unrelated to the victim or the situation complained of, may bring a case – this provision suggested that similar rules of standing would apply. But, it soon

---

Government, before the treaty is opened for ratification. Approval by the Council of Ministers (which is composed of all the foreign ministers of the OAU Member States and meets every six months) is required of any document or action that is to be placed on the agenda of the OAU Assembly of Heads of State and Government, the body that must ultimately approve all new OAU treaties.

[18] Note Verbale, CAB/LEG/66.5/16/vol. I of 14 December 1995.

[19] Mauritius on 8 March 1996, Lesotho on 13 March 1996, and Burkina Faso on 21 March 1996.

[20] The additional seven States were Senegal on 30 April 1996, Tunisia on 2 June 1996, Sierra Leone on 30 July 1996, Benin on 4 September 1996, Cote d'Ivoire on 13 September 1996, Madagascar on 26 September 1996, and Ethiopia on 7 October 1996.

[21] Lesotho and Senegal were concerned about the question of resources for the Court's functioning, given the constraints already imposed on the Commission by limited funds. Madagascar was concerned that the relationship between the Court and the Commission was not clear, notwithstanding that Article 8 of the Cape Town draft provided four paragraphs of conditions addressing the circumstances in which the Court would take cases from the Commission. Tunisia felt that more specifics should be included in the Protocol, such as the functions of the President and Vice-President of the Court and how judges would be designated to sit in panels of five. There were also comments over how best to formulate the terms ensuring the independence of judges, and whether judges should be permitted to deliberate on cases against their countries of citizenship, which was provided for in Article 19 of the Cape Town draft. The draft provided for one renewal of the judges' six-year terms.

became apparent that OAU Member States were unwilling to create a human rights body which matched such broad rules of standing with stronger enforcement.

Of the ten States that submitted comments on the Cape Town draft, six of them commented on this Article. The comment of Mauritius was most honest and to the point, specifying that it favoured limiting exceptional jurisdiction to NGOs and individuals belonging to States Parties, to avoid 'inundation of the Court by applications from international watchdogs'.[22] Burkina Faso, no doubt with the same concern, commented more laconically that, no matter what the circumstances, all cases should go to the Commission first.[23] Sierra Leone said simply that it would place a general reservation on this Article, without giving a reason,[24] although it is unclear if such a reservation might have been impermissible as undermining the purpose of the treaty. Tunisia wished to insert a proviso that the Court would search for amicable resolutions of cases,[25] rather than condemning States. Côte d'Ivoire preferred to specify that the Court must consult with the Commission before taking any such cases.[26]

The 65th Session of the OAU Council of Ministers did not refer the draft to the Assembly of Heads of State and Government, but decided to convene a second government experts' meeting in April 1997. No doubt this decision was due both to the relatively low rate of participation by States in the process, as well as to the fact there had not been a consensus on the Cape Town draft. The second government legal experts' meeting was thus held in Nouakchott, Mauritania, in April 1997, immediately prior to the 21st Session of the African Commission and nearly a year and a half after the Cape Town meeting.[27] The Nouakchott meeting,

---

[22] See note 14, CM/1996(LXV), Annex III(a).

[23] *Ibid.*, Annex III(c).   [24] *Ibid.*, Annex III(f).

[25] *Ibid.*, Annex III(e).   [26] *Ibid.*, Annex III(h).

[27] Once again, NGOs were involved, and the official report of the meeting records that it was conducted 'in collaboration with the African Commission on Human and Peoples' Rights and with the support of the International Commission of Jurists'. See Second Government Legal Experts Meeting on the Establishment of an African Court on Human and Peoples' Rights, 11–14 April 1997, Nouakchott, Mauritania, Report, OAU/LEG/EXP/AFC/HPR/RPT(2), reproduced in *African Journal of International and Comparative Law* 9(2) (1997) 423–39. The active involvement of the International Commission of Jurists in the process is particularly clear: its Secretary-General delivered a message of solidarity at the opening ceremonies of both the Cape Town and Nouakchott meetings, an important honour for a representative of an NGO in a process where NGO participation was so systematically downplayed.

unlike the Cape Town meeting, adopted a text of the draft Protocol by consensus.[28]

A variety of changes were made which reflected the concerns already expressed by States,[29] and on the vexed question of *locus standi* for individuals and NGOs provided for in Article 6, the Nouakchott draft added some extra conditions. The new draft Article 6(1) specified that 'the Court may entitle NGOs with observer status before the Commission and individuals to institute directly before it, urgent cases or serious, systematic or massive violations of human rights'. Additionally, a new Article 6(5) was inserted, requiring States to make a declaration accepting the competence of the Court to receive petitions from individuals and NGOs under Article 6(1). Thus, instead of leaving the question entirely to the discretion of the Court as in the Cape Town draft, *locus standi* was limited to NGOs with observer status with the Commission and to individuals within the jurisdiction of States that had made the special declaration. Such cases must also concern 'urgent cases or serious, systematic or massive violations' in order for the Court to be empowered to hear them.

Although the draft was adopted by consensus, only 36 per cent of OAU Member States sent delegations to Nouakchott.[30] Seven of the ten States that submitted comments prior to the 65th Session of the Council of Ministers attended at least one of the two meetings. Thus, the impression gleaned from the reports of the meetings and the written comments from States is that a relatively small number of interested OAU Member States participated actively,[31] while a majority of States failed to follow the drafting process at all closely. Perhaps it was this consideration that caused the 66th Session of the Council of Ministers, meeting in Zimbabwe in May 1997, to fail once again to refer the now unanimously adopted Nouakchott draft Protocol to

[28] Draft (Nouakchott) Protocol to the African Charter on Human and Peoples' Rights on the establishment of an African Court on Human and Peoples' Rights, OAU/LEG/EXP/AFCHPR/PROT(2).

[29] A new Article 8 on amicable settlement was added, presumably in response to Tunisia's comments. Article 19 on the right of judges to hear cases against their countries of origin was removed and replaced by Article 21 which prohibited judges from deliberating on such cases.

[30] Attendance at the Nouakchott meeting, as recorded in the report, consisted of '33 delegates from 19 Member States, members of the African Commission and other resource persons'. See Second Government Legal Experts Meeting on the Establishment of an African Court on Human and Peoples' Rights, 11–14 April 1997, Nouakchott, Mauritania, Report, para. 3.

[31] Nine States attended both meetings: Algeria, Burundi, Cote d'Ivoire, Egypt, The Gambia, Gabon, South Africa, Sudan and Togo.

the Heads of State and Government. Instead, the 66th Session of the OAU Council of Ministers called for a third meeting of governmental legal experts, this time to be held in Addis Ababa, where the vast majority of OAU Member States have permanent missions.[32]

An important feature of the Addis Ababa meeting, held in December 1997, was that it was enlarged to include diplomats.[33] This was intended to ensure that those States with no 'legal experts' in their Addis Ababa missions could participate by sending representatives who had only diplomatic qualifications. Of course, the move to include diplomats also had political implications, moving the work away from the (superficially) technical legal work of drafting into the realm of political interests and negotiations. In the event, the Addis Ababa meeting was attended by '113 delegates from forty-five States'.[34]

The Addis Ababa experts' meeting, 'enlarged to include diplomats', revisited the question of *locus standi* and produced what became the final formulation. Draft Article 5(3) provided that both NGOs with observer status with the Commission and individuals would have standing to bring cases against any State that, at the time of its ratification, lodged an optional declaration accepting the jurisdiction of the Court over such cases.[35] The

---

[32] In its decision to hold this meeting, the Council of Ministers requested 'all Member States especially those not represented in Addis Ababa to ensure that they are duly represented' at the Addis Ababa meeting and even requested the Secretary-General to 'explore the possibility of raising extra-budgetary funds to cover some of the expenses relating to the above meetings', which implies travel expenses for those States without representation there. See CM/Dec.348(LXVI).

[33] Report of the Experts Meeting, Third Government Legal Experts Meeting (Enlarged to Include Diplomats) on the Establishment of the African Court on Human and Peoples' Rights, 8–11 December 1997, Addis Ababa, Ethiopia, OAU/LEG/EXP/AFCHPR/RPT.(III) Rev.1.

[34] Comoros, Guinea Bissau, Liberia, Mali, Sao Tomé and Principe, Seychelles and Somalia were the only States that did not attend. The number of others, i.e. non-State representatives, who were present is unclear. The report of the meeting mentions simply 'African resource persons invited by the OAU General Secretariat' whose attendance was financed by the ICJ (CM/Dec.348(LXVI), para. 5). The Report on the Progress Made Towards the Establishment of an African Court on Human and Peoples' Rights, which was tabled at the OAU Ministerial Conference on Human Rights in April 1999, seems to imply that all 113 participants were part of State delegations (MIN/CONF/HRA/4(I), para. 31). This seems rather unlikely as it means that the average State represented would have sent more than two delegates. It is more likely that the 113 includes a number of non-State representatives, but their presence is not elaborated upon in the report.

[35] Third Government Legal Experts Meeting (Enlarged to Include Diplomats) on the Establishment of the African Court on Human and Peoples' Rights, 8–11 December 1997, Addis Ababa, Ethiopia, OAU/LEG/EXP/AFCHPR/RPT(III) Rev.1, para. 17.

provision which provides for the making of such a declaration is hidden away in Article 34(6), towards the end of the Protocol. This relaxes the strict conditions of the Nouakchott draft by removing the requirement that such cases be urgent or concern serious or massive violations, but this is a small concession in an otherwise considerably limited regime of access, as will be seen when the matter is considered in greater detail below.

The exclusion of judges from hearing cases concerning their countries of origin was retained, and, perhaps in a bid to strengthen their independence further, their term of office was made non-renewable. A further significant change concerned Article 8, which sets out the conditions which must be fulfilled before the Court can consider cases. The earlier drafts had been four paragraphs long but the Addis Ababa meeting cut this to a single sentence. The Cape Town and Nouakchott drafts had provided that the Court could not hear inter-State cases until the Commission had prepared a report under Article 52 of the Charter; that it could not hear Article 55 cases until the Commission had adopted a decision or report; that all cases had to be brought to the Court within three months of the Commission's decision; and that the Court could at any time reject a case as inadmissible even if it had been previously found to be admissible. The report of the Addis Ababa meeting stated: 'it was generally observed that Article 8 . . . had not catered for all cases envisaged to be brought before the court.'[36] This decision was probably the result of concern that the extensive conditions of the previous drafts created the appearance of comprehensiveness, whereas the meeting did not really have time to consider all the possible scenarios under which cases might be brought. Similarly, other procedural issues, such as those raised in the comments made by Tunisia, were left for the Court to sort out in its Rules of Procedure. Some of the issues thus glossed over are fundamental to the effective functioning of the Court. The failure to properly address them may prove to be detrimental – if not fatal – to its prospects of success.

The experts' meeting 'unanimously recommended the Draft Protocol'[37] but the Addis Ababa meeting of governmental experts was not the last word. Immediately afterwards a 'Conference of Ministers of Justice/Attorneys-General' was held, attended by nineteen Ministers of Justice and forty-five States – no doubt the same forty-five States who had been present the previous days, and very probably the same individuals. In the event, this

---

[36] *Ibid.*, para. 19.   [37] *Ibid.*, para. 32.

Ministerial Conference made 'a minor amendment to one of the Articles'[38] and then proceeded to adopt the draft protocol by consensus, recommending it to the Council of Ministers and the Heads of State and Government. The 67th Session of the Council of Ministers in February 1998 finally approved the Protocol and placed it before the OAU Assembly of Heads of State and Government, meeting in Yaoundé in July 1998. Neither the Council of Ministers nor the Assembly of Heads of State and Government made any changes to what emerged from the Conference of Ministers of Justice/ Attorneys-General.

How, then, would one characterise the drafting process overall? 'Prolonged' is one adjective that comes to mind. Officially, it lasted nearly three years, from September 1995 to July 1998. In reality, as we have seen, drafts were circulating for several years prior to the official drafting process. The process was also contentious, although no more so than is typical at the international level.

What is particularly interesting is how African States seemed carried along almost despite themselves. There were no coherent protests against the concept of the creation of the Court. Resistance manifested itself in the form of non-participation in the process, which was, in the early stages, considerable. Given that lack of enthusiasm, it is surprising that the drafting process proceeded as quickly as it did.

The key to there being a protocol at all, when the States were clearly so ambivalent, probably lies in strong NGO pressure. Non-State participation in the drafting process is intentionally played down in the text of the Preamble to the Protocol, yet careful reading of the documents concerning the drafting process points to important NGO influences. This may also explain why the final provision on *locus standi* for individuals and NGOs was so negative, even regressive. Government representatives and Ministers of Justice had the last word and although they did indeed approve the establishment of a Court their reluctance became manifest in their attempts to limit its power, a compromise that must have been accepted by many NGOs themselves. The Protocol was a verdict or commentary by African leaders on the experience of the African Commission, and it expresses their unease about some aspects of its operation.

---

[38] Report of the Secretary-General on the Conference of Ministers of Justice/Attorneys-General on the Draft Protocol on the Establishment of the African Court on Human and Peoples' Rights, CM/2051(LXVII), para. 22.

The text of the Protocol at face value

It is now necessary to consider the text of the Protocol itself in more detail in order to see what the mix of 'government experts', diplomats, attorneys-general and unnamed NGOs, meeting over the course of several years, have bequeathed to the continent. Paragraph 8 of the Preamble to the Protocol specifies that 'the attainment of the objectives of the African Charter on Human and Peoples' Rights requires the establishment of an African Court on Human and Peoples' Rights to complement and reinforce the functions of the African Commission'. First, we must question the nature of this 're-inforcement' as codified in the text.

THE RELATIONSHIP BETWEEN THE COURT AND THE COMMISSION

Article 2, entitled 'Relationship between the Court and the Commission', states that the Court is to 'complement the protective mandate of the African Commission on Human and Peoples' Rights'.[39] Yet this formulation does not actually take us any further than the Preamble. What is most striking about the formulation is its vagueness: what does 'complement' mean, and how is it to be achieved? The specifics of the relationship between the Commission and the Court, a relationship that will profoundly shape the work and role of the Court, are left undefined. The drafters devoted an Article to the 'Relationship between the Court and the Commission' and ended up telling us almost nothing.

It is worth considering whether the drafters thought the question of the relationship was so overwhelmingly straightforward that there was no point in wasting time and ink over it. To be sure, the European and Inter-American systems for human rights protection,[40] both of which pre-date the African system, originally had commissions and courts. The drafters might have thought it natural that the African system would simply follow the same pattern.

---

[39] Protocol, Article 2.

[40] The Inter-American Commission on Human Rights was created prior to the adoption of the Inter-American Convention on Human Rights. This treaty consolidated the position of the Commission and also provided for a Court (Article 33). The European human rights system was created by the European Convention of Fundamental Rights and Freedoms (1951) which created a Commission and a Court simultaneously (Article 19).

But this is hardly a satisfactory explanation. In the first place, it is generally accepted that the African Charter was intended to be different from other human rights treaties, having distinctly African features[41] which expressed African culture and history, and the absence of a court was a reflection of this. It is not plausible that fifteen years later, in the midst of the exercise that would determine the future of the African system, the African drafters could have entirely forgotten this legacy and lapsed into pure mimicry. In the second place, even if slavish imitation of the European and inter-American systems was intended, it would be both difficult and foolhardy. The European system had abolished its human rights commission several years earlier in favour of a full-time court.[42] The Inter-American system provides a different lesson: under its bifurcated system in which cases had to be passed from the Commission to the Court, the Court heard no cases under its contentious jurisdiction for its first ten years and was confined to issuing advisory opinions, since the Commission, apparently in the grip of jealous territorialism, refused to forward cases.[43]

Why then is the relationship between the African Commission and Court not more clearly defined? The most likely answer is that the details were too technical, and possibly too controversial, for the drafters to work out in the time available. Article 8 of the Cape Town and Nouakchott drafts provided some details of how cases should be passed between the two organs, but these were deleted at the Addis Ababa meeting. Some of the drafters were no doubt aware of the troubled relationship between the Commission and the Court in the Inter-American system, but for the want of any simple solution and lacking the ambition to rework the system as comprehensively as has been done in Europe, they took the easy way out and essentially dodged the issue. Some provisions of the Protocol do cast some light on the relationship between the Court and Commission, at least by implication, but most issues are left to the two institutions to work out between themselves.

---

[41] The provisions on individual duties and peoples' rights are commonly accepted to be expressions of the more communal, collective nature of society in Africa: see M'Baye, *Les Droits de l'Homme en Afrique* (1994). The mention of 'Zionism' in the preamble also reflects particular historical sensibilities.

[42] See Eleventh Protocol to the European Convention on Human Rights, ETS No. 155.

[43] See, for example, C. A. Trindade, 'The Operation of the Inter-American Court of Human Rights (1979–1996)', in D. Harris and S. Livingstone (eds.), *The Inter-American System of Human Rights* (Oxford University Press, 1998), Chapter 5.

SUBSTANTIVE JURISDICTION

Article 3 of the Protocol provides that the jurisdiction of the Court covers 'all cases and disputes submitted to it concerning the interpretation and application of the Charter; this Protocol and any other relevant Human Rights instrument ratified by the States concerned'.[44] This is a very broad, almost unlimited substantive jurisdiction. Since it is not confined to the African Charter, it potentially makes the Court an enforcement body for other human rights treaties ratified by African States, although this may not be the most desirable outcome given that most UN treaties have their own implementation machinery. It might be assumed, however, that the African Court would avoid issuing interpretations which are at odds with those of the UN treaty bodies. The Court also has the mandate to issue advisory opinions at the request of OAU Member States, the OAU or any of its organs on 'any legal matter relating to the Charter or any other relevant human rights instruments, provided that the subject-matter of the opinion is not related to a matter being examined by the Commission'.[45] The substantive mandate of the Court is considerably broader than that of the Commission,[46] indicating that the drafters of the Protocol were intent on giving the Court the widest possible jurisdiction.

LOCUS STANDI BEFORE THE COURT

As seen in the account of the drafting process, Articles 5 and 6, which deal with *locus standi*, were the most controversial Articles in the Protocol. Article 5 provides for the following to submit cases to the Court:

(a) the Commission;
(b) the State Party which has lodged a complaint to the Commission;
(c) the State Party against which the complain has been lodged at the Commission;

---

[44] Protocol on the African Court, Article 3(1).   [45] *Ibid.*, Article 4(1).

[46] This is governed by (a) Article 45(3) of the Charter and is to '[i]nterpret all the provisions of the present Charter at the request of a State Party, an institution of the OAU or an African Organization recognised by the OAU' (this is effectively an advisory capacity, although it has never been used since no requests for interpretation under this Article have been received from any of the relevant parties since the entry into force of the Charter); and (b) Article 55, which sets out the criteria for admissibility, the conditions of which are also applicable to cases before the Court.

(d) the State Party whose citizen is a victim of [a] human rights violation;
(e) African intergovernmental organisations.

As described in the previous section, this Article was rewritten several times during the drafting process. The striking omission in the final text is the absence of any provision for victims of human rights violations, individuals and NGOs to bring cases as of right. Instead, Article 5(3) provides that:

> The Court may entitle relevant Non-Governmental Organizations (NGOs) with observer status before the Commission, and individuals to institute cases directly before it in accordance with Article 34(6) of this Protocol.

However, it is not the Court which grants this entitlement. Article 34(6) specifies that States may make 'declaration[s] accepting the competence of the Court to receive cases under Article 5(3) of this Protocol. The Court shall not receive any petition under Article 5(3) involving a State Party which has not made such a declaration.' It is rather strange that the conditions for direct petition to the Court are divided between two distant Articles, one of which is buried nearly at the end of the document. It is either an oversight in drafting or a strange public relations ploy to make the most odious condition as inconspicuous as possible. The result is that individuals, including victims, and NGOs can only access the Court directly with the consent of the State concerned.

One need not be extensively versed in African politics to gauge the likelihood of African States making an extra effort to provide their citizens and civil society groups with avenues through which to hold them accountable. Unsurprisingly, of the five ratifications deposited so far, only one has made any such declaration under Article 34(6). The drafters of the Charter surely knew this would be the result. The limitation on *locus standi* must be understood as a cynical move to diminish what power the Court might have over States by making it less accessible to those most likely to bring cases. A reading of Article 5 leaves the impression that the Court is to be a mechanism for use by States alone.

The exclusion of individuals and NGOs from bringing cases before the Court is all the more striking when compared with the *locus standi* provisions applicable to the Commission. The Charter does not place any restrictions on who can submit cases to the Commission: any non-State actor, be it a legal or natural person, can bring cases under the Article 55 communication procedure.[47] This generous approach to *locus standi* has been attributed to a recognition that victims themselves, and even victims' families – indeed, anyone within the borders of the State in which the violation occurred – may in practice be unable to launch cases, and all the more so in situations of the gravest abuse. The Charter may thus be seen as a progressive document that takes into account the gravity of abuses to be addressed.

Why should the Court Protocol reverse the progressive provisions of the African Charter? Obviously, and understandably, States would like to limit the number of cases brought against them, and the most efficient way in which to do so is by limiting the number of potential complainants. An examination of the Commission's work, however, does not reveal any great number of communications, despite the generous *locus standi* provisions. Although a majority of the communications reported upon[48] have been brought by individuals and NGOs, these still average fewer than twenty per year over the fourteen years of the Commission's operation. This is a tiny number relative to the number of States, not to mention the scale of human rights violations, in Africa. Indeed, the dearth of communications brought before it has been a continuing subject of concern for the Commission, and seems to reflect either widespread ignorance of the existence of the procedure, lack of faith in it, or both.

So what are African States really afraid of? Perhaps the explanation for the regressive nature of the Protocol on this point lies not so much in the general attitude of African States, although that was surely a factor, but in an accident of historical moment. While most African States have never been the object of a communication before the Commission, at least fifteen cases have been brought against Nigeria alone. This can be explained not only by the enormous number of human rights violations committed by the military governments of Generals Babangida and Abacha, but also by the very active, well-informed and skilful human rights community in Nigeria. The Nigerian Government in fact created the ideal climate for submission of cases to the Commission by entirely ousting the jurisdiction of the national courts in all human rights cases, thus making Nigerian cases almost automatically

---

[47] Article 55 of the Charter simply specifies: 'Before each session, the Secretary of the Commission shall make a list of the Communications other than those of States Parties to the present Charter.'

[48] The Eighth through to the Thirteenth Activity Reports contain annexes on the communications examined by the Commission. These annexes include details of 148 communications, of which 91 were brought by NGOs.

admissible before the Commission.[49] As one might expect, Nigeria has thus been condemned by the Commission several times.

Unfortunately, at the time of the drafting of the Protocol, the government of General Abacha, which had already given dramatic evidence of its disregard for human rights in general and the African Commission in particular,[50] was still in power, and Nigeria participated in the drafting process. No detailed *travaux préparatoires* of the debates themselves have yet been published, so we cannot know how Nigeria used its influence. However, as the largest country in Africa and one of the most powerful in the OAU, Nigeria surely made its presence felt. Ironically, less than a year after the adoption of the Protocol by the OAU, General Abacha was dead and Nigeria was in transition to democracy. In hindsight, one might wish that the drafters had decided to deliberate for one more year, and a far more rational and useful text might have emerged.

The most positive view one can take of the present Protocol is that it creates a similar situation as exists in the Inter-American system, where all cases for the Court must pass through the Commission first. The Inter-American Commission for Human Rights has developed a procedure for deputising NGOs to appear on its behalf before the Inter-American Court, thus preserving the rights of those with the greatest interest in the case to argue it at the highest level. However, embedded in this system is the

---

[49] For example, see the 'Admissibility' sections of the decisions in Communication 60/91, *Constitutional Rights Project (in respect of Wahab Akamu, G. Adega and others) v. Nigeria*, Eighth Activity Report 1994–1995, Annex VI, R. Murray and M. Evans (eds.), *Documents of the African Commission on Human and Peoples' Rights* (Oxford: Hart Publishing, 2001), p. 385 (hereinafter *Documents of the African Commission*); Communication 87/93, *Constitutional Rights Project (in respect of Zamani Lakwot and 6 Others) v. Nigeria*, Eighth Activity Report 1994–1995, Annex VI (*Documents of the African Commission*, p. 391); Communication 101/93, *Civil Liberties Organisation in respect of the Nigerian Bar Association v. Nigeria*, Eighth Activity Report 1994–1995, Annex VI (*Documents of the African Commission*, p. 394); Communications 105/93, 128/94, 130/94 and 152/96, *Media Rights Agenda and Constitutional Rights Project v. Nigeria*, Twelfth Activity Report 1998–1999, Annex V (*Documents of the African Commission*, p. 718).

[50] Between 1993 and 1995, four cases were lodged with the African Commission respecting Ken Saro-Wiwa, a Nigerian writer and minority rights activist who was first detained by the government in 1993, tried, sentenced to death, and finally executed in November 1995. The Commission had invoked provisional measures under Rule 109 of its then Rules of Procedure, asking that no irreparable prejudice be done to Mr Saro-Wiwa before it completed its consideration of the cases. This request was ignored and all the cases were still pending at the time of Saro-Wiwa's execution. In response, the Commission held an extraordinary session on the human rights situation in Nigeria in December 1995.

necessity that the Commission does its work actively and efficiently, or else the stream of potential cases that might eventually come before the Court will be choked off at the source. The relationship between the Court and the Commission becomes of paramount importance. The restricted scope of *locus standi* before the Court may preclude the possibility of having the Commission become primarily a mediation or political body, thus leaving adjudication to the Court, which some felt was the most logical course. The modalities of this relationship will be discussed further below.

CONSIDERATION OF CASES: ADMISSIBILITY, SOURCES OF LAW, HEARINGS, EVIDENCE AND FINDINGS

The provisions of Articles 6–9 of the Protocol, in contrast to Article 5, are comparatively uncontroversial. Article 6, 'Admissibility of cases', refers to Article 56 of the Charter, making admissibility conditions the same for both bodies. The only peculiarity is the possibility that Article 6 leaves it open for the Court to 'request the opinion of the Commission' on the admissibility (Article 6(1)) of cases or to 'transfer them to the Commission' (Article 6(3)). These provisions seem inappropriate for communications referred by the Commission and thus, presumably, already found admissible and fully considered. Thus, these provisions must be intended to apply to communications brought by States, or by whatever NGOs are eligible, directly to the Court under Articles 5(1)(b), (c), (d) and (e), 5(3) and 34(6).

Article 7, 'Sources of law', provides that the Court shall apply the provisions of the Charter 'and any other relevant human rights instruments ratified by the States concerned'. This is somewhat narrower than the Commission's mandate, in Articles 60 and 61 of the Charter, which is to consider international law generally,[51] but these Articles themselves may be

---

[51] Article 60 reads: 'The Commission shall draw inspiration from international law on Human and Peoples' Rights, particularly from the provisions of various African instruments on Human and Peoples' Rights, the Charter of the United Nations, the Charter of the Organization of African Unity, the Universal Declaration of Human Rights, other instruments adopted by the United Nations and by African countries in the field of Human and Peoples' Rights as well as from the provisions of various instruments adopted within the Specialised Agencies of the United Nations of which the parties to the present Charter are members.' Article 61 reads: 'The Commission shall also take into consideration, as subsidiary measures to determine the principles of law, other general or special international conventions, laying down rules expressly recognised by Member States of the Organization of African Unity, African practices consistent with international norms of Human and Peoples' Rights,

considered as incorporated into the mandate of the Court through the reference to the Charter which is found in Article 7.

Article 8, 'Consideration of cases', expresses what has already been concluded: that the Court's Rules of Procedure will have to fill in the extensive gaps in the Protocol. Unsurprisingly, Article 33 provides that these rules should be drawn up by the Court itself. Article 9 then provides for the possibility of amicable settlement between the parties but does not oblige the Court to adopt this approach.

The real differences between the Commission and the Court, and the evidence of the wish of the drafters to create a judicial as opposed to a 'quasi-judicial' body, are found in Article 10, 'Hearings and representation', and in Articles 26–30 on evidence, findings, judgment, notification of judgment, and execution of judgments. These Articles go much further than the Charter in setting out a judicial-style procedure.

To begin with, the Charter itself makes no mention of hearings, and, although the Commission has developed this practice on its own, it is still not codified. The Commission's hearings take place in private sessions. Article 10(1) of the Protocol provides that '[t]he Court shall conduct its proceedings in public', although it leaves open the possibility that the Court might conduct proceedings *in camera* if it provides for this in its Rules of Procedure. The composition of the first Court and the political climate of the time of the drafting of the Rules will thus be of critical importance, since it is possible for the rules to devise an open and well-publicised procedure or a procedure which is shrouded in secrecy, as is currently the case with the Commission.

Similarly, there are no written rules on representation before the Commission, although the Commission has stated that the principles of a fair trial apply in its proceedings[52] which means that parties have the right to representation if they wish it – and can afford it. The Protocol provides that: 'Any party to a case shall be entitled to be represented by a legal representative of the party's choice. Free legal representation may be provided where the interests of justice so require.'[53] While this is far from promising

---

customs generally accepted as law, general principles of law recognised by African States as well as legal precedents and doctrine.'

[52] Dakar Declaration and Recommendations on the Right to a Fair Trial in Africa, adopted at the Seminar on the Right to a Fair Trial in Africa, DOC/OS(XXVI)INF.19, Dakar, September 1998, held by the African Commission in cooperation with Interights and the African Society of International and Comparative Law.

[53] Article 10(2) of the Protocol.

free representation, it is important that it is mentioned at all. Presumably, it refers to representation of complainants, not States Parties. One difficulty that has slowed the procedures of the Commission is the submission of poorly written and unclear cases which may very likely allege serious violations of the Charter but which are nearly impossible to process due to their format. Although representation is mentioned here in the context of hearings, it would be logical for representation to extend to the filing of briefs as well – and in any event, effective representation at a hearing would not be possible without serious prior study of the facts of a case. It can be assumed that this is what the drafters had in mind, and it is to be hoped that this will be how the provision is interpreted in practice.

Article 26, on evidence, is less clear. It provides that: 'The Court shall hear submissions by all parties and if deemed necessary, hold an enquiry.' It is debatable whether this means that the Court should receive submissions in writing, and if necessary hold a hearing, or that, after having the parties present their submissions in a hearing, the Court should conduct its own investigations. The latter interpretation would bring it nearer the wide mandate given to the Commission under Article 46 of the Charter ('The Commission may resort to any appropriate method of investigation'); but neither interpretation says much about evidence *per se*. Article 26(2), which provides that '[t]he Court may receive written and oral evidence including expert testimony and shall make its decisions on the basis of such evidence', is basically a statement that the Court should not base its decisions on information that is not 'on the record'. There is no suggestion here of the Byzantine common law rules of evidence that, for example, exclude hearsay but make an exception for 'dying declarations'. It appears that, unless the Court decides otherwise in its Rules of Procedure, it can admit any type of evidence it wants, from third-hand reports to videotape to DNA tests.

Article 27, 'Findings', might be more appropriately titled 'Remedies'. A confusion that has beset the African Commission since it first began to issue decisions on communications under its Article 55 procedure has concerned the question of whether it is able to specify remedies for the violations it finds, and in particular whether it may order monetary compensation. At times the Commission has prescribed monetary compensation but refrained from stating the amount. This will not pose any problems for the Court since Article 27(1) specifically instructs that the Court shall 'make appropriate orders to remedy the violation, including the payment of fair compensation or reparation'.

Article 27 also gives the Court a mandate to adopt provisional measures, a procedure which the Commission has developed under its Rules of Procedure.[54] What the Protocol fails to specify is whether States are bound to respect the provisional measures adopted by the Court, in the same way that Article 30 binds States 'to undertake to comply with the judgment in any case in which they are parties within the time stipulated by the Court and to guarantee its execution'. The Commission has, unfortunately, had its provisional measures ignored in a few high-profile cases,[55] and there may be a few government lawyers on hand in the future to argue that respecting the Court's judgments does not necessarily include respect for provisional measures.[56]

One of the most significant Articles of the Protocol is Article 28 on 'Judgment' which goes far beyond the Commission's Article 55 procedure. The Court is to render its judgment within ninety days of having completed its deliberations. Presumably, 'deliberations' means 'hearings'; otherwise it would be impossible to say from when the ninety days begin to run. In any event, this provision is clearly designed to address the situation that has arisen with the Commission, where lengthy, unexplained periods occur between the Commission's final hearings in a case and the release of a decision, which can run into years.

The Court's decisions are to be decided by a majority and are not subject to appeal – unless it decides to allow for the review of decisions in the light of new evidence in its Rules of Procedure.[57] Article 28(4), which provides that '[t]he Court may interpret its own decision', probably means that the Court may refer to, and clarify, its decisions in subsequent ones, but there is no hint as to whether the Court should follow the common law tradition of reasoning from precedents, or follow the civil law practice of addressing each case solely on its facts and in the light of the text of the Charter. Article

---

[54] Rule 111.

[55] For example, see, in relation to Ken Saro-Wiwa, Communications 137/94, 139/94, 154/96 and 161/97, *International Pen, Constitutional Rights Project, Interights on behalf of Ken Saro-Wiwa Jr and Civil Liberties Organisation* v. *Nigeria*, Twelfth Activity Report 1998–1999, Annex V (*Documents of the African Commission*, p. 729).

[56] The Commission has now, however, held that in failing to respect its provisional measures the State had violated Article 1 of the Charter: *ibid.*

[57] Articles 28(2) and (3) of the Protocol.

28(6), which provides that '[r]easons shall be given for the judgment of the Court', simply guarantees that the Court's decisions are indeed reasoned. In a few instances the Commission has been guilty of issuing decisions without any information on the facts of the cases,[58] let alone reasoning of a legal sort, although it must be acknowledged that its decisions have been growing in length and detail over the years.[59] The Court needs to do even better if it is to be taken seriously. Article 28 also provides for dissenting opinions,[60] which is not a feature of the Commission's practice.

Another clear break with the practice of the Commission is the provision for reading out the judgment in open court; the Commission's decisions are quietly annexed to its annual activity report, and the concerned parties are lucky if they receive copies of this and thus learn of the decision on their case months after it has been taken.[61] Article 29 of the Protocol specifies that not only should the parties to a case before the Court be notified of a judgment, but that it should be transmitted to the Member States of the OAU[62] and to the Commission.[63]

The Articles on procedure and enforcement make it clear that the Court is intended to go well beyond the Commission in the depth and formality of its inquiries and is entitled to expect the OAU to enforce its decisions. Although much remains to be determined by the Court itself, these Articles signal the intention of the drafters to create a more legally structured body than the Commission.

NOMINATION, ELECTION AND TERMS OF SERVICE OF JUDGES

Ultimately, it is unclear what protection the Protocol provides the Court against the institutional weaknesses that have plagued the Commission.

---

[58] For example, Communication 59/91, *Embga Mekongo Louis* v. *Cameroon*, Eighth Activity Report 1994–1995, Annex VI (*Documents of the African Commission*, p. 385).

[59] This can be clearly seen from the chronological arrangement of decisions in the Compilation of Decisions of the African Commission 1994–9, published by the Institute for Human Rights and Development, April 2000.

[60] Article 28(7) of the Protocol.

[61] If, for example, a decision is taken at the October session of the Commission and not transmitted to the parties until the Activity Report of the Commission has been approved by the OAU summit the following June or July, the time lag could run to nine months.

[62] Whether this means all of the OAU members is not clear.

[63] Article 29(1) of the Protocol. Article 29(2) reads: 'The Council of Ministers shall also be notified of the judgment and shall monitor its execution on behalf of the Assembly.' 'Assembly' refers to the OAU Assembly of Heads of State and Government.

Articles 11–16 deal with the nomination, election and terms of office of judges. These provisions are very similar to those of the Charter concerning the Commission: eleven members, nominated by OAU States, elected by secret ballot for six-year terms. The only interesting differences to the Charter's provisions for Commission members are two references to considerations of 'adequate gender representation' in Articles 12(2) and 14(3), and a reference in Article 14(2) to ensuring that the judges represent the main regions of Africa and their principal legal traditions. None of these clauses involves any concrete or binding action.

The Protocol leaves undisturbed a situation which has vexed the Commission from its inception, namely, the independence of Commissioners from their governments and the incompatibility of Commissioners holding certain positions within their States while serving on the Commission. The oath of office provided for in Article 16 is identical to that taken by the Commissioners, to discharge their duties 'impartially and faithfully'.[64] Although it is not explicitly stated, judges serve, like Commissioners, in their private capacity. Article 17, 'Independence', provides for the immunity of judges from liability for any decision or opinion issued in the exercise of their functions.

The Commission's credibility has suffered significantly from the appointment of Commissioners who serve their country's executive branch in political capacities, i.e. as ambassadors or attorneys-general. Although the issue has been much discussed at sessions of the Commission, the Commission has no means by which to prevent the nomination or election of such individuals, and, indeed, the presence of Commissioners holding such positions has meant that even passing a resolution on the issue has been out of the question.

Article 18 of the Protocol provides: 'The position of judge of the Court is incompatible with any activity that might interfere with the independence or impartiality of such a judge or the demands of the office, as determined in the Rules of Procedure of the Court.' This does leave open the possibility that the Court may make explicit which activities or positions are incompatible with independence and impartiality. But the Rules of Procedure of the Court, like those of the Commission, will be drafted by the first Court that is constituted and this will be considered under the provisions of Article 18 alone. Judges who are also ambassadors, ministers of justice or attorneys-general

---

[64] See Article 38 of the African Charter.

are unlikely to draft rules of procedure indicating that they themselves should resign – notwithstanding the Article 17(4) guarantee of immunity.

Here, as with the *locus standi* provisions, the drafters of the Protocol have put State interest before professionalism, or else struck a devil's bargain by calculating that such formulations were necessary to get the Protocol approved by the OAU Heads of State and Government. It would have been more honest to draft the necessary provisions to ensure a legitimate, functional court, leaving the opprobrium on the Heads of State and Government if they failed to approve the Protocol as a consequence.

The only advance the Protocol can be said to make over the Charter provisions relating to the Commission in this regard is in recognising that, in principle, incompatibility may exist. Article 22, 'Exclusion', also provides that a national of any State which is a party in a case submitted to the Court cannot sit in judgment on that case, which has never been the policy in the Commission, although it is the practice in the Inter-American system.

OFFICERS AND STAFF

In addition to the provisions for procedures and execution of judgments described above, the Protocol goes beyond the Charter in two other important respects. One of these is that in Article 21 the Protocol provides that the President of the Court is to be a full-time appointee and he or she is to reside at the seat of the Court. The other is in Article 24 which provides that the Court shall appoint its own Registrar and other staff. The origins and importance of these provisions are clear to anyone familiar with the work of the Commission and how it has struggled to accomplish its work while meeting for only a maximum of four weeks a year and with staff over whom the Commissioners themselves have no real authority. What OAU staff there are at the Commission's Secretariat seem to be designated by the Secretary-General in Addis Ababa without much consultation with Commissioners. Under the Protocol, the Court will have only itself to blame if its employees fail to carry out their duties. The presence at the seat of the Court of a full-time president who should understand precisely what needs to be done between sessions of the Court and who has a personal interest in accomplishing it should also make a great difference to the efficiency of the Court's administration.

In limiting the office of the President of the Court to a maximum of four years (two years, renewable once) the Protocol also tackles the situation of having a Chairman repeatedly re-elected, which has occurred within the Commission. At one time a Chairman of the Commission served for six consecutive years. The competition to be President of the Court may also not be so keen as it is within the Commission, since it will involve changing residence during the period of office, which is certainly an inconvenience – the more so if the Court is headquartered in one of Africa's less glamorous capitals.

AMENDMENTS

Finally, the Protocol leaves open the possibility of its being amended by a relatively simple process. Article 35 provides that a State Party to the Protocol may propose a draft amendment to the Assembly, which can adopt it by a simple majority. The Court may also propose amendments through the Secretary-General of the OAU. The difficulty presented by this procedure is that, according to Article 35(3), amendments shall come into force 'for each State Party which has accepted' them. Whether this means 'for each State Party that has voted in favour of the amendment in the Assembly', or whether an additional acceptance in the form of a declaration is required, is not clear. Similarly, it is not apparent what will happen if States that originally voted against an amendment change their minds, or if those that originally accepted an amendment subsequently wish to denounce it.

AN ASSESSMENT

Overall, the Protocol on the African Court shows a lack of innovation or creativity, in distinct contrast to the African Charter, which fascinated and infuriated commentators with its quirky formulations and occasionally radical departures from international precedent. The Court Protocol is, fundamentally, a conservative document. It adds the minimum provisions necessary to distinguish it from the Commission as a more formal legal body with theoretically binding judgments, but in several ways it seems to retract the promise of progressiveness held out by the African Charter. The Protocol – and it has this in common with the Charter – is also vague on several essential points that cannot be resolved until the Court is constituted and begins its practice. It also seems clear that the Commission will play a critical role in the Court's operation and this raises a number of questions which will be explored in the following section.

Making text manifest: directions the court may take

The Court's essential function is to consider alleged violations of the African Charter. If one looks at the experience of the African Commission, such cases are very rarely brought by States against other States.[65] As discussed above, it is unlikely that many States will make the declaration necessary for cases to be brought directly to the Court by NGOs or individuals. Thus, if the Court is to be a body of any consequence, it will be so because it receives a good number of significant cases via the African Commission. It is therefore necessary to return to the question of the functioning of the Commission and the relationship between the Commission and the Court and ask what sorts of cases the Commission might send to the Court. It could send cases of 'serious or massive violations'. However, the definition of what is 'serious or massive' is not straightforward and it must be remembered that a question of law raised in a case concerning a single individual can have major repercussions.

It is more likely that the Commission will forward to the Court cases in which the States have failed to respect its recommendations. At the moment the Commission has almost nothing in the way of a follow-up procedure for communications, although persistent complainants may keep it informed of delinquent States who fail to comply. Referring such cases to the Court would be a way of pressing for enforcement. On the other hand, it might seem unnecessary for cases in which the State concerned had responded positively to the Commission's recommendation to be put before the Court.

Another possibility is that the Commission might permit States and/or complainants to indicate if they wish to pursue the case further, and refer only those which the parties request. At the moment, a majority of communications before the Commission involve quite self-evident violations and have ended with the Commission finding this to be the case. Depending on the composition of the Court and its legal rigour, States might be tempted to think that adverse decisions could be reversed or mitigated after a rehearing by the Court. One can also imagine cases of far greater legal complexity, such as are argued in the other regional systems, in which the Commission

[65] The first State-against-State communication was brought by Libya against the United States in the late 1980s, but was inadmissible since the US is not a party to the Charter. The next State communication was not brought until 1999 when the Democratic Republic of the Congo lodged complaints against Rwanda, Burundi and Uganda for their part in the Congolese civil war.

would find no violation and the complainants would wish to have the matter reconsidered.

If the Court is considered as an appeals body for the African Commission, as it seems likely to become, other questions must be answered. First, it is not clear what will be its standard of review, and whether the Court will hear cases coming from the Commission *de novo*, or give some weight to what the Commission has decided, overruling it only in more or less exceptional instances.

Then there is the question of hearings: holding hearings in the African regional system is extremely costly, simply because the geographical jurisdiction of the mechanisms is so vast: to travel from one end of the continent to another, even in the twenty-first century, can take two or three days. To require rehearing, without significant financial aid to complainants, would *de facto* favour States. The Court, in the manner of a true appeals court, could leave findings of fact to the Commission and decide chiefly on the basis of the written record. Hearings could thus be restricted to oral arguments by counsel, rather than the examination of witnesses. This is the practice of many national appeals tribunals.

However, a fundamental prerequisite for the adoption of such an approach would be for the Commission to regularise its filing and briefing procedures, prepare written records of its proceedings, and write more detailed and carefully reasoned decisions. The rules of evidence (none of which is presently codified by the Commission)[66] should be the same for the two bodies. Although the Commission holds hearings, it does not hold them regularly and does not make official transcripts of them. The Commission has even, on one occasion, expressed a reluctance to wade into fact-finding, observing that this should be done by national-level tribunals.[67] A written, certified record will be essential if the Court is to rely upon it. Finally, the Commission's decisions, although having increased in length and complexity since the first reasoned decisions were given in 1994, are still all too often cursory and poorly drafted.

A further obstacle to access to the Court will be the length of time that it takes to get a case through the Commission. At the moment months of time are lost at every step of the communications procedure, from receiving

---

[66] See Chapter 4 above for a discussion of the rules of evidence.
[67] See Communication 40/90, *Bob Ngozi Njoku v. Egypt*, Eleventh Activity Report 1997–1998, Annex II (*Documents of the African Commission*, p. 604).

acknowledgments of receipt to holding hearings and issuing decisions. If complainants are to go through another process subsequent to this, the Commission will have to streamline its procedures.

Alternatively, once the Court is established, the Commission could cease to hold hearings. Although no provision is to be found in the Charter itself, it has simply evolved out of the Article 55 procedure. Indeed, the Commission could even cease deciding cases on their merits altogether, and, by arrangement with the Court, work as a screening body to decide which cases are admissible, and refer these cases directly to the Court. There has been a gesture in this direction in the form of Article 6(1) of the Protocol, which gives the Court the right to ask for the opinion of the Commission on questions of admissibility. If, as is to be expected, the overwhelming majority of potential cases come from NGOs and individuals, they will have to come via the Commission in any event. The two institutions could divide the consideration of communications between them, with the Commission deciding the admissibility and the Court the merits.

The Court does not have the Commission's promotional mandate nor is it involved in the examination of State reports. The Commission could stay busy without holding hearings, or deciding communications on their merits. Dividing the work in this manner would also reduce dramatically the time it would take to make its way through the system: the Commission could decide admissibility in six months[68] and then the Court could begin its work. However, to come to such an agreement would require a certain determination on the part of both the Court and Commission, and would be in the face of the clear intention of OAU States at the time when the Protocol was adopted to prevent individuals and NGOs going directly to the Court. A division of labour may be justifiable and the Rules of Procedure for both bodies could be redrafted to provide for it, but it would be a bold, if logical, step.

Another key aspect of the Commission/Court relationship which is left unspecified by the Protocol is whether the two bodies should be located

---

[68] At the moment, the Commission's Rules of Procedure Rule 117(4) specifies that a State has three months after it has been notified of a communication in which to send the Commission its observations on admissibility. In principle, then, the Commission could choose to notify a State at one session, and consider the response and take a decision at the following session. In practice, States never respect the three-month deadline and the Commission habitually grants several extensions. Because the Commission meets bi-annually, each postponement entails an additional six months of delay.

in the same place. The Commission is in The Gambia and its location has occasioned much criticism over the years for its relative inaccessibility and isolation due to the dearth of diplomatic missions in Banjul. But if the Commission and the Court were to have the close relationship proposed above, becoming essentially two chambers of one institution, it would be infinitely more practical if they were in the same location. On the other hand, if the Commission jealously guards its protective mandate and refers to the Court a minimum number of cases, and/or if the Court decides to hear cases *de novo*, thus removing the need for a transfer of records, the proximity of the two bodies would be less important.

While some of this speculation may seem radical, current developments within the OAU have the potential to affect the Court as envisioned in the Protocol more dramatically than any arrangement that might be entered into with the Commission. This development is the evolution of the OAU into the African Union, as set out in the Constitutive Act of the African Union of July 2000.[69] Article 3(h) of the Act makes the promotion of human and peoples' rights one of the objectives of the Union, and Article 18 of the Act provides for the establishment of a Court of Justice. The statute, composition and functions of the Court of Justice will be defined by a protocol that has yet to be drafted. No mention is made of the fate of existing institutions, aside from the OAU Secretariat which is to become the interim Secretariat of the Union. The Act provides for numerous new institutions to be created. It remains to be seen whether the new African Union will maintain the already existing institutions of the OAU. Certainly, the drafting of protocols is – as we have seen – a time-consuming process, so the fate of the Commission and the Court will not be altered immediately, even though the Union came into existence in June 2001. Timing may ultimately be the determining factor. If the Protocol on the Court comes into force before the Protocol on the Court of Justice is drafted, no doubt the drafting of the latter will take this into account. If, however, the Protocol has not by then come into force, those planning a Court of Justice may decide to integrate the two. If the two institutions are maintained, their respective mandates will have to be disentangled, which could be a more difficult task than apportioning functions between the African Commission and the African Court.

[69] Constitutive Act of the African Union, adopted by the 36th Ordinary Session of the Assembly of Heads of State and Government, Lomé, Togo, 11 July 2000, AHG/Dec.143 (XXXVI).

Conclusion

By agreeing in principle to establish a court, African leaders accepted that the human rights system needed more formality, more legalism, more force and more 'teeth'. The African Commission established by the African Charter has been seen chiefly as a body for promotion, mediation and reconciliation; at best quasi-judicial, in spite of its Article 55 communications procedure. The very word 'court' suggests a forum for the handing down of authoritative judgments, making clear determinations, compliance with which is obligatory. As the above analysis illustrates, however, the Protocol does not provide for a straightforward 'strengthening' of the African system. African States are the parties who chiefly bear the consequences of international adjudication regarding human rights and in the Protocol they did their best to protect themselves from penetrating scrutiny.

There are clear indications from the text of the Protocol that the African Court is intended to be a more structured and powerful legal body than the Commission: the provisions on evidence, findings, judgment, notifications and execution are all more specific than those in the Charter and the full-time presidency is an important step. Yet the restrictions on *locus standi* before the Court, the vague relationship between the Court and Commission, and the weaknesses they share – such as permitting members to be in the political employ of States – could mean that the Court is held hostage by the very confusions that it is supposed to address.

The African Union, as it now is, will have to renew its commitment to providing adequate funds for both these institutions to function more effectively than has the Commission. It must also integrate the human rights mechanisms into its new structures. These are the first requirements if there is to be an effective Court. Its fate will then rest with the women and men who serve on the Court and Commission. The Protocol provides an opportunity for the creation of an important force for human rights protection in Africa but this is conditional upon the intelligence, creativity and dedication to human rights that future judges and Commissioners bring to their task.

11

THE PROMOTIONAL ROLE OF THE AFRICAN COMMISSION ON HUMAN AND PEOPLES' RIGHTS

VICTOR DANKWA

Introduction

The promotion and protection of human and peoples' rights are the two main functions assigned to the African Commission on Human and Peoples' Rights under the African Charter on Human and Peoples' Rights.[1] Articles 45(1)(a), (b) and (c) state how the promotional mandate should be undertaken, namely, that the Commission should:

(a) collect documents, undertake studies and researches on African problems in the field of human and peoples' rights, organise seminars, symposia and conferences, disseminate information, encourage national and local institutions concerned with human and peoples' rights and, should the case arise, give its views or make recommendations to Governments;

(b) formulate and lay down, principles and rules aimed at solving legal problems relating to human and peoples' rights and fundamental freedoms upon which African Governments may base their legislations;

(c) co-operate with other African and international institutions concerned with the promotion and protection of human and peoples' rights.

The Commission has discharged its obligation to promote human rights and peoples' rights[2] in a variety of ways.

---

[1] Article 30. Unless it is otherwise stated, all Articles cited hereinafter are provisions from the Charter.

[2] Hereinafter 'human rights' include 'peoples' rights'.

Promotional responsibility of the Commission

PLANS OF ACTION

In order to fulfil its obligation under the Charter, the Commission adopted a Preliminary Plan of Action in 1988,[3] and a subsequent Plan of Action for 1992–6.[4] After an evaluation of their implementation, the Commission adopted, on the tenth anniversary of the entry into force of the Charter, 21 October 1996, on the island bearing its name, the 'Mauritius Plan of Action for the Period 1996–2001'.[5] Part II of the Plan is devoted to the 'Promotional Mission of the African Commission'. The tasks which the Commission set itself were realistic and attainable and much has been accomplished within the timeframe of the Plan. For example, it was to work towards the ratification of the African Charter on the Rights and Welfare of the Child. This instrument entered into force in September 2000 and the Commission can take credit for playing a part in getting the requisite ratification.

PUBLICATIONS

Regrettably, the Commission does not have much to show by way of publications. With the assistance of UNESCO, more copies of the Charter have been printed and they are being distributed as widely as possible. These copies have added to earlier ones printed in 1990 by the United Nations,

---

[3] Programme of Action of the African Commission on Human and Peoples' Rights, First Annual Activity Report of the African Commission on Human and Peoples' Rights 1987–1988, ACHPR/RPT/1st, Annex VIII; R. Murray and M. Evans (eds.), *Documents of the African Commission on Human and Peoples' Rights* (Oxford: Hart Publishing, 2001), p. 167 (hereinafter *Documents of the African Commission*). It called for the establishment of an African library and documentation centre; printing and dissemination of the Charter and its Rules of Procedure; publication of a journal; periodical radio and TV programmes on human rights; integration of teaching into syllabi of secondary education; a human rights day; getting States to ratify the Charter and introducing the Charter provisions into States' constitutions; co-operation with international and non-government organisations and with African organisations.

[4] Programme of Activities 1992–1996, Sixth Annual Activity Report of the African Commission on Human and Peoples' Rights 1992–1993, ACHPR/RPT/6th, Annex VII (*Documents of the African Commission*, p. 257). It noted similar activities in this Programme as well as training courses.

[5] *Documents of the African Commission*, p. 579.

and later ones, both with the Rules of Procedure of the Commission, printed with the assistance of the European Union.

A fairly respectable documentation centre has been set up at the Secretariat of the Commission. It is noteworthy that it was with funds provided by the Government of Denmark through the Danish Centre for Human Rights, Copenhagen, that a documentalist, who must be credited with building up the Documentation Centre to its present level, was recruited. Although primary responsibility for financial support lies with the parent body, the OAU,[6] its own financial constraints have resulted in much support being provided by outside sources, particularly Denmark.[7] Thus, OAU documents have been catalogued as the Commission set out to do and copies of the Charter and the activity report have been printed and distributed. The Review of the Commission continues to be published regularly. A 'Bulletin' has replaced the 'Newsletter' of the Commission and it is hoped that this will be produced on a continual basis. A compilation of past resolutions of the Commission is available. Seminars and conferences should also be followed with the publication of reports on them. The publication of State reports begun by the Danish Centre for Human Rights should be also continued.[8] Work has started towards the publication of the decisions of the Commission in the communications, and reports of protective missions undertaken by the Commission have also been produced,[9] but it is necessary that the Commission avoid the long lapse of time between missions and the publication of reports. A series of 'Information Sheets' provide further detail on

---

[6] Article 41 provides: 'The Secretary-General of the Organization of African Unity shall provide the staff and services necessary for the effective discharge of the duties of the Commission.'

[7] Although it should not have been so, outside support is greater than that provided by the OAU.

[8] See, for example, African Commission on Human and Peoples' Rights, *Examination of State Reports: Ghana, 14th Session, December 1993* (Copenhagen: Danish Centre for Human Rights, 1995).

[9] Report on Mission of Good Offices to Senegal of the African Commission on Human and Peoples' Rights (1–7 June 1996), Tenth Annual Activity Report of the African Commission on Human and Peoples' Rights, 1996–7, ACHPR/RPT/10th, Annex VIII (*Documents of the African Commission*, p. 518); Report of the Mission to Mauritania of the African Commission on Human and Peoples' Rights, Nouakchott, 19–27 June 1996, Tenth Annual Activity Report of the African Commission on Human and Peoples' Rights, 1996–7, ACHPR/RPT/10th, Annex IX (*Documents of the African Commission*, p. 538).

the functions of the Commission[10] and other small pamphlets have been produced.[11]

It has been noted that, with the financial assistance of the Government of Norway and the administrative support of Penal Reform International, the reports of the Special Rapporteur on Prison Conditions in Africa have been published.[12] The first publication of the Commission in Arabic is a translation of the report on prisons in Mali.

With assistance from the European Union and the Danish Centre for Human Rights, the Commission has printed and distributed widely its 13th Annual Activity Report (1999–2000). It is important that this publication is maintained in order that the general public will know of the African system for the protection of human rights, and how it can be used and improved upon.

Considerable work still needs to be done on the promotion of the Charter and the dissemination of the work of the Commission. The Human Rights Commission in Bangui, Central African Republic, for instance, did not have a copy of the Charter when I visited it last year and it was the same in the Ministries of Justice and Foreign Affairs in Monrovia, Liberia, where the original decision was taken to prepare a draft African Charter on Human and Peoples' Rights.

RESOLUTIONS AND PRESS RELEASES

Resort to resolutions has been an important mode for promoting human rights. Where the human rights situation gives cause for concern, the Commission has not hesitated in passing resolutions condemning actions of governments and stating what ought to be done to improve the situation.[13]

[10] For example, Information Sheet No. 1 summarises the establishment and functions of the Commission. Information Sheet No. 2 presents Guidelines on the Submission of Communications. Funding from the European Union made possible the printing and distribution of the two Information Sheets.

[11] Such as 'The African Commission on Human and Peoples' Rights – One Decade of Challenge' and 'African Charter on Human and Peoples' Rights: Tenth Anniversary Celebration of Its Coming into Force' (1986–96), Grand Bay, Mauritius, 21 October 1996, which provide a useful summary of the activities of the Commission from 1987 to 1997.

[12] See Chapter 9 above.

[13] For recent examples, see the Resolution on the Peace Process in the Democratic Republic of Congo; the Resolution on the Peace and National Reconciliation Process in Somalia; the Resolution on Western Sahara, Thirteenth Activity Report of the African Commission on Human and Peoples' Rights, 1999–2000, ACHPR/RPT/13th, Annex IV.

Conscious of the fact that the government and people of Africa must be aware of the existence of the Charter and know its contents before the rights and freedoms enshrined in it may be respected, the Commission passed a 'Resolution on Celebration of an African Day of Human Rights'.[14] Governments and Commissioners were expected to engage in activities on 21 October, the day on which the Charter entered into force, with the aim of raising awareness of human rights generally and the Charter in particular.

It may also be a good idea for the Commission occasionally to produce press releases on burning human rights situations like the plight of Sierra Leonean refugees in Guinea and internally displaced Guineans arising from the border war between Guinea and Liberia. Admittedly, a much more effective communication network among Commissioners than obtains now will be needed for such press releases to be made between sessions of the Commission. It is a measure of the potency of the Commission's resolutions that State representatives and others at the sessions of the Commission and elsewhere have lobbied against either the passing of the entire resolution or its text. For its independence and integrity, the Commission must not be swayed by considerations other than the best interest of human rights in Africa in the passage of resolutions. The extent to which the Commission has succeeded in undertaking its functions in promoting human rights in Africa may be partly measured by the tasks it has set itself.

LECTURES AND CONFERENCES

Lectures on the Charter and the Commission at universities and other organisations in the host countries have been attended during promotional visits of Commissioners.[15] The need to examine in depth human rights problems in Africa, and to point the way forward, owe a great deal to the specific inclusion of the organisation of seminars, symposia and conferences within the promotional mandate of the Commission.

[14] Resolution on Celebration of an African Day of Human Rights, Second Annual Activity Report of the African Commission on Human and Peoples' Rights 1988–1989, ACHPR/RPT/2nd, Annex VII (*Documents of the African Commission*, p. 183).

[15] The present writer recalls his lectures at the Universities of Nairobi, Botswana and Addis Ababa, as well as outside the university setting. A significant section of the audience at one of two lectures I gave in Harare on 'The African Charter and its Commission' were diplomats, including two High Commissioners (Ghana and Botswana); four First Secretaries (Mozambique, Botswana and Namibia); and one Third Secretary (South Africa). See E. V. O. Dankwa, Report on Promotional Visit to Zimbabwe and Malawi, 19–27 February 1995.

In collaboration with other institutions, the Commission itself has held a number of conferences. These have included conferences on women's rights,[16] which resulted in the development of a draft Protocol on the Rights of Women[17] and the appointment of the Special Rapporteur on the Rights of Women. There have also been seminars on impunity[18] and prison conditions in Africa,[19] the latter prompting the appointment of a Special Rapporteur on Prisons and Detention Centres in Africa. More recently, the Commission held a seminar to consider further elaboration of Article 7 and the right to fair trial, and thereby fulfilled one of the functions expected of the Commission, namely, 'to formulate and lay down principles and rules aimed at solving legal problems relating to human and peoples' rights and fundamental freedoms upon which African Governments may base their legislations'.[20]

Many more conferences have been held by the Commission than have been noted above, and others are planned for the future,[21] taking account of the concerns of human rights protection in Africa. The topics and themes for conferences are those which the Commission consider critical for reflection and action. The availability of finance and the swiftness with which

---

[16] In collaboration with WILDAF and the United Nations Centre for Human Rights, 'Human Rights of the African Woman and the African Charter on Human and Peoples' Rights', in Lomé, Togo, 8–9 March 1995.

[17] Draft Protocol to the African Charter on Human and Peoples' Rights on the Rights of Women in Africa, Final Version, 13 September 2000, CAB/LEG/66.6.

[18] A workshop on 'Impunity in Africa' was held in Ouagadougou, Burkina Faso, in collaboration with the International Centre for Human Rights and Democratic Development, Canada, 22–23 March 1996.

[19] The Commission joined Penal Reform International and other organisations to have a seminar on 'Prison Conditions in Africa' in Kampala, Uganda, 19–21 September 1996. 'The Kampala Declaration on Prison Conditions in Africa' was a product of the seminar. Uganda Prison Services, the International Committee of the Red Cross (ICRC), the Foundation for Human Rights Initiative and the Observatoire International des Prisons were the other organisers of the seminar. The proceedings of the seminar with introductory notes have been compiled and published as 'Prison Conditions in Africa. Report of a Pan-African Seminar', Kampala, Uganda 19–21 September 1996.

[20] Article 45(1)(b), Seminar on the Right to Fair Trial in Africa, in collaboration with the African Society of International and Comparative Law and Interights, Dakar, Senegal, 9–11 September 1999.

[21] See Mauritius Plan of Action 1996–2001, paras. 18–21. These include comparison of the Charter with other regional systems; freedom of expression, association and assembly; economic, social and cultural rights; rights of the child in Africa; freedom of movement and the right to asylum; ethnic conflict resolution in a human rights context and the problem of mass expulsions, among others.

the Commission's partners in the organisation of conferences have moved, largely explain why some conferences have been held while others have remained on the drawing board for a long time.

The participants to the Commission's conferences are selected according to expertise and interest. Accordingly, the participants at the seminar on 'Prison Conditions in Africa' came from the Prison Service while those at the Lomé Conference on the Rights of Women in Africa were largely women. It is the fervent hope of the Commission that participants at its seminars will pass on the lessons learnt to as many persons and organisations as will utilise such lessons. What is required are widely distributed reports of the conferences and seminars for greater awareness of the findings, and the implementation of the recommendations of the conferences.

RESEARCH

A major task yet to be undertaken is a study on the impact of the 'applicable principles' provided for under Articles 60 and 61 of the Charter.

Venue of the sessions

The holding of many of the sessions of the Commission outside its headquarters in Banjul, The Gambia, is dictated by the need to promote human rights across the length and breadth of the continent. As was evidenced by the experience during and after the 21st Ordinary Session in Nouakchott, Mauritania, in April 1997, nationals of the host country take an active part in the work of the Commission, including the submission of communications.

Promotional visits

Very early in its work, the Commission decided that it was necessary to encourage States Parties to the Charter to implement their obligations under the Charter, as they have undertaken to do under Article 1.[22] At that stage countries which had not ratified the Charter were encouraged to do so.[23]

---

[22] Article 1 reads: 'The Member States of the Organization of African Unity parties to the present Charter shall recognise the rights, duties and freedoms enshrined in this Charter and shall undertake to adopt legislative or other measures to give effect to them.'

[23] For example, Draft Resolution on Ratification of the African Charter, Fifth Annual Activity Report of the African Commission on Human and Peoples' Rights, 1991–1992, ACHPR/RPT/5th, Annex VIII (*Documents of the African Commission*, p. 226).

All OAU States have now ratified the Charter and, although the work of Commissioners must have contributed to this end, it is acknowledged that many others worked towards this universal ratification, the International Commission of Jurists and Amnesty International being examples.

To achieve these ends, Member States of the OAU were divided among the Commissioners for promotional purposes.[24] Each Commissioner is to visit the countries assigned to him or her and meet officials whose schedules cover the protection of human rights, such as judges, Ministers of Justice and the Interior, and heads of the police or high-ranking officers of this force. The law and practice as regards the respect of human rights will be elicited from these officials. Being areas where African countries are known to fall short of international standards, the lawful period for detention without trial and the treatment of prisoners, for example, are issues which are likely to be covered at the meetings.

As noted above, 'it is the duty of the Commission to collect documents... [and to] encourage national and local institutions concerned with human and peoples' rights'.[25] Commissioners have returned from promotional visits with copies of constitutions, legislation and other publications on human rights from the host countries. Reports of the activities of non-governmental organisations, which have observer status with the Commission, have also been brought along by Commissioners from their promotional visits. Although a small part, the documents collected by Commissioners on their promotional visits form part of the Commission's Documentation Centre.

It is a pity that written accounts of all promotional visits by Commissioners cannot be obtained at the Secretariat. Former Commissioner, Professor Umozurike, for instance, visited all countries which were assigned to him for promotional activities. I recall his reports to the Commission on his work in Cameroon, Swaziland, Lesotho, South Africa and Nigeria. The Ghana Human Rights Committee, which presented an alternate report to the African Commission in November 1993 in Addis Ababa at the 14th Ordinary Session on the occasion of the presentation of Ghana's initial report, was formed at his suggestion on a promotional visit to Ghana. He continues to speak about the Charter and the Commission at universities and other fora. The submission of State reports to the Commission and the

---

[24] See Geographical Distribution of Countries Among Commissioners, DOC/OS/36e (XXIII).
[25] Article 45(1)(a).

incorporation of the Charter within municipal law are, *inter alia,* matters he brought to the attention of his hosts in all his travels.

In recent times the pace of promotional activity has heightened. Increased funding from the OAU and continued funding for promotional activity by the Government of Sweden have made it possible for Commissioners to be accompanied on their promotional visits by legal officers.[26] It is a development which has contributed to more detailed reports being submitted to the Commission shortly after promotional visits.[27]

In their promotional visit to Chad in September 2000, Commissioners Rezzag-Bara and Ondziel-Gnelenga (the latter is also the Special Rapporteur on the Rights of Women) worked to gain a broad picture of the human rights situation in that country. To this end, meetings were held with government officials, United Nations agencies, the press, NGOs and other sections of civil society.[28] Matters of concern for the Commissioners included the security and liberty of Chadians, extrajudicial executions, impunity on the part of the security forces and the rights of women. Evidence gathered by the mission showed that the judicial process was slow and partial and access to the courts was expensive. Consequently, there was little confidence in the judiciary. Legal aid was limited to criminal cases. The problems in this area were compounded by the paucity of judges – 130 in the whole country – with some parts not covered at all. The government noted how the concerns were being addressed.

Commissioner Rezzag-Bara was able to confirm, during his promotional visit to Djibouti from 26 February to 5 March 2000, that one communication,[29] which was brought by a Djiboutian NGO against the Government of Djibouti, had been resolved amicably. Similarly, on his visit to Mozambique on 7–9 August 2000,[30] Commissioner Pityana stressed to government

---

[26] See, for instance, Report on a Mission to the Republic of Chad, Commissioner Rezzag-Bara, DOC/OS (XXVIII)/187/6; Report on the Promotional Mission Undertaken by Commissioner Rezzag-Bara to the Republic of Djibouti (26 February to 5 March 2000); and Report of Mission to Tanzania, Dr Vera Chirwa, DOC/OS (XXVIII)/187/6.

[27] See also Report of Promotional Visit to the Republic of Mozambique, 7–9 August 2000, DOC/OS (XXVIII)/187/5; Activity Report of Dr N. Barney Pityana; Promotional Activity Report of Commissioner Vera M. Chirwa for Submission to the 28th Ordinary Session of the African Commission on Human and Peoples' Rights.

[28] See Report on a Mission to Chad.

[29] Communication 133/94, *Association pour la Défense des Droits de l'Homme et des Libertés v. Djibouti*, Thirteenth Activity Report 1999–2000, Annex V.

[30] Report of Promotional Visit to the Republic of Mozambique, 7–9 August 2000, DOC/OS (XXVIII)/187/5.

officials the need for timely submission of State reports to the Commission and an active involvement in the work of the Commission by State delegates. Overcrowding in and the dilapidated nature of Macheva prison led to a recommendation that it be closed. Torture, police brutality and extrajudicial executions, as well as the establishment of a national human rights commission, also engaged his attention. As in other countries he canvassed for the ratification of the Protocol on the Establishment of an African Court on Human Rights.

In Swaziland, Namibia and South Africa, where he has lectured on topics in human rights, Commissioner Pityana also promoted the Charter and the Commission in particular and human rights generally.[31] As far as possible, he would meet with high State officials, President Sam Nujoma of Namibia included, and urge measures whose implementation would advance the cause of human rights in Africa.

In his promotional visits to Zimbabwe, Malawi, Botswana, Namibia, Uganda, Kenya, Ethiopia and Sierra Leone,[32] the present writer inquired into these critical areas. Recommendations for changes and improvement in the law and practice in respect of human rights were made wherever necessary. It would appear that the recommendations were received in good faith, but how to follow up and ascertain whether there has indeed been a change for the better is a problem that has bedevilled the work of the Commission. Nevertheless, it may be partly addressed in the course of the examination of State reports, as the Commission, against the background of material gathered by itself, or from credible third parties, seeks to hold the State Party to its Charter obligations. In this regard, it is important that the submission of reports to the Commission by States Parties is raised during promotional visits.

Promotional and protective activities united

Despite the distinction drawn between the promotional and protective functions of the Commission, as is evidenced by Articles 30 and 45 of the

[31] Activity Report of Dr N. Barney Pityana.

[32] Written reports on these visits are available at the Secretariat of the Commission in Banjul, The Gambia, see, for example, 19th Session, Promotional Activities of Professor E. V. O. Dankwa, October 1995 to March 1996 (no reference) The Commission plans to publish the reports of the promotional visits of Commissioners.

Charter,[33] matters falling under the latter may be, and have been, taken up during promotional visits. The distinction is of less relevance where there is co-operation from the host country. On a promotional visit to Botswana, the present writer took up with the relevant authorities a communication by J. K. Modise on the alleged deprivation of his citizenship.[34] The assurance given to me that the President of Botswana had granted citizenship to Modise turned out to be true, although the communication lingered before the Commission thereafter for years because the complainant was not satisfied with the type of citizenship granted to him. Counsel for Modise persuasively argued later that he was entitled to citizenship by birth, which placed no limitation on his civil and political rights.

During the promotional visit to Uganda, inquiries were made of matters that may well be said to be strictly within the province of the protection of human rights. They included torture by the police during interrogation and detention; the peaceful settlement of the rebellions by, on the one hand, Kony in northern Uganda and, on the other hand, by the Allied Democratic Front in western Uganda, with their attendant massive violations of human rights; violation of human rights by the Uganda Defence Force; the use of the police to harass the opposition; and the breaking up of a rally of the Democratic Party.

Thus, promotional visits can be used to detect impending conflicts or potential abuses and these are brought to the attention of both the Commission and the host government. In Cameroon allegations of extrajudicial executions in Maroua in the north-west province of the country had been brought to the attention of the Secretariat of the Commission. These allegations were repeated at the start of the promotional visit by a number of Cameroonians and I was ready to undertake an on-site investigation. When, for various reasons, including the late finalisation by government officials of my programme, the visit to the *locus in quo* proved impossible, the issue of extrajudicial executions was taken up with the appropriate ministries and the *gendarmeries* in Yaoundé. Similarly, allegations of cruel, degrading and

---

[33] Article 30 reads: 'An African Commission on Human and Peoples' Rights . . . shall be established within the Organization of African Unity to promote human and peoples' rights and ensure their protection in Africa.'

[34] Communication 97/93, *John K. Modise v. Botswana*, Seventh Activity Report 1993–1994, Annex IX; Tenth Activity Report 1996–1997, Annex X (*Documents of the African Commission*, p. 349 and 567). It was finally concluded at the 28th Ordinary Session of the Commission held in Cotonou, Benin 23 October to 6 November 2000.

inhuman treatment of detainees from the north-west province, who were being held in Kondegui and Mfou prisons in Yaoundé, leading to the death of some of them, ware taken up. Permission was sought and granted for a visit to the two prisons in order to ascertain their conditions. However, arrangements were never finalised by the officials in charge of my visit to make the prison visit possible. Representations were made to me about the marginalisation of the Anglophones, Cameroon having both French and English speakers. I spoke to the complainants and the government, although the latter denied charges of marginalisation.[35] Anger at marginalisation and its consequences may lead to thoughts of secession, as was voiced by some Anglophones who had a meeting with me. Hardly any African government will countenance secession and, as is evidenced by the war over 'Biafra' in Nigeria in the 1960s, force will be used to prevent the secession. The violations of human rights which war inevitably produces are antithetical to the promotion of human rights. Therein lies the value of promotional visits in prompting governments to take steps to address developments which will not make for the promotion of human rights.

State reports[36]

Although mandated to promote human rights, the extent to which a body of eleven persons, working part-time, can achieve this end in the fifty-three States Parties is limited. A great contribution towards this goal must be made by the States Parties themselves and by institutions within these countries. It is through State reports that the Commission may determine how far human rights are being promoted and suggest how the fundamental obligation outlined in Article 25 of the Charter will be faithfully carried out.

Article 62 of the Charter obliges States Parties 'to submit every two years...a report on the legislative or other measures taken with a view to giving effect to the rights and freedoms recognised and guaranteed by the present Charter'. As noted elsewhere,[37] despite repeated appeals from

---

[35] Professor Augustin Kontehou Kouomegni, Foreign Minister of Cameroon, denied any marginalisation, citing, as an illustration, how an Anglophone, John Fru Ndi, nearly won a presidential election.

[36] Further information on the State reporting mechanism is found in Chapter 2 above.

[37] See Chapter 2 above.

the Commission for compliance with such a fundamental obligation,[38] the record of compliance has been poor.[39] The pressure which is brought to bear on States Parties during promotional visits as regards the submission of reports should be sustained, because the mechanism has the potential to contribute to a more effective protection of human rights in Africa. It is also submitted that the programme for promotional visits should include follow-up of recommendations arising out of the examination of State reports.

Special Rapporteurs

An important component of the work of the Special Rapporteurs of the Commission is undertaking studies and researches on African problems in the field of human and peoples' rights, with particular reference to their subject areas.[40] The studies are followed by recommendations to governments, and thus meet a desideratum of Article 45(1)(a).

The recommendations of, for example, the Special Rapporteur on prisons and conditions of detention aim at getting States Parties, for example, to improve the conditions of their prisons and their treatment of offenders in order to bring them up to standards envisaged under the Charter. The recommendations are thus a way of promoting respect of human rights. Since the reports of the Special Rapporteur are distributed to all States Parties, it is expected that States yet to be visited will take steps to address the shortcomings in their prison regime, based on the recommendations, and thus promote respect of human rights beyond the borders of the particular country to which the recommendations are addressed.

---

[38] See, for example, Recommendation on Periodic Reports, First Annual Activity Report of the African Commission on Human and Peoples' Rights, 1987–1988, ACHPR/RPT/1st, Annex IX (*Documents of the African Commission*, p. 168); Draft Resolution on Overdue Reports for Adoption, Fifth Annual Activity Report of the African Commission on Human and Peoples' Rights, 1991–1992, ACHPR/RPT/5th, Annex IX (*Documents of the African Commission*, p. 226).

[39] States' compliance with their obligation is now provided in a regular document: see Status of Submission of Periodic Reports by States Parties, DOC/OS (XXVIII)/184a.

[40] See Chapter 9 above. Both the Special Rapporteur on Prisons and that on Women's Rights are mandated to conduct studies on the situation of the relevant rights in Africa, advocate adherence to the Charter and encourage governments to implement promotion and protection for those particular rights.

Role of and relationship with other actors

ROLE OF STATES AND NATIONAL COURTS

The enjoyment of the rights and freedoms guaranteed under the Charter may be better realised if the Charter were part of the municipal law of States Parties. It was to achieve this end that in conjunction with the Raoul Wallenberg Institute in Lund, Sweden, the Commission organised a seminar on the 'National Implementation of the African Charter in the Internal Legal Systems in Africa' in Banjul, The Gambia, on 26–30 October 1992.[41]

As enjoined by Article 25, 'States Parties to the present Charter shall have the duty to promote and ensure through teaching, education and publication, the respect of the rights and freedoms contained in the present Charter and to see to it that these freedoms and rights as well as corresponding obligations and duties are understood'. In this respect, some judges in legal systems where incorporation is required, before treaties become part of municipal law, have relied on provisions of the Charter without such incorporation. To illustrate, in the Ghanaian case of *N. P. P.* v. *Inspector General of Police*,[42] Archer CJ partly relied on the Charter to hold unconstitutional legislation which required a police permit for a demonstration. In so doing, the Chief Justice stated:

> Ghana is a signatory to this African Charter and Member States of the OAU and parties to the Charter are expected to recognise the rights, duties and freedoms enshrined in the Charter and to undertake to adopt legislative or other measures to give effect to the rights and duties. I do not think that the fact that Ghana has not passed specific legislation to give effect to the Charter, means that the Charter cannot be relied upon.[43]

[41] Sixth Annual Activity Report of the African Commission on Human and Peoples' Rights 1992–1993, ACHPR/RPT/6th, Annex VIII (*Documents of the African Commission*, p. 270). See also Resolution on the Integration of the Provisions of the African Charter on Human and Peoples' Rights into National Laws of States, Second Annual Activity Report of the African Commission on Human and Peoples' Rights, 1988–1989, ACHPR/RPT/2nd, Annex XI (*Documents of the African Commission*, p. 186).

[42] Writ No. 4/93. See also E. V. O. Dankwa, 'Implementation of International Human Rights Instruments: Ghana as an Illustration', *Proceedings of the Third Annual Conference of the African Society of International and Comparative Law* (1991) 57.

[43] Other national courts have similarly shown some willingness to use the Charter: see F. Viljoen, 'Application of the African Charter on Human and Peoples' Rights by Domestic Courts in Africa', *Journal of African Law* 43 (1999) 1–17.

The right to assemble freely with others which is guaranteed by Article 12 of the Charter was not promoted by the restriction imposed on it before the Supreme Court decision.

The primary responsibility that States Parties have in the promotion of human rights through education was expressed by the Commission in its 'Recommendation on Some Modalities for Promoting Human and Peoples' Rights'.[44] The recommendation covered, *inter alia*, the teaching of human rights at all levels of education and the establishment of human rights research institutes.

A recognition by the Commission that many actors have a part in the promotion of human rights was made clear by its 'Draft Resolution on Promotional Activities'[45] which reinforced its earlier appeal for the inclusion of human rights in the curricula of educational institutions, emphasising on this occasion the training of law enforcement officials. But a measure of the Commission's effectiveness in the discharge of its promotional mandate is not the number of resolutions it passes but the implementation by States Parties and those to whom the resolutions are addressed, of the recommendations in the resolutions. No study has been carried out to determine the extent to which this is done. Arguably, the needs of promotion of human rights may be better served by ensuring that past resolutions of the Commission on the subject are implemented than by piling resolution upon resolution at each session.

NON-GOVERNMENTAL ORGANISATIONS AND NATIONAL INSTITUTIONS

Since a separate chapter in this volume is devoted to the work of non-governmental organisations within the African system for the protection of human rights,[46] a brief indication of their role in the promotional mandate of the Commission will suffice. Alternate reports and other sources of information supplied by NGOs have increased the knowledge and understanding

---

[44] Recommendation on Some Modalities for Promoting Human and Peoples' Rights, Second Annual Activity Report of the African Commission on Human and Peoples' Rights 1988–1989, ACHPR/RPT/2nd, Annex IX (*Documents of the African Commission*, p. 185).

[45] Draft Resolution on Promotional Activities, Fifth Annual Activity Report of the African Commission on Human and Peoples' Rights 1991–1992, ACHPR/RPT/5th Annex X (*Documents of the African Commission*, p. 227).

[46] See Chapter 8 above.

of the Commission on the human rights situation in Africa, and, thus equipped, have better prepared it for the examination of State reports and meetings with State officials. While State officials have arranged and facilitated meetings of Commissioners on promotional visits with NGOs, the latter have also made suggestions towards a more effective programme during promotional visits.

Equally, the Commission has seen it as important that civil society should be aroused to appreciate the importance of working towards the realisation of human and peoples' rights. The insistence on the submission of reports by NGOs with observer status with the Commission[47] is dictated by the need to keep NGOs active in their human rights work, which furthers the work of the Commission and thus partly fulfils one of the promotional functions of the Commission, namely, to 'encourage national and local institutions concerned with human and peoples' rights'.[48] In meeting NGOs in their host countries to learn of their work and to recommend the way forward, and in suggesting that those NGOs which do not have observer status with the Commission seek it, the Commission furthers its duty in this respect. Observer status with the Commission enables non-governmental organisations to propose items for inclusion in the provisional agenda of the sessions of the Commission.[49] Additionally, representatives of such NGOs may 'participate in the public sessions of the Commission and of its subsidiary bodies'.[50] Allowing their voices to be heard in the assembly of Africa's principal human rights institution should encourage NGOs to continue their work of promoting human rights in Africa.

In practical matters, the assistance of NGOs has contributed to effective promotional visits. It was the Kenya Human Rights Commission which welcomed me at Kenyatta Airport and drove me to the hotel it had arranged for me on 17 July 1998 at the start of my promotional visit to that country.[51]

---

[47] See Resolution on the Criteria for Granting and the Maintenance of Observer Status with the African Commission on Human and Peoples' Rights to Non-Governmental Organizations Working in the Field of Human Rights, Twelfth Activity Report of the African Commission on Human and Peoples' Rights, 1998–9, ACHPR/RPT/12th, Annex IV (*Documents of the African Commission*, p. 705).

[48] Article 45(1)(a).

[49] Rules of Procedure of the African Commission On Human and Peoples' Rights, Rule 5(a).

[50] *Ibid.*, Rule 75.

[51] See E. V. O. Dankwa, Report on Promotional Visits to Uganda and Kenya on 12–21 July 1998, available at the Secretariat of the Commission, Banjul, The Gambia.

A few weeks later, a similar reception was accorded me at Douala, Cameroon.[52] As noted previously, almost all our conferences and seminars have been held in collaboration with NGOs, and they have borne the brunt of raising funds and organising these meetings.

Following the passing by the Commission of a 'Resolution on Granting Observer Status to National Human Rights Institutions in Africa',[53] affiliate status was granted to some of these institutions at the 27th Session of the Commission in Algiers. National institutions may be counted upon to facilitate the promotional work of the Commission, as the NGOs have been doing. The submission of State reports, the implementation of recommendations of the Commission, the incorporation of the Charter into domestic law and the ratification of the Protocol on the Court, which have been taken up by Commissioners on promotional matters, are issues which can be followed up by the national institutions with affiliate status, and even by those yet to be so recognised.

INTERNATIONAL INSTITUTIONS

By virtue of Article 45(1)(c) the Commission is mandated to co-operate with international institutions in its promotional mandate. But, were it not so mandated, necessity would have forced the Commission into such a relationship. The defunct European Commission on Human Rights and the Inter-American Commission on Human Rights have contributed positively to the work of the Commission. Commissioners from the African Commission have visited the Inter-American Commission on Human Rights and observed its sessions, prompting ideas for their work in Africa. Seminars organised by the African Commission have been enriched with the contributions of those from other regional systems.[54]

Financial support for our work has come from the United Nations Centre for Human Rights/United Nations High Commissioner for Human Rights

---

[52] On 13 September 1998, I embarked on a five-day promotional visit to Cameroon. See E. V. O. Dankwa, Report of Promotional Visit to Cameroon, September 13–19, available at the Commission's Secretariat.

[53] Twelfth Annual Activity Report of the African Commission on Human and Peoples' Rights 1998–9, ACHPR/RPT/12th, Annex IV (*Documents of the African Commission*, p. 705).

[54] For example, the seminar on Early Warning Mechanism, in Nairobi, saw the participation of a member of the Legal Division of the Inter-American Commission.

and the European Union, among other institutions. In providing funding for promotional activities such as conferences, promotional visits, publications and the personnel who assist the Commission in carrying out its promotional mandate, the Swedish, Danish and Norwegian Governments, as well as the United Nations and the European Union, have made important contributions towards the promotion of human rights in Africa.

Conclusion

A culture of respect of human rights is vital if the rights and freedoms guaranteed under the Charter are to be enjoyed on a wide scale in Africa. Such an aim cannot be realised without the political will of the countries which have ratified the Charter to close the gap between adherence to the obligations under the Charter and the assurance of the rights and freedoms in their respective jurisdictions. The commitment of civil society to the realisation of the aims of the Charter is equally important. The task assigned to the Commission within the province of promotional activities, if faithfully executed, will contribute in no small measure towards the building of a culture of respect for human rights in Africa.

Within its limited human and material resources, the African Commission on Human and Peoples' Rights has made a modest contribution through its publications, conferences, examination of State reports, establishment of a Documentation Centre, cataloguing of human rights materials (the Commission and OAU included), promotional visits, and collaboration with international institutions, non-governmental organisations and national institutions, towards developing respect for human and peoples' rights in Africa. Work, however, towards the publication of the Commission's decisions and reports of its promotional activities should be accelerated. Nevertheless, hope for a more effective protection of human and peoples' rights in Africa is not misplaced.

It is a mark of the awareness of the work of the Commission that over fifty State delegates attended the 27th Session of the Commission in Algiers in April/May 2000. But knowledge of the Charter and the work of the Commission among the ordinary women and men in Africa has a long way to go. Despite what has been achieved, and even as we draw to the end of the period envisaged by the Mauritius Plan of Action, much remains to be done.

AFRICAN CHARTER ON HUMAN AND PEOPLES' RIGHTS

Preamble

The African States members of the Organization of African Unity, parties to the present convention entitled 'African Charter on Human and Peoples' Rights',

Recalling Decision 115 (XVI) of the Assembly of Heads of State and Government at its Sixteenth Ordinary Session held in Monrovia, Liberia, from 17 to 20 July 1979 on the preparation of a 'preliminary draft on an African Charter on Human and Peoples' Rights providing inter alia for the establishment of bodies to promote and protect human and peoples' rights';

Considering the Charter of the Organization of African Unity, which stipulates that 'freedom, equality, justice and dignity are essential objectives for the achievement of the legitimate aspirations of the African peoples';

Reaffirming the pledge they solemnly made in Article 2 of the said Charter to eradicate all forms of colonialism from Africa, to coordinate and intensify their cooperation and efforts to achieve a better life for the peoples of Africa and to promote international cooperation having due regard to the Charter of the United Nations and the Universal Declaration of Human Rights;

Taking into consideration the virtues of their historical tradition and the values of African civilisation which should inspire and characterise their reflection on the concept of human and peoples' rights;

Recognising on the one hand, that fundamental human rights stem from the attributes of human beings which justifies their national and international protection and on the other hand that the reality and respect of peoples rights should necessarily guarantee human rights;

Considering that the enjoyment of rights and freedoms also implies the performance of duties on the part of everyone;

Convinced that it is henceforth essential to pay a particular attention to the right to development and that civil and political rights cannot be dissociated from economic, social and cultural rights in their conception as well as universality and that the satisfaction of economic, social and cultural rights is a guarantee for the enjoyment of civil and political rights;

Conscious of their duty to achieve the total liberation of Africa, the peoples of which are still struggling for their dignity and genuine independence, and undertaking to eliminate colonialism, neo-colonialism, apartheid, zionism and to dismantle aggressive foreign military bases and all forms of discrimination, particularly those based on race, ethnic group, colour, sex, language, religion or political opinion;

Reaffirming their adherence to the principles of human and peoples' rights and freedoms contained in the declarations, conventions and other instrument adopted by the Organization of African Unity, the Movement of Non-Aligned Countries and the United Nations;

Firmly convinced of their duty to promote and protect human and people' rights and freedoms taking into account the importance traditionally attached to these rights and freedoms in Africa;

Have agreed as follows:

Part I   Rights and duties

CHAPTER I   HUMAN AND PEOPLES' RIGHTS

Article 1
The Member States of the Organization of African Unity parties to the present Charter shall recognise the rights, duties and freedoms enshrined in this Chapter and shall undertake to adopt legislative or other measures to give effect to them.

Article 2
Every individual shall be entitled to the enjoyment of the rights and freedoms recognised and guaranteed in the present Charter without distinction of any kind such as race, ethnic group, color, sex, language, religion, political or any other opinion, national and social origin, fortune, birth or other status.

Article 3
1. Every individual shall be equal before the law.
2. Every individual shall be entitled to equal protection of the law.

Article 4
Human beings are inviolable. Every human being shall be entitled to respect for his life and the integrity of his person. No one may be arbitrarily deprived of this right.

Article 5

Every individual shall have the right to the respect of the dignity inherent in a human being and to the recognition of his legal status. All forms of exploitation and degradation of man particularly slavery, slave trade, torture, cruel, inhuman or degrading punishment and treatment shall be prohibited.

Article 6

Every individual shall have the right to liberty and to the security of his person. No one may be deprived of his freedom except for reasons and conditions previously laid down by law. In particular, no one may be arbitrarily arrested or detained.

Article 7

1. Every individual shall have the right to have his cause heard. This comprises:

   (a) the right to an appeal to competent national organs against acts of violating his fundamental rights as recognised and guaranteed by conventions, laws, regulations and customs in force;
   (b) the right to be presumed innocent until proved guilty by a competent court or tribunal;
   (c) the right to defence, including the right to be defended by counsel of his choice;
   (d) the right to be tried within a reasonable time by an impartial court or tribunal.

2. No one may be condemned for an act or omission which did not constitute a legally punishable offence at the time it was committed. No penalty may be inflicted for an offence for which no provision was made at the time it was committed. Punishment is personal and can be imposed only on the offender.

Article 8

Freedom of conscience, the profession and free practice of religion shall be guaranteed. No one may, subject to law and order, be submitted to measures restricting the exercise of these freedoms.

Article 9

1. Every individual shall have the right to receive information.
2. Every individual shall have the right to express and disseminate his opinions within the law.

Article 10

1. Every individual shall have the right to free association provided that he abides by the law.

2. Subject to the obligation of solidarity provided for in 29 no one may be compelled to join an association.

Article 11

Every individual shall have the right to assemble freely with others. The exercise of this right shall be subject only to necessary restrictions provided for by law in particular those enacted in the interest of national security, the safety, health, ethics and rights and freedoms of others.

Article 12

1. Every individual shall have the right to freedom of movement and residence within the borders of a State provided he abides by the law.

2. Every individual shall have the right to leave any country including his own, and to return to his country. This right may only be subject to restrictions, provided for by law for the protection of national security, law and order, public health or morality.

3. Every individual shall have the right, when persecuted, to seek and obtain asylum in other countries in accordance with laws of those countries and international conventions.

4. A non-national legally admitted in a territory of a State Party to the present Charter, may only be expelled from it by virtue of a decision taken in accordance with the law.

5. The mass expulsion of non-nationals shall be prohibited. Mass expulsion shall be that which is aimed at national, racial, ethnic or religious groups.

Article 13

1. Every citizen shall have the right to participate freely in the government of his country, either directly or through freely chosen representatives in accordance with the provisions of the law.

2. Every citizen shall have the right of equal access to the public service of his country.

3. Every individual shall have the right of access to public property and services in strict equality of all persons before the law.

Article 14

The right to property shall be guaranteed. It may only be encroached upon in the interest of public need or in the general interest of the community and in accordance with the provisions of appropriate laws.

Article 15

Every individual shall have the right to work under equitable and satisfactory conditions, and shall receive equal pay for equal work.

Article 16

1. Every individual shall have the right to enjoy the best attainable state of physical and mental health.

2. States Parties to the present Charter shall take the necessary measures to protect the health of their people and to ensure that they receive medical attention when they are sick.

Article 17

1. Every individual shall have the right to education.

2. Every individual may freely, take part in the cultural life of his community.

3. The promotion and protection of morals and traditional values recognised by the community shall be the duty of the State.

Article 18

1. The family shall be the natural unit and basis of society. It shall be protected by the State which shall take care of its physical health and moral.

2. The State shall have the duty to assist the family which is the custodian of morals and traditional values recognised by the community.

3. The State shall ensure the elimination of every discrimination against women and also ensure the protection of the rights of the woman and the child as stipulated in international declarations and conventions.

4. The aged and the disabled shall also have the right to special measures of protection in keeping with their physical or moral needs.

Article 19

All peoples shall be equal; they shall enjoy the same respect and shall have the same rights. Nothing shall justify the domination of a people by another.

Article 20

1. All peoples shall have the right to existence. They shall have the unquestionable and inalienable right to self-determination. They shall freely determine their political status and shall pursue their economic and social development according to the policy they have freely chosen.

2. Colonised or oppressed peoples shall have the right to free themselves from the bonds of domination by resorting to any means recognised by the international community.

3. All peoples shall have the right to the assistance of the States parties to the present Charter in their liberation struggle against foreign domination, be it political, economic or cultural.

Article 21

1. All peoples shall freely dispose of their wealth and natural resources. This right shall be exercised in the exclusive interest of the people. In no case shall a people be deprived of it.

2. In case of spoliation the dispossessed people shall have the right to the lawful recovery of its property as well as to an adequate compensation.

3. The free disposal of wealth and natural resources shall be exercised without prejudice to the obligation of promoting international economic cooperation based on mutual respect, equitable exchange and the principles of international law.

4. States parties to the present Charter shall individually and collectively exercise the right to free disposal of their wealth and natural resources with a view to strengthening African unity and solidarity.

5. States parties to the present Charter shall undertake to eliminate all forms of foreign economic exploitation particularly that practiced by international monopolies so as to enable their peoples to fully benefit from the advantages derived from their national resources.

Article 22

1. All peoples shall have the right to their economic, social and cultural development with due regard to their freedom and identity and in the equal enjoyment of the common heritage of mankind.

2. States shall have the duty, individually or collectively, to ensure the exercise of the right to development.

Article 23

1. All peoples shall have the right to national and international peace and security. The principles of solidarity and friendly relations implicity affirmed by the Charter of the United Nations and reaffirmed by that of the Organization of African Unity shall govern relations between States.

2. For the purpose of strengthening peace, solidarity and friendly relations, States parties to the present Charter shall ensure that:

(a) any individual enjoying the right of asylum under 12 of the present Charter shall not engage in subversive activities against his country of origin or any other State party to the present Charter;

(b) their territories shall not be used as bases for subversive or terrorist activities against the people of any other State party to the present Charter.

Article 24

All peoples shall have the right to a general satisfactory environment favourable to their development.

Article 25

States parties to the present Charter shall have the duty to promote and ensure through teaching, education and publication, the respect of the rights and freedoms contained in the present Charter and to see to it that these freedoms and rights as well as corresponding obligations and duties are understood.

Article 26

States parties to the present Charter shall have the duty to guarantee the independence of the Courts and shall allow the establishment and improvement of appropriate national institutions entrusted with the promotion and protection of the rights and freedoms guaranteed by the present Charter.

CHAPTER II   DUTIES

Article 27

1. Every individual shall have duties towards his family and society, the State and other legally recognised communities and the international community.

2. The rights and freedoms of each individual shall be exercised with due regard to the rights of others, collective security, morality and common interest.

Article 28

Every individual shall have the duty to respect and consider his fellow beings without discrimination, and to maintain relations aimed at promoting, safeguarding and reinforcing mutual respect and tolerance.

Article 29

The individual shall also have the duty:

1. To preserve the harmonious development of the family and to work for the cohesion and respect of the family; to respect his parents at all times, to maintain them in case of need;
2. To serve his national community by placing his physical and intellectual abilities at its service;
3. Not to compromise the security of the State whose national or resident he is;
4. To preserve and strengthen social and national solidarity, particularly when the latter is threatened;

5. To preserve and strengthen the national independence and the territorial integrity of his country and to contribute to its defence in accordance with the law;
6. To work to the best of his abilities and competence, and to pay taxes imposed by law in the interest of the society;
7. To preserve and strengthen positive African cultural values in his relations with other members of the society, in the spirit of tolerance, dialogue and consultation and, in general, to contribute to the promotion of the moral well being of society;
8. To contribute to the best of his abilities, at all times and at all levels, to the promotion and achievement of African unity.

Part II   Measures of safeguard

CHAPTER I   ESTABLISHMENT AND ORGANISATION OF THE AFRICAN COMMISSION ON HUMAN AND PEOPLES' RIGHTS

Article 30
An African Commission on Human and Peoples' Rights, hereinafter called 'the Commission', shall be established within the Organization of African Unity to promote human and peoples' rights and ensure their protection in Africa.

Article 31
1. The Commission shall consist of eleven members chosen from amongst African personalities of the highest reputation, known for their high morality, integrity, impartiality and competence in matters of human and peoples' rights; particular consideration being given to persons having legal experience.
2. The members of the Commission shall serve in their personal capacity.

Article 32
The Commission shall not include more than one national of the same State.

Article 33
The members of the Commission shall be elected by secret ballot by the Assembly of Heads of State and Government, from a list of persons nominated by the States parties to the present Charter.

Article 34
Each State party to the present Charter may not nominate more than two candidates. The candidates must have the nationality of one of the States parties to the present Charter. When two candidates are nominated by a State, one of them may not be a national of that State.

Article 35

1. The Secretary General of the Organization of African Unity shall invite States parties to the present Charter at least four months before the elections to nominate candidates;

2. The Secretary General of the Organization of African Unity shall make an alphabetical list of the persons thus nominated and communicate it to the Heads of State and Government at least one month before the elections.

Article 36

The members of the Commission shall be elected for a six year period and shall be eligible for re-election. However, the term of office of four of the members elected at the first election shall terminate after two years and the term of office of three others, at the end of four years.

Article 37

Immediately after the first election, the Chairman of the Assembly of Heads of State and Government of the Organization of African Unity shall draw lots to decide the names of those members referred to in Article 36.

Article 38

After their election, the members of the Commission shall make a solemn declaration to discharge their duties impartially and faithfully.

Article 39

1. In the case of death or resignation of a member of the Commission the Chairman of the Commission shall immediately inform the Secretary General of the Organization of African Unity, who shall declare the seat vacant from the date of death or from the date on which the resignation takes effect.

2. If, in the unanimous opinion of other members of the Commission, a member has stopped discharging his duties for any reason other than temporary absence, the Chairman of the Commission shall inform the Secretary General of the Organization of African Unity, who shall then declare the seat vacant.

3. In each of the cases anticipated above, the Assembly of Heads of State and Government shall replace the member whose seat became vacant for the remaining period of his term unless the period is less than six months.

Article 40

Every member of the Commission shall be in office until the date his successor assumes office.

Article 41

The Secretary General of the Organization of African Unity shall appoint the Secretary of the Commission. He shall also provide the staff and services necessary for the effective discharge of the duties of the Commission. The Organization of African Unity shall bear the costs of the staff and services.

Article 42

1. The Commission shall elect its Chairman and Vice Chairman for a two-year period. They shall be eligible for re-election.

2. The Commission shall lay down its rules of procedure.

3. Seven members shall form the quorum.

4. In case of an equality of votes, the Chairman shall have the casting vote.

5. The Secretary General may attend the meetings of the Commission. He shall neither participate in the deliberations nor shall he be entitled to vote. The Chairman of the Commission may, however, invite him to speak.

Article 43

In discharging their duties, members of the Commission shall enjoy diplomatic immunities provided for in the General Convention on the Privileges and Immunities of the Organization of African Unity.

Article 44

Provision shall be made for the emoluments and allowances of the members of the Commission in the Regular Budget of the Organization of African Unity.

CHAPTER II MANDATE OF THE COMMISSION

Article 45

The functions of the Commission shall be:

1. To promote Human and Peoples' Rights and in particular:
   (a) to collect documents, undertake studies and researches on African problems in the field of human and peoples' rights, organise seminars, symposia and conferences, disseminate information, encourage national and local institutions concerned with human and peoples' rights, and should the case arise, give its views or make recommendations to Governments.
   (b) to formulate and lay down, principles and rules aimed at solving legal problems relating to human and peoples' rights and fundamental freedoms upon which African Governments may base their legislations.
   (c) co-operate with other African and international institutions concerned with the promotion and protection of human and peoples' rights.

2. Ensure the protection of human and peoples' rights under conditions laid down by the present Charter.
3. Interpret all the provisions of the present Charter at the request of a State party, an institution of the OAU or an African Organization recognised by the OAU.
4. Perform any other tasks which may be entrusted to it by the Assembly of Heads of State and Government.

CHAPTER III   PROCEDURE OF THE COMMISSION

Article 46

The Commission may resort to any appropriate method of investigation; it may hear from the Secretary General of the Organization of African Unity or any other person capable of enlightening it.

COMMUNICATIONS FROM STATES

Article 47

If a State party to the present Charter has good reasons to believe that another State party to this Charter has violated the provisions of the Charter, it may draw, by written communication, the attention of that State to the matter. This communication shall also be addressed to the Secretary General of the OAU and to the Chairman of the Commission. Within three months of the receipt of the communication, the State to which the communication is addressed shall give the enquiring State, written explanation or statement elucidating the matter. This should include as much as possible relevant information relating to the laws and rules of procedure applied and applicable, and the redress already given or course of action available.

Article 48

If within three months from the date on which the original communication is received by the State to which it is addressed, the issue is not settled to the satisfaction of the two States involved through bilateral negotiation or by any other peaceful procedure, either State shall have the right to submit the matter to the Commission through the Chairman and shall notify the other States involved.

Article 49

Notwithstanding the provisions of 47, if a State party to the present Charter considers that another State party has violated the provisions of the Charter, it may refer the matter directly to the Commission by addressing a communication to the Chairman, to the Secretary General of the Organization of African Unity and the State concerned.

Article 50

The Commission can only deal with a matter submitted to it after making sure that all local remedies, if they exist, have been exhausted, unless it is obvious to the Commission that the procedure of achieving these remedies would be unduly prolonged.

Article 51

1. The Commission may ask the States concerned to provide it with all relevant information.
2. When the Commission is considering the matter, States concerned may be represented before it and submit written or oral representation.

Article 52

After having obtained from the States concerned and from other sources all the information it deems necessary and after having tried all appropriate means to reach an amicable solution based on the respect of Human and Peoples' Rights, the Commission shall prepare, within a reasonable period of time from the notification referred to in 48, a report stating the facts and its findings. This report shall be sent to the States concerned and communicated to the Assembly of Heads of State and Government.

Article 53

While transmitting its report, the Commission may make to the Assembly of Heads of State and Government such recommendations as it deems useful.

Article 54

The Commission shall submit to each ordinary Session of the Assembly of Heads of State and Government a report on its activities.

OTHER COMMUNICATIONS

Article 55

1. Before each Session, the Secretary of the Commission shall make a list of the communications other than those of States parties to the present Charter and transmit them to the members of the Commission, who shall indicate which communications should be considered by the Commission.

2. A communication shall be considered by the Commission if a simple majority of its members so decide.

Article 56

Communications relating to human and peoples' rights referred to in 55 received by the Commission, shall be considered if they:

1. Indicate their authors even if the latter request anonymity,
2. Are compatible with the Charter of the Organization of African Unity or with the present Charter,
3. Are not written in disparaging or insulting language directed against the State concerned and its institutions or to the Organization of African Unity,
4. Are not based exclusively on news discriminated through the mass media,
5. Are sent after exhausting local remedies, if any, unless it is obvious that this procedure is unduly prolonged,
6. Are submitted within a reasonable period from the time local remedies are exhausted or from the date the Commission is seized of the matter, and
7. Do not deal with cases which have been settled by these States involved in accordance with the principles of the Charter of the United Nations, or the Charter of the Organization of African Unity or the provisions of the present Charter.

Article 57

Prior to any substantive consideration, all communications shall be brought to the knowledge of the State concerned by the Chairman of the Commission.

Article 58

1. When it appears after deliberations of the Commission that one or more communications apparently relate to special cases which reveal the existence of a series of serious or massive violations of human and peoples' rights, the Commission shall draw the attention of the Assembly of Heads of State and Government to these special cases.

2. The Assembly of Heads of State and Government may then request the Commission to undertake an in-depth study of these cases and make a factual report, accompanied by its findings and recommendations.

3. A case of emergency duly noticed by the Commission shall be submitted by the latter to the Chairman of the Assembly of Heads of State and Government who may request an in-depth study.

Article 59

1. All measures taken within the provisions of the present Chapter shall remain confidential until such a time as the Assembly of Heads of State and Government shall otherwise decide.

2. However, the report shall be published by the Chairman of the Commission upon the decision of the Assembly of Heads of State and Government.

3. The report on the activities of the Commission shall be published by its Chairman after it has been considered by the Assembly of Heads of State and Government.

CHAPTER IV   APPLICABLE PRINCIPLES

Article 60

The Commission shall draw inspiration from international law on human and peoples' rights, particularly from the provisions of various African instruments on human and peoples' rights, the Charter of the United Nations, the Charter of the Organization of African Unity, the Universal Declaration of Human Rights, other instruments adopted by the United Nations and by African countries in the field of human and peoples' rights as well as from the provisions of various instruments adopted within the Specialized Agencies of the United Nations of which the parties to the present Charter are members.

Article 61

The Commission shall also take into consideration, as subsidiary measures to determine the principles of law, other general or special international conventions, laying down rules expressly recognised by member states of the Organization of African Unity, African practices consistent with international norms on human and people's rights, customs generally accepted as law, general principles of law recognised by African states as well as legal precedents and doctrine.

Article 62

Each state party shall undertake to submit every two years, from the date the present Charter comes into force, a report on the legislative or other measures taken with a view to giving effect to the rights and freedoms recognised and guaranteed by the present Charter.

Article 63

1. The present Charter shall be open to signature, ratification or adherence of the member States of the Organization of African Unity.

2. The instruments of ratification or adherence to the present Charter shall be deposited with the Secretary General of the Organization of African Unity.

3. The present Charter shall come into force three months after the reception by the Secretary General of the instrument of ratification or adherence of a simple majority of member States of the Organization of African Unity.

Part III   General provisions

Article 64

1. After the coming into force of the present Charter, members of the Commission shall be elected in accordance with the relevant Articles of the present Charter.

2. The Secretary General of the Organization of African Unity shall convene the first meeting of the Commission at the Headquarters of the Organization within three months of the constitution of the Commission. Thereafter, the Commission shall be convened by its Chairman whenever necessary but at least once a year.

Article 65

For each of the States that will ratify or adhere to the present Charter after its coming into force, the Charter shall take effect three months after the date of the deposit by that State of its instruments of ratification or adherence.

Article 66

Special protocols may, if necessary, supplement the provisions of the present Charter.

Article 67

The Secretary General of the Organization of African Unity shall inform member States of the Organization of the deposit of each instrument of ratification or adherence.

Article 68

The present Charter may be amended if a State party makes a written request to that effect to the Secretary General of the Organization of African Unity. The Assembly of Heads of State and Government may only consider the draft amendment after all the States parties have been duly informed of it and the Commission has given its opinion on it at the request of the sponsoring State. The amendment shall be approved by a simple majority of the States parties. It shall come into force for each State which has accepted it in accordance with its constitutional procedure three months after the Secretary General has received notice of the acceptance.

Adopted by the Eighteenth Assembly of Heads of State and Government, June 1981, Nairobi, Kenya

PROTOCOL TO THE AFRICAN CHARTER ON THE ESTABLISHMENT OF THE AFRICAN COURT ON HUMAN AND PEOPLES' RIGHTS

The Member States of the Organization of African Unity hereinafter referred to as the OAU, States Parties to the African Charter on Human and Peoples' Rights.

Considering that the Charter of the Organization of African Unity recognises that freedom, equality, justice, peace and dignity are essential objectives for the achievement of the legitimate aspirations of the African Peoples;

Noting that the African Charter on Human and Peoples' Rights reaffirms adherence to the principles of Human and Peoples' Rights, freedoms and duties contained in the declarations, conventions and other instruments adopted by the Organization of African Unity, and other international organizations;

Recognising that the two-fold objective of the African Commission on Human and Peoples' Rights is to ensure on the one hand promotion and on the other protection of Human and Peoples' Rights, freedom and duties;

Recognising further, the efforts of the African Charter on Human and Peoples, Rights in the promotion and protection of Human and Peoples' Rights since its inception in 1987;

Recalling resolution AHG/Res.230 (XXX) adopted by the Assembly of Heads of State and Government in June 1994 in Tunis, Tunisia, requesting the Secretary-General to convene a Government experts' meeting to ponder, in conjunction with the African Commission, over the means to enhance the efficiency of the African commission and to consider in particular the establishment of an African Court on Human and Peoples' Rights;

Noting the first and second Government legal experts' meeting held respectively in Cape Town, South Africa (September, 1995) and Nouakchott, Mauritania (April 1997), and the third Government Legal Experts meeting held in Addis Ababa, Ethiopia (December, 1997), which was enlarged to include Diplomats;

Firmly convinced that the attainment of the objectives of the African Charter on Human and Peoples' Rights requires the establishment of an African Court on Human and Peoples' Rights to complement and reinforce the functions of the African Commission on Human and Peoples' Rights.

Have agreed as follows:

Article 1 Establishment of the Court
There shall be established within the Organization of African Unity an African Court Human and Peoples' Rights hereinafter referred to as 'the Court', the organization, jurisdiction and functioning of which shall be governed by the present Protocol.

Article 2 Relationship between the Court and the Commission
The Court shall, bearing in mind the provisions of this Protocol, complement the protective mandate of the African Commission on Human and Peoples' Rights hereinafter referred to as 'the Commission', conferred upon it by the African Charter on Human and Peoples' Rights, hereinafter referred to as 'the Charter'.

Article 3 Jurisdiction
1. The jurisdiction of the Court shall extend to all cases and disputes submitted to it concerning the interpretation and application of the Charter, this Protocol and any other relevant Human Rights instrument ratified by the States concerned.

2. In the event of a dispute as to whether the Court has jurisdiction, the Court shall decide.

Article 4 Advisory opinions
1. At the request of a Member State of the OAU, the OAU, any of its organs, or any African organisation recognised by the OAU, the Court may provide an opinion on any legal matter relating to the Charter or any other relevant human rights instruments, provided that the subject matter of the opinion is not related to a matter being examined by the Commission.

2. The Court shall give reasons for its advisory opinions provided that every judge shall be entitled to deliver a separate of dissenting decision.

Article 5 Access to the Court
1. The following are entitled to submit cases to the Court:

    (a) Commission
    (b) The State Party, which had lodged a complaint to the Commission
    (c) The State Party against which the complaint has been lodged at the Commission
    (d) The State Party whose citizen is a victim of human rights violation
    (e) African Intergovernmental Organisations

2. When a State Party has an interest in a case, it may submit a request to the Court to be permitted to join.

3. The Court may entitle relevant Non Governmental organisations (NGOs) with observer status before the Commission, and individuals to institute cases directly before it, in accordance with article 34 (6) of this Protocol.

Article 6 Admissibility of cases

1. The Court, when deciding on the admissibility of a case instituted under article 5 (3) of this Protocol, may request the opinion of the Commission which shall give it as soon as possible.

2. The Court shall rule on the admissibility of cases taking into account the provisions of article 56 of the Charter.

3. The Court may consider cases or transfer them to the Commission.

Article 7 Sources of law

The Court shall apply the provision of the Charter and any other relevant human rights instruments ratified by the States concerned.

Article 8 Consideration of cases

The Rules of Procedure of the Court shall lay down the detailed conditions under which the Court shall consider cases brought before it, bearing in mind the complementarity's between the Commission and the Court.

Article 9 Amicable settlement

The Court may try to reach an amicable settlement in a case pending before it in accordance with the provisions of the Charter.

Article 10 Hearings and representation

1. Court shall conduct its proceedings in public. The Court may, however, conduct proceedings in camera as may be provided for in the Rules of Procedure.

2. Any party to a case shall be entitled to be represented by a legal representative of the party's choice. Free legal representation may be provided where the interests of justice so require.

3. Any person, witness or representative of the parties, who appears before the Court, shall enjoy protection and all facilities, in accordance with international law, necessary for the discharging of their functions, tasks and duties in relation to the Court.

Article 11 Composition

1. The Court shall consist of eleven judges, nationals of Member States of the OAU, elected in an individual capacity from among jurists of high moral character

and of recognised practical, judicial or academic competence and experience in the field of human and peoples' rights.

2. No two judges shall be nationals of the same State.

Article 12 Nominations

1. States Parties to the Protocol may each propose up to three candidates, at least two of whom shall be nationals of that State.

2. Due consideration shall be given to adequate gender representation in nomination process.

Article 13 List of candidates

1. Upon entry into force of this Protocol, the Secretary-general of the OAU shall request each State Party to the Protocol to present, within ninety (90) days of such a request, its nominees for the office of judge of the Court.

2. The Secretary-General of the OAU shall prepare a list in alphabetical order of the candidates nominated and transmit it to the Member States of the OAU at least thirty days prior to the next session of the Assembly of Heads of State and Government of the OAU hereinafter referred to as 'the Assembly'.

Article 14 Elections

1. The judges of the Court shall be elected by secret ballot by the Assembly from the list referred to in Article 13 (2) of the present Protocol.

2. The Assembly shall ensure that in the Court as a whole there is representation of the main regions of Africa and of their principal legal traditions.

3. In the election of the judges, the Assembly shall ensure that there is adequate gender representation.

Article 15 Term of office

1. The judges of the Court shall be elected for a period of six years and may be re-elected only once. The terms of four judges elected at the first election shall expire at the end of two years, and the terms of four more judges shall expire at the end of four years.

2. The judges whose terms are to expire at the end of the initial periods of wo and four years shall be chosen by lot to be drawn by the Secretary-General of the OAU immediately after the first election has been completed.

3. A judge elected to replace a judge whose term of office has not expired shall hold office for the remainder of the predecessor's term.

4. All judges except the President shall perform their functions on a part-time basis. However, the Assembly may change this arrangement as it deems appropriate.

Article 16 Oath of office
After their election, the judges of the Court shall make a solemn declaration to discharge their duties impartially and faithfully.

Article 17 Independence
1. The independence of the judges shall be fully ensured in accordance with international law.

2. No judge may hear any case in which the same judge has previously taken part as agent, counsel or advocate for one of the parties or as a member of a national or international court or a commission of enquiry or in any other capacity. Any doubt on this point shall be settled by decision of the Court.

3. The judges of the Court shall enjoy, from the moment of their election and throughout their term of office, the immunities extended to diplomatic agents in accordance with international law.

4. At no time shall the judges of the Court be held liable for any decision or opinion issued in the exercise of their functions.

Article 18 Incompatibility
The position of judge of the court is incompatible with any activity that might interfere with the independence or impartiality of such a judge or the demands of the office as determined in the Rules of Procedure of the Court.

Article 19 Cessation of office
1. A judge shall not be suspended or removed from office unless, by the unanimous decision of the other judges of the Court, the judge concerned has been found to be no longer fulfilling the required conditions to be a judge of the Court.

2. Such a decision of the Court shall become final unless it is set aside by the Assembly at its next session.

Article 20 Vacancies
1. In case of death or resignation of a judge of the Court, the President of the Court shall immediately inform the Secretary General of the Organization of African Unity, who shall declare the seat vacant from the date of death or from the date on which the resignation takes effect.

2. The Assembly shall replace the judge whose office became vacant unless the remaining period of the term is less than one hundred and eighty (180) days.

3. The same procedure and considerations as set out in Articles 12, 13 and 14 shall be followed for the filling of vacancies.

Article 21 Presidency of the Court

1. The Court shall elect its President and one Vice-President for a period of two years. They may be re-elected only once.

2. The President shall perform judicial functions on a full-time basis and shall reside at the seat of the Court.

3. The functions of the President and the Vice-President shall be set out in the Rules of Procedure of the Court.

Article 22 Exclusion

If the judge is a national of any State, which is a party to a case, submitted to the Court, that judge shall not hear the case.

Article 23 Quorum

The Court shall examine cases brought before it, if it has a quorum of at least seven judges.

Article 24 Registry of the Court

1. The Court shall appoint its own Registrar and other staff of the registry from among nationals of Member States of the OAU according to the Rules of Procedure.

2. The office and residence of the Registrar shall be at the place where the Court has its seat.

Article 25 Seat of the Court

1. The Court shall have its seat at the place determined by the Assembly from among States parties to this Protocol. However, it may convene in the territory of any Member State of the OAU when the majority of the Court considers it desirable, and with the prior consent of the State concerned.

2. The seat of the Court may be changed by the Assembly after due consultation with the Court.

Article 26 Evidence

1. The Court shall hear submissions by all parties and if deemed necessary, hold an enquiry. The States concerned shall assist by providing relevant facilities for the efficient handling of the case.

2. The Court may receive written and oral evidence including expert testimony and shall make its decision on the basis of such evidence.

Article 27 Findings

1. If the Court finds that there has been violation of a human or peoples' rights, it shall make appropriate orders to remedy the violation, including the payment of fair compensation or reparation.

2. In cases of extreme gravity and urgency, and when necessary to avoid irreparable harm to persons, the Court shall adopt such provisional measures as it deems necessary.

Article 28 Judgment

1. The Court shall render its judgment within ninety-(90)-days of having completed its deliberations.

2. The judgment of the Court decided by majority shall be final and not subject to appeal.

3. Without prejudice to sub-article 2 above, the Court may review its decision in the light of new evidence under conditions to be set out in the Rules of Procedure.

4. The Court may interpret its own decision.

5. The judgment of the Court shall be read in open court, due notice having been given to the parties.

6. Reasons shall be given for the judgment of the Court.

7. If the judgment of the court does not represent, in whole or in part, the unanimous decision of the judges, any judge shall be entitled to deliver a separate or dissenting opinion.

Article 29 Notification of judgment

1. The parties to the case shall be notified of the judgment of the Court and it shall be transmitted to the Member States of the OAU and the Commission.

2. The Council of Ministers shall also be notified of the judgment and shall monitor its execution on behalf of the Assembly.

Article 30 Execution of judgment

The States Parties to the present Protocol undertake to comply with the judgment in any case to which they are parties within the time stipulated by the Court and to guarantee its execution.

Article 31 Report

The Court shall submit to each regular session of the Assembly, a report on its work during the previous year. The report shall specify, in particular, the cases in which a State has not complied with the Court's judgment.

Article 32 Budget

Expenses of the Court, emoluments and allowances for judges and the budget of its registry, shall be determined and borne by the OAU, in accordance with criteria laid down by the OAU in consultation with the Court.

Article 33 Rules of procedure

The Court shall draw up its Rules and determine its own procedures. The Court shall consult the Commission as appropriate.

Article 34 Ratification

1. This Protocol shall be open for signature and ratification or accession by any State Party to the Charter.

2. The instrument of ratification or accession to the present Protocol shall be deposited with the Secretary-General of the OAU.

3. The Protocol shall come into force thirty days after fifteen instruments of ratification or accession have been deposited.

4. For any State Party ratifying or acceding subsequently, the present Protocol shall come into force in respect of that State on the date of the deposit of its instrument of ratification or accession.

5. The Secretary-General of the OAU shall inform all Member States of the entry into force of the present Protocol.

6. At the time of the ratification of this Protocol or any time thereafter, the State shall make a declaration accepting the competence of the Court to receive cases under article 5 (3) of this Protocol. The Court shall not receive any petition under article 5 (3) involving a State Party which has not made such a declaration.

7. Declarations made under sub-article (6) above shall be deposited with the Secretary-General, who shall transmit copies thereof to the State parties.

Article 35 Amendments

1. The present Protocol may be amended if a State Party to the Protocol makes a written request to that effect to the Secretary-General of the OAU. The Assembly may adopt, by simple majority, the draft amendment after all the State Parties to the present Protocol have been duly informed of it and the Court has given its opinion on the amendment.

2. The Court shall also be entitled to propose such amendments to the present Protocol, as it may deem necessary, through the Secretary-General of the OAU.

3. The amendment shall come into force for each State Party, which has accepted it thirty days after the Secretary-General of the OAU has received notice of the acceptance.

GRAND BAY (MAURITIUS) DECLARATION
AND PLAN OF ACTION

The First OAU Ministerial Conference on Human Rights in Africa, meeting from 12 to 16 April 1999 in Grand Bay, Mauritius;

Solemnly adopts this Grand Bay (Mauritius) Declaration and Plan of Action;

Considering that the promotion and protection of human rights is a matter of priority for Africa, and that the Conference provides a unique opportunity to carry out a comprehensive analysis of, and reflection on, the mechanisms for the protection of human rights to guarantee human rights for accelerated development of the continent;

Recalling the Declaration on the Political and Socio-Economic Situation in Africa and the Fundamental Changes Taking Place in the World adopted by the Assembly of Heads of State and Government of the OAU in Addis Ababa, Ethiopia, in 1990, as well as the Declaration on the Establishment, within the OAU, of a Mechanism for Conflict Prevention, Management and Resolution adopted by the Assembly of Heads of State and Government of the OAU in Cairo, Egypt, in June 1993;

Acknowledging that observance of human rights is a key tool for promoting collective security, durable peace and sustainable development as enunciated in the Cairo Agenda for Action on Relaunching Africa's Socio-economic Transformation adopted by the extraordinary session of the Council of Ministers held in Cairo, Egypt, from 25 to 28 March 1995;

Taking note of the growing recognition that violations of human rights may constitute a burden for the international community;

Reaffirming its commitment to the purposes and principles contained in the OAU Charter, the UN Charter, the Universal Declaration of Human Rights as well as the African Charter on Human and Peoples' Rights;

Deeply Concerned about acts of genocide and other crimes against humanity perpetrated in certain parts of Africa;

Emphasising that respect for human rights is indispensable for the maintenance of regional and international peace and security and the elimination of conflicts, and that it constitutes one of the fundamental bedrocks on which development efforts should be realised.

Considering the democratisation processes taking place on the continent and the expressed desires of African peoples to live in a state of law which secures the full enjoyment of human rights and fundamental freedoms for all peoples, regardless of their gender, race, place of origin, religion, social status, ethnic background, political opinions or language;

Further considering the importance of the right to development, the right to international peace and security and the principles of solidarity and friendly relations between States provided for in the African Charter on Human and Peoples' Rights;

Recalling the determination of the collective leadership in Africa to establish conditions which will ensure social justice and progress and thus enable African peoples to enjoy better standards of living in greater freedom and in the spirit of tolerance towards all;

Reiterating the need to examine constructively human rights issues in a spirit of justice, impartiality and non-selectivity, avoiding their use for political purposes;

Recognising the progress achieved by African States in the domain of human rights and the significant contribution of the African continent to the universalisation of human rights;

Further recognising the contribution made by African non-governmental organisations (NGOs) to the promotion and protection of human rights in Africa;

Recalling the recommendations made by the Second Conference of National Human Rights Institutions held in Durban, South Africa, in 1998;

Determined to consolidate the gains made in Africa in the promotion and protection of human and peoples' rights;

1. The Ministerial Conference affirms the principle that human rights are universal, indivisible, interdependent and inter-related and urges governments, in their policies, to give parity to economic, social and cultural rights as well as civil and political rights;

2. The Conference also affirms that the right to development, the right to a generally satisfactory healthy environment and the right to national and international peace and security are universal and inalienable rights which form an integral part of fundamental human rights;

3. The Conference further affirms the interdependence of the principles of good governance, the rule of law, democracy and development.

4. The Conference recognises that the development of the rule of law, democracy and human rights calls for an independent, open, accessible and impartial judiciary, which can deliver justice promptly and at an affordable cost. To this end, such a

system requires a body of professional and competent judges enjoying conducive conditions.

5. The Conference recognises that the core values on which human rights are founded, particularly (a) respect for the sanctity of life and human dignity (b) tolerance of differences, and (c) desire for liberty, order, fairness, prosperity and stability, are shared across all cultures. In this connection, integrating positive traditional and cultural values of Africa into the human rights debate will be useful in ensuring their transmission to future generations.

6. The Conference notes that women and children's rights issues remain of concern to all. The Conference, therefore, welcomes the decision to elaborate a protocol tot he African Charter for the more effective protection of women's rights and calls on the OAU to convene a meeting of government experts to examine the instrument. It urges all African States to work assiduously towards the elimination of discrimination against women and the abolition of cultural practices which dehumanise or demean women and children. The Conference also recommends to States to take the necessary measures to stop the phenomenon and use of child-solidiers and to reinforce the protection of civilian populations, particularly children in conflict situations. The Conference further recommends that States adopt measures to eradicate violence against women and children, child labour, sexual exploitation of children, trafficking in children and to protect children in conflict with the law as well as refugee children.

7. The Conference notes that the rights of people with disability and people living with HIV-AIDS, in particular women and children, are not always observed and urges all African States to work towards ensuring the full respect of these rights.

8. The Conference is aware that violations of human rights in Africa are caused, among others, by:

(a) Contemporary forms of slavery;
(b) Neo-colonialism, racism and religious intolerance;
(c) Poverty, disease, ignorance and illiteracy;
(d) Conflicts leading to refugee outflows and internal population displacement;
(e) Social dislocations which may arise from the implementation of certain aspects of structural adjustment programmes;
(f) The debt problem;
(g) Mismanagement, bad governance and corruption;
(h) Lack of accountability in the management of public affairs;
(i) Monopoly in the exercise of power;

(j) Harmful traditional practices;
(k) Lack of independence of the judiciary;
(l) Lack of independent human rights institutions;
(m) Lack of freedom of the press and association;
(n) Environmental degradation;
(o) Non-compliance with the provisions of the OAU Charter on territorial integrity and inviolability of colonial borders and the right to self-determination;
(p) Unconstitutional changes of governments;
(q) Terrorism;
(r) Nepotism; and
(s) Exploitation of ethnicity.

There is, therefore, need to adopt a multi-faceted approach to the task of eliminating the causes of human rights violations in Africa.

9. While welcoming the improvements which have taken place in addressing the refugee problem, the Conference believes that the high number of refugees, displaced persons and returnees in Africa constitutes an impediment to development. It recognises the link between human rights violations and population displacement and calls for redoubled and concerted efforts by States and the OAU to address the problem.

10. The Conference recognises that the development and energisation of civil society, the strengthening of the family unit as the basis of human society, the removal of harmful traditional practices and consultation with community leaders should all be seen as building blocs in the process of creating an environment conducive to human rights in Africa and as tools for fostering solidarity among her peoples.

11. Deeply concerned about the acts of genocide, crimes against humanity and other war crimes being perpetuated in certain parts of Africa, the Conference appeals to African States to ensure that such acts are definitively eradicated on the continent and recommends that these serious acts of violation be adequately dealt with.

12. Also concerned by the scourge of terrorism as a source of serious human rights violations, especially the most basic of such rights, namely the right to life, the Conference urges African countries to formulate and implement an African convention for cooperation in combating this scourge.

13. The Conference reaffirms the commitment of Africa to the promotion, protection and observance of human rights obligations. In this framework, the

Conference requests those States which have not yet done so to give consideration to the ratification of all major OAU and UN human rights conventions, in
particular:

(a) The African Charter on Human and Peoples' Rights;

(b) The African Charter on the Rights and Welfare of the Child;

(c) The Convention Governing Specific Aspects of Refugee Problems in Africa;

(d) The Protocol to the African Charter on Human and Peoples Rights on the
Establishment of an African Court on Human and Peoples' Rights;

(e) International Covenant on Economic, Social and Cultural Rights;

(f) International Covenant on Civil and Political Rights;

(g) United Nations Covention on the Rights of the Child;

(h) United Nations Convention Relating to the Status of Refugees and its
Protocol;

(i) Convention on the Elimination of All Forms of Discrimination Against
Women;

(j) The Four Geneva Conventions of 1949 as well as the two Additional
Protocols;

(k) UN Convention Against Torture;

(l) UN Convention on the Elimination of All Forms of Racial Discrimination;
and

(m) The Statute of the International Criminal Court.

14. The Conference recognises the necessity for States to give effect to the African
Charter on Human and Peoples' Rights, international humanitarian law and other
major international human rights instruments which they have ratified in their
national legislations for wider effect throughout Africa.

15. The Conference reiterates the fact that the primary responsibility for the
promotion and protection of human rights lies with the State. It therefore urges
States to establish national human rights institutions and to provide them with
adequate financial resources and ensure their independence.

16. The Conference recognises that the reporting obligation of States Parties
under the African Charter on Human and Peoples' Rights provides an important
mechanism and an opportunity for African governments to engage in the process of
continuous dialogue with the African Commission on Human and Peoples' Rights.
Accordingly, the Conference recommends that States Parties take appropriate measures to meet their reporting obligations under the Charter.

17. The Conference recognises the importance of promoting an African civil
society, particularly NGOs, rooted in the realities of the African continent and

calls on African governments to offer their constructive assistance with the aim of consolidating democracy and durable development.

18. The Conference calls upon all international organisations – governmental, inter-governmental and non-governmental – to cooperate and harmonise their initiatives with the OAU and its relevant organs as well as the various sub-regional bodies within Africa for a more coordinated approach to the implementation of human rights in Africa and for maximum effect of such programmes and initiatives.

19. The Conference notes that the adoption of the UN Declaration on the Protection of Human Rights Defenders by the 54th Session of the UN Commission on Human Rights marks a significant turning point, and calls on African governments to take appropriate steps to implement the Declaration in Africa.

20. The Conference appeals to the Secretary General of the OAU and the African Commission on Human and Peoples' Rights to develop appropriate strategies and take measures to sensitise and raise the awareness of African peoples about human rights and international humanitarian law through formal and non-formal educational processes comprising, among others, a special module in school curricula.

21. The Conference recognises that the media are important actors for building bridges between governments and peoples; it, therefore, urges States to guarantee a free and independent press within their national borders to enable it play a role in the promotion of human rights in Africa. To this end, the Conference appeals to the Secretary General of the OAU to look into the possibility of providing assistance to media organisations on the continent.

22. To ensure that human rights considerations are integrated into all OAU activities; the Conference recognises the need for human rights to be reflected in the programmes of the Organisation.

23. The Conference, noting that the working of the African Commission on Human and Peoples' Rights is critical to the due observance of human rights in Africa, believes that there is a need to evaluate the structure and functioning of the Commission and to ascertain the extent to which it is implementing the Mauritius Plan of Action during the period 1996–2001, and to assist it to remove all obstacles to the effective discharge of its functions. There is also an urgent need to provide the Commission with adequate human, material and financial resources.

24. The Conference notes that, under the African Charter on Human and Peoples' Rights, it is the Assembly of Heads of State and Government that is authorised to take decisive action on the activity reports of the African Commission on Human and

Peoples; Rights and expresses the hope that he Assembly would consider delegating this task to the Council of Ministers.

25. The Conference underscores the fact that cooperation between the African Commission and national human rights institutions will greatly enhance respect for human rights in Africa. In that regard, the Conference welcomes the decision by the African Commission on Human and Peoples' Rights to grant affiliated status to national human rights institutions.

26. Concerned by the fact that the external debt burden is crippling the development efforts of Africa and undermining the fostering and sustenance of respect for human rights, the Conference appeals to the international community, especially multilateral financial agencies, to alleviate the external debt and take all steps necessary to reduce this burden on State to enable them to realise fully the economic emancipation of their peoples and enhance the maximum enjoyment of human rights by African peoples.

27. The Conference requests the Secretary General of the OAU to submit this Declaration to the Assembly of Heads of State and Government, all Member States, the African Commission on Human and Peoples' Rights, the UN High Commissioner for Human Rights and other relevant UN organs and agencies and to examine the feasibility of making this conference a regular feature of OAU activities.

28. The conference recommends to States to formulate and adopt national action plans for the promotion and protection of human rights.

29. Finally, the Conference requests the Secretary General of the OAU to submit a report to the next session of the Council of Ministers on the outcome of this Conference.

Adopted at Grand Bay Mauritius, on 16 April, 1999.

BIBLIOGRAPHY

Abdullahi, A. N. M., 'Human Rights Protection in Africa: Towards Effective Mechanisms', *East African Journal of Peace and Human Rights* 3 (1997) 1

Ajibola, B., and Van Zyl, D. (eds.), *The Judiciary in Africa* (Cape Town: 1998)

Alston, P., 'Purposes of Reporting', in 'United Nations Manual on Human Rights Reporting Under Six Major International Human Rights Instruments', UN Doc. HR/PUB/91/1 (1991), pp. 13–16

Alston, P., and Quinn, G., 'The Nature and Scope of States Parties' Obligations Under the International Covenant on Economic, Social and Cultural Rights', *Human Rights Quarterly* 9 (1987) 156

Amate, C. O. C., *Inside the OAU: Pan-Africanism in Practice* (London: 1986)

Amerasinghe, C. F., *Local Remedies in International Law* (1990)

Amoah, P., 'The African Charter on Human and Peoples' Rights – An Effective Weapon for Human Rights?', RADIC 4 (1992) 226

Ankhumah, E. A., *The African Commission on Human and Peoples' Rights* (The Hague: 1996)

An-Na'im, A. A., 'The Cultural Mediation of Human Rights: The Al-Arqam Case in Malaysia', in Bauer, J. E., and Bell, D. A. (eds.), *The East Asian Challenge for Human Rights* (Cambridge and New York: 1999)

Anyangwe, C., 'Obligations of States Parties to the African Charter on Human and Peoples' Rights', RADIC 10 (1998) 625

Arts, K. C. J. M., 'The International Protection of Children's Rights in Africa: The 1990 OAU Charter on the Rights and Welfare of the Child', RADIC 5 (1993) 139

Badawi El-Sheikh, I., 'The African Commission on Human and Peoples' Rights: Prospects and Problems', NQHR 7 (1989) 272

Baldwin J., 'My Dungeon Shook: Letter to My Nephew on the One Hundredth Anniversary of the Emancipation', in J. Baldwin (ed.), *The Fire Next Time* (London: 1963)

Benedek, W., 'The African Charter and Commission on Human and Peoples' Rights: How to Make it More Effective', NQHR 11 (1993) 25

Berlin, I., 'Two Concepts of Liberty', in Berlin, I. (ed.), *Four Essays on Liberty* (Oxford: 1969)

Beyani, C., 'Toward a More Effective Guarantee of Women's Rights in the African Human Rights System', in Cook, R. (ed.), *Human Rights of Women: National and International Perspectives* (Pennsylvania: 1994), p. 285

Bloed, A., 'The Human Dimension of the OSCE: Past, Present and Prospects', *OSCE Office for Democratic Institutions and Human Rights (ODIHR) Bulletin* 3 (1995) 16

Bradley, A. W., 'Social Security and the Right to Fair Hearing: The Strasbourg Perspective', *Public Law* (1987) 3

Brower, C. N., 'Evidence Before International Tribunals: The Need for Some Standard Rules', *International Law* 28 (1994) 47

Brownlie, I. (ed.), *Basic Documents on Human Rights* (3rd edn, Oxford: 1992)

Buergenthal, T., 'Judicial Fact-Finding: Inter-American Human Rights Court', in Lillich, R. (ed.), *Fact-Finding Before International Tribunals* (New York: 1991), pp. 261–74

Busia, N. K. A., Jr, and Mbaye, B. G., 'Filing Communications on Economic, Social and Cultural Rights Under the African Charter on Human and Peoples' Rights (the Banjul Charter)', *East Africa Journal of Peace and Human Rights* 3 (1997) 188

Butegwa, F., 'Using the African Charter on Human and Peoples' Rights to Secure Women's Access to Land in Africa', in Cook, R. (ed.), *Human Rights of Women: National and International Perspectives* (Pennsylvania: 1994), p. 495

Butler, A. S., 'Legal Aid Before Human Rights Treaty Monitoring Bodies', *International and Comparative Law Quarterly* 49 (2000) 360–89

Cerna, C., 'The Inter-American Commission on Human Rights: Its Organisation and Examination of Petitions and Communications', in Harris, D., and Livingstone, S. (eds.), *The Inter-American System of Human Rights* (Oxford: 1998)

Chapman, A. R., 'A "Violations Approach" for Monitoring the International Covenant on Economic, Social and Cultural Rights', *Human Rights Quarterly* 18 (1996) 23

Chaskalson, A., 'Human Dignity as a Foundational Value of the Constitutional Order', 3rd Bram Fischer Memorial Lecture, Johannesburg, May 2000

Churchill, R. R., 'Environmental Rights in Existing Human Rights Treaties', in Boyle, A. E., and Anderson, M. R. (eds.), *Human Rights Approaches to Environmental Protection* (Oxford: 1996), p. 89

Clapham, A., 'UN Human Rights Reporting Procedures: An NGO Perspective', in Alston, P., and Crawford, J. (eds.), *The Future of UN Human Rights Treaty Monitoring* (Cambridge: 2000), pp. 175–200

Clapham, C., *Africa and the International System: The Politics of State Survival* (Cambridge: 1996)

Cobbah, J. A. M., 'African Values and the Human Rights Debate: An African Perspective', *Human Rights Quarterly* 9 (1987) 309

Craven, M., 'The Protection of Economic, Social and Cultural Rights Under the Inter-American System of Human Rights', in Harris, D., and Livingstone, S. (eds.), *The Inter-American System of Human Rights* (Oxford: 1998), p. 289

Crawford, J., 'The UN Human Rights Treaty System: A System in Crisis?', in Alston, P., and Crawford J. (eds.), *The Future of UN Human Rights Treaty Monitoring* (Cambridge: 2000), p. 1

Danielsen, A., *The State Reporting Procedure Under the African Charter* (Danish Centre for Human Rights, 1994)

Dankwa, V., 'The African Charter on Human and Peoples' Rights: Hopes and Fear', in Dankwa, V. (ed.), *The African Charter on Human and Peoples' Rights: Development, Context, Significance* (Marburg: African Law Association, 1990)

Davidson, S., *The Inter-American Court of Human Rights* (Dartmouth: 1992)

Downs, J., 'A Healthy and Ecologically Balanced Environment: An Argument for a Third Generation Right', *Duke Journal of Comparative and International Law* 3 (1993) 351

D'Sa, R. M., 'The African Charter on Human and Peoples' Rights: Problems and Prospects for Regional Action', *Australian Yearbook of International Law* 10 (1981–83), p. 101

' "Human and People" Rights: Distinctive Features of the African Charter', *Journal of African Law* 19 (1985) 72

Duxbury, A., 'Rejuvenating the Commonwealth: The Human Rights Remedy', ICLQ 46 (1997) 344

Elias, T. O., *Africa and the Development of International Law* (2nd edn by Akinjide, R., Dordrecht, Boston and London: 1988)

Elmadmad, K., 'The Rights of Women Under the African Charter on Human and Peoples' Rights', in Benedek, W., and Heinz, W. (eds.), *Regional Systems of Human Rights in Africa, America and Europe: Proceedings of the Conference* (Friedrich Naumann Stiftung, 1992), p. 17

Fish, S., *There's No Such Thing as Free Speech and It's a Good Thing Too* (Oxford: 1994)

Franck, T., *Fairness in International Law and Institutions* (Oxford: 1995)

Gittleman, R., 'The African Charter on Human and Peoples' Rights: A Legal Analysis', *Virginia Journal of International Law* 22 (1982) 667

Gormley, W. P., 'The Legal Obligation of the International Community to Guarantee a Pure and Decent Environment: The Expansion of Human Rights Norms', *Georgetown International Environmental Law Review* 3 (1990) 85

Gutto, S., 'The New Mechanism of the Organization of African Unity for Conflict Prevention, Management and Resolution, and the Controversial Concept of Humanitarian Intervention in International Law', *South African Law Journal* 113 (1996) 314

Gye-Wado, O., 'The Rule of Admissibility Under the African Charter on Human and Peoples' Rights', *African Journal of International and Comparative Law* 3 (1991) 742–55

Harris, D. J., O'Boyle, M., and Warbrick, C., *Law of the European Convention on Human Rights* (London: 1995)

Harvey, E., 'A Mockery of Our Constitution', *Mail and Guardian* (South Africa), 15–22 July 2000

Hefny, M. A., 'Enhancing the Capabilities of the OAU Mechanism for Conflict Prevention, Management and Resolution: An Immediate Agenda for Action', *Proceedings of the African Society of International and Comparative Law* 7 (1995) 176

Heyns, C. H., 'African Human Rights Law and the European Convention', *South African Journal of Human Rights* 11 (1995) 252–63

'Extended Medical Training and the Constitution: Balancing Civil and Political Rights and Socio-Economic Rights', *De Jure* 30 (1997) 1–17

Human Rights Law in Africa, vol. II, *1997* (The Hague: 1999)

Higgins, R., 'Derogations Under Human Rights Treaties', *British Yearbook of International Law* 48 (1976–7) 281

Problems and Process: International Law and How We Use It (Oxford: 1994)

Highet, K., 'Evidence and the Proof of Facts', in Damrosch, L. F. (ed.), *The International Court of Justice at a Crossroad* (New York: 1987), pp. 355–75

Hood, R., *The Death Penalty* (2nd edn, Oxford: 1996)

Howard, R., 'The Full Belly Thesis: Should Economic Rights Take Priority Over Civil and Political Rights? Evidence from Sub-Saharan Africa', *Human Rights Quarterly* 9 (1987) 467

Kannyo, E., 'The Banjul Charter on Human and Peoples' Rights: Genesis and Political Background', in Welch, C. E., Jr, and Meltzer, R. I. (eds.), *Human Rights and Development in Africa* (Albany: 1984), p. 184

Kirsch, N., 'The Establishment of an African Court on Human and Peoples' Rights', *Zeitschrift für auslandisches offentliches Recht und Volkerrecht* 58 (1998) 713

Klerk, Y., 'Forced Labour and the African Charter on Human and Peoples' Rights', in Dankwa, V. (ed.), *The African Charter on Human and Peoples' Rights: Development, Context, Significance* (Marburg: African Law Association, 1990)

Kois, L., 'Article 18 of the African Charter on Human and Peoples' Rights: A Progressive Approach to Women's Human Rights', *East Africa Journal of Peace and Human Rights* 3 (1997) 92

Kokott, J., *The Burden of Proof in Comparative and International Human Rights Law. Civil and Common Law Approaches with Specific Reference to American and German Legal Systems* (Kluwer, 1998)

Kufuor, K. O., 'Safeguarding Human Rights: A Critique of the African Commission on Human and Peoples' Rights', *Africa Development* 18 (1993) 65

Kunig, P., Benedek W., and Mahalu, C. R. (eds.), *Regional Protection of Human Rights by International Law: The Emerging African System* (Baden Baden: 1985)

Magliveras, K. D., *Exclusion from Participation in International Organisations* (The Hague: 1999)

Magnarella, P. J., *Justice in Africa: Rwanda's Genocide, Its Courts and the UN Criminal Tribunal* (Aldershot: 2000)

Maluwa, T., 'The Peaceful Settlement of Disputes Among African States, 1963–1983: Some Conceptual Issues and Practical Trends', ICLQ 38 (1989) 299

International Law in Post-Colonial Africa (The Hague: 1999)

McBride, J., 'Access to Justice Under International Human Rights Treaties', *Parker School Journal of East European Law* 5 (1998) 3

McGoldrick, D., *The Human Rights Committee. Its Role in the Development of the International Covenant on Civil and Political Rights* (Oxford: 1991)

The Human Rights Committee (Oxford: 1994)

Medina, C., 'The Role of Country Reports in the Inter-American System of Human Rights', in Harris, D., and Livingstone, S. (eds.), *The Inter-American System of Human Rights* (Oxford: 1998), pp. 115–32

Motala, Z., 'Human Rights in Africa: A Cultural, Ideological, and Legal Examination', *Hastings International and Comparative Law Review* 12 (1989) 373

Murray, R., 'Decisions by the African Commission on Human and Peoples' Rights on Individual Communications Under the African Charter on Human and Peoples' Rights', ICLQ 46 (1997) 431

'Digest of Foreign Cases: African Commission on Human and Peoples' Rights', SAJHR 13 (1997) 666

'The 1997 Sessions of the African Commission on Human and Peoples' Rights', HRLJ 19 (1998) 169–87

'Africa', NQHR 17 (1999) 350

'On-Site Visits by the African Commission on Human and Peoples' Rights: A Case Study and Comparison with the Inter-American Commission on Human Rights', *African Journal of International and Comparative Law* 11 (1999) 460–73

'Serious or Massive Violations Under the African Charter on Human and Peoples' Rights: A Comparison with the Inter-American and European Mechanisms', NQHR 17 (1999) 109

Naim, A. A., and Deng, F. M. (eds.), *Human Rights in Africa* (Washington DC: 1990)

Naldi, G. J. (ed.), *Documents of the Organization of African Unity* (London: 1992)

The Organization of African Unity (2nd edn, London: 1999)

Naldi, G. J., and Magliveras, K. D., 'Reinforcing the African System of Human Rights: The Protocol on the Establishment of a Regional Court of Human and Peoples' Rights', NQHR 16 (1999) 431

'The African Economic Community: Emancipation for African States or Yet Another Glorious Failure?', *North Carolina Journal of International Law and Commercial Regulation* 24 (1999) 601

Nhlapo, T., 'International Protection of Human Rights and the Family: African Variations on a Common Theme', *International Journal of Law and the Family* 3 (1989) 11

Nowak, M., 'The International Covenant on Civil and Political Rights', in Hanski, R., and Suksi, M. (eds.), *An Introduction to the International Protection of Human Rights: A Textbook* (Abo Akademi University, 1997)

Nwabueze, B. O., *The Presidential Constitution of Nigeria* (London: 1982)

Obinna Okere, B., 'The Protection of Human Rights in Africa and the African Charter on Human and Peoples' Rights: A Comparative Analysis with the European and American Systems', *Human Rights Quarterly* 6 (1984) 141

Odinkalu, C. A., 'The Individual Complaints Procedures of the African Commission on Human and Peoples' Rights: A Preliminary Assessment', *Transnational Law and Contemporary Problems* 8 (1998) 359

Odinkalu, C. A., and Christensen, C., 'The African Commission on Human and Peoples' Rights: The Development of Its Non-State Communications Procedures', *Human Rights Quarterly* 20 (1998) 235

Odinkalu, C. A., and Mdoe, R., *Article 58 of the African Charter on Human Rights: A Legal Analysis and Proposals for Implementation* (Interights, 1996)

Ojo, O., and Sesay, A., 'The OAU and Human Rights: Prospects for the 1980s and Beyond', *Human Rights Quarterly* 8 (1989) 101

Oloka-Onyango, J., 'Beyond the Rhetoric: Reinvigorating the Struggle for Economic and Social Rights in Africa', *California Western International Law Journal* 26 (1995) 1

Österdahl, I., 'The Jurisdiction Ratione Materiae of the African Court of Human and Peoples' Rights', *Review of the African Commission on Human and Peoples' Rights* 7 (1998) 132–50

O'Sullivan, D., 'The Allocation of Scarce Resources and the Right to Life Under the European Convention on Human Rights', *Public Law* (1995) 389

Ouguerouz, F., *La Charte Africaine des Droits de l'Homme et des Peuples* (Paris: 1993)

Parry, C., *The Sources and Evidence of International Law* (Manchester: 1965)

Parsons, A., *From Cold War to Hot Peace: UN Interventions 1994–5* (London: 1995)

Paust, J. J., 'The Complex Nature, Sources and Evidence of Customary Human Rights', *Journal of International and Comparative Law* 25 (1995–6) 235

Peter, C. M., *Human Rights in Africa: A Comparative Study of the African Human and Peoples' Rights Charter and the New Tanzanian Bill of Rights* (1990)

'The Proposed African Court of Justice – Jurisprudential, Procedural, Enforcement Problems and Beyond', *East Africa Journal of Peace and Human Rights* 1 (1993) 117

Ratner, S. R., and Abrams, J. S., *Accounting for Human Rights Atrocities in International Law – Beyond the Nuremberg Legacy* (Oxford: 1997)

Reid, K., *A Practitioner's Guide to the European Convention on Human Rights* (London: 1998)

Reidy, A., Hampson, F., and Boyle, K., 'Gross Violations of Human Rights: Invoking the European Convention on Human Rights in the Case of Turkey', *Netherlands Quarterly on Human Rights* 15 (1997) 161

Reisman, M., and Levit, J. K., 'Fact-Finding Initiatives for the Inter-American Court of Human Rights', in Navia, R. (ed.), *La Corte y el Sistema Interamericanos de Derechos Humanos* (Costa Rica: 1994), pp. 443–57

Robertson, G., *Crimes Against Humanity: The Struggle for Global Justice* (London: 1999)

Robertson, R. E., 'Measuring State Compliance with the Obligation to Devote "Maximum Available Resources" to Realizing Economic, Social and Cultural Rights', *Human Rights Quarterly* 16 (1994) 694

Sandifer, D., *Evidence Before International Tribunals* (Charlottesville, VA: 1975)

Scott, C., 'Reaching Beyond (Without Abandoning) the Category of Economic, Social and Cultural Rights', *Human Rights Quarterly* 21 (1999) 633

Scott, C., and Macklem, P., 'Constitutional Ropes of Sand or Justiciable Guarantees? Social Rights in a New South African Constitution', *University of Pennsylvania Law Review* 141 (1992) 1, 43–75

Shaw, M., 'Dispute Settlement in Africa', *The Yearbook of World Affairs* 37 (1983) 149 *International Law* (Grotius, 1997)

Shelton, D., 'Human Rights, Environmental Rights, and the Right to the Environment', *Stanford Journal of International Law* 28 (1991) 103

Shue, H., *Basic Rights: Subsistence, Affluence and US Foreign Policy* (Princeton: 1980)

Sieghart, P., *The Lawful Rights of Mankind* (Oxford: 1986)

Sinjela, M., 'Constitutionalism in Africa: Emerging Trends', *The Review* (International Commission of Jurists) 60 (1998) 23

Tapper, C., *Cross and Tapper on Evidence* (London: 1999)

Thirlway, H., 'Evidence Before International Courts and Tribunals', in Bernhardt, R. (ed.), *Encyclopaedia of Public International Law* (1995), vol. II, p. 302

Thompson, B., 'Africa's Charter on Children's Rights: A Normative Break with Cultural Traditionalism', ICLQ 41 (1992) 434

Trindade, A., 'The Operation of the Inter-American Court of Human Rights', in Harris, D., and Livingstone, S., *The Inter-American System of Human Rights* (Oxford: 1998), pp. 133–51

Umozurike, U. O., 'The Protection of Human Rights Under the Banjul (African) Charter on Human and Peoples' Rights', *African Journal of International Law* 1 (1988) 65

'The Protection of Human Rights Under the Banjul (African) Charter on Human and Peoples' Rights', in M. Theodoropoulas (ed.), *Human Rights in Europe and Africa* (Athens: 1992)

The African Charter on Human and Peoples' Rights (The Hague: 1997)

van Hoof, G. J. H., 'The Legal Nature of Economic, Social and Cultural Rights: A Rebuttal of Some Traditional Views', in P. Alston and K. Tomasevski (eds.), *The Right to Food* (Utrecht: 1984)

Vierdag, E., 'The Legal Nature of the Rights Granted by the International Covenant on Economic, Social and Cultural Rights', *Netherlands Yearbook of International Law* 9 (1978) 69

Viljoen, F., 'Review of the African Commission on Human and Peoples' Rights: 21 October 1986 to January 1997', in Heyns, C. H. (ed.), *Human Rights Law in Africa 1996* (Kluwer, 1997)

'Review of the African Commission on Human and Peoples' Rights', in Heyns, C. H. (ed.), *Human Rights Law in Africa 1997* (Kluwer, 1999)

'The Relevance of the Inter-American Human Rights System for Africa', *African Journal of International and Comparative Law* (1999) 659

wa Mutua, M., 'The African Human Rights System in Comparative Perspective', *Review of the African Commission on Human and Peoples' Rights* 3 (1993) 5

'The Banjul Charter and the African Cultural Fingerprint: An Evaluation of the Language of Duties', *Virginia Journal of International Law* 35 (1995) 339

Welch, C. E., Jr, 'The African Commission on Human and Peoples' Rights: A Five-Year Report and Assessment', *Human Rights Quarterly* 14 (1992) 43

'The African Charter and Freedom of Expression in Africa', *Buffalo Human Rights Law Review* 4 (1998) 103

Zwart, T., *The Admissibility of Human Rights Petitions* (Kluwer, 1994)

INDEX

Index

Printed in the United States
98578LV00003BB/3/A